Political Science Research Methods

Political Science Research Methods

SECOND EDITION

Janet Buttolph Johnson
University of Delaware

Richard A. Joslyn
Temple University

A Division of Congressional Quarterly Inc.
Washington, D.C.

Printed in the United States of America
Second Printing

Cover design: Paula Anderson

Library of Congress Cataloging-in-Publication Data

Johnson, Janet Buttolph, 1950—
    Political science research methods / Janet Buttolph Johnson, Richard A. Joslyn. -- 2nd ed.
    p. cm.
    Includes bibliographical references and index.
    ISBN 0-87187-556-X :
    1. Political science—Research—Methodology. I. Joslyn, Richard.
II. Title.
JA73.J64   1991   90-29056
320'.072 -- dc20   CIP

To our families
Art, Ross, and Ned
Kathy, Erin, and Andrew

CONTENTS

TABLES AND FIGURES

Tables

Figures

PREFACE

This new edition of *Political Science Research Methods* was prompted by our desire to continue to meet the three primary objectives that guided us in the original edition. The first objective was to demonstrate that the research methods we describe here have been used by political scientists to produce worthwhile knowledge about significant political phenomena. To that end, we have chosen four new case studies to illustrate important aspects of the research process: the stability of political regimes, how congressional elections are financed, the relationship between public opinion and public policy, and the judicial decision making of selected U.S. Supreme Court justices in civil liberties cases.

Fulfilling our other two objectives—giving readers the tools necessary not only to conduct empirical research projects of their own but also to evaluate others' research, and helping students with modest mathematical backgrounds to understand statistical calculations that are part of social science research—required fewer changes, although we have updated examples and added new material in response to requests from users of the first edition. New exercises for readers also have been added throughout the book.

Chapter 1 introduces the four new case studies, which, as in the first edition, are integrated into our discussion of the research process in the subsequent chapters. Chapter 2 examines the definition of scientific research and the development of empirical political science. In this second edition, we have given more recognition to the role of theory in the research process and have enlarged our discussion of modern political science, particularly postbehavioralism and the feminist critiques of political science.

In Chapters 3 and 4 we introduce the building blocks of scientific research. Chapter 3 explores concepts, hypotheses, variables, units of analysis, and the relationship between social theories and hypotheses. Our discussion of how researchers deduce specific hypotheses from more general theories has been expanded. Changes in Chapter 4 include new examples that illustrate a variety of decisions and difficulties about conceptualization and the measurement of abstract political phenomena and an expanded section on multi-item measures to illustrate more fully the Guttman, Likert, Thurstone, and semantic differential scales.

Chapter 5 addresses research design to alert readers to some of the important decisions that should be made before a research project reaches an advanced stage. This new edition gives greater emphasis to case study designs.

In Chapter 6 we discuss how and why to conduct background research. And, in response to changes in research technology, a section on computerized bibliographic searches has been added.

Sampling is the topic of Chapter 7. How a sample is selected and the limits to extrapolation are some of the issues discussed.

Collecting data is discussed in Chapters 8 through 10 by focusing on the research methods that are frequently used by political scientists and that students are likely to find useful in conducting or evaluating empirical research.

The subject of Chapters 11 through 13 is data analysis: how to interpret data and present it to others. Chapter 11 contains a more complete description of frequency distribution, including numerous examples from published research reports and additional examples of graphic displays of univariate information. All three chapters contain updated examples, and Chapters 11 and 12 include tables showing the output from SPSS-X, the most commonly used computer software package for political science research.

Finally, in Chapter 14, we evaluate an actual research report, using an entirely new example from the field of international relations, noting how it addresses each step of the research process.

We would like to thank several people who have contributed to this second edition: our anonymous reviewers who mercifully mixed praise with insightful criticism of the first edition; our editors at CQ Press: Joanne Daniels, Ann O'Malley, Nola Healy Lynch, and Margaret Benjaminson; Gini Alvord, Geneva Tabb, and Alicia Jackson of Temple University, and Teresa Brower of the University of Delaware who helped to prepare the manuscript; and all those readers who helped to make the response to the first edition far better than we had dared to hope.

We again dedicate this book to our families, especially to Erin, Andrew, Ross, and Ned who were too young to appreciate the dedication the first time around, but who are now old enough to eat up the royalties.

Janet Buttolph Johnson
Richard A. Joslyn

CHAPTER 1

Introduction

Political scientists are interested in acquiring knowledge about and understanding a variety of important political phenomena. Some of us are interested, for example, in the conditions that lead to stable and secure political regimes without civil unrest, rebellion, or governmental repression. Others are more interested in the relationship between the populace and public officials in democratic countries, and in particular with the question of whether public opinion influences the policy decisions made by public officials. Still others are more concerned with how particular political institutions function; they conduct research on questions such as, Does Congress serve the interests of organized groups rather than of the general populace? Do judicial decisions depend upon the personal values of individual judges and the group dynamics of judicial groups? To what extent can American presidents influence the behavior of the members of the federal bureaucracy? Do political parties enhance or retard democratic processes?

This book is an introduction to the process and methods of using *empirical research*—research based on the actual, "objective" observation of phenomena—to achieve scientific knowledge about political phenomena. Scientific knowledge, which will be discussed in more detail in Chapter 2, differs from other types of knowledge, such as intuition, common sense, superstition, or mystical knowledge. One difference stems from the way in which scientific knowledge is acquired. In conducting empirical research the researcher adheres to certain well-defined principles for collecting, analyzing, and evaluating information. *Political science*, then, is simply the application of these principles to the study of phenomena that are political in nature.

There are two major reasons for students to learn about how political scientists conduct empirical research. First, citizens in contemporary American society are often called upon to evaluate empirical research about political phenomena. Debates about the wisdom of the death penalty, for example, frequently hinge on whether it is an effective deterrent to crime, and debates about using busing to achieve racial desegregation of the nation's schools involve conclusions about the effects of segregated schools on student performance. Similarly, evaluating current developments in Eastern Europe, Southeast Asia, Central America, and South Africa requires an understanding of the role of competitive elections, rights of expression, religious tolerance, and the ownership of private property in the development of democratic institutions and beliefs. In these and many other cases, thoughtful and concerned citizens find that they must evaluate the accuracy and adequacy of the theories and research of political (and other social) scientists.

A second reason for learning these research methods is that students often need to acquire scientific knowledge of their own, whether for a term paper for an introductory course on American government, a research project for an upper-level seminar, or a series of assignments in a course devoted to learning empirical research methods. Familiarity with empirical research methods is generally a prerequisite to making this a profitable endeavor.

The prospect of learning empirical research methods is often intimidating to students. Sometimes students dislike this type of inquiry because it involves numbers and statistics. Although to understand research well one must have a basic knowledge of statistics and how to use statistics in analyzing and reporting research findings, the empirical research process that we will describe here is first and foremost a way of thought and a prescription for disciplined reasoning. Statistics will be introduced only after an understanding of the thought process involved in scientific inquiry is established, and then in a nontechnical way that should be understandable to any student familiar with basic algebra.

Students are also sometimes uneasy about taking a course in social science research methods because they view it as unrelated to other courses in their political science curriculum. But an understanding of the concepts normally included in a course in social science research methods is integrally related to a student's assimilation, evaluation, and production of knowledge in other courses. An important result of understanding the scientific research process is that a student may begin to think more independently about concepts and theories presented in other courses and readings. For example, a student might say, "That may be true under the given conditions, but I believe it won't remain true under the following conditions ... " Or, "If this theory is correct, I would expect to be able to observe the following ... " Or, "Before I'm going to accept that interpretation, I'd like to have this additional information ... " Students who can specify what information is needed and what relationships between phenomena must be observed in support of an idea are more likely to develop an understanding of the subjects they study.

Researchers conduct empirical research studies for two primary reasons. One reason is to accumulate knowledge that will apply to a particular problem in need of solution or to a condition in need of improvement. Research on the causes of crime, for example, may be useful for reducing crime rates, and research on the reasons for poverty may help governments devise successful income maintenance and social welfare policies. Such research is often referred to as *applied research* because it has a fairly direct, immediate application to a real-world situation.

Researchers also conduct empirical research to satisfy their intellectual curiosity about a subject, regardless of whether the research will lead to changes in governmental policy or private behavior. Many political scientists, for example, study the process by which citizens decide for whom to vote not because they are interested in giving practical advice to political candidates but because they want to know if elections allow the populace to have some measure of influence over the behavior of elected public officials. Such research is sometimes referred to as *pure, theoretical,* or *recreational research* to indicate that it is not concerned primarily with practical applications.[1]

In this chapter we will describe four social science research projects that were designed to produce scientific knowledge about significant political phenomena. These examples illustrate a variety of actual research topics and methods of investigation. They also show how decisions about various aspects of the research process affect the conclusions that may be drawn about the phenomena under study. And they represent attempts by political scientists to acquire knowledge by building on the research of others, in order to arrive at increasingly complete explanations of political behavior and processes.

Research on Regime Stability

One of the most interesting political phenomena in the world today is the stability of political regimes. We seem to be living in a time of rapid change around the globe, with governmental change and civil unrest prevalent in Central America, Eastern Europe, Southern Africa, and Southeast Asia. In contrast the United States has recently embarked on its third century of relatively stable politics, and many other nation-states have also experienced long periods of political calm and continuity. It is only natural, then, for political scientists and others to wonder why some governments are more stable than others and to attempt to provide systematic explanations for the observed variation in regime stability.

Attempts to discover the factors leading to civil unrest and governmental change have been made for decades. One of the first such attempts to use empirical research methods may be found in *Why Men Rebel* by Ted Robert Gurr.[2] Gurr developed the concept of relative deprivation to explain and predict the amount of political violence in different countries. The concept is based on the belief that frustration leads to aggression. Gurr states that a gap may exist between the goods and conditions to which people believe they are rightfully entitled (people's *expectations*) and those that they think they are capable of attaining or maintaining (people's *capabilities*). The larger this gap, or relative deprivation, the greater the frustration and the greater the chances of political violence. Increases in relative deprivation can result from (1) a decline in capabilities while expectations increase, (2) a decline in capabilities while expectations remain the same, or (3) an increase in expectations while capabilities of attaining these expectations are perceived to remain constant. Thus absolute deprivation in objective terms does not lead to frustration if expectations are equally low; it is relative deprivation that is important.

To test his theory Gurr produced a measure of relative deprivation in thirteen nations based on the responses of individuals to opinion polls administered from 1957 to 1963. The polls asked respondents how they compared their past, present, and future position with their ideal of a good life. When this measure of relative deprivation was related to the magnitude of turmoil in the countries between 1961 and 1965, a fairly strong relationship was found, supporting the theory that the greater the relative deprivation, the greater the internal violence.

Gurr goes on to suggest that relative deprivation is influenced by a number of factors, including economic well-being, power values such as physical security and ability to participate in politics, and interpersonal values such as social status, family happiness, and moral and ethical standards. Whether or not relative deprivation leads to political violence (defined by Gurr as violent political strikes, riots, coups d'état, civil wars, and revolutions) depends upon the extent and intensity of shared discontent by members of a society and the degree to which the political system and political actors are blamed. Moral and social attitudes toward violence and the expression of aggression, the use of alternative methods of redress, the expected utility of violence, and the extent of coercive measures practiced by the ruling regime also affect the likelihood of political violence.

Group expectations are related to the greatest gains experienced by other groups perceived to be socioeconomically similar, Gurr suggests. For instance, wage and benefit demands by one set of municipal workers are related to the gains of similar sets of municipal workers more than they are related to similar or dissimilar groups of workers in the private sector. Gurr also takes note of the theory that exposure to Western ways of life makes non-Westerners discontented with their own way of life and that migration to urban areas raises expectations unreasonably and hence leads to violence.

Although Gurr was able to find some empirical evidence in support of his relative deprivation hypothesis, his research did not result in a definitive or complete explanation of civil unrest or regime instability. Consequently many other political scientists have attempted to provide their own explanations for these phenomena. Recent issues of the *American Political Science Review,* for example, contain two interesting attempts to account for violent political change in Latin America and Africa.

Explanations of political violence in Latin America often center on the distributions of land ownership and of land inequality.[3] To date, however, research on the topic has failed to produce a consensus about this relationship. One problem is that it is unclear what kind of land ownership pattern is likely to lead to political violence. Some believe the most salient pattern occurs when a few people own most of the land and most people own little land; others focus on the pattern in which many people are without land. Consequently how one measures land ownership is important.

Another challenge for research in this area is whether land inequality leads directly to political rebellion or whether there exist other factors that either inhibit or exacerbate this connection. Land inequality may lead to political violence, for example, only when governmental authorities are disliked or viewed with suspicion. As a result, researchers are constantly reexamining the theories that lead them to expect relationships between such phenomena as land inequality and political violence in order to develop more complete explanations for such complicated behaviors.

Political scientists have also been interested in attempting to explain regime instability on the African continent. Over the past twenty-five years many African nations have seen changes in regime, often accomplished by military coups, while several other nations have kept the same leader for many years. This situation has attracted the interest of scholars curious about the factors that distinguish stable from unstable regimes.

It is common to explain regime change in African systems of personal rule with factors such as the social, economic, and political characteristics of the countries and the leadership styles and personal characteristics of the leaders. Therefore such phenomena as a country's colonial experience, rate of economic growth, income level, and degree of ethnic conflict and a leader's means of achieving power, military background, and age have been measured and investigated by researchers.

One recent analysis of regime stability in Africa, however, has found that one of the best predictors of a ruler's persistence is the length of time he has been in power. Generally, the longer a ruler has been in power the more apt a ruler is to continue in power regardless of other characteristics of the country and leader. The researchers believe that the length of time a ruler has been in power captures phenomena that are difficult to observe directly, such as a leader's ability to build and wield "networks of information, repression, and patronage." [4]

Political scientists investigate the causes of civil unrest and regime instability primarily out of intellectual curiosity. Although corporations and investment groups that must decide where to locate plants or invest overseas sometimes hire specialists to predict whether particular foreign countries are apt to experience political unrest and economic disruption, more often researchers work in this area not for money but because political scientists are intrigued by governmental change, political unrest, and the transfer of political authority. No doubt civil unrest and regime instability will be an enduring topic of interest in decades to come.

A Study of How Congressional Elections Are Financed

A second topic of enduring concern to political scientists is the behavior of political institutions, like the U.S. Congress, which are designed to give the populace some influence on government. In the United States we often expect citizens to vote for the congressional candidates who are closest to their own political beliefs and preferences—and thereby influence lawmaking indirectly. For congressional elections to work that way, however, voters must be presented with candidates who are able to compete on fairly even terms for popular support. If voters ordinarily choose between an experienced and gifted candidate and an inexperienced and unwise one, or if only one candidate has the resources necessary to conduct a robust and visible campaign, then voters in reality do not have much of a choice and do not gain political influence through elections.

Because the competitiveness of congressional elections is important, political scientists are interested in how congressional candidates get recruited, the resources they have for campaigning, and the quality and impact of the campaigns they run. One of the most salient campaign resources is, of course, money. Therefore a number of recent studies have been done of the impact of money on the conduct and outcomes of congressional elections. One such study, Gary Jacobson's *Money in Congressional Elections,* provides convincing evidence that money in congressional elections is vitally important, especially to challengers trying to unseat incumbents.[5]

Elections to the House of Representatives have not been very competitive in recent years. Most incumbents seek and win reelection each year (the percentage of first-term House members has declined steadily since the Civil War), and incumbents are winning reelection by greater electoral margins than ever before. Jacobson discusses institutional changes in Congress and in voting behavior that explain this increase in incumbent security and that point to the importance of campaign spending by challengers.

Congressional reforms have given members opportunities to advertise their names, to take credit for desirable government decisions, and to take positions on policies favored by constituents without necessarily taking any effective action. Official perquisites—such as congressional staff, trips home to the district, franking privileges, and media access to constituents back home—have all increased. These changes help incumbents develop greater visibility and name recognition and improve their reelection chances.

In addition, voters' ties to political parties have been weakening. Party affiliation is being replaced by name recognition as a voting cue—a reason to choose one candidate over another. Since voters are more likely to recognize the names of incumbents than the names of challengers, incumbents have an edge. Even though information about candidates does not always evoke a positive response by voters, name recognition itself is an important resource for incumbents. To make up for this advantage, challengers must try to increase their recognition during the election campaign by meeting or exceeding incumbent spending levels.

Using data for 1972, 1974, and 1976, Jacobson found that campaign expenditures were—as expected—more important to challengers than to incumbents. Challengers for U.S. House seats in 1972 and 1974 gained slightly more than 1 percent of the vote for every $10,000 they spent. Among challengers for U.S. Senate seats, as spending per voter increased, a challenger's vote percentage also increased. In 1972, as spending per voter increased from nothing to 6.25 cents, the Senate challengers' vote share increased by 11.5 percentage points; thereafter, each time spending doubled, an additional 4.4 percentage point increase was observed. (Similar calculations were made for 1974 and 1976.) The incumbents' increase in vote percentages for a given increase in spending was less than that of challengers. In fact, heavy spending by incumbents was positively related in some cases to *challengers'* victories. In these cases, spending by incumbents was a reaction to the seriousness of the challenge they were facing, and even though they increased their spending, they lost the election.

Jacobson considers the possibility that votes and expenditures are related because more money is contributed to candidates who are expected to do well, and the very characteristics that help candidates attract votes help them attract money. Even after taking into account this reciprocal relationship, however, campaign spending was still shown to be more useful to challengers than to incumbents in gaining voter recall of candidates' names. In 1972, challengers who spent more than $150,000 were as likely as incumbents to be remembered by voters. Thus, the benefits of incumbency in terms of exposure were overcome in these contests, and other differences between the incumbent and challenger determined the outcomes.

Jacobson's research provides useful information for prospective congressional candidates and for citizens. It allows challengers to estimate how much money has to be spent to overcome the incumbents' prior advantage in name recognition. And it enables citizens to gain a clearer understanding of national policy regarding campaign finance. Jacobson concludes that subsidies to candidates would enhance electoral competition and limits on campaign expenditures would decrease it, since limits could prevent challengers from mounting a viable campaign.

Several precautionary notes about Jacobson's conclusions are in order. He had to rely on candidates' campaign finance reports filed with the Federal Election Commission. But these reports may not accurately reflect the amount of money actually spent: money spent independently on behalf of candidates, for example, is not included in candidates' reports. Such independent spending—that is, spending by individuals and groups unaffiliated with a particular candidate—has increased since Jacobson conducted his research in the 1970s. Another limitation to the study is that other factors besides money may have accounted, at least in part, for the success or failure of challengers, even though Jacobson considered many factors in addition to spending in the races he studied.

Investigating Popular Influence on Public Policy

Another concern of researchers is the matter of how much influence public opinion has on the policy decisions made by public officials. Most versions of democratic theory incorporate the idea that public officials should take the preferences of the populace into consideration when making policy decisions and that a democratic political system should give the populace an opportunity to express its preferences and constrain the behavior of public officials.

Investigating the relationship between public opinion and public policy decisions, though, is a difficult enterprise. Measuring what the public desires or prefers on any public policy question is challenging, especially when we attempt to compare the public's views with the types of legislative and administrative decisions made by public officials. Policy decisions are usually too complicated to ask the populace to approve or disapprove, and most public opinion surveys do not ask the public about the policy choices and priorities faced by public officials. Even if we could measure both public opinion and public policy in comparable ways, however, we would also face the difficult job of determining when and why they are congruent.

Yet the question of the relationship between public opinion and public policy is so important for evaluating democratic theory that measurement difficulties have not discouraged researchers. Benjamin Page and Robert Shapiro, for example, have investigated the relationship between changes in public opinion and changes in public policy.[6] By sorting through thousands of public opinion questions asked of nation-wide samples of adults between 1935 and 1979, Page and Shapiro were able to find 357 instances in which opinion changed significantly (that is, by 6 percentage points or more from one time to the next). They then developed measures of public policy to evaluate the same 357 items in the period from two years before through four years after the measures of public opinion. Their framework allowed them to compare the amount of policy change that coincided with opinion change, to tell whether opinion change preceded policy change, and to measure the length of time that usually elapsed between opinion change and policy change.

Their research found significant congruence between the direction of opinion change and the direction of policy change. In the 231 cases in which some policy change occurred, 66 percent of the changes were in the same direction as the opinion change. Furthermore, taking into consideration opinion changes that were relatively small, policy measures that were less than ideal, and time lags that were longer than one year, the portion of opinion/policy changes that were congruent increases to 87 percent.

This finding is important, for it suggests that for some reason public officials do respond to changes in public opinion, at least when those changes are large and stable. Although this single research report does not reveal why or how policy changes are related to opinion changes, it does suggest that public opinion is a significant influence in the American political process and that democratic processes may be at work.

A Look into Supreme Court Decision Making

When the decisions of public officials clearly and visibly affect the lives of the populace, political scientists are interested in the process by which those decisions are reached. The decision-making behavior of the nine justices of the U.S. Supreme Court is especially intriguing because they are not elected officials, their deliberations are secret, they serve for life, and their decisions constrain other judges and public officials. As a result, political scientists have been curious for some time about how Supreme Court justices reach their decisions.

One school of thought on judicial decision making holds that decisions are shaped primarily by legal doctrine and precedent. Since most Supreme Court judges have spent many years rendering judicial decisions on lower courts and since judges in general are supposed to respect the decisions made by previous courts, this approach posits that the decisions of Supreme Court justices depend on a search for, and discovery of, the relevant legal precedent.

Another, more recent, approach to judicial decision making proposes that judges, like other politicians, make decisions in part because of their own personal political beliefs and values. Furthermore, because Supreme Court judges are not elected, serve for life, seldom seek any other office, and are not expected to justify their decisions to the public, it may be that they are in an ideal position for acting on their personal value systems.

One of the obstacles to discovering the relationship between the personal attitudes and the decisions of Supreme Court justices is the difficulty of measuring judicial attitudes. Supreme Court justices do not often consent to give interviews to researchers while they are on the bench, nor do they fill out attitudinal surveys. Their deliberations are secret, they seldom make public speeches during their terms, and their written publications consist mainly of their case decisions. Consequently, about all we can observe of the political attitudes of Supreme Court judges during their terms are the written decisions they offer, and that is what researchers seek to explain.

A recent inventive attempt to overcome this obstacle is contained within Jeffrey A. Segal and Albert D. Cover's "Ideological Values and the Votes of U.S. Supreme Court Justices." [7] They decided that an appropriate way in which to measure the attitudes of judges, independent of the decisions they make, would be to analyze the editorial columns written about them in four major U.S. daily newspapers after their nomination by the president but before their confirmation by the Senate. This data source, the researchers argued, provided a comparable measure of attitudes for all justices studied, independent of the judicial decisions rendered and free of systematic errors. Here, too, though, the researchers had to accept a measure that was not ideal, for the editorial columns reflected journalists' perceptions of judicial attitudes rather than the attitudes themselves.

Despite this limitation, the editorial columns do provide an independent measure of Supreme Court justice attitudes, and when this measure was related to the decisions rendered by the last eighteen justices on cases dealing with civil liberties between 1953 and 1987, a strong relationship was found. Hence those justices who were perceived to be liberal *before* their term on the Supreme Court acted that way once they got on the Court. Judicial attitudes, then, do seem to be an important source of judicial decisions.

Conclusion

As these few examples illustrate, empirical research in political science is useful for satisfying intellectual curiosity and for evaluating real-world political conditions. Conducting empirical research is not a simple process, however. The information a researcher chooses to use, the method that he or she follows to investigate a research question, and the statistics used to report research findings may affect the conclusions that are drawn. For example, some of these examples used sample surveys to measure important phenomena such as relative deprivation and public opinion on a variety of public policy issues. Yet surveys are not always an accurate reflection of people's beliefs and attitudes. In addition, how a researcher measures the phenomena of interest can affect the conclusions that are reached. Researchers studying the effect of land inequality on civil unrest in Latin America have disagreed about whether to measure landlessness, discrepancies in land ownership between the smallest and largest land owners, or land inequality across the entire range of land ownership. To some extent conclusions about the importance of land inequality have depended on how it was measured.

Several researchers in our examples were also unable to measure political phenomena themselves and had to rely on information collected by others, particularly government agencies. Can we always find readily available data to investigate a topic? If not, do we choose a different topic or collect our own data? How do we collect data firsthand? Finally, do research findings based on the study of particular people, communities, or countries have general applications to all people, communities, or countries? To develop answers to these questions we need to understand the process of scientific research, the subject of this book.

Notes

1. *Recreational research* is a term used by Shively. See W. Phillips Shively, *The Craft of Political Research,* 2d ed. (Englewood Cliffs, N.J.: Prentice-Hall, 1980), chap. 1.
2. Ted Robert Gurr, *Why Men Rebel* (Princeton, N.J.: Princeton University Press, 1970).
3. See Manus I. Midlarsky, "Rulers and the Ruled: Patterned Inequality and the

Onset of Mass Political Violence," *American Political Science Review* 82 (June 1988): 491-509, and the exchange between Edward Muller, Mitchell Seligson, Hung-der Fu, and Midlarsky in the June 1989 *American Political Science Review*, 577-595.

4. Henry Bienen and Nicolas van de Walle, "Time and Power in Africa," *American Political Science Review* 83 (March 1989): 19-34.

5. Gary C. Jacobson, *Money in Congressional Elections* (New Haven, Conn.: Yale University Press, 1980).

6. Benjamin I. Page and Robert Y. Shapiro, "Effects of Public Opinion on Policy," *American Political Science Review* 77 (March 1983): 175-190.

7. Jeffrey A. Segal and Albert D. Cover, "Ideological Values and the Votes of U.S. Supreme Court Justices," *American Political Science Review* 83 (June 1989): 557-565.

Terms Introduced

Applied research. Research designed to produce knowledge useful in altering a real-world condition or situation.

Empirical research. Research based on actual, "objective" observation of phenomena.

Political science. The application of the methods of acquiring scientific knowledge to the study of political phenomena.

Pure, theoretical, or recreational research. Research designed to satisfy one's intellectual curiosity about some phenomenon.

Exercises

1. Go to the library at your school and locate the following major political science journals: the *American Political Science Review*, the *American Journal of Political Science*, the *Journal of Politics*, and *Comparative Politics*. Browse through the table of contents of several back issues of these journals to get an idea of what the articles are about. Then read several of the abstracts that appear at the beginning of the articles. What are some of the major topics or phenomena with which the research published in these journals is concerned?

2. Ask to speak with several of the political/social scientists at your school about the research they are conducting. What political phenomena are they interested in understanding? What questions are they trying to answer? Do they employ empirical research methods in their research?

3. Find the articles referred to in endnotes 3, 4, 6, and 7 (we will refer to these articles throughout this book), and read the abstract at the beginning of each of these articles. What questions are the researchers trying to answer?

CHAPTER 2

Studying Politics Scientifically

As Chapter 1 explained, empirical research employs scientific principles and methods of observation and results in scientific knowledge. In this chapter we shall explore the ways in which scientific knowledge is different from other types of knowledge, with respect to both the kind of knowledge it is and the method by which it is acquired. Important features of the scientific research process and the scientific study of politics also will be discussed. The chapter concludes with a brief history of political science as a discipline.

Characteristics of Scientific Knowledge

In our daily lives we "know" things in many different ways. For example, we know that the bus will get us to work more quickly than the train, and that small towns are safer than big cities. We also may "know" that blondes are more fun than brunettes, and that there is life after death. In some cases we know something because we believe what someone has told us. In other cases we know something through personal observation or because it appears to be logical or consistent with common sense.

One particular way in which knowledge is acquired is through a *scientific* process. As we noted earlier, scientific knowledge differs from knowledge derived from myth, casual observation, intuition, belief, or common sense. It has certain characteristics that these other types of knowledge do not share completely: it is empirical and subject to empirical verification, nonnormative, transmissible, general, explanatory, and provisional. Each of these characteristics will be examined in turn.

When we say that scientific knowledge is *empirical* we mean that it is "grounded in observation and experience." [1] We can use our senses to observe actual occurrences of some phenomenon (such as political protests, votes cast in the U.S. Senate, invasions of the territory of one nation by another) and to record those observations as accurately as we can. In the examples in Chapter 1, for example, researchers recorded actual occurrences of land ownership, political disorder and violence, voting and spending in congressional campaigns, public opinion, policy changes, and judicial decisions.

By *empirical verification,* we mean that our acceptance or rejection of a statement must be influenced by observation. [2] Thus if we say that New York State has mandatory seatbelt use legislation, we must be able to provide tangible evidence, such as a copy of the law, to verify the statement. Similarly, as Chapters 3 and 5 will make clear, proposed explanations (that is, statements that claim that the occurrence of a phenomenon is caused by another phenomenon) must be tested scientifically and logically; they cannot simply be assumed to be true.

The empirical nature of scientific knowledge distinguishes it from mystical knowledge; in the latter case only "true believers" are able to observe the phenomena that support their beliefs and observations that would disprove their beliefs are impossible to specify. Knowledge derived from superstition and prejudice is usually not subjected to thorough empirical verification either. Superstitious or prejudiced persons are likely to note only phenomena that reinforce their beliefs while ignoring or dismissing those that do not. Thus their knowledge is based on selective and biased experience and observation. Superstitious people are often fearful of empirically testing their superstitions and resist doing so.

Common sense knowledge as well as knowledge derived from casual observation (for example, we might observe among our friends that pigeon-toed people are more athletic than those whose feet point outward) may be valid, yet they do not constitute scientific knowledge until they have been empirically verified in a systematic and unbiased way. Alan Isaak notes that common sense knowledge is often accepted "without question, as a matter of faith," which means that facts are accepted without being explained properly. Common sense knowledge is, therefore, limited and superficial. [3]

Sometimes scrutiny of common sense knowledge can have surprising results. In Ted Gurr's study of civil strife, for example, common sense might have led us to predict that civil violence will occur whenever economic conditions are poor or worsen. [4] The evidence accumulated by Gurr, however, indicated that violence is likely to occur when expectations and attainment do not coincide—in other words, when *relative* deprivation (not deprivation itself) is felt. Consequently, contradicting common sense knowledge, he concluded that conditions can be quite bad and a society relatively peaceful if poor conditions are expected and accepted.

Another good example of the limitations of common sense may be found in a study of presidential campaign rhetoric. In 1960 four televised debates took place between the Republican party's nominee, Richard M. Nixon, and the Democrats' presidential candidate, John F. Kennedy. In the first debate Kennedy was generally considered to have given the better performance and to have benefited from his more aggressive debating style and attractive appearance. Common sense might lead one to expect that a significant portion of the electorate would have decided to vote for Kennedy after that first debate. Evidence collected during the 1960 campaign, however, has indicated that that one debate did not greatly influence voters' candidate preferences. Although there was a noticeable postdebate surge for Kennedy, it was neither of great size nor necessarily a result of the debate itself. Most people retained their predebate vote intentions. What little surge there was for Kennedy came mainly from wavering Democrats who might have decided to vote for Kennedy anyway before the end of the campaign.[5] In this case, then, common sense might have led to an overestimation of the ease and rapidity with which a single campaign event could alter voters' intentions.

In the examples given in Chapter 1, each of the researchers subjected their ideas and explanations to empirical verification. They observed the phenomena they were trying to understand, recorded instances of the occurrence of these phenomena, and looked for a pattern in their observations that was consistent with their expectations. In other words, a body of empirical evidence was accumulated and presented that gave others an empirical basis for acquiring knowledge about some political phenomenon.

Scientific knowledge is also distinctive in terms of its scope and immediate purpose. The empirical research used to acquire scientific knowledge addresses what is, why, and what might be in the future. It does not typically address whether what is, is good or bad, or what ought to be, although it may be useful in making these types of determinations. Political scientists use the words *normative* and *nonnormative* to express the distinction. Normative knowledge evaluates what is and prescribes what ought to be. Empirical knowledge is nonnormative.

This is not to say that empirical research is conducted in a valueless vacuum. A researcher's values and concerns will determine the topic of research interest, and his or her beliefs will affect the focus of the research or the population chosen for observation. For example, a researcher may feel that crime is a serious problem and that stiffer penalties for those who commit crimes will deter would-be criminals, thereby reducing the crime rate. But the test of the proposition that stiffer penalties will reduce the crime rate should be conducted in such a way that the values of the researcher do not bias the results of the study. It is the responsibility of the researcher to test the proposition without prejudice. It is the responsibility of others to evaluate the research to ascertain whether the conclusions drawn by the researcher are justified and based on valid information. Scientific principles and methods of observation help both the researcher and those who evaluate the researcher's conclusions to perform their tasks. Within the discipline of political science as well as in other disciplines, the relationship between values and scientific research is frequently debated. We shall have more to say about the subject later in this chapter.

Even though political scientists may strive to minimize the impact of biases when conducting their research, it is difficult, if not impossible, to achieve total objectivity. A fourth characteristic of scientific knowledge, however, helps to identify and weed out biases that may enter research activities.[6] Scientific knowledge is *transmissible,* by which we mean that the method of knowing is made explicit so that the research can be analyzed and replicated. Scientific knowledge is transmissible "because science is a social activity in that it takes several scientists, analyzing and criticizing each other, to produce more reliable knowledge."[7] The researcher must specify what data were collected and how they were analyzed. A clear description of research procedures allows others to independently evaluate the worth of the research. It also allows other researchers to collect the same information and test the original propositions themselves. If the original results are not replicated using the same procedures, they may be incorrect.

This does not mean that scientific knowledge is accumulated primarily through the exact repetition of research by many researchers. Often research procedures are changed intentionally to see whether similar results are obtained under different conditions. Consider, for example, two studies concerning the connection between TV violence and antisocial aggressive behavior among children who view TV.[8] One study compared children in two Canadian towns, one with TV, one without. The researchers found that younger children (ages eleven and twelve) from the TV town were less, not more, aggressive; for older children (ages fifteen and sixteen) there was no difference. This research was subsequently criticized because the two towns were not matched closely enough and because other factors related to aggressiveness among children, such as differences in school discipline, were not considered. Another study was then conducted involving children in a single town, thus avoiding the problem of matching. Children were divided into "high" and "low" TV viewers, with high viewers found to be slightly more aggressive than low viewers. Yet in this study no attempt was made to assess the amount of violence seen on TV. Low viewers could have watched particularly violent programs, so that the difference between the groups would have been minimized. The method of measuring aggressiveness was also suspect.

Thus flaws in a research study often lead others to doubt the results and to design their own tests. This would not be possible, however, if the researchers did not clearly specify their research design and methods. This description of methods and results permits a better assessment of results and allows others to conduct further studies with adjustments in design and measurement. The results of these new studies can then be compared with the earlier results and a body of evidence concerning the political phenomena in question may be accumulated. In each of the examples in Chapter 1, the researchers revealed enough information about their methods and procedures that others could evaluate the strengths and weaknesses of their research. The way of measuring certain phenomena could be questioned and improved, the range of situations studied could be broadened, and alternate explanations could be tested by other researchers. In this way evidence on a particular aspect of social and political life may be accumulated and, it is hoped, become increasingly informative.

Another important characteristic of scientific knowledge is that it is *general*. Knowledge that describes, explains, and predicts many phenomena is more valuable than knowledge that addresses few phenomena. For example, the knowledge that states with easier voter registration systems have higher election turnout rates than states with more difficult systems is preferable to the knowledge that Wisconsin has a higher turnout rate than Alabama. To know that familiarity with a candidate, rather than similarity of party affiliation, increasingly influences how people vote is general knowledge. It is more useful to someone seeking to understand the outcomes of elections than is the knowledge that John Doe, a Democrat, voted for the Republican candidate for Congress and knew the Republican's name but not the Democrat's. Knowing that Pennsylvania, which has a safety inspection program, has a lower automobile fatality rate than Georgia, which does not, is less useful to the legislator debating the worth of inspection programs than knowing that inspected states in general have lower average fatality rates than uninspected states. General knowledge is preferred, then, because it accounts for a wider range of phenomena than specific knowledge and helps us understand more of the world in which we live.

Statements that communicate general knowledge are called *empirical generalizations;* they summarize relationships between individual facts.[9] For example, the statement that states with easier voter registration systems have higher turnout rates than states with more burdensome systems connects information about voter registration systems and voter turnout rates in individual states and summarizes that information for many states.

Another characteristic of scientific knowledge is that it is *explanatory*. It provides a reason for a behavior, attitude, or event; it answers a "why" question. For example, one might explain differences in voter turnout among states by differences in the complexity of their voter registration systems. As we have seen, scientific knowledge requires the accurate description of attributes and behaviors based on careful observation and measurement. Knowing facts is important—for example, that 45 percent of registered voters voted in a particular election, that 11.2 percent of all teenagers in a city are unemployed, or that the amount of money spent on national defense rose by 2.5 percent. But most political scientists are not content just to describe a factual situation. They are usually interested in identifying the factors that account for or explain patterns in human behavior.

For example, Gurr's theory of relative deprivation offers an explanation of why political violence occurs and why certain combinations of expectations and value attainment are associated with political violence. It is more than a description of where violence occurs. Other political scientists may try to explain why legislatures in some states adopt particular policies, why some people run for office, and why some cities are fiscally more solvent than others.

Accurate description is the basis for observing patterns and regularities in phenomena and for explaining them. One must have as accurate a picture as possible of what *is* before one can determine *why* it is so. History is replete with examples of erroneous explanations that were developed on the basis of inadequate observation. These explanations have been rejected and new ones have taken their place often as the result of technological advances. Recent space exploration, for example, has made it possible to observe many more phenomena in astronomy than ever before and has led to the reappraisal of many theories regarding Saturn's rings, Jupiter's moons, and Mars's canals. In political science the development of sample surveys has allowed political scientists to study a wide range of human attitudes that previously had been virtually impossible to observe.

Explanatory knowledge is important because it is the basis for *prediction*, the application of explanation to events in the future. In fact, many consider the ultimate test of an explanation to be its usefulness in prediction. Prediction is an extremely valuable type of knowledge since it may be used to avoid undesirable and costly events and to achieve desired outcomes.[10]

But exactly how accurate do scientific explanations need to be? Do they have to account for or predict phenomena 100 percent of the time? Some accept the idea of probabilistic or statistical explanation in which it is not necessary to explain or predict a phenomenon with 100 percent accuracy. But others believe an explanation is acceptable only if it explains or predicts what it purports to explain or predict all the time. In political science, explanations rarely account for all of the variation observed in attributes or behavior. Probabilistic explanations are usually considered acceptable, as they are in other disciplines as well.

Explanation is the primary purpose of a *theory*. A "theory's major function is ... to explain singular facts and occurrences, but perhaps more importantly to explain empirical generalizations." [11] Empirical generalizations linking phenomena are a basis for developing explanations. Theories go beyond empirical generalizations, however; they are more powerful and abstract. As Isaak states, "A theory can explain empirical generalizations because it is more general, more inclusive than they are." [12] Theories also have two other functions: "to organize, systematize, and coordinate existing knowledge in a field" and to "predict an empirical generalization—predict that a particular relationship holds." [13] For example, a theory of voting may explain voter turnout by proposing that people generally weigh the costs and benefits of voting: the higher an individual's cost of voting in comparison with the benefits, the less likely he or she is to vote. [14] The more empirical generalizations a theory systematizes and organizes, and the more of them it suggests or predicts, the stronger the theory.

Theories of politics generate the excitement in political science research and stimulate our study of politics. In our quest to understand our lives and the world around us, to create order out of complexity, even chaos, we turn to theories. Not all of us turn to the same theories, however, and that contributes to the excitement of studying politics. Each theory offers a different view of politics or focuses our attention on a different set of political phenomena.

For example, Bruce A. Williams and Albert R. Matheny evaluate several competing theories in their examination of variation in state regulation of hazardous waste disposal. [15] Regulation of hazardous waste disposal is an example of "social regulation" which imposes costs on a concentrated group in order to benefit a wider latent group—the public. Improper waste disposal imposes costs on the environment and human health. These costs, known as negative externalities, are not reflected in the price of a product. Avoiding or preventing negative externalities means imposing substantial costs on industry for safe disposal. There are at least three theories to explain and predict the reaction to negative externalities in terms of the amount of social regulation.

According to economic theory, negative externalities are a type of market failure, that is, the market fails to allocate resources efficiently. When this happens, government regulation of the market is justified. The market failure theory of government regulation would predict that social regulation would be related to the severity of the market failure and that the costs to regulated industries should be equal to the costs or harms created by unsafe hazardous waste disposal.

Others would argue that social regulation does not correspond to the presence or magnitude of market failures. Rather, social regulation is the result of politics with several distinct outcomes. Some predict that exaggerated claims about dangers imposed by market failures must be made in order to generate enough public awareness and support for regulation and, that consequently, the resulting regulations impose unnecessarily high costs on industry. In contrast, others argue that industries oppose regulation and can dominate the regulatory process by threatening economic slowdown, unemployment, even change of location. The political strength of an industry is related to its importance to the economy and level of government considering the regulation. Threats to relocate have more of an impact at the local or state level than at the national. Thus regulation is related to conditions of industry dominance, not the extent of market failure or actual pollution.

A third theoretical position states that industry dominates the regulatory process, but it does not necessarily oppose all regulation. According to this perspective, industry supports regulation as long as the costs of regulation can be shifted to government away from industry. This regulatory outcome is called the socialization of the costs of production and is predicted by neo-Marxists who maintain that many private industries could not make a profit without evading actual production costs. They also argue that effective regulation and avoidance of negative externalities is not possible without fundamental institutional reform of both government and the economy.

These, then, are quite different views of why and how much regulation occurs. Each view has something different to say about the power of public interest groups and industry groups and the outcome of social regulatory efforts. The conflicting beliefs about politics they represent fuel many a debate about environmental regulations and the performance of government and the economy. Researchers investigating examples of social regulation may be far more interested in determining which theory seems to fit than in the actual amount and consequence of particular regulatory programs. Researchers may become quite attached to a particular theory and be convinced that it is the correct theory, even if they are aware of our final characteristic of scientific knowledge.

This final characteristic is that scientific knowledge is *provisional.* Future research may demonstrate the inadequacy of our understanding of a phenomenon up to that point. New observations, more accurate measurements, improvements in research design, and the testing of alternative explanations may always reveal the limitations or empirical inadequacies of a body of scientific knowledge.[16] One must always remain open to the alteration and improvement of the understanding of human phenomena. To say that scientific knowledge is provisional does not mean that the evidence accumulated to date can be safely ignored. It does mean, however, that future research could always significantly alter our present understanding. Often when people think of science and scientific knowledge they think of scientific "laws." A scientific law is a "generalization that was tested and confirmed through empirical verification." [17] Generally *law* refers to generalizations that have held up under repeated testing. The provisional nature of scientific knowledge alerts us to the possibility that future observations may contradict currently accepted laws.

So far we have described the characteristics of scientific knowledge. In the next section we will discuss two ways in which this knowledge is typically produced: induction and deduction. Empirical observation and theories are key elements in both of them.

Acquiring Scientific Knowledge: Induction and Deduction

Induction is the process of reasoning from specific observation to general principle or theory. In induction, observation precedes theory. The researcher objectively observes the phenomena of interest and records those observations. Upon studying them, the researcher notices a pattern or regularity in the data and develops a theory that explains why the pattern has occurred. This theory may also offer an explanation for patterns in other related observations. For example, imagine that you have made the following three observations. First, the Bemba of South Central Africa live a life of marginal subsistence consisting of nine months of abundance and three months of hunger. Despite deplorable conditions, there is no outbreak of violence or protest among the tribe during the three-month hunger period.[18] Second, the income of American blacks compared with that of whites of equal education rose rapidly during the 1940s and early 1950s but then declined so that half the relative gains were lost by 1960. Violence broke out among blacks in the 1960s.[19] Third, political violence in Europe occurred during the growth of industrial and commercial centers, despite the fact that opportunities for alternatives to the hard life of peasants were created.[20]

In two cases the objective well-being of people declined, but in only one did violence break out. In the other there was no decline in the objective well-being of the people yet violence did occur. Let's assume that in seeking an explanation in the first case, you reason that the cycle of the seasons and its ensuing periods of feast and famine had been experienced for many years and was unlikely to change. In the second case you reason that blacks expected to maintain and continue the gains they had made in the past decade. And in the third case you reason that perhaps all people expected to improve their living conditions, yet some in society were benefiting much more from increased industry and commerce than others. Based on this reasoning, you could conclude that the two last cases were similar because there was a discrepancy between expected and actual conditions, while in the first there was no discrepancy. From this you might develop the general theory that a discrepancy between expectations and attainable conditions causes discontent, which leads to political violence. Thus you might induce the theory of relative deprivation from a few observations of specific cases of deprivations and violence. Generally speaking, it is difficult to point to examples of pure induction since often a researcher will start with a hunch and proceed to collect information that he or she expects to show certain patterns in line with the hunch. A hunch is not a full-blown theory, yet it is more than starting with observations alone.

In the second mode of scientific inquiry, *deduction,* theory precedes observation. Deduction is the process of proceeding from general principle or theory to specific observations. On the basis of theory certain phenomena are predicted. Then events are observed and measured to see if they occur as predicted. For example, to test the theory that the earth is flat, it should be possible to find the earth's edge and to sail in a straight line directly from a starting point to the edge of the earth and back. Or take the theory in psychology—the theory of imitation—that new behavior is partly acquired by copying others. If this theory is correct, an increase in the portrayal of sex and violence on TV could be expected to lead to an increase in such behavior among viewers.[21] To test this theory one might take two groups with similar sex habits or levels of aggression, and expose one group but not the other to TV programs with sex and violence. If the former group exhibits an increase in sexual activity and aggressive or violent behavior, but the latter does not, then one could conclude that TV did affect viewer behavior in accordance with the theory of imitation.

Scientific research typically involves both deduction and induction. Thus a researcher may start with a theory and deduce certain phenomena that he or she will attempt to observe. If the observations are not quite as expected, some modification of the theory will be made and the revised theory subjected to further testing. Sometimes the theory may have to be discarded, and on the basis of observations a new theory will be induced.

For example, Ptolemy's theory that the heavens revolved around the earth was initially developed two centuries before Christ.[22] It was quite successful at predicting the changing positions of planets and stars, but it was not completely successful at predicting other astronomical phenomena. There were many discrepancies between actual astronomical observations and predictions derived from Ptolemy's theory. Astronomers responded at first by making adjustments in Ptolemy's system of compounded circles. Changes in the theory to correct discrepancies in one place created discrepancies in other places, however. Over the centuries the theory became increasingly more complex yet no more accurate. Finally, by the sixteenth century, it was concluded that the Ptolemaic system was so complex and inaccurate that it couldn't be true of nature. Copernicus then suggested an alternative heliocentric theory, that the planets revolved around the sun. This theory was simpler and more accurately accounted for a variety of astronomical phenomena.

A good example of social science research that involves both induction and deduction is the work of two psychologists regarding news coverage and social trust.[23] For some time they had been studying the rate at which people would return wallets dropped in the streets of New York City to the addresses of the owners identified inside. To observe this phenomenon the researchers would periodically drop a number of wallets in various locations and wait and see how many were returned. Typically, half the wallets dropped were eventually returned. However, one day something happened that had never happened before: none of the wallets was returned. This unexpected result led them to search for a plausible explanation for the result. Hence, they were involved in developing an explanation based on an observation—induction.

It so happened that the day this particular wallet drop occurred was the day Robert Kennedy was assassinated in June 1968. They wondered: Could the assassination have something to do with the failure to recover any of the dropped wallets? Perhaps the news coverage of the event made people upset, socially mistrustful of strangers, and unwilling to help people whom they did not know or had not seen. Hence they hypothesized that exposure to "bad" news makes people less socially trusting and cooperative.

To test this hypothesis the researchers devised a series of experiments in which people were divided into two groups and were subtly exposed to "bad" or "good" news broadcasts. Then they were asked to reveal their attitudes toward other people and to play a game with other people that allowed the observation of their cooperativeness. Thus a general theory was being tested with research designed to measure the occurrence of certain predicted observations—deduction.

The experiments demonstrated that those exposed to bad news were, indeed, less socially trusting and cooperative, confirming the researchers' expectations. Both induction and deduction had been involved in accumulating an empirical, verifiable, transmissible, explanatory, general (yet provisional) body of evidence regarding an important social phenomenon.

Applying an existing theory to new situations, deciding which phenomena to observe and how to measure them, and developing a theory that explains many more things than the specific observations that led to its discovery are all creative enterprises. Unfortunately it is difficult to teach creativity. But being aware of the processes of induction and deduction, and keeping in mind the characteristics of scientific knowledge, will make your own evaluation and conduct of research more worthwhile.

Can Politics Be Studied Scientifically?

We have implied throughout this chapter that politics can and should be studied scientifically. Some people question this assumption, however. Political science involves the study of human beings and the discovery of explanations for the political behavior that they exhibit. This discovery of regularities and patterns of behavior in politics requires that human beings act consistently or in a nonrandom, nonidiosyncratic, or discoverable manner. But if human beings do not act predictably, political scientists cannot explain and predict their political behavior.

Even if we accept that human beings are generally predictable, some persons may deliberately act in an unpredictable or misleading way. This problem may be encountered among subjects "cooperating" in a research project. For example, a person may figure out that he or she is part of an experiment to test a theory about how people will behave when faced with a particular situation. That person may deliberately act in a fashion not predicted by or in conflict with the theory, or that person may alter his or her behavior to conform to what the researcher is looking for. Similarly, a person may never reveal what he or she is really thinking, or what his or her behavior in the past has been or would be in the future. In other words, our ability to observe accurately the attributes of people may be severely limited. For example, it is difficult to develop explanations for why some people use certain drugs when measures of how often people use drugs (especially illegal ones) are notoriously inaccurate.

Measurement problems also arise in political science because the concepts of interest to many political scientists are value laden. Thus it is difficult to measure objectively these concepts, and value disagreements lead to conflict over which measure to use. For example, one measure of unemployment counts persons who are out of work and actively seeking employment. Some argue that this measure underestimates unemployment because it does not include those who are so discouraged from failure to find a job that they no longer are actively seeking employment.

Political scientists must also deal with the fact that human beings and their behavior are complex, perhaps fundamentally more complex than the subject matter of other sciences (bacteria, elements, subatomic particles, insects, and so on). This complexity poses difficulties for the researcher. For example, the complexity of human behavior has been an obstacle to political scientists' discovery of general theories to accurately explain and predict a wide range of political behavior. A theory with broad applicability might be extremely cumbersome. Specification of many variables might well be necessary to apply the theory to a large number of situations with any acceptable degree of accuracy. On the other hand, due to the complexity of human behavior, a theory that appears to be relatively simple and elegant may be attacked on the ground that it is fairly easy to find exceptions to it. Certainly no empirically verified propositions in political science match the simplicity and explanatory power of $E=mc^2$.[24]

Political scientists, like other scientists, must deal as well with obstacles to empirical observation.[25] Because political science is concerned with human behavior and its products, data needed to test theories may be extremely hard to obtain. For instance, those who have the needed information may not want to release it for political or personal reasons. Moreover, because human beings are the subjects of analysis in the social sciences, researchers must contend with ethical considerations. Obtaining certain information may interfere with an individual's right to privacy, for example. In many studies, individuals are informed about the purpose of the research; consequently, some people may not answer questions honestly or may not behave naturally. Others who know the true purpose of a study may not be willing to participate at all. Similarly, some critical experiments to test a theory may manipulate human subjects. Testing the impact of incarceration on subsequent lawful behavior, for example, could conceivably involve placing innocent people in prison. Fortunately, researchers are not given such power to interfere in people's lives. Other obstacles to observation may arise from technological limitations on measurement and analysis. For example, computers have facilitated the storage and analysis of more information than ever before, yet it is still difficult to measure accurately attitudes and behavior that are socially undesirable or that typically occur in private.

Despite the difficulties of studying politics scientifically, the scientific approach has had a profound effect on the discipline of political science. This can be seen by taking a look at the differences between the scientific approach and other approaches to the study of politics. Even if one agrees that politics can be studied scientifically, important criticisms can be made concerning the application of scientific methods to the study of politics. These are discussed in the remainder of this chapter.

Political Science as a Discipline

The study of politics is often divided into two historical periods: the period of traditional political inquiry and the period of modern or behavioral political science, which did not appear until the 1950s in the United States, although certain developments that are responsible for its appearance took place earlier.

Traditional Political Science

There were three major approaches to the study of politics during the period of traditional political inquiry: historical, legalistic, and institutional.[26] The historical approach produced detailed descriptions of the historical developments leading to political events and other phenomena. The legalistic approach involved the study of constitutions and legal codes. The institutional approach yielded descriptions of the powers and functions of political institutions (legislatures, executive branches, or courts, for example). In general, traditional political science focused on formal governmental institutions and their formal powers. Legal and historical documents, such as constitutions, proclamations, and treaties, were studied to trace the development of international organizations and key concepts, such as sovereignty, the state, federalism, and imperialism. Informal political processes, the exercise of informal power, and the internal dynamics of institutions were generally ignored.

Under the traditional approach, the study of politics was usually subsumed in academia under the disciplines of history and philosophy. Political theories concerning the nature of man and politics, the purpose and most desirable form of government, and the philosophy of law were the province of philosophy departments. When separate departments for the study of politics appeared, they were frequently called departments of government, reflecting the emphasis on governmental institutions rather than on political processes and behavior. In fact, some universities still have government departments.

Traditional political science was primarily descriptive rather than explanatory. While political theorists offered intriguing and well-reasoned theories of politics, these theories or explanations were usually not subjected to extensive empirical verification. Knowledge in political science was not acquired scientifically, nor was there a felt need to produce knowledge that had the characteristics of scientific knowledge.

Modern Political Science

The appearance of the scientific study of politics in the United States can be attributed to several developments.[27] First, numerous

European social scientists and theorists came to the United States in the 1930s, many of whom were skilled in the use of new, more scientific research methods.[28] Second, war-related social research in the following decade promoted the exchange of ideas among scientifically minded persons from the disciplines of political science, sociology, psychology, and economics. This research effort was aided by a related development: the collection of large amounts of empirical data and the development of technology and practices to store and process this information. For example, Paul Lazarsfeld pioneered in the development of large-scale survey research while working for the federal government during World War II. In 1940 he conducted the first study of voting behavior based on sample surveys.[29]

Much of the new research focused on the political behavior of individuals and groups, hence the term *behavioral political science*. Unlike traditional political science, modern political science embraces the scientific method.[30] This relationship to the scientific method is illustrated by the assumptions and objectives of behavioralism, which David Easton outlined in his article "The Current Meaning of 'Behavioralism.'" A few of them are listed here:

> There are discoverable uniformities in political behavior. These can be expressed in generalizations or theories with explanatory and predictive value. Means for acquiring and interpreting data ... need to be examined self-consciously, refined, and validated. Precision in the recording of data and the statement of findings requires measurement and quantification. Ethical evaluation and empirical explanation involve two different kinds of propositions that, for the sake of clarity, should be kept analytically distinct. Research ought to be systematic.[31]

Behavioral political science assumes and advocates the search for fundamental units of analysis that can provide a common base for the investigation of man by all social scientists. For example, some political scientists suggest that groups are an important unit on which to focus, while others suggest that decision making and decisions are.[32] There is hope that a few units of analysis will be found and focused upon much the same as physicists and chemists focus on atoms, molecules, and the like.

The reaction to behavioral and empirical political science has not been entirely positive. Critics of empirical political science point to the trivial nature of applications of scientific methods to politics. Common sense would have told the average person the same thing, they argue. As explained earlier, however, there is a difference between common sense knowledge and scientific knowledge. In order to build a solid base for further research and accumulation of scientific knowledge in politics, common sense knowledge must be empirically verified. Common sense is, after all, frequently wrong.

Some political scientists have also been concerned about the prominence of nonpolitical factors in explanations of political behavior. Psychological explanations that stress the effect of personality on political behavior or economic explanations that attempt to show how people behave in terms of costs and benefits, incentives and disincentives, offer competing ways of understanding political phenomena for those used to studying political institutions and political philosophies. To them it looks like political inquiry is being fundamentally altered by the concepts, language, and methods of other disciplines.

A more serious criticism of the scientific study of politics is that it leads to a failure to focus enough scholarly research attention on important social issues and problems. Not only is this research conducted in an objective, value-free, scientific fashion, some say, but the values, moral questions, and philosophical topics to which the research can be related are seldom considered. The implications of research findings for important public policy choices are rarely addressed. Some also argue that the quest for scientific knowledge of politics has led to a focus on topics that are quantifiable and relatively easy to verify empirically but that are not related to significant, enduring, and relevant social concerns.[33]

The reaction and challenge to behavioralism by the late 1960s led the president of the American Political Science Association to declare a "postbehavioral revolution." [34] Postbehavioralism included the following tenets:

1. Substance must precede technique. If one *must* be sacrificed for the other—and this need not always be so—it is more important to be relevant and meaningful for contemporary urgent social problems than to be sophisticated in the tools of investigation....
2. Behavioral science conceals an ideology of empirical conservatism. To confine oneself exclusively to the description and analysis of facts is to hamper the understanding of these same facts in their broadest context. As a result empirical political science must lend its support to the maintenance of the very factual conditions it explores. It unwittingly purveys an ideology of social conservatism tempered by modest incremental change.
3. Behavioral research must lose touch with reality. The heart of behavioral inquiry is abstraction and analysis and this serves to conceal the brute realities of politics. The task of post-behavioralism is to break the barriers of silence that behavioral language necessarily has created and to help political science reach out to the real needs of mankind in time of crisis.
4. Research about and constructive development of values are inextinguishable parts of the study of politics. Science cannot be and never has been evaluatively neutral despite protestations to the contrary. Hence to understand the limits of our knowledge we need to be aware of the value premises on which it stands and the alternatives for which this knowledge could be used.

5. Members of a learned discipline bear the responsibilities of all intellectuals. The intellectuals' historical role has been and must be to protect the humane values of civilization. This is their unique task and obligation. . . .

6. To know is to bear the responsibility of acting and to act is to engage in reshaping society. The intellectual as scientist bears the special obligation to put his knowledge to work. . . .

7. If the intellectual has the obligation to implement his knowledge, those organizations composed of intellectuals—the professional associations—and the universities themselves, cannot stand apart from the struggles of the day. Politicization of the professions is inescapable as well as desirable.[35]

The postbehavioral revolution has brought about renewed interest in normative political philosophy, that is, in questions of "what ought to be" rather than "what is." [36] Others have responded by turning their attention to public policy, the policy-making process, and policy analysis.[37] Many political scientists who study these topics apply scientific methods to socially relevant and important questions.

Postbehavioralism has not silenced critical reflection upon political science as a discipline and the impact of incorporating scientific method in the study of politics.[38] New concerns continue to surface. For example, some lament the failure of government to benefit from the knowledge and perspectives of political scientists and the overreliance on economists and econometric methods in policy making.[39]

One important challenge to research in political science (as well as in other social science disciplines such as sociology) has come from feminist social scientists. Among the criticisms that have been raised is that "the nature of political action and the scope of political research have been defined in ways that, in particular, exclude *women as women* from politics." [Emphasis added.][40] Accordingly, "What a feminist political science must do is develop a new vocabulary of politics so that it can express the specific and different ways in which women have wielded power, been in authority, practised citizenship, and understood freedom." [41] Even short of arguing that political science concepts and theories have been developed from a male-only perspective, it is all too easy to point to examples of gender bias in political science research, such as failure to focus on policy issues of importance to women, assuming that findings apply to everyone when the population studied was predominantly male, and bias in survey question wording.[42]

Conclusion

In this chapter we have described the characteristics of scientific knowledge and the scientific process of investigation. We have presented reasons why political scientists are attempting to become more scientific in their research and have discussed some of the difficulties associated with empirical political science. We have also touched on questions that exist about the value of the scientific approach to the study of politics. Despite these difficulties and questions, the empirical approach is widely embraced, and students of politics need to be familiar with it. In the next chapter we shall begin to examine how to take a general topic or question about some political phenomenon and develop a strategy for investigating that topic scientifically.

Notes

1. Alan C. Isaak, *Scope and Methods of Political Science,* 4th ed. (Homewood, Ill.: Dorsey, 1985), 106.
2. Ibid., 107.
3. Ibid., 66; see also 67.
4. Ted Robert Gurr, *Why Men Rebel* (Princeton, N.J.: Princeton University Press, 1970).
5. Kurt Lang and Gladys Engel Lang, *Politics and Television* (Chicago: Quadrangle, 1968), chap. 6.
6. Isaak, *Scope and Methods,* 30.
7. Ibid., 31.
8. The studies are reported in H. J. Eysenck and D. K. B. Nias, *Sex, Violence and the Media* (London: Temple Smith, 1978), 103-104.
9. Isaak, *Scope and Methods,* 103.
10. For a discussion of prediction, see Edward R. Tufte, *Data Analysis for Politics and Policy* (Englewood Cliffs, N.J.: Prentice-Hall, 1974), chap. 2, 36-40.
11. Isaak, *Scope and Methods,* 167.
12. Ibid.
13. Ibid., 167, 169.
14. See Raymond E. Wolfinger and Steven J. Rosenstone, *Who Votes?* (New Haven, Conn.: Yale University Press, 1980).
15. Bruce A. Williams and Albert R. Matheny, "Testing Theories of Social Regulation: Hazardous Waste Regulation in the American States," *Journal of Politics* 46 (May 1984): 428-458.
16. For discussion of the process of changing scientific knowledge, see Thomas Kuhn, *The Structure of Scientific Revolutions,* 2d ed. (Chicago: University of Chicago Press, 1971).
17. Isaak, *Scope and Methods,* 297.
18. Gurr, *Why Men Rebel,* 57.
19. Ibid., 54.
20. Ibid., 51.
21. For a discussion of the theory of imitation and its role in explaining possible effects of increased sex and violence on TV, see Eysenck and Nias, *Sex, Violence and the Media,* 56-59.
22. This example is based on the discussion in Kuhn, *Scientific Revolutions,* 68-69.

23. The wallet episode is described in Stephen Holloway and Harvey A. Hornstein, "How Good News Makes Us Good," *Psychology Today*, December 1976, 76-78. The results of the subsequent experiments are discussed in Stephen Holloway, Lyle Tucker, and Harvey A. Hornstein, "The Effects of Social and Nonsocial Information on Interpersonal Behavior of Males: The News Makes News," *Journal of Personality and Social Psychology* 35 (July 1977): 514-522; and in Harvey A. Hornstein, Elizabeth Lakind, Gladys Frankel, and Stella Manne, "Effects of Knowledge about Remote Social Events on Prosocial Behavior, Social Conception, and Mood," *Journal of Personality and Social Psychology* 32 (December 1975): 1038-1046.

24. For further discussion of complete and partial explanations, see Isaak, *Scope and Methods*, 143.

25. See Charles A. McCoy and John Playford, eds., *Apolitical Politics: A Critique of Behavioralism* (New York: Thomas Y. Crowell, 1967).

26. Isaak, *Scope and Methods*, 34-38.

27. Ibid., 38-39. For a history of the development of survey research, see also Earl F. Babbie, *Survey Research Methods* (Belmont, Calif.: Wadsworth, 1973), 42-45.

28. For early American sources of behavioralism, see Charles E. Merriam, *New Aspects of Politics* (Chicago: University of Chicago Press, 1924).

29. Paul F. Lazarsfeld, Bernard Berelson, and Hazel Gaudet, *The People's Choice* (New York: Duell, Sloane and Pearce, 1944).

30. David B. Easton, "The Current Meaning of 'Behavioralism,'" in James C. Charlesworth, ed., *Contemporary Political Analysis* (New York: Free Press, 1967), 11-31.

31. Easton, "Behavioralism," 16-17.

32. David B. Truman, *The Governmental Process* (New York: Knopf, 1951), and Robert A. Dahl, *Who Governs? Democracy and Power in an American City* (New Haven, Conn.: Yale University Press, 1961).

33. See McCoy and Playford, eds., *Apolitical Politics*.

34. David Easton, "The New Revolution in Political Science," *American Political Science Review* 63 (December 1969): 1051.

35. Easton, "The New Revolution," 1052.

36. Isaak, *Scope and Methods*, 45.

37. Ibid., 46.

38. For example, see David M. Ricci, *The Tragedy of Political Science: Politics, Scholarship, and Democracy* (New Haven, Conn.: Yale University Press, 1984).

39. See Richard P. Nathan, *Social Science in Government: Uses and Misuses* (New York: Basic Books, 1988).

40. Kathleen B. Jones and Anna G. Jonasdottir, "Introduction: Gender as an Analytic Category in Political Science," in Kathleen B. Jones and Anna G. Jonasdottir, eds., *The Political Interests of Gender* (Beverly Hills, Calif.: Sage, 1988), 2.

41. Kathleen B. Jones, "Towards the Revision of Politics," in Kathleen B. Jones and Anna G. Jonasdottir, eds., *The Political Interests of Gender*, 25.

42. Margrit Eichler, *Nonsexist Research Methods: A Practical Guide* (Boston: Allen & Unwin, 1987).

Terms Introduced

Behavioralism. The study of politics that focuses on political behavior and embraces the scientific method.

Deduction. A process of reasoning from a theory to specific observations.

Empirical generalization. A statement that summarizes the relationship between individual facts and that communicates general knowledge.

Empirical verification. Demonstration by means of objective observation that a statement is true.

Explanation. A statement that provides a reason for a phenomenon.

General. Applicable to many rather than a few cases.

Induction. A process of reasoning from specific observations to general principle.

Nonnormative knowledge. Knowledge concerned not with evaluation or prescription but with factual or objective determinations.

Normative knowledge. Knowledge that is evaluative, value-laden, and concerned with prescribing what ought to be.

Postbehavioralism. The reaction to behavioralism in political science that called for political science research to be more relevant to important current political issues.

Prediction. The application of explanation to events in the future. The ability to correctly anticipate future events.

Probabilistic explanation. An explanation that does not explain or predict events with 100 percent accuracy.

Provisional. Subject to revision and change.

Theory. A statement or series of statements that organize, explain, and predict knowledge.

Transmissible knowledge. Knowledge for which the method of knowing is made explicit.

Suggested Readings

Eichler, Margrit. *Nonsexist Research Methods: A Practical Guide.* Boston: Allen & Unwin, 1987.

Isaak, Alan C. *Scope and Methods of Political Science,* 4th ed. Homewood, Ill.: Dorsey, 1985.

McCoy, Charles A., and John Playford, eds. *Apolitical Politics: A Critique of Behavioralism.* New York: Thomas Y. Crowell, 1967.

Nielsen, Joyce McCarl, ed. *Feminist Research Methods: Exemplary Readings in the Social Sciences.* Boulder, Colo.: Westview, 1990.

CHAPTER 3

The Building Blocks
of Social Scientific Research:
Hypotheses, Concepts, and Variables

Chapters 1 and 2 discussed what it means to acquire scientific knowledge and presented a number of examples of political science research intended to produce this type of knowledge. In this chapter we will begin the process of evaluating and acquiring scientific knowledge by explaining the initial steps in an empirical research project. These steps require a researcher to (1) specify the question or problem with which the research is concerned; (2) propose a suitable explanation for the phenomena under study; (3) define the concepts thought to be useful in this explanation; and (4) formulate testable hypotheses. Although we will discuss these steps as if they represent a logical sequence of thought, in the conduct of actual research the order may vary. They must all be accomplished eventually, however, before a research project can be completed successfully. The sooner the issues and decisions involved in each of the steps are addressed, the sooner the other portions of the research project can be completed.

Specifying the Research Question

One of the most important purposes of social scientific research is to answer questions about social phenomena. The research projects summarized in Chapter 1, for example, all attempt to answer questions about some important political behavior. Why are some political regimes more stable than others? Why do some candidates for U.S. Congress receive more votes than other candidates do? Why do public officials make the public policy decisions they do? And why do Supreme

Court justices take the positions they take on the cases that come before them? In every case the researchers identified some political phenomenon that interested them and tried to answer questions about that phenomenon.

The phenomena investigated by political scientists are diverse and are limited only by whether they are significant (that is, would advance our understanding of politics and government), observable, and political. Political scientists attempt to answer questions about the political behavior of individuals (voters, citizens, residents of a particular area, Supreme Court justices, presidents), groups (political parties, interest groups, labor unions, ethnic organizations), institutions (state legislatures, city governments, bureaucracies, district courts), and nations.

The first task of a researcher is to specify the "why" question with which the research is concerned. That will identify the phenomenon being investigated and will point the research project in the direction of providing an explanation for that phenomenon. Failure to specify the "why" question clearly can lead to confused researchers as well as confused readers.

Where do the research questions of political scientists originate? There are many answers. Some researchers become interested in a topic because of personal observation or experience. For example, a researcher who works for a candidate who loses a political campaign may wonder what factors are responsible for electoral success, and a researcher who fled his country of birth during a period of civil unrest may be drawn to conducting research on the causes of political disorder. Some researchers are drawn to a topic because of the research and writing of others. A scholar familiar with studies of congressional decision making may want to investigate the reasons for the success and failure of different public policy proposals. Still others select a research topic because of their interest in some broader social theory, as in the researcher whose fascination with economic theories of rational decision making prompted the study of federal bureaucrats' behavior; similarly, researchers concerned in general with democratic theory often conduct research on what causes people to participate in politics. Finally, it must be admitted, researchers sometimes select research topics for less lofty reasons: because grant money for a particular subject is available, or because demonstrating expertise in a particular area will advance their professional career objectives.

The framing of an engaging and appropriate research question will get a research project off to a good start. Any of the following questions would probably lead to a politically significant and informative research project:

Why are some cities fiscally healthier than others?
Why are some ethnic groups more cohesive than others?
Why are some U.S. senators more liberal than others?
Why are some judges more protective of the rights of the accused than others?
Why do some nations spend more on weapons systems than others?
Why do some states have more extensive welfare systems than others?
Why are some governments more stable than others?

Students sometimes have difficulty formulating interesting and appropriate research questions. Researchers also occasionally pose questions that are simplistic, trivial, or impossible to answer. A research project will get off on the wrong foot if the question that shapes it is inappropriate, unduly concerned with discrete facts, or focused on reaching normative conclusions.

Political scientists seek knowledge about political phenomena. Although the definition of political phenomena is vague, it does not include the study of all human characteristics or behavior. For example, research studies guided by questions such as "Why do some people drink coffee and others do not?" or "Why did dinosaurs become extinct?" might be interesting studies, but they would be unlikely to yield fresh insights into political phenomena. Questions such as those would be inappropriate for the study of politics and would be better addressed by people in fields other than political science.

Research questions may also limit the significance of a research project if they are unduly focused on discrete facts. Questions such as "Who is the secretary of state?" or "Which interest groups contribute the most money to political campaigns?" or "How many nuclear warheads does the Soviet Union possess?" may yield important factual knowledge, but they will not sustain a research project of the type developed in this book. Each of them asks for one discrete piece of information or fact. While facts are important, they alone will not yield scientific knowledge—knowledge about patterns, relationships, and explanations. Scientific knowledge should be consistent with facts, but facts are not enough to yield scientific explanations. Instead we are interested here in advancing and testing generalizations relating one phenomenon to another. In the absence of such generalizations, factual knowledge of the type called for by the preceding research questions will be fundamentally limited in scope.

Another type of question that is inconsistent with the research methods discussed in this book is a question calling for a normative conclusion. Questions such as "Should the United States deploy nuclear missiles in Europe?" or "Is the 'actual malice test' too stringent a guideline for the solution of libel suits?" or "Were Ronald Reagan's public policies unfair to the working poor?" are important and suitable for the attention of political scientists (indeed, for any citizen), but they, too, are inappropriate as presently framed. They ask for a normative response, seeking an indication of what is good or of what should be done. Although scientific knowledge may be helpful in answering questions like these, it cannot provide the answers without regard for an individual's personal values or preferences. What someone ultimately likes or dislikes, values or rejects, is involved in the answers to these questions.

Proposing Explanations

Once a researcher has developed a suitable research question or topic, the next step is to propose an explanation for the phenomenon the researcher is interested in understanding. In the previous section we said that most political science research is concerned with answering questions about some political phenomenon. As noted earlier, these questions are normally "why" questions in which the researcher is trying to explain the variation in political phenomena—in other words, why political characteristics and behavior occur at some times rather than others, or why they are more likely to be exhibited in some circumstances than in others.

To advance our understanding of political behavior, we propose explanations for a phenomenon and then produce evidence bearing on those explanations. Proposing an explanation involves identifying other phenomena that we think will help us account for the object of our research and then specifying how these two (or more) phenomena are related.

In the research examples described in Chapter 1 the researchers proposed explanations for the political phenomena they were studying. Ted Gurr thought that political violence might be affected by a population's sense of relative deprivation. Gary Jacobson thought that congressional election outcomes might be influenced by campaign spending. Benjamin Page and Robert Shapiro wondered if public policy decisions made in the United States over a forty-year period were influenced by the amount of popular support for those decisions. And Jeffrey Segal and Albert Cover tried to find out if the personal attitudes of Supreme Court justices affect their judicial decisions.

Those phenomena that we think will help us explain the political characteristics or behavior that interest us are called independent variables. Independent variables are the measures of the phenomena that are thought to influence, affect, or cause some other phenomenon. Dependent variables are thought to be caused, to depend upon, or to be a function of the independent variables. Thus, if a researcher has hypothesized that acquiring more formal education will lead to increased income later on (in other words, that income may be explained by education), then years of formal education would be the independent variable and income would be the dependent variable.

Proposed explanations for political phenomena are often more complicated than the simple identification of one independent variable that is thought to explain a dependent variable. More than one phenomenon is usually needed to account adequately for most political behavior. For example, suppose a researcher proposes that an individual's income and an individual's attitude toward busing are related, with the higher the income (independent variable), the more liberal the attitude (dependent variable). The insightful researcher would realize the possibility that another phenomenon, such as whether the individual has school-age children, might also affect his or her attitude toward busing. The proposed explanation for attitudes toward busing, then, would involve an alternative variable in addition to the original independent variable, and the researcher would be interested in determining the relative effect of each variable on the dependent variable. This is done by "controlling for" or "holding constant" one of the independent variables so that the effect of the other may be observed. This process will be discussed in more detail in Chapter 13.

Sometimes researchers are also able to propose explanations for how the independent variables are related to each other. In particular, we might want to distinguish between which independent variables come before other independent variables and indicate which have a more direct, as opposed to indirect, effect on the phenomenon we are trying to explain (the dependent variable). Variables that occur prior to all other variables and that may affect other independent variables are called *antecedent variables*. Variables that occur closer in time to the dependent variable and are themselves affected by other independent variables are called *intervening variables*. The roles of antecedent and intervening variables in the explanation of the dependent variable differ significantly. Consider these examples.

Suppose a researcher hypothesizes that a person who favors increased military spending is more likely to vote for a Republican presidential candidate than a person who does not favor military spending increases. In this case the attitude toward military spending would be the independent variable and the presidential vote the dependent variable. The researcher might wonder what causes the attitude toward military spending and might propose that those people who believe that the Soviet Union is an expansionist regime are more apt to favor increased military spending. This new variable would then be an antecedent variable since it comes before and affects (we think) the independent variable. Thinking about antecedent variables pushes our explanatory scheme further back in time and, it is hoped, will lead to a more complete understanding of a particular phenomenon (in this case presidential voting). Notice how the independent variable in the original hypothesis (favoring increased defense spending) becomes the dependent variable in the hypothesis involving the antecedent variable (beliefs about the Soviet Union). Also notice that in this example beliefs about the Soviet Union are thought to exert an indirect effect on the dependent variable (presidential voting) via its impact on attitudes toward military spending.

Now let us consider a second example. Suppose a researcher hypothesizes that the number of years of formal education affects one's chances of turning out to vote. In this case education would be the independent variable and turnout the dependent variable. If the researcher then begins to think about what it is about formal education that has this effect, he or she has begun to identify the intervening variables between education and turnout. For example, the researcher might hypothesize that formal education causes a sense of civic duty, which in turn causes voter turnout, or that formal education causes an ability to deal with bureaucratic details, which in turn causes voter turnout. Intervening variables come between an independent and dependent variable and help explain the process by which one influences the other.

Explanatory schemes that involve numerous independent, alternative, antecedent, and intervening variables can become quite complex. An arrow diagram is a handy device for presenting and keeping track of such complicated explanations. It specifies the phenomena of interest; indicates which variables are independent, alternative, antecedent, intervening, and dependent; and shows which variables are thought to affect which other ones. Figure 3-1 presents arrow diagrams for the two examples we just considered.

In both diagrams the dependent variable is placed at the end of the time line, with the independent, alternative, intervening, and antecedent variables placed in their appropriate locations to indicate which ones come first. Arrows indicate that one variable is thought to explain or be related to another; the direction of the arrow indicates which variable is independent and which is dependent in that proposed relationship.

Figure 3-2 shows two examples of actual arrow diagrams that have been proposed and tested by political scientists. Both are thought to explain presidential voting behavior. In the first diagram the ultimate dependent variable is the Vote, and is thought to be explained by Candidate Evaluations and Party Identification. Candidate Evaluations, in turn, is explained by Issue Losses, Party Identification, and Perceived Candidate Personalities. These, in turn, are explained by other concepts in the diagram. The variables at the top of the diagram tend to be antecedent variables; the ones in the center tend to be intervening

Figure 3-1   Arrow Diagrams of Military Spending and Voter Turnout
Examples

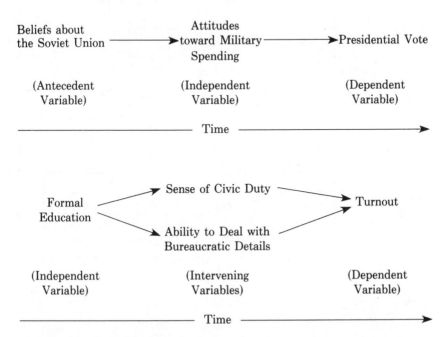

variables. Nine independent variables of one sort or another figure in the
explanation of the vote.

The second diagram also has the Vote as the ultimate dependent
variable, which is explained directly by only one independent variable,
Comparative Candidate Evaluations. The latter variable, in turn, is
dependent upon six independent variables: Personal Qualities Evaluations,
Comparative Policy Distances, Current Party Attachment, Region, Religion,
and Partisan Voting History. In this diagram sixteen variables figure, either
indirectly or directly, in the explanation of the vote, with the antecedent
variables located around the perimeter of the diagram and the intervening
variables closer to the center. Both of these diagrams clearly represent
complicated and extensive attempts to explain a dependent variable.

Defining Concepts

One of the primary purposes of political science research is to
provide scientific explanations for political phenomena. In this section we
will consider what these phenomena are and how our research can be
sharpened so that the knowledge we acquire is transmissible, empirical,
and general.

Figure 3-2   Two Causal Models of Vote Choice

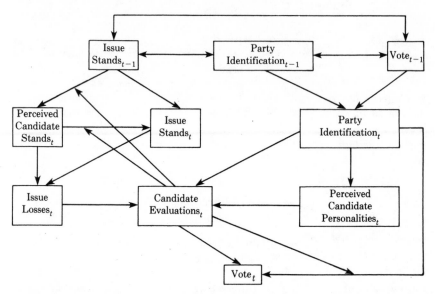

Source: Gregory B. Markus and Philip E. Converse, "A Dynamic Simultaneous Equation Model of Electoral Choice," *American Political Science Review* 73 (December 1979): 1059. Reprinted with permission.

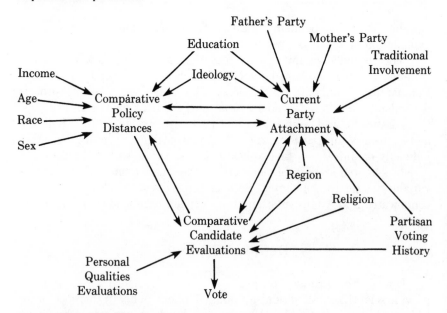

Source: Benjamin I. Page and Calvin C. Jones, "Reciprocal Effects of Policy Preferences, Party Loyalties and the Vote," *American Political Science Review* 73 (December 1979): 1083. Reprinted with permission.

Political scientists are interested in why people or social groupings (organizations, political parties, legislatures, states, countries) behave in a certain way or have particular attributes or properties. The words that we choose to describe these behaviors or attributes are called concepts. Concepts should be accurate, precise, and informative.

In our daily life we use concepts frequently to name and describe features of our environment. For example, we describe some snakes as poisonous and others as nonpoisonous, some politicians as liberal and others as conservative, some friends as shy and others as extroverted. These attributes or concepts are useful to us because they help us observe and understand aspects of our environment, and they help us communicate with others.

Concepts also contribute to the identification and delineation of the scientific disciplines within which research is done. In fact, to a large extent a discipline maintains its identity because different researchers within it share a concern for the same concepts. Physics, for example, is concerned with the concepts of gravity and mass (among others); sociology with social class and social mobility; psychology with personality and deviance. By contrast, political science is concerned with concepts such as democracy, power, representation, justice, and equality. The boundaries of disciplines are not well defined or rigid, however. Political scientists, developmental psychologists, sociologists, and anthropologists all share an interest in how new members of a society are "socialized" into the norms and beliefs of that society, for example. Nonetheless, because a particular discipline has some minimal level of shared consensus concerning its significant concepts, researchers can usually communicate more readily with other researchers in the same discipline than with researchers in other disciplines.

Concepts are developed through a process by which some human group (tribe, nation, culture, profession) agrees to give a phenomenon or property a particular name. The process is ongoing and somewhat arbitrary and does not ensure that all peoples everywhere will give the same phenomena the same names. In some areas of the United States, for example, a "soda" is a carbonated beverage, while in other areas it is a drink with ice cream in it. Likewise, the English language has only one word for love, whereas the Greeks have three words to distinguish between romantic love, familial love, and generalized feelings of affection.[1] Concepts disappear from a group's language when they are no longer needed, and new ones are invented as new phenomena are noticed that require names (for example, computer "programs" and "software," "cultural imperialism," and "hyperkinetic" behavior).

Some concepts—such as "car," "chair," and "vote"—are fairly precise because there is considerable agreement about their meaning. Others are more abstract and lend themselves to differing definitions—for example, "liberalism," "crime," "democracy," "equal opportunity," "human rights," "social mobility," and "alienation." A similar concept is "orange." Although there is considerable agreement about it (orange is not usually confused with purple), the agreement is less than total (whether a particular object is orange or red is not always clear).

Unfortunately, most interesting concepts that political scientists deal with lack a completely precise, shared meaning. This hinders communication concerning research and creates uncertainty regarding the measurement of a phenomenon. Consequently, a researcher must explain what is meant by the concept so that a measurement strategy may be developed and so that those reading and evaluating the research can decide if the meaning accords with their own understanding of the term. Although some concepts that political scientists use—such as "amount of formal education," "presidential vote," and "amount of foreign trade"—are not particularly abstract, other concepts—such as "partisan realignment," "political integration," and "regime support"—are far more abstract and need more careful consideration and definition.

Suppose, for example, that a researcher is interested in the kinds of political systems that different countries have and, in particular, why some countries are more democratic than others. "Democracy" is consequently a key concept and one that needs definition and measurement. The word contains meaning for most of us; that is, we have some idea what is democratic and what is not. But once we begin thinking about the concept, we quickly realize that it is not as clear as we thought originally. To some, a country is democratic if it has "competing political parties, operating in free elections, with some reasonable level of popular participation in the process." [2] To others, a country is democratic only if there are legal guarantees protecting free speech, press, religion, and the like. To others, a country is democratic if the political leaders make decisions that are acceptable to the populace. And to still others, democracy implies economic equality among the citizenry. If a country has all of these attributes, it would be called a democracy by any of the criteria and there would be no problem classifying the country. But if a country possesses only one of the above attributes, its classification would be uncertain, since by some definitions it would be democratic but by others it would not. Different definitions require different measurements and may result in different research findings. Hence defining one's concepts is important, particularly when the concept is so abstract as to make shared agreement difficult.

Concept definitions have a direct impact on the quality of knowledge produced by research studies. Suppose, for example, that a researcher is interested in the connection between economic development and democracy, the working hypothesis being that countries with a high level of economic development will be more likely to have democratic forms of government. And suppose that there are two definitions of economic development and two definitions of democracy that might be used in the research. Finally, suppose that the researcher has data on twelve countries (A-L) included in the study (Table 3-1). This table shows that the definition selected for each concept has a direct bearing on how different countries are categorized on each attribute. By definition 1, countries A, B, C, D, E, F are economically developed; while by definition 2, countries A, B, C, G, H, I are. By definition 1, countries A, B, C, D, E, F are democracies; by definition 2, countries D, E, F, J, K, L are.

This is only the beginning of our troubles, however. When we look for a pattern involving the economic development and democracy of countries, we find that our answer depends mightily on how we have defined the two concepts. If we use the first definitions of the two concepts, we find that all economically developed countries are also democracies (A, B, C, D, E, F), which supports our hypothesis. If we use the first definition for economic development and the second for democracy (or vice-versa), half of the economically developed nations are democracies and half are not. If we use the second definitions of both concepts, none of the economically developed countries is a democracy while all of the undeveloped countries are (D, E, F, J, K, L). In other words, because of our inability to formulate a precise definition of the two concepts, and because the two definitions of each concept yield quite different categorizations of the twelve countries, our hypothesis could be either confirmed or disconfirmed by the data at hand. Our conceptual confusion has put us in a difficult position.

Consider another example. Suppose a researcher is interested in why some people are liberal and some are not. In this case one needs to define what is meant by liberal so that those who are liberal can be identified. *Liberal* is a frequently used term, but it has many different meanings: one who favors change, one who favors redistributive income or social welfare policies, one who favors increased government spending and taxation, or one who opposes government interference into the political activities of its citizens. If a person possessed all these attributes, there would be no problem deciding that he or she was a liberal. A problem arises, however, when a person possesses some of these attributes but not others.

The previous examples illustrate the elusive nature of concepts and the need to define them. The empirical researcher's responsibility to "define terms" is a necessary and challenging one. Unfortunately, many of the concepts used by political science researchers are fairly abstract and need careful thought and extensive elaboration.

Researchers can clarify the concept definitions they use simply by making the meanings of key concepts explicit. This requires researchers to think carefully about the concepts used in their research and to share

Table 3-1   Concept Development: The Relation between Economic
Development and Democracy

1. *Is the country economically developed?*

		By definition 1: Yes	No
By definition 2:	*Yes*	A, B, C	G, H, I
	No	D, E, F	J, K, L

2. *Is the country a democracy?*

		By definition 1: Yes	No
By definition 2:	*Yes*	D, E, F	J, K, L
	No	A, B, C	G, H, I

their meanings with others. Other researchers often challenge concept definitions, requiring researchers to elaborate upon and justify their meanings.

Another way in which researchers get help in defining concepts is by reviewing the definitions used by others and revising or borrowing those definitions. This is one of the reasons why researchers conduct literature reviews of pertinent research, a task we take up in detail in Chapter 6. For example, a researcher interested in the political attitudes and behavior of the American public would find the following definitions of key concepts in the existing literature:

Political participation. Those activities by private citizens that are more or less directly aimed at influencing the selection of governmental personnel and/or the actions they take.[3]
Political violence. All collective attacks within a political community against the political regime, its actors—including competing political groups as well as incumbents—or its policies.[4]
Political efficacy. The feeling that individual political action does have, or can have, an impact upon the political processes—that it is worthwhile to perform one's civic duties.[5]
Belief system. A configuration of ideas and attitudes in which the elements are bound together by some form of constraint or functional interdependence.[6]

Each of these concepts is somewhat vague and lacks complete shared agreement about its meaning. Furthermore, it is possible to raise questions about each of these concept definitions. Notice, for example, that the definition of political participation excludes the possibility that government employees (presumably "nonprivate citizens") engage in political participation, and the definition of political efficacy excludes the impact of collective political action on political processes. Consequently, we may find these and other concept definitions inadequate and revise them to capture more accurately what we mean by the terms.

Over time a discipline cannot proceed very far unless there is some minimal agreement about the meanings of the concepts with which scientific research is concerned. Researchers must take care to think about the phenomena named in a research project and make explicit the meanings of any problematic concepts.

Formulating Hypotheses

Thus far we have discussed three stages in the research process: identifying the research question, proposing explanations for the phenomena of interest, and defining the concepts used to describe these phenomena. By this point, then, the researcher (or reader of social science research) is ready to state what his or her hypotheses are. *Hypotheses* are explicit statements that indicate how a researcher thinks the phenomena of interest are related. They are guesses (but of an "educated" nature) that represent the proposed explanation for some phenomena and that indicate how an independent variable is thought to affect, influence, or alter a dependent variable. Since hypotheses are proposed relationships, they may turn out to be incorrect. To test a hypothesis adequately and persuasively, it must be properly formulated.

Actually, our everyday language is filled with hypotheses (though they may not be properly formulated). When we wonder why a particular child is shy, for example, and we assert that it is because he is the baby of the family, we are actually proposing an explanation for a concept (shyness) that relies on another concept (birth order). When we wonder why a local public official turned down our request for a new street light, and we suspect that it's because we are from different political parties, we are suggesting a hypothesis relating partisan identification and official responsiveness. When we wonder why a particular country is experiencing social turmoil, and we decide that it is because the population is illiterate, poor, and ethnically diverse, we are proposing hypotheses relating literacy, wealth, ethnic homogeneity, and political stability. In fact, whenever we propose an explanation for any phenomenon, we are engaging in the preliminary stages of hypothesis formulation. One of the differences between doing this in everyday conversation and doing it as part of a scientific research project is that in research, hypothesis formulation is only the beginning of a process that will include a test of our hypotheses. In everyday life we seldom test our hypotheses systematically.

Types of Hypotheses

There are essentially four different types of hypotheses, depending upon what the researcher is willing to propose about the relationship between concepts. Hypotheses can be null, correlative, directional, or causal.

A *null hypothesis* is simply a hypothesis that states that there is no relationship between two variables. When we analyze data to test a hypothesis, we often work with the null hypothesis and attempt to disprove it. A null hypothesis posits the absence of a relationship between two or more variables and usually represents the opposite of the hypothesis we are actually trying to confirm. (Null hypotheses will be discussed more fully in Chapter 12.)

A *correlative hypothesis* states that there is a relationship between two (or among more) concepts. However, it does not specify the nature of this relationship. "There is a relationship between age and political cynicism" and "there is a relationship between cultural homogeneity and civil unrest" are two correlative hypotheses. Notice that they do not tell us whether it is the old or the young who are thought to be more cynical, nor whether civil unrest is thought to be more or less likely when cultural homogeneity is present.

With a *directional hypothesis,* the researcher makes a guess about the direction of the relationship between concepts. If the researcher thinks that concepts are apt to increase in size together or decrease in size together, then there is a *direct relationship* hypothesized between them. Consider these examples:

> As a person's years of formal education increase, that person's income increases.
> As the percentage of a country's population that is literate increases, the country's political process becomes more democratic.
> The older a person gets, the more conservative the person becomes.
> The less newspaper reading a person does, the less informed about current events the person will be.

If, on the other hand, the researcher thinks that as one concept increases in size or amount another one will decrease in size or amount, then an *inverse relationship* is suggested. Here are some examples:

> The older a person is, the less tolerant of social protest the person becomes.
> The more income a person has, the less concerned about mass transit the person will become.
> The more affluent a country becomes, the less property crime that country will have.

Both types of directional hypotheses specify the existence and the direction of the proposed relationship. Consequently, the researcher's hypothesis will be disproved if there is no relationship between the two concepts or if the relationship is in the opposite direction of that hypothesized. On the other hand, if the hypothesis is supported by the evidence, then we have learned more than simply that there is a relationship between two concepts. To know that there is a relationship between income and education does not tell us whether income goes up or down with increased education. To learn that there is a relationship between the size of a country's population and the amount of democracy that exists in the country's political process does not tell us whether large or small populations have more democratic political processes. To discover that there is a relationship between age and political participation does not tell us whether the young or the old are more likely to participate. In all three of these cases, the direction of the relationship is also illuminating.

Directional hypotheses do not necessarily specify either a simple direct or inverse linear relationship between two concepts, however. There are many other possibilities. For example, the relationship between age and political participation might be *curvilinear,* with the youngest and the oldest populations being the least participatory (due to the geographical mobility of the young and the poor health of the elderly) and the middle-aged participating the most. Or the relationship between two concepts might be *logarithmic,* with increasing amounts of one concept having less and less effect on the other concept. An example of this is the relationship between campaign spending and votes received: the initial amount of money is the most crucial; at higher levels of spending each dollar spent has less and less impact.[7] Basically, a directional hypothesis may specify any type of mathematical function relating the independent and dependent variables. Most directional hypotheses in political science, however, are simple linear ones.

A *causal hypothesis* makes the boldest claim about the relationship between two or more variables, yet it is also the most difficult to confirm. Causal hypotheses may take a number of forms. They may simply state that one variable is a cause of another, as in "literacy, affluence, and cultural homogeneity cause democratic movements in countries." Or they may be stated in "if/then" terms, as in "if a congressional challenger spends less than $200,000, then he will lose." Finally, a causal hypothesis may be stated negatively, as in "if it were not for the large security forces maintained by modern national governments, civil strife would be much more prevalent."

What is distinctive about a causal hypothesis is not so much its form as the nature of the claim it makes. Null, correlative, and directional hypotheses are primarily concerned with relationships, correlations, or covariations between variables. They posit either the absence or the presence of a connection between one phenomenon and another. Causal hypotheses, on the other hand, advance this proposition but also make two other important claims: that one phenomenon (the cause) preceded the other phenomenon (the effect) in time and that the effect was dependent upon or could not have occurred in the absence of the cause. Researchers evaluating causal hypotheses must present evidence concerning both these claims.

It is possible to confirm a relationship between two phenomena without one being the cause of the other. There is a relationship between the amount of television individuals watch, for example, and how fearful they are, but we do not know which phenomenon comes first in time. There is also a relationship between the height of major-party presidential candidates and their electoral success, but the relationship may well be accidental (that is, not necessary or dependent) rather than causal. And there is a relationship between income and voter turnout, but it is largely due to the impact of education on both income and turnout and hence not due to the causal influence of income.

Deciding whether an observed relationship is causal is one of the most challenging aspects of scientific research. A causal hypothesis makes a distinctive and more significant assertion than any of the other types of hypotheses do. Consequently, the evaluation of a causal hypothesis requires extraordinary research designs and data analysis. The knowledge derived from the confirmation of a causal hypothesis is so valuable, however, that researchers are often intent on evaluating such hypotheses. All of the researchers mentioned in Chapter 1 wanted to discover the causes of various phenomena although their particular research studies may not have provided evidence adequate for such a task.

Political scientists often speak about causal hypotheses, construct causal models, and perform causal analysis, but we seldom achieve causal knowledge. The world of politics is so complex and our ability to test causal hypotheses so limited that causal knowledge remains elusive, and causal hypotheses are rare. But since a causal hypothesis posits the most informative form of scientific knowledge, it is in many respects the most desirable type of hypothesis.

Characteristics of Good Hypotheses

So far we have discussed what a hypothesis is and identified four types of hypotheses. The characteristics and wording of a good hypothesis will now be examined.

First, hypotheses should be *empirical* statements, that is, they should be educated guesses about relationships that exist in the real world, not statements about what ought to be true or about what a researcher believes should be the case. Statements such as "South Africa should respect the civil rights of its nonwhite residents" are *normative* statements, and they cannot be evaluated with the research methods discussed here. Although empirical findings may be pertinent to the formulation and evaluation of a normative statement, they can never tell us for certain whether the normative statement is justified.

Let us return to our example of the researcher interested in the causes of democracy. By now, this researcher ought to have defined the central concept (democracy) and those concepts thought to be related to democracy (such as literacy, size of population, geographical isolation, and economic development). If the researcher then hypothesizes that "democracy is the best form of government," he or she has formulated a normative, nonempirical statement that cannot possibly be tested in its present form. The statement states the preference of the researcher rather than an explanation for a phenomenon. To produce an acceptable hypothesis, the researcher ought to make an educated guess about the way the real world is, for example: "Democracy exists only where the population is literate and affluent." This hypothesis now proposes an explanation for a phenomenon that can be empirically observed. Whether the hypothesis is confirmed is not necessarily related to whether the researcher thinks the phenomenon (in this case democracy) is good or bad. Some proposed hypotheses need to be revised because they are nonempirical and cannot be evaluated with empirical observations alone. Consider these two examples:

> Increasing the size of the navy would be better for the United States than increasing the number of stationary antiballistic missiles.
> Democrats ought to reject their New Deal liberalism philosophy and develop an alternative view.

This does not mean, however, that empirical knowledge is completely irrelevant for normative inquiry. Often people have reached normative conclusions based on their evaluation of empirical relationships. Someone might reason, for example, that:

1. Current government welfare programs lead to family disintegration.
2. Family disintegration is bad.
3. Therefore, current government welfare programs are bad.

The first statement could be considered a research hypothesis and could be investigated using the techniques developed in this book. The results could then be used to evaluate the third statement. However, the second statement, which is a normative statement of preference, cannot be tested, as it stands, using these techniques.

Normative thinking is useful because it forces an individual to clarify his or her values, and it encourages research on significant empirical questions. For example, a normative distaste for crime encourages empirical research on the causes of crime. Consequently, the two modes of inquiry—normative and empirical—should be viewed as complementary rather than contradictory.

A second characteristic of a good hypothesis is *generality*. It should explain a general phenomenon rather than one particular occurrence of the phenomenon. For example, one might hypothesize that the cause of World War II was economic upheaval in Germany. If the hypothesis were confirmed, what would be the extent of our knowledge? We would know the cause of one war. This knowledge is valuable, but it would be more useful to know if economic upheaval *in general* causes wars. That would be knowledge pertaining to many occurrences of a phenomenon (in this case many wars), rather than knowledge about just one occurrence. A more general hypothesis, then, might be "the greater the economic upheaval experienced by a country, the more likely that country is to become involved in a war." Knowledge about the causes of particular occurrences of a phenomenon could be helpful in formulating more general guesses about the relationships between concepts, but with a general hypothesis we attempt to expand the scope of our knowledge beyond individual cases.

Below are four hypotheses that are too narrow, followed by four acceptable hypotheses that are more general:

Senator X voted for that bill because it is the president's bill and they are both Republicans.	Senators are more likely to vote for bills sponsored by the president if they belong to the same political party as the president.
The United States is a democracy because its population is affluent and literate.	Affluence and literacy are necessary conditions for democracy.
The United States has more murders than other countries because so many people own guns there.	The more guns per capita a country possesses, the more murders that country will experience.
Joe is a liberal because his mother is one too.	If a person's mother is liberal, then that person is apt to be liberal also.

A third characteristic of a good hypothesis is that it should be *plausible*; that is, there should be some logical reason for thinking that it might be confirmed. Of course, since a hypothesis is a guess about a relationship, whether it will be confirmed cannot be known for certain. Any number of hypotheses could be thought of and tested, but there are many fewer plausible ones. For example, if a researcher hypothesized that "people who eat dry cereal for breakfast are more likely to be liberal than people who eat eggs," we would question his or her logic even though the form of the hypothesis may be perfectly acceptable. It is difficult to imagine why this hypothesis would be confirmed.

But how do we make sure that a hypothesis has a good chance of being confirmed? Sometimes the justification is provided by specific instances in which the hypothesis was supported (going from specific to general knowledge in the manner discussed in Chapter 2—that is, induction). For example, a researcher may have observed a particular election in which a hotly contested primary campaign damaged the eventual nominee's chances of winning the general election. The researcher may then have concluded that "the more difficult it is for candidates to secure their party's nomination, the more poorly those candidates will do in the general election."

A hypothesis also may be justified through the process of deduction. A researcher may deduce from more general theories that a particular hypothesis is sensible. For example, there is a general psychological theory that frustration leads to aggression. Some political scientists have adapted this general theory to the study of political violence or civil unrest and hypothesized that civil unrest occurs when a civilian population is frustrated. A population may feel frustrated when many people believe that they are economically or politically worse off than they should be, than they used to be, or than other people like themselves are. This feeling has been called "relative deprivation" and it has figured prominently in hypotheses that relative deprivation leads to civil unrest. (We first discussed this line of research in Chapter 1.) In this way the general frustration-aggression theory led to a more specialized, deduced hypothesis for the occurrence of civil unrest.

Formulating plausible hypotheses is one of the reasons why researchers conduct a literature review early in their research projects. Literature reviews (discussed in more detail in Chapter 6) can acquaint researchers both with general theories and with specific hypotheses advanced by others. In either case, reading the literature on a subject can improve the chances that a hypothesis will be confirmed. There are no hard and fast rules to ensure plausibility, however. After all, people used to think that "germs cause diseases" was an implausible hypothesis and that "dirt may be turned into gold" was a plausible one.

The fourth characteristic of all good hypotheses is that they are *specific*. The concepts used in a hypothesis should be carefully defined. For example, a hypothesis that suggests that "there is a relationship between personality and political attitudes" is far too ambiguous. What is meant by personality? Which political attitudes? A more specific reformulation of this hypothesis might be "the more self-esteem a person has, the less likely a person is to be an isolationist." Now personality has been narrowed to self-esteem, and the political attitude has been defined as isolationism, both more precise concepts. Eventually, of course, even these two terms must be given more precise definitions when it comes to measuring them. (We will return to the problem of measuring concepts in Chapter 4.)

Following are four examples of ambiguous hypotheses that have been made more specific:

How a person votes for president depends on the information he or she is exposed to.	The more information favoring candidate X a person is exposed to during a political campaign, the more likely that person is to vote for candidate X.
A country's geographical location matters for the type of political system it develops.	The more borders a country shares with other countries, the more likely that country is to have a nondemocratic political process.
A person's capabilities affect his or her political attitudes.	The more intelligent a person is, the more likely he or she is to support civil liberties.
Guns do not cause crime.	People who own guns are less likely to be the victims of crimes than persons who do not own guns.

Finally, a good hypothesis is *testable*; there must be some evidence that is obtainable and that will indicate whether the hypothesis is correct. Hypotheses for which either confirming or nonconfirming evidence is impossible to gather are untestable.

Consider this example of a promising yet untestable hypothesis: "The more supportive of political authorities a child is, the less likely that child will be to engage in political dissent as an adult." This hypothesis is general, plausible, fairly specific, and empirical, but it is currently untestable because no data exist to test the proposition. The hypothesis requires data that measure a set of attitudes for individuals when they are children and a set of behaviors when they are adults. Survey data do exist that include the political attitudes and behavior of seventeen-and eighteen-year-olds and their parents in 1965 and many of the same people in 1973.[8] These data lack childhood measures for the parents, however, and for the others there are only late adolescent and early adulthood (mid-twenties) measures. Consequently, a frustrating practical barrier prevents the testing of an otherwise acceptable hypothesis.

Students in one-semester college courses on research methods often run up against this constraint. A semester is not usually long enough to collect and analyze data, and some data may be too expensive to acquire. Many interesting hypotheses go untested simply because researchers do not have the resources to collect the data necessary to test them.

Hypotheses stated in tautological form are also untestable. A tautology is a statement linking two concepts that mean essentially the same thing: for example, "the less support there is for a country's political institutions, the more tenuous the stability of that country's political system." This hypothesis would be difficult to disconfirm because the two concepts are so similar. To provide a fair test one would have to measure independently—in different ways—the support for the political institutions and the stability of the political system.

"Conspiracy" theories are often tautological. The typical conspiracy theory states that "group X always gets its way when political decisions are made." If a skeptic provides a disconfirming case of a decision where Group X was apparently the loser, the conspiracy theorists typically respond, "They allowed that decision in order to disguise their power." If decisions on which Group X "wins" are evidence for a conspiracy theory and decisions on which Group X "loses" are also evidence for the same conspiracy theory, then it is impossible for any evidence to disconfirm the hypothesis. A hypothesis that cannot be disconfirmed is not a hypothesis at all, and it is not suitable for empirical data analysis.

There are many hypotheses, then, that are not formulated in a way that permits an informative test of them with empirical research. Readers of empirical research in political science, as well as researchers themselves, should take care that research hypotheses are empirical, general, plausible, specific, and testable. Hypotheses that do not share these characteristics are likely to cause difficulty for the researcher and reader alike and make a minimal contribution to scientific knowledge.

Specifying Units of Analysis

In addition to proposing a relationship between two or more variables, a hypothesis also specifies the types or levels of political actor to which the hypothesis is thought to apply. This is called the *unit of analysis* of the hypothesis, and it also must be selected thoughtfully.

As noted in Chapter 2, political scientists are interested in understanding the behavior or properties of all sorts of political actors: individuals, groups, states, governmental agencies, regions, and nations. The particular type of actor whose political behavior is named in a hypothesis is the unit of analysis for the research project. For example, the individual member of the House of Representatives is the unit of analysis in the following hypothesis:

> Members of the House of Representatives who belong to the same party as the president are more likely to vote for legislation desired by the president than members who belong to a different party.

In the following hypothesis the city is the unit of analysis since it is attributes of cities that are being explored:

> Northeastern cities are more likely to have mayors, while western cities have city managers.

Finally, consider this hypothesis:

> The more affluent a country is, the more likely the country is to have democratic political institutions.

Here the unit of analysis is the country. It is the attributes of countries—affluence (the independent variable) and democratic political institutions (the dependent variable)—that will need to be empirically observed. In sum, the research hypothesis indicates what the researcher's unit of analysis is and what behavior or attributes must be measured for that unit.

A discrepancy between the unit of analysis specified in a hypothesis and the entities whose behavior is actually empirically observed can cause problems. For example, suppose a researcher wants to test the hypothesis "blacks are more likely to support female candidates than Italians are." He or she might select an election with a female candidate and obtain data on the voting returns in election precincts with varying proportions of blacks and Italians. If it is found that female candidates received more votes in precincts with a high proportion of blacks than in the precincts with a high proportion of Italians, the researcher might conclude that there was evidence in support of the hypothesis.

There is a fundamental problem with this approach, however. In the original hypothesis the unit of analysis is the individual voter, yet the data apply to election precincts, a different unit of analysis. Unless a district is 100 percent black or Italian, the researcher cannot necessarily draw conclusions about the behavior of individuals from the behavior of election districts. It could be that a female candidate's support in a district with a high proportion of black voters came mostly from nonblacks, and that most of the female candidate's votes in the Italian districts came from Italians.

Let us take two hypothetical election precincts to illustrate this fallacy. Suppose we have Precinct 1, a "black" district, and Precinct 2, an "Italian" district. If the black district voted 67 percent to 33 percent in favor of the female candidate, and the Italian district voted 53 percent to 47 percent in favor of the female candidate, we might be tempted to conclude that blacks voted more heavily for the female candidate than Italians did.

But suppose we peek inside each of the election precincts to see how individuals of different ethnicities behaved (Table 3-2). In the black district, blacks split 25-25 for the woman, Italians voted 18-2 for her, and others voted 24-6 for her. This resulted in the 67-33 edge for the woman

Table 3-2 Voting by Blacks, Italians, and Others for a Female Candidate

		Raw Vote		*Percent Vote*	
Ethnicity	Number	For Male	For Female	For Male	For Female
Precinct 1					
Blacks	50	25	25	50.0	50.0
Italians	20	2	18	10.0	90.0
Other	30	6	24	20.0	80.0
Total	100	33	67	33.0	67.0
Precinct 2					
Blacks	40	24	16	60.0	40.0
Italians	50	20	30	40.0	60.0
Other	10	3	7	30.0	70.0
Total	100	47	53	47.0	53.0
Voting of Individuals					
Blacks	90	49	41	54.4	45.6
Italians	70	22	48	31.4	68.6
Other	40	9	31	22.5	77.5
Total	200	80	120	40.0	60.0

Source: Hypothetical data.

in Precinct 1. In the Italian district, blacks voted 16-24 against the woman, Italians split 30-20 for her, and others voted 7-3 in her favor. This resulted in the 53-47 margin for the woman in Precinct 2. When the individual votes are counted by ethnicity, however, we find that all the blacks in the two districts split 41-49 against the woman. Italians voted 48-22 in her favor, and others voted 31-9 for her. In other words, more Italians as individuals voted for the woman candidate than did blacks as individuals (68.6 percent to 45.6 percent, respectively), even though the precinct-level data gave the opposite impression.

Whenever a researcher uses the behavior of groups to draw inferences about the behavior of individuals, the danger of just such an ecological fallacy exists. An *ecological fallacy* occurs when the attributes of groups lead to a misleading assessment of the attributes of individuals. Sometimes data from a group can be used as evidence regarding the characteristics of individual members of the group. Generally, however, the unit of analysis of the measures and of the hypothesis should match.

Similarly, one cannot necessarily use the characteristics of individuals as measures of the attributes of groups. Suppose a researcher is interested in how much cooperation or conflict exists in two groups (say a group of ten Democratic committee members and a group of eight

Republican committee members). The researcher devises a questionnaire designed to measure cooperation and administers it to the eighteen subjects. Individual scores on the questionnaire can vary from 1 (for a very cooperative person) to 7 (for a very uncooperative person).

Suppose the results of the questionnaire are as follows:

Scores of Ten *Democratic Committee Members*	*Scores of Eight* *Republican Committee Members*
1	3
2	4
3	3
2	2
1	5
7	4
1	3
2	4
1	___
7	Average: 3.5
___	
Average: 2.7	

The Democrats look more cooperative. Forty percent of them are very cooperative (score of 1), 70 percent are cooperative (scores of 1 or 2), and their average score is well to the cooperative side of the scale. The Republicans have no one who is very cooperative, only 12 percent who are cooperative, and an average score that is near the middle of the scale. When cooperation is measured for individuals, then, and aggregated to make an inference about the group, the Democrats look more cooperative.

Cooperation is not only an attribute of individuals, however; it is also an attribute of a group. It would not be difficult to imagine that when the Democrats get together they might have a difficult time cooperating. Not only is the size of their group larger, which might jeopardize cooperation, but it also includes two very uncooperative individuals (score of 7), who might make cooperation among the group impossible. In other words, the Republicans as a group might be able to cooperate more than the Democrats, even though our individual level measures indicated otherwise.

Another mistake sometimes made by researchers is to mix different units of analysis in the same hypothesis. "The more education a person has, the more democratic his country is" doesn't make much sense since it mixes the individual and country as units of analysis. However, "the smaller a government agency, the happier its workers" concerns an attribute of an agency and an attribute of individuals, but in a way that makes sense. The size of the agency in which individuals work may be an important aspect of the context or environment in which the individual phenomenon occurs and may influence the individual attribute. In this case the unit of analysis is clearly the individual, but a phenomenon that is experienced by many cases is used to explain the behavior of individuals, some of whom may well be identically "situated."

In short, a researcher must be careful about the unit of analysis specified in a hypothesis and its correspondence with the unit measured. In general, a researcher should not mix units of analysis within a hypothesis.

Conclusion

In this chapter we have discussed the beginning stages of a scientific research project. A research project must provide—to both the producer and the consumer of social scientific knowledge—the answers to these important questions: What phenomenon is the researcher trying to understand and explain? What explanation has the researcher proposed for the political behavior or attributes in question? What are the meanings of the concepts used in this explanation? What specific hypotheses relating two or more variables will be tested? What is the unit of analysis for the observations? If all of these questions are answered adequately, then the research will have a firm foundation.

Notes

1. Kenneth R. Hoover, *The Elements of Social Scientific Thinking* (New York: St. Martin's Press, 1980), 18-19.
2. W. Phillips Shively, *The Craft of Political Research* (Englewood Cliffs, N.J.: Prentice-Hall, 1980), 33.
3. Sidney Verba and Norman H. Nie, *Participation in America* (New York: Harper & Row, 1972), 2.
4. Ted Robert Gurr, *Why Men Rebel* (Princeton, N.J.: Princeton University Press, 1970), 3-4.
5. Angus Campbell, Gerald Gurin, and Warren E. Miller, *The Voter Decides* (Evanston, Ill.: Row, Peterson, 1954), 187.
6. Philip E. Converse, "The Nature of Belief Systems in Mass Publics," in David E. Apter, ed., *Ideology and Discontent* (New York: Free Press, 1964), 207.
7. Gary C. Jacobson, *Money in Congressional Elections* (New Haven, Conn.: Yale University Press, 1980).
8. For a description of this dataset, see M. Kent Jennings and Richard G. Niemi, *Generations and Politics* (Princeton, N.J.: Princeton University Press, 1981).

Terms Introduced

Antecedent variable. An independent variable that precedes other independent variables in time.

Arrow diagram. A pictorial representation of a researcher's explanatory scheme.

Causal hypothesis. A hypothesis in which the independent variable is thought to be a cause of the dependent variable.

Concept. The definition or meaning of a phenomenon used in empirical research.

Correlative hypothesis. A hypothesis that proposes a relationship between two variables without indicating the nature of that relationship.

Curvilinear relationship. A relationship between two variables that may best be described by a curved, rather than a straight, line.

Dependent variable. The phenomenon thought to be influenced, affected, or caused by some other phenomenon.

Direct relationship. A relationship in which the values of one variable increase as the values of another variable increase.

Directional hypothesis. A hypothesis that specifies the expected relationship between two or more variables.

Ecological fallacy. The fallacy of deducing the attributes or behavior of individuals from the attributes or behavior of the group to which they belong.

Explanation. A systematic, empirically verified understanding of why a phenomenon occurs as it does.

Hypothesis. A statement proposing a relationship between two or more variables.

Independent variable. The phenomenon thought to influence, affect, or cause some other phenomenon.

Intervening variable. A variable coming between an independent and a dependent variable in an explanatory scheme.

Inverse relationship. A relationship in which the values of one variable increase as the values of another variable decrease.

Logarithmic relationship. A mathematical relationship in which increasing amounts of one variable have less and less effect on another variable.

Null hypothesis. A hypothesis that proposes no relationship between two variables.

Relationship. The association, dependence, or covariance of the values of one variable with the values of another variable.

Tautology. A hypothesis in which the independent and dependent variables are identical, making it impossible to disconfirm.

Unit of analysis. The type of actor (individual, group, institution, nation) specified in a researcher's hypothesis.

Exercises

1. Read Ada Finifter, "Dimensions of Political Alienation," *American Political Science Review* 64 (June 1970): 389-410. What concept is she attempting to define? How many different meanings of the concept does she give? Do these definitions capture what the concept means to you?

2. Read "Land Inequality and Political Violence," by Edward N. Muller, Mitchell A. Seligson, and Hung-der Fu, in *American Political Science Review* 83 (June 1989): 577-586. What concept is the focus of this article? Why is this concept

thought to be important? What are the different aspects of this concept that different researchers have emphasized?

3. Read Jeffrey A. Segal and Albert D. Cover, "Ideological Values and the Votes of U.S. Supreme Court Justices," *American Political Science Review* 83 (June 1989): 557-565. What is the major hypothesis tested in this article? What kind of hypothesis is it? What are the independent and dependent variables?

4. Read Robert D. Putnam, Robert Leonardi, Raffaella Y. Nanetti, and Franco Pavoncello, "Explaining Institutional Success: The Case of Italian Regional Government," *American Political Science Review* 77 (March 1983): 55-74. What dependent variables are the authors attempting to explain? What independent variables do they use? What hypotheses are advanced by the researchers? Draw an arrow diagram that summarizes the explanatory scheme proposed and evaluated in this piece of research.

5. For the following hypotheses, identify the *type of hypothesis* (null, correlative, directional, or causal); *unit of analysis;* and *independent and dependent variables.*
   a. The more education a person has, the more politically active that person is.
   b. City governments provide more benefits for neighborhoods with strong community organizations.
   c. People who are experiencing economic distress are likely to vote against candidates from the same party as the incumbent president.
   d. When the two chambers of a legislature are controlled by different parties, it is difficult to pass major pieces of legislation.
   e. If a young person watches a lot of television he or she will engage in antisocial behavior.
   f. The severity of punishment has no effect on the amount of violent crime.
   g. There is a relationship between the amount of political freedom in a nation and the size of the domestic police force.
   h. Insecure relations with neighboring countries lead to political repression.

6. Can you suggest a way of turning each of these assertions into a testable research hypothesis?
   a. All politicians are crooks and liars.
   b. You cannot fight city hall (unless you are rich).
   c. Many countries in the world are not ready for democracy.
   d. If we outlaw guns, only the outlaws will have guns.
   e. You can accomplish more by protesting than you can by voting in elections.
   f. When the Democrats are in office, we end up with higher taxes and unbalanced budgets.
   g. Political advertisements can make voters believe almost anything.

7. Read Benjamin I. Page and Robert Y. Shapiro, "Effects of Public Opinion on Policy," *American Political Science Review* 77 (March 1983): 175-190. What do the authors say about the causal hypothesis advanced in their article? Do they discuss (a) the temporal sequence of their two variables, and (b) whether the effect could have been caused by some other factor? What do they ultimately conclude about whether public opinion causes public policy?

8. What is the unit of analysis in the research reported in the articles in exercises 2, 3, 4, and 7?

9. Think of a political phenomenon that you are interested in understanding. Define the phenomenon as completely and carefully as possible. Now think about other phenomena or concepts that you think might help you explain the

phenomenon you chose. Pick one of these concepts and state how it is related to the first phenomenon. Draw an arrow diagram to summarize your explanatory scheme.

Suggested Readings

Blalock, Hubert M., Jr. *Causal Inferences in Nonexperimental Research.* New York: W. W. Norton, 1964.

Hoover, Kenneth R. *The Elements of Social Scientific Thinking.* New York: St. Martin's, 1984.

Isaak, Alan C. *Scope and Methods of Political Science.* Homewood, Ill.: Dorsey, 1985.

Jacob, Herbert, and Robert Weissberg. *Elementary Political Analysis.* New York: McGraw-Hill, 1975.

Kerlinger, Fred N. *Behavioral Research.* New York: Holt, Rinehart & Winston, 1979.

Shively, W. Phillips. *The Craft of Political Research.* Englewood Cliffs, N.J.: Prentice-Hall, 1980.

Simon, Julian L., and Paul Burstein. *Basic Research Methods in Social Science.* New York: Random House, 1985.

CHAPTER 4

The Building Blocks of Social Scientific Research: Measurement

In the previous chapter we discussed the beginning stages of political science research projects: the choice of research topics, the formulation of scientific explanations, the development of testable hypotheses, and the definition of concepts. In this chapter we show how to test empirically the hypotheses we have advanced. This entails understanding a number of issues involving the *measurement* of the variables we have decided to investigate.

In Chapter 1 we said that scientific knowledge is based upon empirical observation. In this chapter we confront the implications of this fact. If we are to test empirically the accuracy and utility of a scientific explanation for a political phenomenon, we will have to observe and measure the presence of the concepts we are using to understand that phenomenon. Furthermore, if this test is to be an adequate one, our measurements of the political phenomena must be as accurate and precise as possible. The process of measurement is important because it provides the bridge between our proposed explanations and the empirical world they are supposed to explain.

The researchers discussed in Chapter 1 measured a variety of political phenomena. Gary Jacobson measured levels of campaign spending by candidates for the U.S. Congress and the number of votes that these candidates received.[1] Ted Gurr measured the level of relative deprivation and the frequency of political violence in different countries, and Manus Midlarsky measured the distribution of land ownership in several societies in order to investigate the impact of land-owning inequality on the stability of political regimes.[2] Benjamin Page and Robert Shapiro measured the change in public opinion on more than 300 political issues and the subsequent change, if any, in public policy on those same issues.[3] And Jeffrey Segal and Albert Cover measured both the political ideologies and the written opinions of Supreme Court justices in cases involving civil rights and liberties.[4] In each case some human behavior or attribute was measured so that a scientific explanation could be tested.

Devising Measurement Strategies

As Chapter 3 pointed out, researchers must define the concepts they use in their hypotheses. Researchers also must decide how they are actually going to measure the presence, absence, or amount of these concepts in the real world. Political scientists refer to this process as providing an *operational definition* of their concepts—in other words deciding what kinds of empirical observations should be made to measure the occurrence of an attribute or behavior.

Let us return, for example, to the researcher trying to explain the existence of democracy in different nations. If the researcher were to hypothesize that higher rates of literacy make democracy more likely, then a definition of two concepts—literacy and democracy—would be necessary. The researcher could then develop a strategy, based on these two definitions, for measuring the existence and amount of both attributes in a number of nations.

Suppose literacy was defined as "the completion of six years of formal education," and democracy was defined as "a system of government in which public officials are selected in competitive elections." These definitions would then be used to develop operational definitions of the two concepts. These operational definitions would indicate what should be observed empirically to measure both literacy and democracy, and they would indicate specifically what data should be collected to test the researcher's hypothesis. In this example, the operational definition of literacy might be "those nations in which at least 50 percent of the population has had six years of formal education, as indicated in a publication of the United Nations," while the operational definition of democracy might be "those countries in which the second place finisher in elections for the chief executive office has received at least 25 percent of the vote at least once in the past eight years."

When a researcher specifies the operational definition of a concept, the precise meaning of that concept becomes clear. In this example, we now know exactly what the researcher means by literacy and democracy. Since different people often mean different things by the same concept, operational definitions are especially important. Someone might argue that defining literacy in terms of formal education ignores the possibility that people who complete six years of formal education might still be unable to read or write well. Similarly, it might be argued that defining democracy in terms of competitive elections ignores other important features of democracy such as freedom of expression and citizen involvement in government actions. In addition, the operational definition of competitive elections is clearly debatable. Is the "competitiveness" of elections based on the number of competing candidates, the size of the margin of victory, or the number of consecutive victories by a single party in a series of elections? Unfortunately, operational definitions are seldom absolutely correct or absolutely incorrect; rather they are evaluated in terms of how well they correspond to the concepts they are meant to measure.

It is useful to think of the operational definition as the last stage in the process of defining a concept precisely. We often begin with an abstract concept (such as democracy), then attempt to define it in a meaningful way, and finally decide in specific terms how we are going to measure it. At the end of this process we hope to attain a definition that is sensible, close to our meaning of the concept, and exact in what it tells us about how to go about measuring the concept.

Let us consider another example: the researcher interested in why some individuals are more liberal than others. The concept of liberalism might be defined as "believing that government ought to pursue policies that provide benefits for the less well off." The task then is to develop an operational definition that can be used to measure whether particular individuals are liberal or not. The researcher might decide that anyone is a liberal who agrees on a public opinion poll with the following statement: "The federal government should increase the amount of money spent on food stamp and free lunch programs."

An abstract concept, liberalism, has now been given an operational definition that can be used to measure the concept for individuals. This definition is also related to the original definition of the concept, and it indicates precisely what observations need to be made. It is not, however, the only operational definition possible. Others might suggest that questions regarding busing, the death penalty, and pornography could be used to measure liberalism. The important thing is to think carefully about the operational definition you choose and to try to ensure that it coincides closely with the meaning of the original concept.

Examples of Political Measurement

Let us take a closer look at the operational definitions used by the researchers mentioned in Chapter 1. Page and Shapiro's article on the relationship between public opinion and public policy contains a number of important decisions about the measurement of abstract political concepts.[5] Ever since democratic theorists first articulated the normative position that in a democracy there should be a relationship between popular preferences and the decisions made by political elites, researchers have been curious about whether such a relationship exists in modern nation-states and, if so, how strong it is. Observing the relationship requires devising proper measures of both popular preferences and public policy decisions, a requirement that effectively stymied empirical research on opinion-policy relationships until recently. For it is difficult to find appropriate measures of popular preferences and of corresponding public policy decisions over an extensive enough period of time.

Page and Shapiro approached this problem by relying on the thousands of public opinion survey questions that have been asked of the American adult population since 1935 for their measures of popular preferences. Since they were interested in the effect of *change* in the distribution of public opinion, they decided to select those survey questions that had been asked in identical form at two or more points in time, and on which there had been at least a 6 percentage point change in public opinion from one survey to another. This left them with 357 instances of public opinion change on public policy questions between 1935 and 1979.

In order to test the relationship between opinion and policy change, Page and Shapiro then had to devise measures of public policy that corresponded to the measures of public opinion. And in order to determine whether opinion change *precedes* policy change (recall our discussion in Chapter 3 of the importance of establishing the temporal sequence when evaluating causal hypotheses), the policy measures needed to cover a period of time at least as broad as the measures of public opinion covered. So Page and Shapiro sought public policy measures that began two years before the first measure of public opinion and continued until four years after the final survey (to allow for a time lag in the policy-making process).

Developing measures of public policy that correspond with public opinion surveys is not an easy task. Suppose, for example, a survey asks whether the populace favors increasing, decreasing, or maintaining the government's defense spending. What would be an appropriate corresponding measure of public policy? Would one use the entire budget of the Defense Department? Should military personnel salaries, benefits, and pensions be included, or just expenditures on weapons systems? Should we use authorized budget figures (as a measure of willingness to spend) or the amount actually expended? Should expenditures on NASA, the CIA, and military foreign aid be included? Should the measure of expenditures correct for inflation? Should it express expenditures as a percentage of the total budget or as a percentage of the Gross National Product? These and other questions have to be answered before one can settle on an appropriate measure of just this one public policy. So the measurement decisions required by the hypothesis relating public opinion and public policy are both numerous and difficult.

Jacobson's research concerned the impact of campaign spending on the number of votes cast for congressional candidates.[6] For this he needed measures of the amount of money spent by congressional candidates and of the votes cast for each candidate. His measure of the amount of money spent by congressional candidates was the amount listed by candidates in their reports to the Federal Election Commission (FEC). (For 1972 and 1974, Jacobson used summaries of the campaign spending reports compiled by Common Cause; 1976 and 1978 data came from FEC publications.) This approach forced Jacobson to limit his inquiry to elections after 1971 (only since April 7, 1972, have candidates for federal elective office been required to report their campaign expenditures to the federal government) and assumes that the amounts reported to the federal government are accurate indicators of actual campaign spending.

Jacobson's measures of congressional election returns also came from readily available, published sources: Richard M. Scammon's *America Votes 11: A Handbook of Contemporary American Election Statistics* (published by Congressional Quarterly) and *Congressional Quarterly's Guide to the 1976 Elections: A Supplement to CQ's Guide to U.S. Elections.* The official returns reported by the state boards of elections are compiled in these books. This is a case, then, of a researcher who was able to measure two significant political phenomena by relying on measurements made and published by others.

The research conducted by Segal and Cover on the behavior of U.S. Supreme Court justices is a good example of an attempt to overcome a serious measurement problem in order to test a scientific hypothesis.[7] Recall that Segal and Cover were interested, as many others have been before them, in the extent to which the votes cast by Supreme Court justices are dependent upon their own personal political attitudes. Measuring the justices' votes on the cases decided by the Supreme Court is no problem; the votes are public information. But measuring the personal political attitudes of judges, *independent of their votes* (remember the discussion in Chapter 3 on avoiding tautologies), is a problem. Many of the judges whose behavior is of interest have died, and it is difficult to get living Supreme Court justices to reveal their political attitudes through personal interviews or questionnaires. Furthermore, ideally one would like a measure of attitudes that is comparable across many judges and that measures attitudes related to the cases decided by the Court.

Segal and Cover decided to limit their inquiry to votes on civil liberties cases between 1953 and 1987, so they needed a measure of related political attitudes for the judges serving on the Supreme Court over that same period of time. They decided to infer each judge's attitudes from the newspaper editorials written about them in four major daily newspapers from the time each justice was appointed by the president until the justice's confirmation vote by the Senate. Trained analysts read the editorials and coded each paragraph for whether it asserted that a justice designate was liberal, moderate, or conservative (or if the paragraph was inapplicable) regarding "support for the rights of defendants in criminal cases, women and racial minorities in equality cases, and the individual against the government in privacy and First Amendment cases." [8] They selected the editorials appearing in two liberal papers and in two conservative papers in order to produce a more accurate measure of judicial attitudes.

Because of practical barriers to ideal measurement, then, Segal and Cover had to rely on a measure of judicial attitudes *as perceived by four newspapers* rather than on a more direct measure of the attitudes themselves. While this approach *may* result in flawed measures, it also permitted the test of an interesting hypothesis about the behavior of Supreme Court justices that had not been tested previously. If the measures that result are both accurate and precise then this measurement strategy will have permitted the empirical verification of an important hypothesis. Without such measurements, the hypothesis would have to go untested.

Finally, consider the research on regime stability described briefly in Chapter 1. Recall that a common hypothesis is that the distribution of income and wealth has an impact on the tendency of populations to protest and rebel and, therefore, on the stability of governmental regimes. More specifically, it is often hypothesized that income/wealth inequality leads to political violence and instability.

In many parts of the world the main form of wealth is land ownership. Consequently, in places such as Latin America, researchers have been investigating the relationship between land inequality and civil unrest. Obviously the task requires an accurate measure of land inequality in a variety of nation-states.

Measuring the distribution of land ownership and especially of the inequality of land ownership is not a simple matter, however. Everyone agrees that equality of land ownership would mean that every adult or family owned the same amount of land, so that 25 percent of the population owned 25 percent of the land, 75 percent of the population owned 75 percent of the land, and so on. But when the pattern of land ownership departs from this strict equality it is not altogether clear what should be measured. If a few people own most of the land and most people own little or no land, there is land inequality. But should the measure of land inequality focus on unequal land holdings throughout the range of land ownership, or on the land owned by those at both ends of the ownership range (the very rich and the very poor) and the gap between them, or on the number of people who own little or no land, regardless of how much is owned by others? The answer is not clear.

Because of this uncertainty over how best to measure land inequality, researchers have used a number of different measures. One commonly used measure is the Gini index, which attempts to take into account inequalities throughout the range of land ownership. More recently, Midlarsky (referred to in Chapter 1) has proposed a different measure which concentrates on the gap between the very rich and the very poor.[9]

There is some evidence that the measure of inequality used affects the conclusions reached about the relationship between land inequality and political violence. Research using the Gini index has generally found a weak relationship between land inequality and political violence and has led researchers to think about the other factors affecting regime stability. Midlarsky's research using the new measure of land inequality, however, reports a much stronger relationship with political violence, at least in Latin America.

This is a good example, then, of how measurement decisions may affect substantive conclusions. Our choice of measures, especially of abstract phenomena such as land inequality, is a crucial part of the entire research process.

The cases we have discussed here are good examples of researchers' attempts to measure important political phenomena (behaviors or attributes) in the real world. Whether the phenomenon in question was public policy decisions, judge's political attitudes, land inequality, or campaign expenditures by congressional candidates, the researchers devised measurement strategies that could detect and measure the presence and amount of the concept in question. These observations were used as the basis for an empirical test of the researchers' hypotheses.

To be useful in providing scientific explanations for political behavior, measurements of political phenomena must correspond closely to the original meaning of a researcher's concepts. They must also provide the researcher with enough information to make valuable comparisons and contrasts. Hence the quality of measurements is judged in terms of both their *accuracy* and their *precision*.

The Accuracy of Measurements

Since we are going to use our measurements to test the validity of explanations for political phenomena, those measurements must be as accurate as possible. Inaccurate measurements may lead to erroneous conclusions since they will interfere with our ability to observe the actual relationship between two or more variables.

Suppose, for example, that you have hypothesized that "courses taught by political scientists are more worthwhile than courses taught by psychologists." During registration time you see a course description for a course in the political science department that looks worthwhile, so you sign up for it. Your friend, on the other hand, signs up for a course in the psychology department. Two weeks after classes start you meet your friend in the campus dining hall and swap evaluations of your courses. Your political science course has turned out to be a dreadful experience, but your friend seems to be enjoying the psychology course.

Does your experience that semester (actually an empirical observation of two cases seemingly relevant to the hypothesis) mean that your hypothesis is wrong? Not necessarily. Suppose the course you had signed up for was not being taught by a political scientist but rather by a historian on loan to the political science department. This would mean that you had inaccurately measured the nature of the course you were taking by assuming that all courses taught in the political science department were taught by political scientists. Thus you were being led to what might, in fact, have been an erroneous conclusion about the quality of courses taught by political scientists. Because of the inaccuracy of your measurement, the comparison you made with your friend turns out to be irrelevant for the hypothesis with which you began.

There are two major threats to the accuracy of measurements. Measures may be inaccurate because they are *unreliable* or because they are *invalid*.

Reliability

Reliability "concerns the extent to which an experiment, test, or any measuring procedure yields the same results on repeated trials.... The more consistent the results given by repeated measurements, the higher the reliability of the measuring procedure; conversely, the less consistent the results, the lower the reliability." [10]

Suppose, for example, you are given the responsibility of counting a stack of 1,000 paper ballots for some public office. The first time you count them, you obtain a particular result. But as you were counting the ballots you might have been interrupted, two or more ballots might have stuck together, some might have been blown onto the floor, or you might have written the totals down incorrectly. As a precaution, then, you count them five more times and get four other people to count them as well. The consistency of the results of all ten counts would be an indication of the reliability of the measure.

Or suppose you design a series of questions to measure how cynical people are and ask a group of people those questions. If a few days later you ask the same questions of the same group of people, the correspondence between the two measures would indicate the reliability of that particular measure of cynicism.

Similarly, suppose you wanted to test the hypothesis that the *New York Times* is more critical of the federal government than the *Wall Street Journal*. This would require you to measure the level of criticism found in articles in the two papers. The reliability of such measures might be assessed by having two people read all the articles, independently measure the level of criticism in them, and then compare their two distinct measures of the news articles. Reliability would be demonstrated if both people reached similar conclusions regarding the content of the articles in question.

The reliability of political science measures can be calculated a number of ways. The *test-retest method* involves applying the same "test" to the same observations after a period of time and then comparing the results of the different measurements. For example, if a series of questions measuring liberalism is asked of a group of respondents two weeks in a row, a comparison of their scores at both times could be used as an indication of the reliability of the measure of liberalism.

This method of measuring reliability is both difficult and problematic since the opportunity to measure the phenomenon at two different points in time is required and the administration of the first measure may affect the second's results. For instance, the difference between Scholastic Aptitude Test scores the first and second times that individuals take the test ought not be assumed to be a measure of the reliability of the test since test takers might alter systematically their behavior the second time as a result of taking the test the first time.

The *alternative-form method* of measuring reliability also involves measuring the same attribute more than once, but uses two different measures of the same concept rather than the same measure. For example, a researcher could devise two different sets of questions to measure the concept of liberalism, ask the two sets of questions of the same respondents at two different times, and compare the respondents' scores. Using two different forms of the measure prevents the second scores from being influenced by the first measure, but it still requires being able to measure the phenomenon twice.

Finally, the *split-halves method* of measuring reliability involves two measures of the same concept, with both measures applied at the same time. The results of the two measures are then compared. For example, one may devise a measure of liberalism consisting of the responses to ten questions on a public opinion survey. Half of these questions could be selected to represent one measure of liberalism and the other half selected to represent a second measure of liberalism. If individual scores on the two measures of liberalism are similar, then the ten-item measure may be said to be reliable by the split-halves approach.

The test-retest, alternative-form, and split-halves methods provide a basis for calculating the similarity of results of two or more applications of the same or equivalent measure. The less consistent the results are, the less reliable the measure is. Frankly, the reliability of the measures used by political scientists is frequently suspect and seldom demonstrated. Respondents' answers to survey questions often vary considerably when given at two different times.[11] Usually political scientists simply assume that their measures are reliable rather than assess that reliability empirically.

Validity

Essentially, a valid measure is one that measures what it is supposed to measure. Unlike reliability, which depends on whether repeated applications of the same or equivalent measure yield the same result, validity involves the correspondence between the measure and the concept it is thought to measure.

Let us consider first some examples of invalid measures. Suppose a researcher hypothesizes that the larger a city's police force is, the less crime that city will have. This requires the measurement of crime rates in different cities. Now also assume that some police departments systematically overrepresent the number of crimes in their cities to persuade public officials that crime is a serious problem and that the local police need more resources. If the researcher relied on official, reported measures of crime, the measures would be invalid because they did not correspond closely to the actual amount of crime in some cities.

Or suppose you hypothesize that the more productive a scholar a faculty member is, the better a teacher he or she is. This requires measuring different faculty members' teaching abilities. The task might be accomplished by asking students to grade their instructors on teaching. But do students know a good teacher when they see one? Is it possible that students will give good grades to instructors who are personable, humorous, approachable, or easy graders, rather than to instructors who teach them something? If so, such a measurement strategy might well produce an invalid measure of good teaching.

Finally, consider the hypothesis that easy voter registration systems get more people to vote than difficult voter registration systems do.[12] Testing this requires the accurate measurement of voter turnout. One way of measuring voter turnout is to ask people if they voted in the last election. However, given the social desirability of voting in the United States, will all the people who did not vote in the previous election admit it to an interviewer? More people might say that they voted than actually did, resulting in an invalid measure of voter turnout. In fact, this is what usually happens. Voter surveys commonly overestimate turnout by several percentage points.[13]

A measure's validity is more difficult to demonstrate empirically than its reliability because validity involves the relationship between the measurement of a concept and the actual presence or amount of the concept itself. Information regarding the correspondence is seldom abundant. Nonetheless, there are a number of ways of evaluating the validity of any particular measure.

Face validity may be asserted (not empirically demonstrated) when the measurement instrument appears to measure the concept it is supposed to measure. To assess the face validity of a measure, we need to know the meaning of the concept being measured and whether the information being collected is "germane to that concept." [14] For example, suppose a researcher wants to measure the concept "identification with a political party" and devises a question that asks whether the respondent usually thinks of himself or herself as a Democrat, Republican, Independent, or something else. If this measure is given to a group of citizens during a presidential election campaign (as it often is), some people might respond to the question in terms of the particular presidential candidate they are supporting. If this happens, then the measure is measuring two concepts (party identification and candidate support) and is a less valid measure of party identification. Similarly, some have argued that the results of many standard IQ tests measure intelligence *and* exposure to middle-class white culture, thus making the test results a less valid measure of intelligence.

In general, measures lack face validity when there are good reasons to question the correspondence of the measure to the concept in question. In other words, assessing face validity is essentially a matter of judgment. If there is no consensus about the meaning of the concept to be measured, the face validity of one's measure is bound to be problematic.

A second kind of validity test, *content validity,* is similar to face validity. This test (actually a logical argument rather than a test) involves determining the full domain or meaning of a particular concept and then making sure that measures of all portions of this domain are included in the measurement technique. For example, suppose you wanted to design a measure of the extent to which a nation's political system is democratic. As noted earlier, democracy means many things to many people. One way of measuring a concept with multiple meanings is to try to determine the various meanings attached to the concept (such as guarantees for free expression, provision for citizen decision making, agreement between public opinion and public policy, and economic equality) and then try to make sure that every one of these meanings is included in the measuring scheme. If this can be accomplished, then the entire domain of the concept has been measured and the measure possesses content validity. Unfortunately, many political science concepts are so abstract and ill-defined that there is little agreement about their domain. This makes content validity less useful to political scientists than it is to other researchers.

A third way to evaluate the validity of a measure is by empirically demonstrating *construct validity*. When a measure of a concept is related to a measure of another concept with which the original concept is thought to be related, construct validity is demonstrated. In other words, a researcher may specify, on theoretical grounds, that two concepts ought to be related (say, political efficacy with political participation, or education with income). The researcher then develops a measure of each of the concepts and determines the relationship between them. If the measures are related, then one measure has construct validity for the other measure. If the measures are unrelated, there is an absence of construct validity. Either the theoretical relationship is in error, one or more of the measures is not an accurate representation of the concept, or the procedure used to test the relationship is inappropriate. The absence of the hypothesized relationship does not tell us for certain that the measure is invalid, but the presence of a relationship gives us some assurance of the measure's validity.

A good example of an attempt to demonstrate construct validity may be found in the Educational Testing Service's (ETS) booklet describing the Graduate Record Exam (GRE), a standardized test required for admission to most graduate schools. Since GRE test scores are supposed to measure a person's aptitude for graduate study, presumably construct validity could be demonstrated if the scores did, in fact, accurately predict the person's performance in graduate school. Over the years ETS has tested the relationships between GRE scores and first-year graduate school grade-point average. The results, shown in Table 4-1, indicate that GRE scores are typically quite poor predictors of this measure of graduate school performance. In short, ETS has found it difficult to demonstrate construct validity for its GRE.[15]

A fourth way in which validity can be demonstrated is through *interitem association*. This is the type of validity test most often used by political scientists. It relies on the similarity of outcomes of more than one measure of a concept to demonstrate the validity of the entire measurement scheme.

Let us return to the researcher who wants to develop a valid measure of liberalism. First the researcher might measure people's attitudes toward (1) school busing, (2) welfare, (3) protection of the rights of the accused, (4) military spending, (5) government employment programs, (6) social security benefit levels, (7) urban renewal programs, and (8) a

Table 4-1 Construct Validity of Graduate Record Examination
Test Scores

Relationship between GRE test scores, undergraduate grade-point average, and first-year graduate grade-point average		(n)
GRE verbal	+.24	(388)
GRE quantitative	+.24	(388)
GRE subject tests	+.32	(144)
Undergraduate GPA	+.28	(366)
GRE verbal + GRE quantitative + undergraduate GPA	+.37	(365)

Source: GRE Information Bulletin, 1985-86, 29. Copyright© 1984 by Educational Testing Service. All rights reserved. Reprinted by permission.

Note: The numbers in this table are product-moment correlations—numbers that can vary between −1.0 and +1.0 and that indicate the extent to which one variable is associated with another. The closer the correlation is to ±1.0, the stronger the relationship between the two variables; the closer the correlation is to 0.0, the weaker the relationship. Since all of the correlations in this table are between .2 and .4, the relationship between GRE scores and first-year graduate grade-point average is not very strong. In other words, knowing a student's GRE scores would not be very helpful in predicting accurately a student's first-year grade-point average.

progressive income tax. Then the researcher could determine how the responses to each question relate to the responses to each of the other questions. The validity of the measurement scheme would be demonstrated if there were strong relationships between people's responses across the eight questions.

The results of such interitem association tests are often displayed in a *correlation matrix* (Table 4-2). Such a display shows how strongly related each of the items in the measurement scheme is to all of the other items. In the hypothetical data shown in Table 4-2, we can see that people's responses to six of the eight measures were strongly related to each other while responses to the questions on protection of the rights of the accused and school busing were not part of the general pattern. Thus the researcher would probably conclude that the first six items all measure a dimension of liberalism and that, taken together, they are a valid measurement of the liberalism concept.

Content and face validity are difficult to assess when there is a lack of agreement on the meaning of a concept, and construct validity, which requires a well-developed theoretical perspective, usually yields a less than definitive result. The interitem association test requires multiple measures of the same concept. Although those validity "tests" provide important evidence, none of them is likely to support an unequivocal decision concerning the validity of particular measures.

An example of research performed at the Survey Research Center at the University of Michigan illustrates the numerous threats to the

Table 4-2 Interitem Association Validity Test of a Measure of Liberalism

	Welfare	Military Spending	Government Spending	Social Security	Urban Renewal	Income Tax	Busing	Rights of Accused
Welfare	x							
Military Spending	.56	x						
Government Spending	.71	.60	x					
Social Security	.80	.51	.83	x				
Urban Renewal	.63	.38	.59	.69	x			
Income Tax	.48	.67	.75	.39	.51	x		
Busing	.28	.08	.19	.03	.30	−.07	x	
Rights of Accused	−.01	.14	−.12	.10	.23	.18	.45	x

Source: Hypothetical data.

Note: The figures in this table are product-moment correlations, explained in the note to Table 4-1. A high correlation indicates a strong relationship between how people answered the two different questions designed to measure liberalism. The figures in the last two rows are considerably closer to 0.0 than are the other entries, indicating that people's answers to the busing and rights of accused questions did not follow the same pattern as their answers to the other questions. Therefore, it looks like busing and rights of the accused are not part of the measure of liberalism accomplished with the other questions.

reliability and validity of political science measures. In 1980 the center conducted interviews with a national sample of eligible voters and measured their income levels with the following question:

Please look at this page and tell me the letter of the income group that includes the income of *all members of your family living here in 1979 before taxes.* This figure should include salaries, wages, pensions, dividends, interest, and all other income.

Respondents were given the following choices:

A. None or less than $2,000
B. $2,000 - $2,999
C. $3,000 - $3,999
D. $4,000 - $4,999
E. $5,000 - $5,999
F. $6,000 - $6,999
G. $7,000 - $7,999
H. $8,000 - $8,999
J. $9,000 - $9,999
K. $10,000 - $10,999
M. $11,000 - $11,999
N. $12,000 - $12,999
P. $13,000 - $13,999
Q. $14,000 - $14,999
R. $15,000 - $16,999
S. $17,000 - $19,999
T. $20,000 - $22,999
U. $23,000 - $24,999
V. $25,000 - $29,999
W. $30,000 - $34,999
X. $35,000 - $49,999
Y. $50,000 and over

Both the reliability and the validity of this method of measuring income are questionable. Threats to the reliability of the measure include the following:

1. Respondents may not know how much money they make and therefore incorrectly guess their income.
2. Respondents may also not know how much money other family members make and guess incorrectly.
3. Respondents may know how much they make but carelessly select the wrong categories.
4. Interviewers may circle the wrong categories when listening to the selections of the respondents.
5. Keypunchers may punch the wrong numbers when entering the answers into the computer.

6. Dishonest interviewers may incorrectly guess the income of a respondent who does not complete the interview.
7. Respondents may not know which family members to include in the income total; some respondents may include only a few family members while others may include even distant relations.
8. Respondents whose income is on the border between two categories may not know which one to pick. Some pick the higher category, some the lower one.

Each of these problems may introduce some error into the measurement of income, resulting in inaccurate measures that are too high for some respondents and too low for others. Therefore, if this measure were applied to the same people at two different times we could expect the results to vary.

In addition to these threats to reliability, there are numerous threats to the validity of this measure:

1. Respondents may have illegal income they do not want to reveal and, therefore, systematically underestimate their income.
2. Respondents may try to impress the interviewer, or themselves, by systematically overestimating their income.
3. Respondents may systematically underestimate their before-tax income if they believe too much money is being withheld from their paychecks.

This long list of problems with both the reliability and the validity of this fairly straightforward measure of a relatively concrete concept is worrisome. Imagine how much more difficult it is to develop reliable and valid measures when the concept is abstract (for example, intelligence, self-esteem, or liberalism), and the measurement scheme is more complicated.

The reliability and validity of the measures used by political scientists are seldom demonstrated to everyone's satisfaction. Most measures of political phenomena are neither completely invalid or valid nor thoroughly unreliable or reliable, but rather are partially accurate. Therefore, researchers generally present the rationale and evidence that are available in support of their measures and attempt to persuade their audience that their measures are at least as accurate as alternative measures would be. Nonetheless, it must be admitted that demonstrating the accuracy of measures is not often a high priority of political scientists. A skeptical stance on the part of the reader toward the reliability and validity of political science measures is often warranted.

Reliability and validity are not the same thing. A measure may be reliable without being valid. One may devise a series of questions to measure liberalism, for example, which yields the same result for the same people every time but which misidentifies individuals. A valid measure, on the other hand, will also be reliable since if it accurately measures the concept in question then it should do so consistently across measurements. It is more important, then, to demonstrate validity than reliability, but reliability is usually more easily and precisely tested.

The Precision of Measurements

Measurements should be not only accurate but also precise; that is, measurements should contain as much information as possible about the attribute or behavior being measured. The more precise our measures, the more complete and informative can be our test of the relationships between two or more variables.

Suppose, for example, that we were measuring the height of political candidates to see if taller candidates usually win elections. Height could be measured in many different ways. We could have two categories of the variable height, tall and short, and assign different candidates to the two categories based on whether they were of above-average or below-average height. Or we could compare the heights of candidates running for the same office and measure which candidate was the tallest, which the next tallest, and so on. Or we could take a tape measure and measure each candidate's height in inches and record that measure. Clearly, the last method of measurement preserves the most information about each candidate's height and is, therefore, the most precise measure of the attribute.

When we consider the precision of our measurements, we refer to the *level of measurement*. The level of measurement involves the type of information that we think our measurements contain and the type of comparisons that can be made across a number of observations on the same variable. The level of measurement also refers to the claim we are willing to make when we assign numbers to our measurements.

There are four different levels of measurement: *nominal, ordinal, interval,* and *ratio.* Very few concepts used in political science research inherently require a particular level of measurement, so the level used in any specific research project is a function of the imagination and resources of the researcher and the decisions made when the method of measuring each of the variables is developed.

A *nominal* level of measurement is involved whenever the values assigned to a variable represent only different categories or classifications for that variable. In such a case, no category is more or less than another category, simply different. For example, suppose we measure the religion of individuals by asking them to indicate whether they are Protestant, Catholic, Jewish, or something else. Since the four categories or values for the variable "religion" are simply different, the measurement is at a nominal level.

Nominal level measures ought to consist of categories that are exhaustive and mutually exclusive; that is, the categories should include all of the possibilities for the measure, and they should be differentiated in such a way that a case will fit into one and only one category. For example, the categories of the measure of religion are exhaustive (because of the "something else" category) as well as mutually exclusive (since presumably an individual cannot be of more than one religion). If one attempted to measure "types of political systems," on the other hand, with the categories democratic, socialist, authoritarian, undeveloped, traditional, capitalist, and monarchical, the categories would be neither exhaustive nor mutually exclusive. (In which category do the Soviet Union, Great Britain, and India belong?) The difficulty of deciding the category into which many countries should be put would hinder the very measurement process the variable was intended to further.

An *ordinal* level of measurement assumes that more or less of a variable can be measured and that a comparison can be made on which observations have more or less of a particular attribute. For example, we could create an ordinal measure of formal education completed with the following categories: "eighth grade or less," "some high school," "high school graduate," "some college," "college degree or more." Notice that we are not concerned here with the exact difference between the categories of education, but only with whether one category is more or less than another. Or suppose we ask individuals three questions designed to measure social trust, and we believe that an individual who answers all three questions a certain way has more social trust than a person who answers two of the questions a certain way, and this person has more social trust than a person who answers one of the questions a certain way, and so on. We could assign a score of 3 to the first group, a 2 to the second group, a 1 to the first group, and a 0 to those who did not answer any of the questions in a socially trusting manner. In this case, the higher the number, the more social trust an individual has. With an ordinal measure it does not matter whether we assign to the four categories the numbers 0, 1, 2, 3; 5, 6, 7, 8; 10, 100, 1000, 10005; or 100, 101, 107, 111. The intervals between the numbers have no meaning; all that matters is that the higher numbers represent more of the attribute than the lower numbers do.

An *interval* level of measurement is a measuring scheme in which the intervals between the categories or values assigned to the observations have meaning. For interval measures, the value of a particular observation is important not just in terms of whether it is larger or smaller than another value (as in ordinal measures), but also in terms of how much larger or smaller it is. For example, suppose we record the year in which certain events occurred. If we have three observations—1950, 1960, and

1970—we know that the event in 1950 occurred ten years before the one in 1960 and twenty years before the one in 1970. We also know that the difference between the 1950 and 1970 observations is twice the difference between the 1950 and 1960 or 1960 and 1970 observations. One unit change (the interval) all along this measurement is identical in meaning: the passage of one year's time. This is not necessarily the case for the measure of social trust discussed earlier, since we are not certain in that example whether the difference between a score of 1 and a score of 2 is identical with the difference between a score of 2 and a score of 3.

Another characteristic of an interval level of measurement that distinguishes it from the next level of measurement (ratio) is that the zero point is arbitrarily assigned and does not represent the absence of the attribute being measured. For example, many time and temperature scales have arbitrary zero points. Thus, the year 0 A.D. does not indicate the beginning of time—if this were true, there would be no B.C. dates. Nor does 0°C indicate the absence of heat but rather the temperature at which water freezes. For this reason, with interval level measurements we cannot calculate ratios; that is, we cannot say that 60°F is twice as warm as 30°F because it does not represent twice as much warmth.

The final and highest level of measurement is a *ratio* level measure. This type of measurement involves the full mathematical properties of numbers. That is, the values of categories order the categories, tell something about the intervals between the categories, and state precisely the relative amounts of the variable that the categories represent. If, for example, a researcher is willing to claim that an observation with 10 units of a variable possesses exactly twice as much of that attribute as an observation with 5 units of that variable, then a ratio level measurement exists.

The key to making this assumption is that a value of zero on the variable actually represents the absence of that variable. Because ratio measures have a true zero point, it makes sense to say that one measurement is x times another. It makes sense to say a 60-year-old person is twice the age of a 30-year-old person (60/30 = 2), while it does not make sense to say that 60°C is twice as warm as 30°C.[16]

Identifying the level of measurement of variables is important since it affects the kinds of hypotheses that can be tested and the data analysis techniques that can be used. However, the decision is not always a straightforward one, and there is often uncertainty and disagreement among researchers concerning these decisions. Very few phenomena inherently require one particular level of measurement. Often a phenomenon can be measured with any level of measurement, depending upon the particular technique designed by the researcher and the claims that the researcher is willing to make about the resulting measure.

Since distinguishing different levels of measurement is sometimes difficult, let us consider an example. Suppose we are interested in measuring how much political freedom exists in different countries. We can design a measure of political freedom by deciding its important dimensions and determining the presence of each in different countries. For example, does the country have privately owned newspapers; the legal right to form political parties; contested elections for significant public offices; voting rights extended to most of the adult population; and limitations on government's ability to incarcerate citizens? From this checklist, suppose we form a summary index of political freedom by summing the number of conditions thought to exist in each country. The index could vary from 0 to 5.

This measure could be a nominal level measure since it groups countries into discrete categories. Could it also be an ordinal measure? That depends on whether the researcher thinks that each of the five activities is equally important for the measurement of political freedom. If so, then the higher the index value, the more political freedom in a country. But if the researcher thinks that some of the attributes are more important than others, then the measure would not be an ordinal one. Does a country with contested elections and privately owned newspapers (an index value of 2) have more political freedom than one with limits on government's ability to incarcerate citizens (an index value of 1)? It is difficult to say.

If it is hard to imagine this measure's being ordinal, it is even more difficult to imagine its being interval or ratio. To do so would require claims about (1) the precise amount of freedom represented by an index interval of one everywhere along the index, and (2) whether it is possible to say that a country has two or three (or whatever) times more freedom than another country. Such claims are highly suspect in this case.

For this measure, then, a nominal level measure is certainly acceptable and an ordinal level measure possible. It is unlikely that the measure could be considered interval or ratio.

Political science researchers have measured many concepts at the ratio level. People's ages, unemployment rates, percent vote for a particular candidate, and crime rates are all examples of measures that contain a zero point and represent the full mathematical properties of the numbers used. However, more political science research has probably relied upon nominal and ordinal level measures than interval or ratio level measures. This has restricted the types of hypotheses and analysis techniques that political scientists have been willing and able to use.

Researchers usually try to devise as high a level of measurement for their concepts as possible (nominal being the lowest level of measurement and ratio the highest). With a higher level of measurement, a hypothesis using the variables will be more informative, and more advanced data analysis techniques can be used. Consequently, one might start with a nominal level measure and think of a way to turn it into an ordinal or interval level measure. For example, a researcher investigating the effect of campaign spending on election outcomes could devise an ordinal level measure that simply distinguished between those candidates who spent more or less than their opponent. However, more information would be preserved if a ratio level variable measuring how much more (or less) a candidate spent than the opposition were devised. Similarly, researchers measuring attitudes or personality traits also often construct a scale or index from nominal level measures that permits at least ordinal level comparisons between observations.

Multi-item Measures

Some of the measures considered so far in this chapter have consisted of a single item. Jacobson's measures of candidate expenditures and vote totals, Page and Shapiro's measures of public opinion change, and Midlarsky's measure of political violence are all based on single measures of each phenomenon in question. Often, however, researchers need to devise measures of more complicated phenomena that have more than one facet, aspect, or dimension. Liberalism, democracy, and even land inequality, for example, are complex phenomena that may be measured in many different ways. In this situation, researchers often develop a measurement strategy that allows them to capture numerous aspects of a complex phenomenon while representing the existence of that phenomenon in particular cases with a single representative value. Usually this involves the construction of a multi-item index or scale representing the several dimensions of a complex phenomenon. These multi-item measures are useful because they enhance the accuracy of a measure, simplify a researcher's data by reducing it to a more manageable size, and increase the level of measurement of a phenomenon. In the remainder of this section we will describe several commonly used types of indexes and scales.

Indexes

An index is a method of accumulating scores on individual items to form a composite measure of a complex phenomenon. The typical index is constructed by assigning a range of possible scores for a number of items, determining the score for each item for each observation, and then combining the scores for each observation across all of the items. The resulting summary score is the representative measurement of the phenomenon.

The researcher interested in measuring how much freedom there is in different countries might construct an index of political freedom by devising a list of items germane to the concept, determining where individual countries score on each of the items, and then adding these scores together to get a summary measure. In Table 4-3 such a hypothetical index is used to measure the amount of freedom in countries A through E.

The index in Table 4-3 is a simple, additive one; that is, each of the items counts equally toward the calculation of the index score, and the total score is the summation of the individual item scores. However, indexes may be constructed with more complicated aggregation procedures and by counting some items as more important than others. In the preceding example a researcher might consider some indicators of freedom more important than others and wish to have them contribute more to the calculation of the final index score. This could be done either by weighting (multiplying) some item scores by a number indicating their importance or by assigning a higher score than 1 for those attributes considered more important.

Indexes are often used with public opinion surveys to measure political attitudes. This is because attitudes are complex phenomena and we usually do not know enough about them to devise single-item measures. So we often ask several questions of people about a single attitude and aggregate the answers to represent the attitude. A researcher might measure attitudes toward abortion, for example, by asking respondents to choose one of five possible responses—strongly agree, agree, undecided, disagree, and strongly disagree to the following three statements:

> Abortions should be permitted in the first three months of pregnancy.
>
> Abortions should be permitted if the woman's life is in danger.
>
> Abortions should be permitted whenever a woman wants one.

An index of attitudes toward abortion could be computed by assigning numerical values to each response (such as 1 for strongly agree, 2 for agree, 3 for undecided, and so on) and then adding the values of a respondent's answers to these three questions. (The researcher would have to decide what to do when a respondent did not answer one or more of the questions.) The lowest possible score would be a 3, indicating the most extreme pro-abortion attitude, and the highest possible score would be a 15, indicating the most extreme anti-abortion attitude. Scores in between would indicate varying degrees of approval of abortion.

Indexes are typically fairly simple ways of producing single representative scores of complicated phenomena such as political attitudes. They are probably more accurate than most single-item measures, but they are also flawed in important ways. Aggregating the scores across several items assumes, for example, that each item is equally important to the

Table 4-3 Index for Measuring Freedom in Countries

	Country A	Country B	Country C	Country D	Country E
Does the country possess:					
Privately owned newspapers	1	0	0	0	1
Legal right to form political parties	1	1	0	0	0
Contested elections for significant public offices	1	1	0	0	0
Voting rights extended to most of the adult population	1	1	0	1	0
Limitations on government's ability to incarcerate citizens	1	0	0	0	1
Index Score	5	3	0	1	2

Source: Hypothetical data.

Note: The score is 1 if the answer is yes, 0 if no.

summary measure of the concept and that the items used faithfully encompass the domain of the concept. Although individual item scores can be weighted to change their contribution to the summary measure, there is often little information upon which to base a weighting scheme.

Several standard indexes are often used in political science research. The FBI Crime Index and the Consumer Price Index, for example, have been used by many researchers. Although simple summation indexes are generally more accurate than single-item measures of complicated phenomena would be, it is often unclear how valid they are or what level of measurement they represent.

Scales

Although indexes are often an improvement over single-item measures, there is also an element of arbitrariness in their construction. Both the selection of particular items making up the index and the way in which the scores on individual items are aggregated are based on the judgment of the researcher. Scales are also multi-item measures, but the selection and combination of items in them is more systematically accomplished than is usually the case for indexes. Four different kinds of multi-item scales are frequently used in political science research: Likert scales, Guttman scales, Thurstone scales, and the semantic differential.

A *Likert scale* score is calculated from the scores obtained on individual items. Each item generally asks a respondent to indicate a degree of agreement or disagreement with the item, as with the abortion questions discussed earlier. A Likert scale differs from an index, however, in that once the scores on each of the items are obtained, some of the items are selected for inclusion in the calculation of the final score. Those items that allow a researcher to distinguish most readily those scoring high on an attribute from those scoring low will be retained, and a new scale score will be calculated based only on those items.

For example, recall the researcher interested in measuring the liberalism of a group of respondents. Since definitions of liberalism vary, the researcher cannot be sure how many aspects of liberalism need to be measured. With Likert scaling the researcher would begin with a large group of questions thought to express various aspects of liberalism and respondents would be asked to indicate how much they agree with each item. A provisional Likert scale for liberalism, then, might look like this:

	Strongly Disagree (1)	Disagree (2)	Undecided (3)	Agree (4)	Strongly Agree (5)
The government should ensure that no one lives in poverty.	——	——	——	——	——
Military spending should be reduced.	——	——	——	——	——
It is more important to take care of people's needs than it is to balance the federal budget.	——	——	——	——	——
Social Security benefits should not be cut.	——	——	——	——	——
The government should spend money to improve housing and transportation in urban areas.	——	——	——	——	——
Wealthy people should pay taxes at a much higher rate than poor people.	——	——	——	——	——
Busing should be used to integrate public schools.	——	——	——	——	——
The rights of persons accused of a crime must be vigorously protected.	——	——	——	——	——

In practice, a set of questions like this would be scattered throughout a questionnaire so that respondents do not see them as related. Some of the questions might also be worded in the opposite way (that is, so an "agree" response is a conservative response) to ensure genuine answers.

The respondents' answers to these eight questions would be summed to produce a provisional score. The scores in this case can range from 8 to 40. Then the responses of the most liberal and the most conservative people to each question would be compared; any questions with similar answers from the disparate respondents would be eliminated—such questions would not distinguish liberals from conservatives. A new summary scale score for all the respondents would be calculated from the questions that remained.

Likert scales are improvements over multi-item indexes because the items that make up the multi-item measure are selected based on the behavior of the respondents rather than on the judgment of the researcher. Likert scales suffer two of the other defects of indexes, however: the researcher cannot be sure that all of the dimensions of a concept have been measured, and the relative importance of each item is still arbitrarily determined.

Guttman scales also employ a series of items to produce a scale score for respondents. Unlike the Likert scale, however, a Guttman scale is designed to present respondents with a range of attitude choices that are increasingly difficult to agree with; that is, the items composing the scale range from those easy to agree with to those difficult to agree with. Respondents who agree with one of the "more difficult" attitude items will also generally agree with the "less difficult" ones. (Guttman scales have also been used to measure attributes other than attitudes. Their main application has been in the area of attitude research, however, so an example of that type is used here.)

Let us return to the researcher interested in measuring attitudes toward abortion. He or she might devise a series of items ranging from "easy to agree with" to "difficult to agree with." Such an approach might be represented by the following items.

Do you agree or disagree that abortions should be permitted:
1. When the life of the woman is in danger.
2. In the case of incest or rape.
3. When the fetus appears to be unhealthy.
4. When the father does not want to have a baby.
5. When the woman cannot afford to have a baby.
6. Whenever the woman wants one.

This array of items seems likely to result in responses consistent with Guttman scaling. A respondent agreeing with any one of the items is likely to also agree with those items numbered lower than that one. This would result in the "stepwise" pattern of responses characteristic of a Guttman scale.

Suppose six respondents answered this series of questions as shown in Table 4-4. Generally speaking, the pattern of responses is as expected; those who agreed with the "most difficult" questions were also likely to agree with the "less difficult" ones. However, responses to the question about the father's preferences do not fit the pattern. Respondent 2 agreed with a more difficult question but disagreed with that one, and respondents 4 and 5 disagreed with a less difficult question but agreed with that one. So the question about the father does not seem to fit the pattern and would be removed from the scale. Once that has been done, the stepwise pattern becomes clearer.

Even after the question about the father is removed, respondent 6 has given answers that do not fit the pattern—an "agree" response to the question about incest or rape is unexpected. Therefore, there is an "error" in this respondent's answers. When the number of errors is small, researchers assume that the scale is an appropriate measure and that the respondent's "error" may be "corrected." In this case either the "agree" in the case of incest or rape or the "disagree" in the case of the life of the woman must be changed if the scale pattern is to be kept. Here we have decided to treat the "agree" as the error and to assign a corrected scale score of 0.

Guttman scales differ from Likert scales in that generally only one set of responses will yield a particular scale score. That is, to get a score of 3 on the abortion scale a particular pattern of responses (or something very close to it) is necessary. In the case of a Likert scale, however, many different patterns of responses can yield the same scale score.

A Guttman scale is much more difficult to achieve than a Likert scale. For a Guttman scale to work, the items must have been ordered and be perceived by the respondents as representing increasingly more difficult responses to the same attitude. If the respondents' patterns of responses fit the Guttman model, however, the resulting scale scores are likely to be an accurate measure of an attitude.

Both Likert and Guttman scales have shortcomings in their level of measurement. The level of measurement produced by Likert scales is, at best, ordinal (since we do not know what the relative importance is of each item and so we cannot be sure that a "5" answer on one item is the same as a "5" answer on another), and the level of measurement produced by Guttman scales is usually assumed to be ordinal. There exist scaling techniques that attempt to produce interval level measures. One of the most common of such scales is a *Thurstone scale*.

Thurstone scales attempt to ensure that the items used in the calculation of the scale score represent equally spaced intervals across the range of an attitude. This is done in the following way. First, the

Table 4-4   Guttman Scale of Attitudes toward Abortion

Respon- dent	Life of Woman	Incest or Rape	Un- healthy Fetus	Father	Afford	Any- time	No. of Agree Answers	Revised Scale Score
1	A	A	A	A	A	A	6	5
2	A	A	A	D	A	D	4	4
3	A	A	A	D	D	D	3	3
4	A	A	D	A	D	D	3	2
5	A	D	D	A	D	D	2	1
6	D	A	D	D	D	D	1	0

Source: Hypothetical data.
Note: A = Agree, D = Disagree.

researcher composes dozens of questionnaire items or statements thought to represent the full range of responses, from unfavorable to favorable, to some object. The object can be a politician, group of people, public policy, or anything about which people usually have positive or negative feelings. Then, a number of respondents (the number is usually between fifty and several hundred depending on the researcher's resources) are selected and asked to evaluate each of the researcher's statements (these people are commonly called the "judges"). These judges are asked to place each of the statements into one of eleven categories, depending on how unfavorable (category 1) or favorable (category 11) each of the statements is to the object in question.

Once the judges have done their evaluations, the category position of each statement is determined by calculating the mean or median value given to each statement by all of the judges. Statements that the judges have placed in many different categories are excluded, as are the evaluations of judges that seem to be quite different from the rest. From the items that remain, the twenty-two or so that best cover the scale range from 1 to 11, and about which there was the most agreement among the judges, are selected to make up the final scale representing attitudes toward the object. These items are thought to represent, as nearly as possible, attitude measures with equally spaced intervals between them. This set of items is then administered to a complete set of respondents, whose responses (agree or disagree) to all the statements may be summed to produce an interval level measure of attitudes toward some object.

The main difference between Thurstone scales and Likert and Guttman scales is that in Thurstone scales a group of respondents is used to help the researcher form a set of equally spaced attitude items. This is thought both to improve the validity of the summary measure and to raise the scale scores to an interval level of measurement.

The last method of producing multi-item summary measures of a complex phenomenon that we will discuss here is a technique called the *semantic differential.* This technique presents respondents with a series of adjective pairs in order to bring out the ways in which people respond to some particular object. These responses may then be used to understand the dimensions or attributes of that object and/or to compare evaluations across objects.

Suppose, for example, that you were a political consultant preparing for the reelection campaign of an incumbent U.S. senator. You would probably be interested in the public's attitude toward your client so that you could identify his or her major strengths and weaknesses. If you were uncertain about the attitudes that people had toward your candidate you might use the semantic differential to explore those attitudes.

In the typical semantic differential application respondents are presented with adjective pairs (opposites) with seven response categories available for each pair, and they are asked to evaluate some object in terms of each adjective pair. So, for example, respondents might be asked to reveal their feelings toward a political candidate in the following way:

Listed below are several pairs of words that could be used to describe Senator X. Between the words in each pair are several blanks. Please put an X in the blank between each pair that best describes how you feel about Senator X.

Senator X

honest	—	—	—	—	—	—	—	dishonest
smart	—	—	—	—	—	—	—	dumb
sincere	—	—	—	—	—	—	—	insincere
superficial	—	—	—	—	—	—	—	profound
good	—	—	—	—	—	—	—	bad
serious	—	—	—	—	—	—	—	humorous
idealistic	—	—	—	—	—	—	—	realistic
strong	—	—	—	—	—	—	—	weak
pleasant	—	—	—	—	—	—	—	unpleasant
helpful	—	—	—	—	—	—	—	unhelpful
powerful	—	—	—	—	—	—	—	powerless
active	—	—	—	—	—	—	—	inactive
young	—	—	—	—	—	—	—	old
nice	—	—	—	—	—	—	—	awful

Research on the use of the semantic differential has discovered that there are three underlying dimensions for attitudes toward most objects: an evaluative dimension (favorable versus unfavorable), a potency dimension (strong versus weak), and an activity dimension (active versus passive). Typically, responses to a set of adjective pairs are analyzed in terms of these three dimensions, allowing a researcher to infer the respondents' attitudes toward one or more objects of interest. In the case pursued here, this measurement strategy would probably allow a political consultant to determine the perceived evaluation, potency, and activity of a candidate in a more accurate way than would any single questionnaire item.

Through indexes and scales, researchers attempt to enhance both the accuracy and the precision of their measures. Although these multi-item measures have received most use in attitude research, they are often useful in other endeavors as well. Both indexes and scales require researchers to make decisions regarding the selection of individual items and the way in which the scores on those items will be combined to produce more useful measures of political phenomena.

Conclusion

To a large extent, a research project is only as good as the measurements that are developed and used in it. Inaccurate measurements will interfere with the testing of scientific explanations for political phenomena and may lead to erroneous conclusions. Imprecise measurements will limit the extent of the comparisons that can be made between observations and the precision of the knowledge that results from empirical research.

Despite the importance of good measurement, political science researchers often find that their measurement schemes are of uncertain accuracy and precision. Abstract concepts are difficult to measure in a valid way, and the practical constraints of time and money often jeopardize the reliability and precision of measurements. The quality of a researcher's measurements makes an important contribution to the results of his or her empirical research and should not be lightly or routinely sacrificed.

Sometimes the accuracy of measurements may be enhanced through the use of multi-item measures. With indexes and scales, researchers select multiple indicators of a phenomenon, assign scores to each of these indicators, and combine those scores into a summary measure. While these methods have been used most frequently in attitude research, they can also be used in other situations to improve the accuracy and precision of single-item measures.

Notes

1. Gary C. Jacobson, *Money in Congressional Elections* (New Haven, Conn.: Yale University Press, 1980).
2. Ted Robert Gurr, *Why Men Rebel* (Princeton, N.J.: Princeton University

Press, 1970); and Manus I. Midlarsky, "Rulers and the Ruled: Patterned Inequality and the Onset of Mass Political Violence," *American Political Science Review* 82 (June 1988): 491-509.

3. Benjamin I. Page and Robert Y. Shapiro, "Effects of Public Opinion on Policy," *American Political Science Review* 77 (March 1983): 175-190.

4. Jeffrey A. Segal and Albert D. Cover, "Ideological Values and the Votes of U.S. Supreme Court Justices," *American Political Science Review* 83 (June 1989): 557-565.

5. Page and Shapiro, "Effects of Public Opinion."

6. Jacobson, *Money in Congressional Elections,* 38-45.

7. Segal and Cover, "Ideological Values."

8. Ibid., 559.

9. Midlarsky, "Rulers and the Ruled."

10. Edward G. Carmines and Richard A. Zeller, *Reliability and Validity Assessment,* Series on Quantitative Applications in the Social Sciences, No. 07-001, Sage University Papers (Beverly Hills, Calif.: Sage, 1979).

11. Philip E. Converse, "The Nature of Belief Systems in Mass Publics," in David E. Apter, ed., *Ideology and Discontent* (New York: Free Press, 1964); D. M. Vaillancourt, "Stability of Children's Survey Responses," *Public Opinion Quarterly* 37 (Fall 1973): 373-387; J. Miller McPherson, Susan Welch, and Cal Clark, "The Stability and Reliability of Political Efficacy: Using Path Analysis to Test Alternative Models," *American Political Science Review* 71 (June 1977): 509-521; and Philip E. Converse and Gregory B. Markus, "The New CPS Election Study Panel," *American Political Science Review* 73 (March 1979): 32-49.

12. Raymond E. Wolfinger and Steven J. Rosenstone, *Who Votes?* (New Haven, Conn: Yale University Press, 1980).

13. Ibid., Appendix A.

14. Kenneth D. Bailey, *Methods of Social Research* (New York: Free Press, 1978), 58.

15. This is a good example of a situation where the absence of a relationship does not necessarily mean the measure lacks construct validity. Because persons with low GRE scores are generally not admitted to graduate school, we lack performance measures for them. Consequently, the people for whom we can test the relationship between test scores and performance may be of similar ability and may not exhibit meaningful variation in their graduate school performance. Hence the test scores may be valid indicators of ability, but only for a less selective sample of test takers. The lack of a relationship in Table 4-1 undercuts claims of test score validity, but it does not necessarily disprove such claims.

16. The distinction between an interval and a ratio level measure is not always clear, and some political science texts do not distinguish between them. Interval level measures in political science are rather rare; ratio level measures (money spent, age, number of children, years living in the same location, for example) are more prevalent.

Terms Introduced

Alternative-form method. A method of calculating reliability by repeating different but equivalent measures at two or more points in time.

Construct validity. Validity demonstrated for a measure by showing that it is related to the measure of another concept.

Content validity. Validity demonstrated by ensuring that the full domain of a concept is measured.

Correlation matrix. A table showing the relationships among a number of discrete measures.

Face validity. Validity asserted by arguing that a measure corresponds closely to the concept it is designed to measure.

Guttman scale. A multi-item measure in which respondents are presented with increasingly difficult measures of approval for an attitude.

Index. A multi-item measure in which individual scores on a set of items are combined to form a summary measure.

Interval measurement. A measure for which a one-unit difference in scores is the same throughout the range of the measure.

Level of measurement. An indication of what is meant by assigning scores or numerals to empirical observations.

Likert scale. A multi-item measure in which the items are selected based on their ability to discriminate between those scoring high and those scoring low on the measure.

Measurement. The process by which phenomena are observed systematically and represented by scores or numerals.

Nominal measurement. A measure for which different scores represent different, but not ordered, categories.

Operational definition. The rules by which a concept is measured and scores assigned.

Ordinal measurement. A measure for which the scores represent ordered categories that are not necessarily equally distant from each other.

Ratio measurement. A measure for which the scores possess the full mathematical properties of the numbers assigned.

Reliability. The extent to which a measure yields the same results on repeated trials.

Semantic differential. A technique for measuring attitudes toward an object in which respondents are presented with a series of opposite adjective pairs.

Split-halves method. A method of calculating reliability by comparing the results of two equivalent measures made at the same time.

Test-retest method. A method of calculating reliability by repeating the same measure at two or more points in time.

Thurstone scale. A multi-item measure in which the goal is to select items that represent the entire range of an attitude at equal intervals.

Validity. The correspondence between a measure and the concept it is supposed to measure.

Exercises

1. Read J. Miller McPherson, Susan Welch, and Cal Clark, "The Stability and Reliability of Political Efficacy: Using Path Analysis to Test Alternative Models," *American Political Science Review* 71 (June 1977): 509-521. With what measurement issue are the authors concerned? What do they conclude about the measure of political efficacy that they analyze?

2. Read Jerald G. Bachman and Patrick M. O'Malley, "When Four Months Equal a Year: Inconsistencies in Student Reports of Drug Use," *Public Opinion Quarterly* 45 (Winter 1981): 536-548. Are the authors concerned with the reliability or validity of their measures? What do they conclude about the adequacy of their measure of drug use? On what is this conclusion based?

3. What would be the level of measurement of the following measures?
    a. The unemployment rates of the fifty American states.
    b. The region of the country in which people were born.
    c. How frequently people attended religious services in the last two months.
    d. The number of employees in different government agencies.
    e. The number of times incumbent senators voted the way the president wanted them to on twenty key pieces of legislation.
    f. The occupation of candidates for public office (for example, lawyer, teacher, farmer, banker).
    g. The percent of different corporations' pretax profit accounted for by overseas sales.
    h. Whether people read the daily newspaper every day, almost every day, frequently, occasionally, seldom, or never.

4. See Benjamin I. Page and Robert Y. Shapiro, "Effects of Public Opinion on Policy," *American Political Science Review* 77 (March 1983): 175-190. What do the authors say about their measures of public policy on page 177? Is this a discussion of reliability or validity? Where can readers find additional information about the measures of public policy used in this analysis?

5. Consider the measurement of the personal ideologies of Supreme Court justices in Jeffrey A. Segal and Albert D. Cover, "Ideological Values and the Votes of U.S. Supreme Court Justices," *American Political Science Review* 83 (June 1989): 557-565. What are some of the obstacles to measuring judicial attitudes directly (pages 558-561)? What do the authors say about the reliability of their measure? What is the evidence "that the scores accurately measure the perceptions of the justices' values at the time of their nominations" (page 559)?

6. In Manus I. Midlarsky, "Rulers and the Ruled: Patterned Inequality and the Onset of Mass Political Violence," *American Political Science Review* 82 (June 1988): 491-509, how did the researcher decide in which countries he would study the relationship between land inequality and political violence?

Suggested Readings

Babbie, Earl R. *Survey Research Methods.* Belmont, Calif.: Wadsworth, 1973.

Carmines, Edward G., and Richard A. Zeller. *Reliability and Validity Assessment.* Series on Quantitative Applications in the Social Sciences. No. 07-001, Sage University Papers. Beverly Hills, Calif.: Sage, 1979.

Kerlinger, Fred N. *Behavioral Research.* New York: Holt, Rinehart & Winston, 1979.

Robinson, John P., Jerrold G. Rusk, and Kendra B. Head. *Measures of Political Attitudes.* Ann Arbor, Mich.: Institute for Social Research, 1969.

Rubin, Herbert J. *Applied Social Research.* Columbus, Ohio: Merrill, 1983.

Smith, Barbara, et al. *Political Research Methods.* Boston: Houghton Mifflin, 1976.

CHAPTER 5

Research Design

A research design is a plan that shows how a researcher intends to fulfill the goals of a proposed study. It indicates what observations will be made to provide answers to the questions posed by the researcher, how the observations will be made, and the analytical and statistical procedures to be used once the data are collected. If the goal of the research is to test hypotheses, a research design will explain how the test is to be accomplished.

A research design has been defined as a plan that "guides the investigator in the process of collecting, analyzing, and interpreting observations. It is a logical model of proof that allows the researcher to draw inferences concerning causal relations among the variables under investigation. The research design also defines the domain of generalizability, that is, whether the obtained interpretations can be generalized to a larger population or to different situations." [1]

Developing the research design is just as important as developing research questions and hypotheses. A poor research design may produce insignificant and erroneous conclusions, no matter how original and brilliant the hypothesis. In this chapter we will discuss various research designs and their advantages and disadvantages and show how a poor research design can result only in tentative and uninformative research.

Many factors affect the choice of a particular research design. One is the purpose of the investigation. Whether the research is intended to be exploratory, descriptive, or explanatory will most likely influence the choice of a research design. Another is the practical limitations on how researchers may test their hypotheses. Some research designs may be unethical, others impossible to implement for lack of data or sufficient time and money. Researchers frequently must balance what is humanly possible to accomplish against what would be ideally done to test a particular hypothesis. Consequently, many of the research designs that researchers actually use are unfortunate but necessary compromises. The conclusions that reasonably may be drawn from most political science research are more tentative and incomplete than they might be.

All research designs to test hypotheses are attempts by researchers to (1) establish a relationship between two or more variables, (2) demonstrate that the results are generally true in the real world, (3) reveal whether one phenomenon precedes another in time, and (4) eliminate as many alternative explanations for a phenomenon as possible. This chapter will explain how various research designs allow or do not allow researchers to accomplish these four objectives. Two different types of designs will be discussed: experimental and nonexperimental.

Experimentation

Experimental research designs differ from nonexperimental designs in that they allow the researcher to have more control over the independent variable, the units of analysis, and the environment in which behavior occurs. Consequently, experimental designs allow researchers to establish causal explanations for political behavior more easily than nonexperimental designs do. However, very few types of significant political behaviors are studied by political scientists with experimentation. Nonetheless, it is important to understand how an experimental research design allows researchers to evaluate causal explanations.

An ideal experiment has five basic characteristics.[2] First, there are experimental groups that receive an experimental or test stimulus and control groups that do not. Second, the researcher determines the composition of the experimental and control groups by choosing the subjects and assigning them to one of the groups. In other words, the researcher can control who experiences the independent variable and who does not. Third, the researcher has control over the introduction of the experimental treatment—the independent variable; that is, the researcher can determine when, and under what circumstances, the experimental group is exposed to the experimental stimulus. Fourth, the researcher is able to measure the dependent variable both before and after the experimental stimulus is given. And finally, the researcher is able to control the environment of the subjects in order to control or exclude extraneous factors that might affect the dependent variable.

In an ideal experiment a researcher can make causal statements and rule out alternative explanations; that is, he or she can argue that manipulation of the experimental stimulus caused the experimental and control groups to differ with respect to the dependent variable. Before we examine some of the types of experimental research designs used by researchers and the advantages and limitations of each, let us consider how we might experimentally test an actual hypothesis.

Suppose you want to test the hypothesis that "watching violence on television causes people to engage in aggressive social behavior." The independent variable, or experimental stimulus, is the amount of violence watched on television, and the dependent variable is the frequency with which people exhibit aggressive social behavior. To test this hypothesis you might ask some people to experience the experimental stimulus (watch a lot of television violence); others you would not permit to experience this same stimulus. In this experiment you would be able to exercise enough control over the participants' lives that you could determine who watched a lot of television violence and who did not. You also could control when, how often, for how long, and under what conditions those in the experimental group would watch violence on television. The next step would be to observe the amount of aggressive social behavior by all participants in the experiment, both before and after the experimental group watched the violent programming. It would be important to ensure that nothing other than the difference in television viewing affected one group and not the other during the course of the experiment.

If all of these conditions could be met, an experiment could be conducted that would shed considerable light on the hypothesis. You would be particularly interested in the amount, and change in the amount, of aggressive behavior for the experimental group compared with the control group and would have some basis for concluding that any difference could be attributed to the experimental stimulus. In other words, if significant differences in the aggressive behavior of the two groups occurred, then you could legitimately conclude that watching television violence was a causal explanation for at least a portion of a group's aggression.

This is a very persuasive kind of evidence for a researcher to have, hence the attraction of experimentation. But problems arise with the conduct of experiments. These problems are often discussed in terms of internal and external validity.[3]

Internal Validity

Internal validity deals with whether the manipulation or variation in the independent variable makes a difference in the dependent variable. The internal validity of experimental research may be adversely affected by history, maturation, testing, statistical regression, and several other factors.

History. As we have seen, one of the characteristics of experimental research is that the researcher has enough control over the environment to make sure that exposure to the experimental stimulus is the only difference between experimental and control groups. Sometimes, however, events other than the experimental stimulus occur between the pretreatment and post-treatment measurements of the dependent variable and these affect the dependent variable. For example, suppose that after an automobile safety inspection program is introduced in a state, a crackdown on drunk driving also begins. A decline in the traffic fatality rate could be due to the inspection program, the drunk driving campaign, or a combination of both.

Maturation. The passage of time may also affect subjects and create differences between experimental and control groups. For example, subjects may grow older, or become tired or hungry during the course of an experiment. These changes may affect their reaction to the test stimulus and introduce an unanticipated effect on post-treatment scores.

Testing. The standard experimental research design includes a measurement of the dependent variable both before and after the experimental stimulus. However, the act of measuring the dependent variable prior to the experimental stimulus may itself affect the post-treatment scores of subjects. For example, suppose individuals who do poorly on the Scholastic Aptitude Test enroll in a course to improve their performance (the experimental stimulus), retake the SATs, and obtain higher scores. The improvement could be due to the course, to the experience that taking the SATs initially provided, or to a combination of the initial test and the course. Similarly, suppose a researcher wanted to see if watching a presidential debate makes viewers better informed than nonviewers. If the researcher measures the political awareness of the experimental and control groups prior to the debate, he or she runs the risk of sensitizing the subjects to certain topics or issues and contributing to a more attentive audience than would otherwise be the case. Consequently, we would not know for sure whether any increase in awareness was due to the debate, the pre-test, or a combination of both. Fortunately, some research designs have been developed to separate these various effects.

Statistical Regression. Sometimes a person is selected for participation in an experimental program because of some extreme characteristic such as very high or low reading test scores. These scores may be temporary deviations—due to illness, fatigue, or emotional upset—from the person's normal scores. After subsequent retesting, the scores would be expected to return to normal and become less extreme regardless of the impact of the person's participation in any special program. If this happens, improvements in scores may be attributed erroneously to the program.

Experimental Mortality. In assigning subjects to experimental and control groups, a researcher hopes that the two groups will be equivalent. If subjects drop out of the experiment, experimental and control groups that may have been the same at the start may no longer be equivalent. Thus differential loss of participants from comparison groups may raise doubts about whether the changes and variation in the dependent variable are due to manipulation of the independent variable.

Instrument Decay. Sometimes the instrument used to measure the dependent variable changes during the experiment so that the pre-test and post-test measures are not made in the same way. For example, a researcher may become tired and not take post-test measurements as carefully as pre-test ones. Or different persons with different biases may conduct the pre-test and post-test. Thus changes in the dependent variable may be due to measurement changes, not to the experimental stimulus.

Selection. If experimental and control group subjects are not equivalent, then differences between the groups at the end of an experiment cannot be attributed conclusively to the independent variable. Bias in the selection of subjects may occur if a researcher does not control assignment of subjects to experimental and control groups or if the researcher personally assigns subjects in a biased manner. A common selection problem occurs when subjects volunteer to participate in a program. Volunteers may differ significantly from nonvolunteers.

Some of the difficulties that may prevent completion of a successful experiment may be anticipated and guarded against by using particular experimental designs. In other cases, however, a researcher cannot rule out all possible threats to internal validity. Nevertheless, because of the characteristics mentioned earlier, experimental research designs are better able to resist threats to internal validity than are other types of research designs.

External Validity

External validity refers to the representativeness of research findings and whether it is possible to generalize from them to other situations. One possible problem is that the same effects may not be found using a different population. For example, findings from an experiment investigating the effects of live television coverage on legislators' behavior in state legislatures with fewer than one hundred members may not be generalizable to larger state legislative bodies or to Congress. In general, if a sample population is not representative of a larger population, the ability to generalize about the larger population will be limited.

Another question is whether slightly different experimental treatments will result in similar findings with small differences or in findings that are fundamentally different. For example, a small increase in city spending for neighborhood improvements may not result in a more positive attitude of residents toward their neighborhood or the city. A slightly larger increase, however, may have an effect, perhaps because it has resulted in more noticeable improvements.

Threats to the external validity of an experiment also may be caused if the artificiality of the experimental setting makes it hard to generalize about findings in more natural settings. For example, subjects may react to a stimulus differently when they know they are being studied than when they are in a natural setting. Finally, subjects' behavior may be affected by testing. For example, if subjects react to the pre-test (not just to the experimental treatment), the findings may not be applicable to other subjects who are not exposed to a pre-test.

Despite these problems with experimental research designs, experiments are still attractive to researchers because they provide control over the subjects and their exposure to various levels of the independent variable.[4] The purpose of an experiment is to isolate and measure the effects of the independent variable or variables and to exclude other factors that might also influence the dependent variable. Control over the assignment of subjects to the experimental and control groups is used by researchers to exclude as many of these other factors as possible.

Control over Assignment of Subjects

Researchers attempt to exclude extraneous factors by assigning subjects to control and experimental groups in three different ways. One way is to assign subjects to the groups at random under the assumption that extraneous factors will affect all groups equally. *Assignment at random* is the practical choice when the researcher is not able to specify possible extraneous factors in advance or when there are so many that it is not possible to assign subjects to experimental and control groups equally.

Even if a researcher assigns subjects at random, extraneous factors may not be randomly distributed and therefore will affect the outcome of the experiment. This is especially true if the number of subjects is small. Prudent researchers do not assume that all significant factors are randomly distributed just because subjects have been assigned at random. In addition to random assignment, researchers often check to see if the control and experimental groups are, in fact, equal with regard to those factors that are suspected of influencing the dependent variable.

Precision matching is another way to assign subjects to groups in order to control extraneous factors. Precision matching is used if the researcher knows ahead of time that certain factors are related to differences in the dependent variable. In precision matching, the researcher matches pairs of subjects who are as similar as possible and assigns one to the experimental group and the other to the control group. Thus the researcher does not take the chance that random assignment will equalize the groups with respect to these factors. One problem with this method is that when there are many factors to be controlled, it becomes difficult to match subjects on all relevant characteristics and a larger pool of prospective subjects is required. A second problem is that not all extraneous factors may be identified ahead of time. To guard against bias in the assignment of pairs, members of the matched pairs should be randomly assigned to the control and experimental groups.

A third method of assigning subjects to groups is by *frequency distribution control.* Instead of matching pairs of subjects, the researcher makes sure that the experimental and control groups are identical in the distribution and average value of an extraneous variable. For example, if one wanted to control income as an extraneous factor, one would make sure that the average income of the control and experimental groups was similar. Frequency distribution control requires a smaller subject pool than precision matching, but it has the disadvantage that it can be done only for one variable at a time. Thus it is possible to equalize groups with respect to income and end up with all doctors in one group and all lawyers in another. If occupation were also a suspected extraneous factor, the experiment would be in jeopardy.

One of the biggest obstacles to experimentation in social science research is the inability of researchers to control assignment of subjects to experimental and control groups. This is especially true when public policies are involved. Even though the point of conducting an experiment is to test whether a treatment or program has a beneficial effect, it is often politically difficult to assign subjects to a control group; people assume that the experimental treatment must be beneficial—otherwise the treatment or program would not have been proposed as a response to a public policy problem. In setting up experimental and control groups, social scientists generally lack sufficient authority or incentives to offer subjects.

Now that we have discussed experimental research in general and some problems associated with it, let us consider some specific experimental research designs. Each one represents a different attempt by the researcher to retain experimental control while also dealing with the various threats to internal and external validity. Students may not have the immediate opportunity to employ these research designs, but knowledge of them will help in evaluating research and in determining whether the research design employed by the researcher supports the conclusions that are reached.

Experimental Designs

Simple Post-test Design

The simplest experimental design involves two groups and two variables, one independent and one dependent. Subjects are assigned to one or the other of the two groups. One group, the experimental group, is exposed to a "treatment" or stimulus that represents the independent variable. The other group, the control group, is not. Then the dependent variable is measured for each group. This design may be diagrammed as follows:

(Random Assignment)	*Treatment*	*Post-treatment Measurement of Dependent Variable*
Experimental Group	Yes	Yes
Control Group	No	Yes

A researcher using this design can make causal inferences because he or she can make sure that the treatment occurred prior to measurement of the dependent variable. Furthermore, the researcher can argue that any difference between the two groups on the measure of the dependent variable is attributed to the difference in the treatment—in other words, to the introduction of the independent variable—between the groups. This design requires random assignment of subjects to the experimental and control groups, and therefore assumes that extraneous factors have been controlled (that is, were the same for both groups). It also assumes that prior to the application of the experimental stimulus, both groups were equivalent with respect to the dependent variable.

A simple example will illustrate this design. Suppose we wanted to test the hypothesis that watching a national nominating convention on television makes people better informed politically. Using this research design, we would take our subjects, randomly assign them to a group that will watch a convention or a group that will not, and measure how well informed the members of the two groups are after the convention is over. Any difference in the level of awareness between the two groups after the convention would be attributed to the impact of watching convention coverage.

The simple post-test experimental design assumes that the random assignment of subjects to the experimental and control groups creates two groups that are identical in all significant ways prior to the introduction of the experimental stimulus. Although this is a safe assumption, it is not always accurate. Post-treatment differences between the two groups may be the result of pre-treatment differences. Since it is impossible with this design to tell how much of the post-treatment difference is simply a reflection of pre-treatment differences, a second research design is often used.

"Classic" Pre-test and Post-test Design

Unlike the simplest experimental design, the classic experimental design provides for a pre-test of the dependent variable before the experimental stimulus is introduced. This design may be diagrammed this way:

	Pre-treatment Measurement of		Post-treatment Measurement of
(Random Assignment)	*Dependent Variable*	*Treatment*	*Dependent Variable*
Experimental Group	Yes	Yes	Yes
Control Group	Yes	No	Yes

In this design it is possible to determine whether the groups actually are equivalent with respect to the dependent variable prior to the experimental treatment. The extra measurement provided by the pre-test strengthens the validity of the experiment by removing the doubt in the simple post-test design that the groups might not have been equivalent despite random assignment of subjects to groups. Furthermore, any pre-test difference between control and experimental groups can be taken into account when calculating the effect of the experimental stimulus.

For example, let's assume that a researcher wants to test the effect of a candidate's televised campaign commercials on the ability of voters to identify important issues in the campaign. In a post-test only experimental design, subjects would be randomly assigned to experimental and control groups, and one group of subjects would be shown the commercials while the other group would not. After the experimental group had seen the commercials, a test measuring the ability to identify campaign issues would be given to subjects in both groups. Suppose the average score on this test was 9.5 for the experimental group and 7.5 for the control group. The effect of having seen the campaign commercials would seem to be the difference in the two scores (2).

Now suppose a pre-test of issue awareness had also been given to both groups. The experimental group might have had a pre-test score of 8 and the control group a score of 7.5. In this case the presence of a pre-test would reveal to the researcher that the random assignment to the two groups did not create perfectly equivalent groups. Furthermore, the researcher would then realize that the gain in awareness for the experimental group was 1.5 (9.5 − 8), while the gain in awareness for the control group was 0 (7.5 − 7.5). Hence the researcher could conclude that the effect of seeing the ads translated into a 1.5 point change on the score of the experimental group, not 2 points as measured in the simple first design.

Pre-test, post-test designs with a control group have another advantage as well. Sometimes a considerable amount of time elapses between the pre-test and the post-test. This increases the possibility that extraneous factors may intrude and cause the dependent variable to change. Historical events or maturation processes may take place, for example. If it can be assumed that extraneous factors affect control and experimental groups equally, then the effect of extraneous factors is measured by the change in the dependent variable for the control group. Therefore, change in the dependent variable due only to the experimental stimulus can be calculated as follows:

$$\text{Experimental effect} = \left(\begin{array}{ll}\text{Post-test} & \text{Pre-test} \\ \text{score for} & \text{score for} \\ \text{experimental} & - \text{ experimental} \\ \text{group} & \text{group}\end{array}\right) - \left(\begin{array}{ll}\text{Post-test} & \text{Pre-test} \\ \text{score for} & \text{score for} \\ \text{control} & - \text{ control} \\ \text{group} & \text{group}\end{array}\right) \quad (5.1)$$

Now assume for a moment that the post-test score for the control group was 8 instead of 7.5 (reflecting the possibility that the control group would increase its issue awareness over time even though it did not watch any political commercials on television). The effect of seeing the campaign commercials would be only a one-point difference in awareness: (9.5 − 8.0) − (8.0 − 7.5) = 1.

Although this classic experimental design allows researchers to assess the pre-treatment equivalence of the experimental and control groups, it, too, is vulnerable to a particular problem—namely, *testing* or *instrument reactivity*. In other words, the pre-test itself may sensitize or otherwise affect respondents and cause a change in the dependent variable for both control and experimental groups. For example, if you are in the control group, taking the pre-test may make you more attentive to information touched on in the test in the days and weeks that follow. To minimize the possibility of the pre-test having an enduring effect, researchers often allow a considerable amount of time to elapse between pre-test and post-test measurements. If the effect of the pre-test is equal for both control and experimental groups, any instrument reactivity caused by the pre-test would be factored out along with any other extraneous factors by Equation 5.1. The pre-test may sensitize both the control and experimental groups, but the effect may be greater for the experimental group. The pre-test may cause the experimental group to react differently to the treatment than it would have if there had been no pre-test. If the pre-test affects the experimental and control groups differently, the pre-test, post-test design does not permit precise measurement and adjustment for the effect of the pre-test.

In addition to instrument reactivity, there is another problem with the classic pre-test, post-test design: measurement error. So far we have assumed that all the measurements taken are precise and reliable measures of the independent and dependent variables. However, measurement error may affect the reliability of the difference measure between the pre-test and the post-test. If the reliability of the instrument used in the pre-test and post-test is imperfect, the reliability of the measurement of the difference between two imperfect measures will be even lower and may be unacceptable for use in drawing any conclusions.[5]

Despite these difficulties, the pre-test, post-test design is useful, particularly where there are several treatment groups with random assignment but no control group. This is often the case in program evaluation studies where researchers are investigating whether the program has produced changes in program participants.[6] If the program is believed to be beneficial, it may be difficult to establish a control group that receives no treatment. The pre-test, post-test design allows the researcher to compare change in two groups receiving different treatments. Any difference in change is attributed to differences in treatments. Without a control group, however, change between a pre-test and post-test does not absolutely establish the factors that caused the change. The researcher can never be sure what might have happened to subjects if no treatment had been given at all.

Multigroup Design

So far we have discussed mainly research involving one experimental and one control group. In multigroup designs the dependent variable is measured for each group, but instead of one experimental group and one control group, more experimental or control groups are added. This is useful if the independent variable can assume several values and if the researcher wants to see the possible effects of manipulating the independent variable in several different ways. Multigroup designs may involve a post-test only or both a pre-test and a post-test.

Suppose you were concerned with the problem of how to increase the proportion of respondents who fill out and return mail questionnaires. The proportion of respondents who return questionnaires in a mail survey is usually quite low. Investigators have attempted to increase these response rates by including an incentive or token of appreciation in the survey. Since these add to the cost of the survey, researchers like to know whether the incentives do increase response rates and which ones are most effective and cost efficient.

To test the effect of various incentives, you could use a multigroup post-test design. If you wanted to test the effects of five treatments, you could randomly assign subjects to six groups. One group would receive no reward (the control group); each of the other groups would receive a different reward—for example, 25¢, 50¢, $1.00, a key ring, or a pen. Response rates (the post-treatment measure of the dependent variable) for the groups could then be compared. Table 5-1 presents the results.

The response rates indicate that rewards increase response rates and that monetary incentives have more effect than do token gifts. Furthermore, it seems that the dollar incentive is not cost effective since it did not yield a sufficiently greater response rate than the 50¢ reward to warrant the additional expense. Other experiments of this type could be conducted to compare the effects of prepaid versus promised monetary rewards or the inclusion or exclusion of a pre-stamped return envelope.

Multigroup Time Series Design

The pre-test must come before the experimental treatment and the post-test must come afterward, but exactly how long before and how long afterward? Researchers seldom know for sure. Therefore, a research design including several pre-treatment and post-treatment measures is often used when a researcher is uncertain exactly how quickly the effect of the independent variable should be observed or when the most reliable pre-test measurement of the dependent variable should be taken.

For example, a three-group, four-measurement design might consist of the following:

(Random Assignment)	Pre-test		Treatment	Post-test	
	First	*Second*		*First*	*Second*
Experimental Group 1	Yes	Yes	Yes	Yes	Yes
Experimental Group 2	Yes	Yes	Yes but different	Yes	Yes
Control Group	Yes	Yes	No	Yes	Yes

One good reason to use this design is to establish pre-treatment trends in the dependent variable. Multiple measurements can be used to check for stability in the dependent variable for all groups prior to treatment. In addition, multiple measurements after treatment allow researchers to see if treatment effects are immediate or delayed and whether the effects are lasting. The issue of lasting effects is often an important one in the evaluation of programs in education, health, and criminal justice. One drawback to this design, however, is that the possibility of instrument reactivity becomes greater when there are multiple measurements of the dependent variable.

Table 5-1   Mail Survey Incentive Experiment

(Random Assignment)	Treatment	Response Rate
Experimental Group 1	25¢	45.0%
Experimental Group 2	50¢	51.0
Experimental Group 3	$1.00	52.0
Experimental Group 4	pen	38.0
Experimental Group 5	key ring	37.0
Control Group	no reward	30.2

Source: Hypothetical data.

An example of a multigroup time series design would be an attempt to test the relationship between watching a presidential debate and support for the candidates. Suppose you conducted a classical experiment, randomly assigning some people to a group that watches a debate and others to a group that does not watch the debate. On the pre- and post-tests you might receive the following scores:

	Pre-debate Support for Candidate X	Treatment	Post-debate Support for Candidate X
Experimental Group 1	60	Yes	50
Control Group	55	No	50

These scores seem to indicate that the control group was slightly less supportive of Candidate X before the debate (that is, the random assignment did not work perfectly) and that the debate led to a decline in support for Candidate X of 5 percent $(60 - 50) - (55 - 50)$.

Suppose, however, that you had the following additional measures.

	Pre-test			Treatment	Post-test		
	First	Second	Third		First	Second	Third
Experimental Group 1	80	70	60	Yes	50	40	30
Control Group	65	60	55	No	50	45	40

It appears that support for Candidate X eroded throughout the whole period for both the experimental and control groups and that the rate of decline was consistently more rapid for the experimental group (that is, the two groups were not equivalent prior to the debate). Viewed from this perspective, it seems that the debate had no effect on the experimental group since the rate of decline both before and after the debate was the same.

Factorial Designs

In experiments where researchers are interested in determining the effects of several independent variables on a dependent variable, alone and in combination, factorial designs are used. The simplest factorial design is the 2 x 2 design. In this design there are two independent variables, each of which takes on two values. Factorial designs may involve more than two dimensions and an independent variable may have any number of values or levels.

An example of a 2 x 2 design is an experiment to test the effectiveness of token gifts and follow-up reminders alone and in combination on the response rate in a mail survey. Four hundred respondents were randomly assigned in equal numbers to the four treatment groups shown in Table 5-2.

To examine the effect of each independent variable singly, ignore the individual cell response rates and observe the response rates at the bottom and along the side of the table. There is a 12.5 percentage point (52.5 percent − 40 percent) increase in response rates when a token is included with the mail survey. Also a follow-up letter improves rates. Therefore, each independent variable has a positive effect on response rates. By looking at the individual cell response rates, you see that the two treatments combine to increase response rates well above any other combination (60 percent).

Solomon Four-Group Design

We have mentioned the possible problem of instrument reactivity caused by using a pre-test. A more complex pattern of reactivity, however, may occur: the pre-test and test stimulus may interact to cause additional change in the dependent variable, beyond the effects attributable to the pre-test and the test stimulus individually.

Consider this example. An experiment is designed to test the effect of a film about water use and supplies on attitudes about water conservation. Subjects are assigned at random to two groups. Both groups are given a pre-test asking them about their attitudes about water conservation. Then the test group, but not the control group, is shown the film. Sometime later both groups are retested on their attitudes toward water conservation. It is possible that the control group will show a change in attitudes if the pre-test made the subjects more aware of water conservation issues. Suppose the experimental group showed a much larger change. The difference between the control and test groups could be due to the film, but it also could be due to the pre-test and the film. The combination might create a much greater effect than simply the sum of the effect of the pre-test alone and the effect of the film alone. The

Table 5-2   Response Rates in Mail Survey Experiment

	No Gift	Token Gift	
No Follow Up	30.0% (30/100)	45.0% (45/100)	37.5% (75/200)
Follow Up	50.0% (50/100)	60.0% (60/100)	55.0% (110/200)
	40% (80/200)	52.5% (105/200)	

experimental group may have watched the film differently and responded to it differently than it would have otherwise because it had been given the pre-test. (Perhaps it is easier to understand the concept of measurement interaction by recalling how you may have felt after consuming a little too much pizza or beer. Now how would you have felt if you had had too much pizza and beer at the same sitting?)

The Solomon four-group design is an experimental design that allows a researcher to measure the interaction between a pre-test and test stimulus. The effect of the treatment, the effect of the pre-test on the post-test, and the effect of other extraneous factors can also be measured.[7] Thus, unlike the two-group pre-test, post-test design, extraneous factors are isolated from pre-test factors.

In this design one group is given the pre-test, test stimulus, and post-test. A second group is given the test stimulus and post-test, but no pre-test. A third group is given a pre-test and post-test, but no experimental stimulus. A fourth group is given only the post-test. The design can be represented as follows:

Random Assignment	*Pre-test*	*Treatment*	*Post-test*
Experimental Group 1	Yes	Yes	Yes
Experimental Group 2	No	Yes	Yes
Control Group 1	Yes	No	Yes
Control Group 2	No	No	Yes

The total change in the first experimental group can be summarized as:

$$\text{Change} = \text{Pre-test effect} + \text{treatment effect} \\ + \text{interaction effect} + \text{other factors} \quad (5.2)$$

Table 5-3 presents the result of this four-group experiment. Total change in Experimental Group 1 equals 10 (20 − 10). The pre-test effect is determined by comparing the post-test scores of the two control groups, one of which had a pre-test. Subtracting the post-test of Control Group 2 from that of Control Group 1, we get (12 − 11) for a pre-test only effect. The treatment effect can be determined by comparing Experimental Group 2, which received no pre-test and saw only the film,

Table 5-3   Water Conservation Test

(Random Assignment)	Pre-test	Treatment	Post-test
Experimental Group 1	10	Yes	20
Experimental Group 2		Yes	15
Control Group 1	10	No	12
Control Group 2	(Assumed to be 10)	No	11

and Control Group 2, which received no pre-test and did not see the film. The treatment effect equals 4 (15 − 11). To calculate the effect of other factors only, we need to compare the post-test score for Control Group 2 with the pre-test scores of the groups given a pre-test. Since subjects were assigned at random to all four groups, we can assume that the pre-test score of Control Group 2 is the average of the pre-test scores of the two pre-tested groups or 10. Thus the effect of other factors affecting the dependent variable is 1 (11 − 10).

Substituting these numbers into Equation 5.2 and rearranging the terms to solve for interaction, we find that 4 points out of the 10 point change were due to the interaction between the pre-test and the test stimulus.

$$10 = 1 + 4 + \text{interaction effect} + 1$$
$$\text{Interaction effect} = 10 - 1 - 4 - 1 = 4$$

In addition to the six types of experimental designs mentioned here—the simple post-test design; the classic pre-test, post-test design; the multigroup design; the multigroup time series design; the factorial design; and the Solomon four-group design—there are numerous others described in the Suggested Readings list at the end of this chapter.

Field Experiments

Field experiments are experimental designs applied in a natural setting; thus they are not really a separate kind of design. In field experiments, researchers try to control the selection of subjects, their assignment to treatment groups, and the manipulation of the independent variable. Field experiments differ from laboratory experiments because the environment in which the subjects behave cannot be completely controlled. Thus there is a greater chance for extraneous factors—such as historical events—to intrude and affect experimental results. It may be possible to choose natural settings that are isolated in some respects, thereby approximating a controlled environment, but the researcher can only hope that the environment remains unchanged during the course of a field experiment.

Field experiments should not necessarily be considered inferior to laboratory experiments. The artificial environment of a laboratory or controlled setting may seriously affect the external validity of an experiment. Something that can be shown only in a laboratory may have limited applicability in the real world. A program or treatment that is successful in a controlled setting may not be successful in a natural setting.

An interesting example of a field experiment in political science is the New Jersey experiment in income maintenance funded by the Office of Economic Opportunity and conducted from 1967 to 1971.[8] This effort was the forerunner of other large-scale social experiments designed to test the effects of new social programs. The experiment is a good illustration of the difficulty of mounting a large social experiment.

At the time of the experiment, dissatisfaction with the existing welfare system was high because of its cost and because it was thought to discourage the poor from lifting themselves out of poverty. Families headed by able-bodied men generally were excluded from welfare programs and the income of welfare recipients was taxed at such a rate that many thought there was little incentive for recipients to work.

In 1965 a negative income tax was proposed that would provide a minimum, nontaxable allowance to all families and that would attempt to maintain work incentives by allowing the poor to keep a significant fraction of their earnings. For example, a family of four might be guaranteed an income of $5,000 and would be allowed to keep 50 percent of all its earnings up to a break-even point where it could choose to remain in the program or opt out. If the break-even income was $10,000, a family earning $10,000 could receive a $5,000 guaranteed minimum plus half of $10,000 ($5,000) for a total of $10,000 or it could keep all the $10,000 earned and choose not to receive any income from the government. The idea was opposed by those who thought a guaranteed minimum income would induce people to reduce their work effort. Others were concerned about how families would use the cash allowances. Numerous questions also were raised about the administration of the program. Because of these uncertainties, an experiment was designed to test the consequences of a guaranteed minimum income system.

The experimental design included two experimental factors. One was the income guarantee level, expressed as a percent of the poverty line. The level is the amount a family received if other income was zero. The other factor was the rate at which each dollar of earned income was taxed. The design showing the experimental conditions is presented in Table 5-4.

This 4 x 3 factorial design allowed researchers to examine the effect of the variation in one factor while the other was held constant. For example, it allowed researchers to examine the effect of varying the tax rate from 30 to 50 to 70 percent while the guarantee remained set at 75 percent of the poverty line.

Table 5-4 Experimental Design of New Jersey Income-
Maintenance Experiment

Guarantee (percent of poverty line)	Tax Rate		
	30%	50%	70%
125		X	
100		X	X
75	X	X	X
50	X	X	

Note: X represents experimental conditions actually tested.

Certain combinations of experimental treatments were not chosen because they were not realistic policy options or because they increased the cost of the study. In assigning families to cells, there was a tradeoff between the number of families that could be included in the study and the number of families assigned to each cell since some cells were more costly than others. The cells with the most likely national policy options (the 100-50 and 75-50 plans) were assigned more families to make sure that enough families completed the experiment. Finally, for some of the less generous combinations, the researchers experienced difficulty in finding eligible families willing to participate in the experiment. Families placed in these cells were likely to receive at most a small payment because they were near the break-even point. This situation created resentment within the community because it was hoped that participants would benefit from participating in the experiment beyond the nominal payment families were given each time they completed an income report. If the researchers had had complete control over their subjects, assignment problems would have been fewer. But in research involving human subjects, such control is understandably lacking.

Only families headed by able-bodied males were eligible for the experiment because of the great interest in the possible impact the program would have on the work effort of poor families. Information about the work behavior of females with dependent children was not considered a good indicator of the work response of able-bodied males to public assistance. Very little was known about the work response of males because, as a group, able-bodied men and their families were not entitled to general public assistance.

In the rest of this section we will explore some of the issues and problems faced during this field experiment.

Generalizability. To limit possible extraneous factors, families were chosen from a fairly homogeneous setting—New Jersey. Because a nationally dispersed sample was not chosen, however, the ability to generalize findings to a national program was limited. Generalizability was also affected by the three-year duration of the experiment. Families knew that the program was not permanent, and this may have affected their behavior.

Instrumentation Difficulties. The experiment encountered income measurement problems. The income reports asked for gross income, but families had trouble distinguishing between net and gross income. Families in the experimental groups learned more quickly how to fill out the reports correctly than control group families because they were asked to report income every month. Control families (that is, other low-income families) were asked only every three months. As a result, the accuracy of income data changed over time and differentially for experimental and control group families. This one month-three month difference arose because researchers were afraid that too much contact with control families would change their behavior (instrument reactivity) and make them less than true controls. Such are the tradeoffs that researchers must make to avoid the numerous threats to the validity of experiments.

Uncontrolled Environment. In field experiments, unlike laboratory experiments, researchers are not in complete control of subjects' environments. This problem was dramatically illustrated during the New Jersey income-maintenance experiment. In the middle of the experiment, New Jersey adopted AFDC-UP, a public assistance program. Eligible families were those with dependent children and an unemployed parent, male or female. One reason New Jersey originally had been chosen was because it did not have this program. AFDC-UP provided an attractive alternative to some of the experimental cell conditions, and thus many families dropped out of the experiment.

Another problem arose because there were not enough eligible families in the New Jersey communities that were chosen to provide sufficient ethnic diversity. As a consequence, an urban area in northeastern Pennsylvania was included. However, the families in that area faced different conditions than the New Jersey families and varied on some important characteristics such as home ownership. One purpose of the study was to examine whether ethnic groups responded differently to the income-maintenance program. Because whites were represented mostly from one site, it became difficult to separate ethnic differences from site-induced differences.

Ethical Issues. Even though participation in the program was voluntary, the researchers were concerned about the effect of termination of the experiment on families that had been receiving payments. At the start of the experiment, families were given a card with the termination date of payments printed on it. Researchers debated tapering off payments and reminding families of the approaching end. It was decided to remind the families once toward the end, and research field offices remained open as referral agencies in case families needed help. But none requested help. Answers to a questionnaire three months after the last payment indicated that there were no serious adverse effects on the families caused by the experiment.

Major Findings. There was only a 5 to 6 percent reduction in average hours worked by the male heads of families who received negative income tax payments. This reduction occurred only among white men. For black men, average hours increased, although not significantly. For Spanish-speaking men, hours decreased but also not significantly. Researchers were unable to explain this unexpected finding, and therefore it may be unreliable. The behavior of black working wives was not affected, while Spanish-speaking and white working wives reduced their work effort considerably. Experimental families made larger investments in housing and durable goods than control families. There was also an indication that experimental families experienced increased educational attainment.

The experiment failed to provide accurate cost estimates for alternative negative income tax plans or conclusive evidence on the work disincentive of various tax rates. Because of these shortcomings, it did not provide conclusive evidence in favor of or against a negative income tax plan.

This is a good example of the difficulty of studying a political phenomenon both experimentally and in a natural setting. Political scientists seldom have the resources or the control over subjects and other phenomena to conduct experiments on political behavior of the type attempted in New Jersey. Consequently, researchers interested in explaining political phenomena usually have to rely on other kinds of approaches.

Nonexperimental Designs

We described experimental research designs in some detail because they capture the logic of testing the effect of an independent variable and are the standard against which research is often evaluated. In practice, however, political scientists seldom use any of these experimental designs. The reason is really quite simple: political scientists seldom have sufficient control over people's behavior and the introduction of experimental stimuli to conduct experimental research.

Suppose, for example, that a researcher wanted to test the hypothesis that poverty causes people to commit robberies. Following the logic of experimental research, the researcher would have to randomly assign people to two groups, measure the number of robberies committed by members of the two groups prior to the experimental treatment, force the experimental group to become poor, and then remeasure the number of robberies committed at some later date. Clearly, people are understandably reluctant to allow researchers to have this much control over their lives. (Witness the difficulties that arose when such an "experiment" was conducted with two people in the movie *Trading Places*.)

As a result of the many obstacles to conducting experimental research, political scientists have developed a number of nonexperimental research designs that are more practical. In these designs only a single group is used or the researcher has no control over the application of the test stimulus or independent variable. A few of these designs are described in the following sections.

Pre-test, Post-test Design

The pre-test, post-test design involves only one group that is given a pre-test, a test stimulus, and a post-test. There is no control group, and it is assumed that any change in the dependent variable is due to the test stimulus. Obviously, there is no way of knowing for sure that a change in the dependent variable was due to the experimental factor and not to other factors. Also there is no way to check for pre-test effects and pre-test, test stimulus interaction.

Suppose, for example, that we measured the level of political interest for a group of people, had them all watch a televised presidential debate, remeasured levels of political interest, and then observed that the amount of interest increased. Would we be justified in concluding that watching the debate caused an increase in political interest? Clearly, the answer is no because we do not know what would have happened in the absence of watching the debate. The increase in political interest could have been the result of any number of other factors, including the pre-test and participation in the project, as well as a secular trend (for example, political interest in general was on the rise).

Interrupted Time Series Design

An improvement over the single group pre-test, post-test design is the interrupted time series design. In this design numerous measures of the dependent variable are taken both before and after the treatment, but still for only one group. The premeasurements allow a researcher to establish trends in the dependent variable. These trends may be linear (either increasing or decreasing) or cyclical, as illustrated in Figure 5-1. After the trends are established, the researcher introduces (or observes)

Figure 5-1 Examples of Pre-treatment Trends in the Dependent
Variable

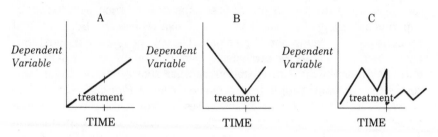

the experimental stimulus. A change in direction of the dependent
variable away from the established trend may indicate that the test
stimulus has had an effect. (In Figure 5-1 such an effect is presumably
present in examples B and C, but not A.) This assumes that nothing else
changed that might have affected the dependent variable and that the
trend would have continued undisturbed if not for the test stimulus.

This research design could be used to study the impact of a program.
For example, one might try to evaluate the impact of sobriety checks on
alcohol-related traffic accidents in states by examining the number of
such accidents for several years before and after the introduction of the
checks. If a decline in accidents was observed, it would be evidence that
sobriety checks have been effective, but one cannot be sure whether the
decline results from the checks alone or at all. Some other factor may
have caused the decline in accidents.

Time series studies may be affected by numerous threats to internal
validity. For example, instrument change may affect the measurement of
the dependent variable over time. This may be a problem if the
researcher has relied on existing data collected by others. For example,
time series studies are often used to investigate the impact of governmental programs. City crime rates may be compared for several years
before and after a change in police patrol practices. Achievement scores
of schoolchildren may be observed before and after a change in the
school's reading program. City budgets may be examined before and after
reorganization of city departments. In these instances, conclusions may
be jeopardized by different ways of recording crimes, different achievement tests, or different accounting methods. The longer the time period
under study is, the more likely instrument change is to occur.

Another problem with time series studies is that subjects may react to
multiple measurements by becoming bored or tired, or by trying to be consistent. In some cases, however, multiple testing may help a respondent to
relax and give more natural answers or to learn what information is desired
by the researcher so that more accurate and valid answers may be given.

Finally, since time series studies also lack a control group, we cannot be certain that all post-treatment changes are due to the experimental stimulus. Other factors that are present or that occur at approximately the same time can also influence the dependent variable. For example, it is difficult to tell how much public opinion was affected by the civil rights movement, the Vietnam War, and the federal government's War on Poverty in the 1960s; there is no control group that was not appreciably "exposed" to all the "experimental stimuli."

Page and Shapiro's study of the relationship between public opinion change and change in policy employs the logic of the interrupted time series design. After identifying cases in which public opinion had changed substantially, the researchers measured government policy outputs at several time points before and after the period of opinion change. With these measurements of policy, they were able to see whether policy changes occurred before or after changes in public opinion and how much of a time lag there was in policy change after a change in public opinion.[9] Page and Shapiro were able to rule out the possibility that policy affected opinion in many of the cases. They argue that it is reasonable to infer that opinion change was a cause of policy change. Of course, it is still possible that both policy and opinion were independently affected by other factors such as world events, elite leadership, interest group campaigns, or technological change.[10]

One of the problems with the two nonexperimental research designs discussed so far is the lack of a control group with which to compare the behavior of the experimental group. In experimental research the researcher can create a control group by preventing exposure to the independent variable. This cannot be done in nonexperimental research, but sometimes researchers can use a control group that exists naturally (that is, without the researcher's interference). For example, an improvement upon the study of the impact of sobriety checks would be to try to introduce a control group by tracking the number of alcohol related traffic accidents in states without sobriety checks. If there was a decline in accidents in these states as well, one would be less confident in attributing all the decline in states with checks to the introduction of the checks.

The cross-sectional and panel study research designs are ones in which a control group of sorts is also present, as we will explain next.

Cross-sectional Design

In a cross-sectional research design, measurements of the independent and dependent variables are taken at the same point in time. The measurements of the independent variable are used to construct quasi-experimental and quasi-control groups that have naturally occurred, and the measurements of the dependent variable are used to assess the differences between the quasi-experimental and quasi-control groups.

For example, to test the hypothesis that "those with more education earn more income" a researcher could divide people into groups with varying amounts of education. In this way the quasi-control group (those with no formal education) and the quasi-experimental group (the others) may be observed. (Notice, however, that the researcher did not control who would be in each group by forcing people to have differing amounts of education. The groups were simply naturally occurring and observed.) The income levels for each of these groups could then be measured and contrasted to assess the impact of education on income.

The cross-sectional design is frequently used in political science research. In a study of attitudes toward busing, for example, researchers used survey data to measure the dependent variable (support for busing) and the independent variables (racial intolerance, political conservatism, and self-interest in the busing issue—that is, whether or not the respondent had a child in school) at the same point in time.[11] They divided people into groups based on the measures of the independent variable and then observed the amount of the dependent variable in each of the groups. They found that measures of racial intolerance and political conservatism inversely correlated with support for busing while measures of self-interest did not.

This study and others of the same type have several limitations. Because all measures were taken at one point in time, the researchers cannot be certain that racial intolerance or political conservatism preceded attitudes toward busing. Therefore, they cannot assert that racial intolerance caused attitudes toward busing, even though there is a strong relationship between the two. The respondents' attitudes toward busing, after all, may have been formed before their racial intolerance. Furthermore, since the subjects were not randomly assigned to treatment groups, any differences between treatment groups may result from factors other than the independent variables under consideration.

Researchers attempt to remove the effects of other factors by controlling for them statistically (a process we will describe in Chapter 13); that is, they attempt to make the comparison groups equivalent by holding relevant extraneous factors constant and then observing the relationship between independent and dependent variables. Yet holding these factors constant is problematic and ultimately impossible, since it is very difficult to be sure that all relevant variables have been controlled for.

Edward Tufte used a cross-sectional design in his study of whether compulsory automobile safety inspection programs help reduce traffic fatalities.[12] The hypothesis tested was "states with inspection programs have fewer automobile deaths than states without inspection programs."

Tufte measured the relevant variables at the same time, even though he used the average of auto fatality rates in three years as the dependent variable. Note also that he did not control the assignment of states to different experimental conditions (that is, inspection program or no inspection program). Rather he observed the naturally occurring groups of states with different inspection programs. This research design affects the conclusions that Tufte was able to draw from his study.

The average number of traffic fatalities per 100,000 people for inspected states was 26.1. For uninspected states it was 31.9. Would we be safe to conclude, therefore, that inspection programs caused the lower death rate? Possibly, but there are some problems with this conclusion. First, since the study lacks a pre-test of the dependent variable, it may be that there has always been a difference in the auto death rates of these two groups of states and that the existence or absence of state inspections is irrelevant. Even before adopting inspection programs, some states may have had very low death rates for reasons that have nothing to do with car inspections. Second, because Tufte did not control the assignment of the states to the two groups, he was not able to equalize average death rates for the two groups of states prior to the addition of inspection programs. Consequently, he could not be sure that the groups of states with and without inspection programs were equivalent or that all relevant extraneous factors were distributed at random. Tufte did statistically control for some relevant differences among states—such as population density and number of miles driven. Yet states with inspection programs may still have differed systematically from states without programs in some other way that was related to traffic fatalities. Hence we cannot be certain that any portion of the difference in fatality rates between the two groups of states can be attributed to the effect of an automobile inspection program.

On the other hand, the difference in average death rates between the two groups of states may understate the benefits of inspection programs, especially if many of the inspection programs were weak or poorly implemented. This possibility is plausible since the treatment given the inspection states was not controlled by Tufte and could not be carefully observed.

Clearly, the lack of a pre-test and of control over the assignment of cases to the experimental and control groups creates difficulties for researchers who use the cross-sectional design. A research design that attempts to address at least the absence of a pre-test is the panel study.

Panel Study Design

A panel study is a cross-sectional design that introduces a time element. In a panel study the researcher takes measurements of the variables of interest on the same units of analysis at several points in time. Panel studies may thus be used to observe changes over time and to provide a pre-test of some phenomenon prior to exposure to the experimental stimulus. A panel study is similar to a cross-sectional study in that measurements of the independent and dependent variables are made at the same time, and the researcher has no control over which subjects are exposed to the experimental stimulus.

Let us return to the classic pre-test, post-test experiment described earlier in this chapter. In that example we were interested in finding out whether exposure to a candidate's televised campaign commercials increased voters' ability to identify the important issues in a campaign. If we used the pre-test, post-test experimental design to test this hypothesis, we would measure pre-exposure issue awareness, randomly assign people to an experimental or control group, expose only the experimental group to the commercials, and then measure post-exposure issue awareness again.

When using a panel research design, a researcher would proceed in a similar way. First, pre-exposure issue awareness would be measured for a group of subjects (presumably before any commercials have been broadcast). The researcher would wait for time to pass, the campaign to begin, and the commercials to be broadcast. Then the researcher would interview the same respondents again and measure both the amount of exposure to commercials and the post-exposure issue awareness for everyone. Finally, the researcher would use the measure of commercial exposure to construct quasi-experimental and quasi-control groups and compare the change in the amount of issue awareness for the two groups.

The major difference between such a study and the classic experiment is that in the panel study the researcher waits for exposure to the experimental stimulus to occur and then uses the amount of exposure to create naturally occurring experimental and control groups. Hence the researcher observes rather than controls exposure to the experimental stimulus.

Since the panel study has a pre-test and a quasi-control group, it allows the researcher to reach more confident conclusions than are possible with any of the other nonexperimental designs. However, the lack of control over who is exposed to the independent variable and under what conditions creates the problem of nonequivalent experimental and control groups. In our example those who are exposed to more commercials may be more likely to develop issue awareness than those who are not for reasons that have nothing to do with commercial exposure itself.

Panel studies are particularly useful in studies of change in individuals over time. One difficulty with panel studies, however, is *panel mortality*. Individuals may die, move away, or decide to drop out of the study. If these persons differ from those who remain in the study, study findings may be biased and unrepresentative.

Case Study Design

The final research design we will discuss is the case study. In a case study the researcher examines one or a few cases of a phenomenon in considerable detail, typically using a number of data collection methods, such as personal interviews, document analysis, and observation. For many years the case study was considered to be an inferior research strategy, but it is now recognized as a "distinctive form of empirical inquiry" and an important design to use for the development and evaluation of public policies as well as for developing explanations for and testing theories of political phenomena.[13]

Robert K. Yin, one of the leading proponents of the case study, defines the case study as an empirical inquiry that (1) investigates a contemporary phenomenon within its real-life context; when (2) the boundaries between phenomenon and context are not clearly evident; and in which (3) multiple sources of evidence are used.[14] Yin distinguishes between histories and case studies, reserving the term case study for the study of contemporary events.[15] Other researchers do not make this distinction, but the study of contemporary events does allow researchers a wider selection of data collection methods, including observation and interviewing.[16]

A case study may be used for exploratory, descriptive, or explanatory purposes. Exploratory case studies may be conducted when little is known about some political phenomenon. Researchers initially may observe only one or a few cases of that phenomenon. Careful observation of a small number of cases may suggest possible general explanations for the behavior or attributes that are observed. These explanations—in the form of hypotheses—can then be tested more systematically by observing more cases. Carefully observing the origins of political dissent within one group at one location may suggest general explanations for dissent, and observing a handful of incumbent representatives when they return to their districts may suggest hypotheses relating incumbent attributes, district settings, and incumbent-constituency relations.[17] In the descriptive case, the purpose of a case study may be to find out and describe what happened in a single or select few situations. The emphasis is not on developing general explanations for what happened.

According to Yin, case studies are most appropriately used to answer "how" or "why" questions.[18] These questions direct our attention toward *explaining* events. The strongest case studies start out with clearly identified theories that are expected to explain the events. Case studies are particularly useful for testing hypotheses deduced from existing theories of politics.

Yin argues that the case study has some distinct advantages over experimental and cross-sectional designs for testing under certain conditions. For example, a case study may be useful in assessing whether a statistical correlation between independent and dependent variables, discovered using a cross-sectional design with survey data, is causal.[19] By choosing a case in which the appropriate values of the independent and dependent variables are present, researchers can try to determine whether and how the independent variable actually caused the dependent variable. That is, they can learn whether there is an actual link between the variables and, therefore, can more likely offer an explanation for the statistical association. Page and Shapiro followed their study of the statistical relationship between public opinion and public policy with a number of case studies.[20]

The case study design differs from experimental designs in that the researcher is neither able to assign subjects or cases to experimental and control groups nor to manipulate the independent variable. Furthermore, the researcher does not control the context or environment as in the case of a laboratory experiment. Yet the researcher can, through the careful selection of a case or cases, achieve a quasi-experimental situation. For example, a researcher may choose cases with different values of an independent variable, but with the same values for important control variables. Cases with similar environments can be chosen. Furthermore, lack of complete control over the environment or context of a phenomenon can be seen as useful. If it can be shown that a theory actually works and is applicable in a real situation, then the theory may more readily be accepted. This may be especially important, for example, in testing theories underlying public policies and public programs.

Like experimental and nonexperimental research designs, the case study design has several variations. In the *single holistic case study* design, the research is focused on a single unit of analysis, such as a single group, neighborhood, bureaucracy, or program. In some situations a single case may represent a critical test of a theory.[21] For example, in a study of organization innovation, a school with a history of innovation was used to test theories that claimed "barriers to innovation" accounted for innovation failure. The researchers showed that even in the school that did not suffer from these barriers, an innovation failed. The result of this case study was to reorient innovation theory away from a focus on barriers.[22]

Another example that demonstrates the explanatory possibilities of a case study is Jeffrey Pressman and Aaron Wildavsky's study of the implementation of an economic development program in Oakland, California.[23] In contrast to other programs whose failure had been documented, the Oakland program lacked certain factors associated with failure: great conflict, excessive publicity, political importance and sensitivity, and insufficient funds. Yet the Oakland program also failed. Pressman and Wildavsky attributed the failure to the fact that numerous approvals and clearances had to be obtained from a variety of participants. These "perfectly ordinary circumstances" led to the unraveling of previous agreements and ultimately the demise of the program.[24]

By choosing a case in which implementation looked as if it would be easy, Pressman and Wildavsky were able to shed considerable light on the process of implementation. This type of case study design has been called the deviant case study, a case that differs from what prevailing theory would lead the researcher to expect. The researcher looks for factors that may explain why the case differs. Research like this may lead to the revision or clarification of existing theories.

Another good example of a deviant case study is discussed in *Union Democracy* by Seymour Martin Lipset, Martin Trow, and James Coleman.[25] It has long been observed that voluntary organizations conform to Michels's "iron law of oligarchy." [26] Lipset, however, observed that the International Typographical Union (ITU) did not conform to the normal oligarchical pattern in which one group "controls the administration, usually retains power indefinitely, rarely faces organized opposition, and when faced with such opposition often resorts to undemocratic procedures to eliminate it." [27] The ITU had an institutionalized two-party system that regularly presented candidates for chief union posts elected in biennial elections. In *Union Democracy*, the authors attempted to understand this anomaly and in doing so helped explain the workings of democratic processes in general.

Single cases studies are also called for where the case represents an extreme or unique case (that is, a rarely occurring phenomenon) and when a researcher has an opportunity to study a phenomenon (not necessarily a rare one) previously inaccessible to researchers which thus serves a "revelatory" purpose.[28] In other uses of single case studies, the single case is either exploratory or otherwise considered to be one case in a multiple case study, not a complete explanatory study on its own.[29]

An *embedded single-case* design involves studying subunits within the single case. Actually Lipset, Trow, and Coleman's study of the ITU involved several units of analysis: the main unit was the ITU, but the researchers also investigated ITU locals, shops, and individual members.[30] Martha Weinberg's study of former Massachusetts governor Francis Sargent was a case study of gubernatorial management and decision-making style, but she investigated several state departments and agencies and their interaction with the governor in depth.[31] Researchers who use this case study design must be careful to remember their main unit of analysis. Weinberg's main unit of analysis was the governor, not the various state agencies. Her case study could have become one that focused on agencies and how and why they resisted or complied with a governor's attempts to influence their behavior. Weinberg, however, was investigating the validity of various theories of executive decision making and thus her focus appropriately remained the governor. This example shows the vital importance of clearly specifying the theory of interest and the unit or units of analysis for which the theory applies. This provides necessary direction and purpose for the investigator as he or she becomes immersed in the details of the case under study.

Case studies may involve more than one case. A *comparative* or *multiple case study* design is more likely to have explanatory power than a single case study design because it provides the opportunity for replication; that is, it enables a researcher to test a single theory more than once. For some cases, similar results will be predicted; for others, different results.[32] Multiple cases should not be thought of as a "sample." Cases are not chosen using a statistical procedure to form a "representative" sample from which the frequency of a particular phenomenon will be calculated and inferences about a larger population made.[33] Rather, cases are chosen for the presence or absence of factors which a political theory has indicated to be important. Multiple case studies may be either holistic or embedded as with the single case study.

Despite the important contribution to our understanding of political phenomena a researcher can make with case study research, some researchers avoid using case study designs and do not give researchers who use the case study as much recognition as those who use other research designs. Yin gives three reasons for the poor reputation of case studies.[34] One concern about case studies is the "lack of rigor" in presenting evidence and the possibility for bias in the use of evidence. Typically researchers sift through enormous quantities of detailed information about their cases. In studying contemporary events, the researcher may be the only one to record certain behavior or phenomena. Certainly, the potential for bias is not limited to case studies. However, as Yin points out, the problems of bias have not been investigated as thoroughly for case studies as they have been for other research strategies, such as survey research (Chapter 8).

A second criticism of case studies is that one cannot generalize from a single case. One response to this criticism is to use multiple-case studies. In fact, however, as Yin points out, the same criticism can be leveled against a single experiment—scientific knowledge is usually based on multiple experiments rather than a single experiment.[35] Yet people do not say that to perform a single experiment is not worthwhile. Furthermore, Yin states: "Case studies, like experiments, are generalizable to theoretical propositions and not to populations or universes. In this sense, the case study, like the experiment, does not represent a 'sample,' and the investigator's goal is to expand and generalize theories (analytic generalization) and not to enumerate frequencies (statistical generalization)."[36]

The third criticism one often hears about case studies is that they take ages to conduct and result in lengthy, unreadable reports. This criticism confuses the case study with particular methods of data collection, such as participant observation (discussed in Chapter 10); furthermore, the evidence collected in a case study can be presented succinctly—even if long reports have been the rule.[37]

Conclusion

In this chapter we have discussed why choosing a research design is an important step in the research process. A research design is a plan that enables the researcher to achieve his or her research objectives. A good research design produces definitive, informative research findings.

Two basic types of research designs—experimental and nonexperimental—were presented along with numerous variations of these designs. We discussed their advantages and disadvantages. Experimental designs—which allow the researcher to have control over the independent variable, the units of analysis, and their environment—are preferred over nonexperimental designs because they enable the researcher to establish more easily causal explanations of the phenomena being studied. Therefore, experimental designs are generally stronger in internal validity than nonexperimental ones. Yet it may not always be possible or appropriate to use an experimental design. Thus nonexperimental observation may be used to test hypotheses in a meaningful fashion, in political science as well as other disciplines.

It is rarely possible to study political phenomena using an experimental research design. Nevertheless, the principles and objectives of research designs, whether experimental or nonexperimental, are the same. It is important to understand the strengths of experimental designs in order to choose an appropriate research design from the remaining options.

A single research design may not be able to avoid all threats to internal and external validity. Researchers often use several designs together so that the weaknesses of one can be overcome by the strengths of another. Also, findings based on research with a weak design are likely to be more readily accepted if they corroborate findings from previous research that used different designs.

In the next chapter we will discuss how to conduct background research on a topic you may be interested in studying. One purpose of this process is to discover and evaluate the research designs that other researchers have used to study the topic. Background research may suggest appropriate research designs for you to employ. You may be able to use a research design that results in an improvement over past research. Later chapters will discuss various methods that you can use to collect the data you need to implement your design.

Notes

1. Four components of an ideal experiment are identified by Kenneth D. Bailey in *Methods of Social Research* (New York: Free Press, 1978), 191.
2. See Donald T. Campbell and Julian C. Stanley, *Experimental and Quasi-Experimental Designs for Research* (Chicago: Rand-McNally, 1966), 5-6; and Paul E. Spector, *Research Designs* (Beverly Hills, Calif.: Sage, 1981), 24-27.
3. Spector, *Research Designs,* 22.
4. This discussion is based on Bailey, *Methods of Social Research,* 204-206; and Jarol B. Mannheim and Richard C. Rich, *Empirical Political Science* (Englewood Cliffs, N.J.: Prentice-Hall, 1981), 76-77.
5. Spector, *Research Designs,* 46-47.
6. Ibid., 45-46.
7. Ibid., 60-61; and Campbell and Stanley, *Experimental and Quasi-Experimental Designs,* 24-25.
8. This discussion of the New Jersey experiment is based on Joseph A. Pechman and P. Michael Timpare, eds., *Work Incentives and Income Guarantees: The New Jersey Negative Income Tax Experiment* (Washington, D.C.: Brookings Institution, 1975), esp. chaps. 2 and 3.
9. Benjamin I. Page and Robert Y. Shapiro, "Effects of Public Opinion on Policy," *American Political Science Review* 77 (March 1983): 175-190.
10. Ibid., 186.
11. David O. Sears, Carl P. Hensler, and Leslie K. Speer, "Whites' Opposition to 'Busing': Self-Interest or Symbolic Politics?" *American Political Science Review* 73 (June 1979): 369-384.
12. Edward R. Tufte, *Data Analysis for Politics and Policy* (Englewood Cliffs, N.J.: Prentice-Hall, 1974), 5-17.
13. Robert K. Yin, *Case Study Research: Design and Methods,* rev.ed. (Beverly Hills, Calif.: Sage, 1989), 21.
14. Ibid., 23.
15. Ibid., 19.
16. Ibid., 19-20.
17. See Richard F. Fenno, Jr., *Home Style: House Members in Their Districts* (Boston: Little, Brown, 1978).
18. Yin, *Case Study Research,* 17-19.
19. Alexander L. George, "Case Studies and Theory Development: The Method of Structured, Focused Comparison," in Paul Gordon Lauren, ed., *Diplomacy: New Approaches in History, Theory and Policy* (New York: Free Press, 1979), 46.
20. Page and Shapiro, "Effects of Public Opinion," 186.
21. Yin, *Case Study Research,* 47.
22. Neal Gross, Joseph B. Giacquinta, and Marilyn Bernstein, *Implementing Organizational Innovations* (New York: Basic Books, 1971). See Yin's discussion in *Case Study Research,* 47.
23. Jeffrey L. Pressman and Aaron B. Wildavsky, *Implementation* (Berkeley: University of California Press, 1973).
24. Ibid., xii.
25. Seymour Martin Lipset, Martin Trow, and James Coleman, *Union Democracy* (Garden City, N.Y.: Anchor, 1962).
26. Robert Michels, *Political Parties* (New York: Dover, 1959).
27. Lipset, Trow, and Coleman, *Union Democracy,* 1.
28. Yin, *Case Study Research,* 47-48.

29. Ibid., 49.
30. Ibid., 50.
31. Martha Wagner Weinberg, *Managing the State* (Cambridge, Mass.: MIT Press, 1977).
32. Yin, *Case Study Research,* 53.
33. Ibid.
34. Ibid., 21-22.
35. Ibid., 21.
36. Ibid., 23.
37. Ibid.

Terms Introduced

Assignment at random. Random assignment of subjects to experimental and control groups.

Case study design. A comprehensive and in-depth study of a single case or several cases. A nonexperimental design in which investigator has little control over events.

Classic experimental design. An experiment with the random assignment of subjects to experimental and control groups with a pre-test and post-test for both groups.

Control group. A group of subjects that does not receive the treatment or test stimulus.

Cross-sectional design. A research design in which measurements of independent and dependent variables are taken at the same time; naturally occurring differences in the independent variable are used to create quasi-experimental and quasi-control groups; extraneous factors are controlled for by statistical means.

Deviant case study. Study of a case that deviates from other cases and from what prevailing theory would lead the researcher to expect.

Experimental effect. Effect of the independent variable on the dependent variable.

Experimental group. A group of subjects receiving treatment or test stimulus.

Experimental mortality. A differential loss of subjects from experimental and control groups that affects equivalency of groups.

Experimentation. Research using an experimental research design in which the researcher has control over the independent variable, the units of analysis, and their environment; used to test causal relationships.

External validity. The ability to generalize from one set of research findings to other situations.

Extraneous factors. Other factors besides the independent variable that may cause change in the dependent variable.

Factorial design. Experimental design used to measure the effect of two or more independent variables singly and in combination.

Field experiments. Experimental designs applied in a natural setting.

Frequency distribution control. The assignment of experimental and control groups in such a way that the frequency distribution of a characteristic is the same in both.

History. A change in the dependent variable due to changes in the environment over time; a threat to internal validity.

Instrument decay. A change in the measurement device used to measure the dependent variable, producing change in measurements.

Instrument reactivity. Reaction of subjects to a pre-test.

Interaction effect. Reaction of subjects to a combination of pre-test and test stimulus.

Internal validity. The ability to show that manipulation or variation of the independent variable causes the dependent variable to change.

Maturation. A change in subjects over time that affects the dependent variable.

Nonexperimental design. A research design characterized by the presence of a single group or lack of researcher control over the assignment of subjects to control and experimental groups.

Panel study. A cross-sectional study in which measurements of variables are taken on the same units of analysis at multiple points in time.

Post-test. Measurement of the dependent variable after manipulation of the independent variable.

Precision matching. Matching of pairs of subjects with one of the pair assigned to the experimental group and the other to the control group.

Pre-test. Measurement of the dependent variable prior to the administration of treatment or manipulation of the independent variable.

Research design. A plan specifying how the researcher intends to fulfill the goals of the study; a logical plan for testing hypotheses.

Selection. Bias in selection of experimental and control groups.

Statistical regression. Change in the dependent variable due to the temporary nature of extreme values.

Test stimulus. The independent variable.

Testing. Effect of a pre-test on the dependent variable.

Time series design. A research design featuring multiple measurements of the dependent variable before or after experimental treatment.

Exercises

1. How would you design a research project to test the effect on the number of abortions of a state's decision to place additional limits on a woman's ability to obtain an abortion legally? Discuss the advantages and disadvantages of your design. Specify why you ruled out other possible designs. What research design would you choose if it were the federal government, not a state government, that enacted the limitations? Would the research design be the same or different? Explain.

2. What is the most appropriate research design to answer the following questions? Is another design appropriate? What control variables would you need to consider? How does your design allow for these controls?

   a. How effective is a particular program for youth gang members in reducing neighborhood gang violence?

   b. What is the effect of state mandatory seatbelt usage legislation on death and injury rates from automobile accidents?

   c. What is the impact on judicial turnover of moving from a system of electing judges to an appointive system? Assume the change was made ten years ago.

3. What research designs are used by the researchers in the following articles?

   a. Kenneth K. Wong, "Policy-Making in the American States: Typology,

Process, and Institutions," *Policy Studies Review* 8 (Spring 1989): 527-548.
  b. John G. Heilman and Gerald W. Johnson, "System and Process in Capital-Intensive Privatization: A Comparative Case Study of Municipal Wastewater Treatment Works," *Policy Studies Review* 8 (Spring 1989): 549-572.
  c. Alwyn R. Rouyer, "Political Capacity and the Decline of Fertility in India," *American Political Science Review* 81 (June 1987): 453-470.

Suggested Readings

Campbell, Donald T., and Julian C. Stanley. *Experimental and Quasi-Experimental Designs for Research.* Chicago: Rand-McNally, 1966.
Hakim, Catherine. *Research Design: Strategies and Choices in the Design of Social Research.* London: Allen and Unwin, 1987.
Spector, Paul E. *Research Designs.* Beverly Hills, Calif.: Sage, 1981.
Yin, Robert K. *Case Study Research: Design and Methods,* rev. ed. Beverly Hills, Calif.: Sage, 1989.

CHAPTER 6

Conducting a Literature Review

So far we have discussed the initial stages of any research project: hypothesis formation, conceptualization, measurement, and the development of a suitable research design. At some point early in the research process it is also important for a researcher to spend some time reading others' reports of similar research. We refer to this enterprise as conducting background research or a literature review.

You should undertake a literature review near the outset of a research effort, if only to make sure that your research does not duplicate someone else's. In this chapter we will discuss reasons for background research and explain how to conduct a review.

Reasons for a Literature Review

All sound research involves reviewing what has been written about a research topic. Among the reasons for such a review are (1) to develop general explanations for observed variations in a behavior or phenomenon; (2) to identify potential relationships between concepts and to identify researchable hypotheses; (3) to learn how others have defined and measured key concepts; (4) to identify data sources that other researchers have used; (5) to develop alternative research designs; and (6) to discover how a research project is related to the work of others. Let us examine some of these reasons more closely.

Often a novice researcher will start out by expressing only a general interest in a topic, such as childhood socialization or the siting of hazardous waste facilities. At this stage the researcher will not have formulated a research question (for example, "How soon in childhood does socialization begin?" or "What are the characteristics of communities most likely to oppose hazardous waste facilities, and what tactics are most commonly used to successfully oppose hazardous waste disposal in a community?") A review of the previous research will help sharpen a research topic by familiarizing the researcher with the major research questions that have been asked by others. After reading the published work in an area, a researcher may decide that previous work has not answered a question satisfactorily. Thus a research project may be designed to answer an "old" question in a new way. Published research reports often are sources of important questions and untested hypotheses that need to be researched. Thus an investigation may follow up on one of these research ideas.

At other times, researchers may begin a research project with a hypothesis or with a desire to explain a relationship that has already been observed. Here a literature review may reveal reports of similar observations by researchers and may also help a researcher develop general explanations for the relationship by identifying theories that explain the phenomenon of interest. The value of one's research will be higher if a general explanation of the observed or hypothesized relationship can be provided rather than simply a report of the empirical verification of a relationship.

In addition to seeking theories that support the plausibility and increase the significance of a hypothesis, a researcher should be alert for competing or alternative hypotheses. One may start out with a hypothesis specifying a simple relationship between two variables. Since it is rare for one political phenomenon to be related to or caused by just one other phenomenon, it is important to look for other possible causes of the dependent variable and to look for other variables that may affect in some way the relationship specified in the researcher's own hypothesis. Data collection should include measurement of these other relevant variables so that in subsequent data analysis the researcher may rule out competing explanations or at least indicate more clearly the nature of the relationship between the variables in the original hypothesis.

For example, suppose a researcher has hypothesized that people become active in politics because they have some serious dissatisfaction with government policy. A review of the literature on political participation might show that participation is related to years of formal education, attitudes of citizen duty, and beliefs in one's own ability to affect political affairs. Thus it would be wise for the researcher to include measures of these variables in the research design so that the policy dissatisfaction explanation may be compared with the other explanations for political participation.

A researcher also may compare his or her concept definitions with those of other researchers. Using the same definitions of a concept as other researchers will lead to greater comparability of research findings on the same topic. Furthermore, the validity of a researcher's measures may be improved if the literature reveals that other researchers' definitions of a concept are ambiguous or combine two or more concepts that need to be treated separately. For example, in his study of political participation of French peasants, Sidney Tarrow found that it was important to separate the concept "support for political parties" from the concept "interest in politics." [1] The concept "interest in politics" was interpreted by French peasants to include the idea of approval of existing parties. Because French peasants did not approve of the parties, they denied that they were interested in politics despite their high levels of voter turnout. Hence in this case it was advisable to measure political interest and party support separately.

A researcher may also discover the opposite problem: he or she may be using overly narrow definitions that fail to capture important dimensions of a concept. For example, if you were conducting a survey to measure support for democratic values, you would be missing numerous definitions of this concept if you simply defined it as a belief in regular elections. A review of other studies on democratic values would alert you to other definitions.

Research reports provide us with valuable information about viable research designs, measurement strategies, and data collection methods. A note of caution is necessary, however. Dead ends and "bonehead" mistakes are rarely reported. Published research reports may lead us to believe that the research process proceeds in an orderly, non-problematical, textbook fashion. Thus some of the more obvious alternatives in research design, measurement, and data collection may have been tried by other researchers and rejected for good reasons. Sometimes, however, an author will discuss possible improvements and explain why they were not incorporated into his or her own research. Although reading previous research will not necessarily tell you everything other researchers have tried and rejected, it may suggest to you ways of improving your research design and measurements and help you turn your study into a more interesting and successful research project.

As an example of the benefits of a literature review, let us look at a review conducted by one of us, Richard Joslyn, who was interested in the impact of television news on the political opinions and behavior of the American public. In particular, he wondered whether watching the news affected people's beliefs about the utility of political participation.

A review of the literature on political participation revealed four main considerations. First, it was discovered that previous researchers had developed a concept that was relevant to the hypothesis. It was called *political efficacy* or *sense of civic competence*. This concept had been defined in a number of similar ways:

the feeling that political and social change is possible, and that the individual citizen can play a part in bringing about this change;[2]

the timeless theme of democratic theory that members of a democratic regime ought to regard those who occupy positions of political authority as responsive agents and that the members themselves ought to be disposed to participate in the honors and offices of the system.[3]

an individual's belief in the value of political action and the probability of success in this action.[4]

belief in the efficacy of one's own political action, consisting of (1) a belief that public officials can be and are influenced by ordinary citizens, (2) some knowledge about how to proceed in making this influence felt, and (3) sufficient self-confidence to try to put this knowledge to work at appropriate times and places.[5]

This looked to the author like a concept that might be influenced by watching television news shows.

Second, it was discovered that political efficacy had recently been divided into two different types of belief: *internal political efficacy,* or "the level of perceived personal power in the political system"[6] and *external political efficacy,* or "the feeling that an individual and the public can have an impact on the political process because government institutions will respond to their needs."[7] This division meant that a researcher might want to specify which aspect of political efficacy was involved in any given hypothesis.

Third, the literature review revealed ways in which both internal and external political efficacy had been measured by other researchers. A set of six to eight questions on public opinion surveys had originally been used to measure efficacy in general; later a smaller set of questions was found to measure internal and external political efficacy separately.

Fourth, the literature review turned up numerous studies that had tested different explanations for variations in people's political efficacy (see Table 6-1). These explanations focused on individuals' personality, social status, social cohesion, and political experiences, and consequently they represented rival hypotheses for efficacy that did not depend upon television news viewing. The researcher was able to include some of these alternative explanations in his research design so that the television news hypothesis could be evaluated more completely.

At the conclusion of this literature review, then, the researcher had become familiar with the conceptualization and measurement of a phenomenon relevant to his original hypothesis, had discovered sources of data that included at least some of the measures of interest, and had been alerted to competing hypotheses that would have to be taken into consideration in testing the link between political efficacy and television news exposure. One can readily see that literature reviews further the conceptual, empirical, and theoretical aims of most research projects.

Table 6-1 Explanations for Political Efficacy Concepts Used as
Independent Variables

Personality

Political cynicism   Self-competence/personal efficacy
Opinion intensity   Political interest
Interpersonal trust   Cosmopolitanism

Social Status

Education   Religion
Region   Sex
Size and place of residence   Race
Age   Relative deprivation
Income   IQ
Occupation

Social Cohesion

Marital status   Organization membership/
Number of children   leadership
Years of residence   Political, social participation
Church attendance   Size of community

Political Environment/Experiences/Interaction

Newspaper exposure   Ideology
Incumbent support   Political milieu (exposure to
Partisan domination   corrupt urban politics)
Partisan competition   Political subculture
Political success   Exposure to political agitation
Events/period/history   Attitudes of friends
Accumulation of democratic experience   Attitudes of parents
Party identification   Attitudes of teachers

Source: Richard Joslyn, "The Portrayal of Government and Nation on Television Network News: Content and Implications" (Paper delivered at the annual meeting of the Midwest Political Science Association, Cincinnati, Ohio, 1981).

Conducting a Literature Review

How you conduct a literature review depends on the main purpose of the review and the stage of development of the research topic. If you are starting with only a general interest in a subject and not a specific hypothesis you want to test, then it might be a good idea to locate a textbook covering the subject, read the appropriate sections, and then check out the sources cited in the footnotes. A perusal of the subject catalog in your library will also help you identify books that broadly address your topic. From there you can begin to develop and refine a more specific research question. Another approach to get you started would be to skim the contents of a few professional journals likely to have articles in your area of interest.

A thorough literature search includes anything published on your topic in professional journals, magazines, books, newspapers, government publications and documents, and conference proceedings. To guide you in this endeavor, we have listed in the remainder of this chapter a number of professional journals in political science, with comments on their content. Also listed are indexes and bibliographies that will help you locate materials related to your topic.[8] Several of these indexes are available as compact disc databases. Your library's reference librarian will undoubtedly be able to provide you with additional information and guidance on the particular library sources available.

Advances in computer technology have significantly improved a researcher's ability to search for and find published material. Computerized literature searches produce more up-to-date citations than printed indexes since the computer data base can be updated more easily and more frequently. Computer-assisted searches can also be quite specific; it is usually possible to use several key words to narrowly identify a subject. This reduces the necessity in most literature searches of eliminating citations that are not really related to the research topic. Finally, a computerized literature search may produce a printed list of citations. This reduces the amount of tedious labor required to do a thorough literature search by hand. Many libraries have their catalog computerized, which makes it easier to search for books related to the research topic and gives the user a printed list of citations.

It is wise to check with a reference librarian in your library on the availability of specialized computerized searches which can identify materials beyond the library's own catalog or journal and government document indexes. Some universities provide this service to students at no charge; others charge a fee. Depending on the time you have and your particular topic and research goals, a computerized search may be well worth the cost.

Although computerized indexes and catalogs are a great advance for literature reviews, it is extremely important for the user to know how to use them well. Knowing what keywords or descriptors to use to find sources related to your topic is essential. Be prepared to spend some time learning how to use the various systems. Otherwise you may end up missing many sources or being overwhelmed with long lists of citations, many of which are not relevant to your research effort.

Professional Journals in Political Science and Related Fields

Any good literature review will include research reports published in professional political science journals. It is a sign of the information explosion and of academic pressures to publish that there are now an increasing number of journals with political science-related articles. The following list is not complete, but it includes the major journals of general political science, a representative selection of journals that specialize in some aspect of political science, multidisciplinary journals, and some major journals in related disciplines.

Journals of National and Regional Political Science Associations

American Journal of Political Science. 1957- . Primarily American government and politics articles.

American Political Science Review. 1906- . The official journal of the American Political Science Association.

Canadian Journal of Political Science/Revue Canadien de Science Politique. 1968- . Focus on Canadian political matters, some articles on international affairs and political theory. Bilingual.

Journal of Politics. 1939- . Primarily American government and politics articles.

Polity. 1968- . Articles on American politics, comparative politics, international relations, and political philosophy.

Social Science Quarterly. 1920- . Articles on a wide range of topics in the social sciences.

Western Political Quarterly. 1948- . Broad coverage of political science and public administration.

Specialized or Multidisciplinary Journals

Academy of Political Science. Proceedings. 1910- . Each issue is devoted to a single theme. Presents divergent views on topics. Articles tend to be expository, rather than analytical or empirical.

American Politics Quarterly. 1973- . Articles on American political behavior.

Annals (American Academy of Political and Social Sciences). 1899- . Each issue focuses on a single topic.

The Brookings Review. 1982- . Articles on public affairs research by scholars associated with the Brookings Institution.

Campaigns and Elections: The Journal of Political Action. 1980- . Articles by academics and practitioners on the contemporary American political scene.

Comparative Political Studies. 1969- . Interdisciplinary articles on cross-national comparative studies.

Comparative Politics. 1968- . Broad coverage of comparative politics topics.

Comparative Strategy: An International Journal. 1970- . Focus on international politics and strategic problems.

Congress and the Presidency. 1972- . Formerly *Congressional Studies; Capitol Studies.* Focus on research on the presidency and Congress.

Electoral Studies. 1982- . International, interdisciplinary journal focusing on voting and elections.

European Journal of Political Science. 1973- . Research on European political matters.

Foreign Affairs. 1922- . Foreign policy focus, especially on current issues in American foreign policy.

Foreign Policy. 1970- . Wide-ranging coverage of foreign affairs.

Government and Opposition: A Quarterly Journal of Comparative Politics. 1965- . Comparative studies of political development.

International Affairs. 1922- . Emphasis on political and social aspects of international affairs.

International Organization. 1947- . Focus on practical and theoretical problems of international organizations.

International Political Science Review. 1980- . Official publication of the International Political Science Association. Each issue focuses on a theme.

International Studies Quarterly. 1957- . Multidisciplinary articles related to transnational phenomena.

Journal of Communist Studies. 1985- . Articles examine historical and current situations throughout the world involving communism.

Journal of Conflict Resolution. 1957- . Articles on international and intranational conflicts.

Journal of Development Studies. 1964- . Interdisciplinary journal with articles on economic and social development of Third World countries.

Journal of Policy Analysis and Management. 1981- . Journal of the Association for Public Policy Analysis and Management.

Legislative Studies Quarterly. 1976- . International journal concentrating on comparative legislative and cross-national studies.

Policy Studies Journal. 1972- . Theoretical and practical articles addressing important public policy problems.

Policy Studies Review. 1981- . Articles related to current public policy issues.

Political Behavior. 1979- . Interdisciplinary journal with articles on political behavior and decision making.

Political Science Quarterly. 1886- . Articles on American politics, comparative politics, and international relations.

Presidential Studies Quarterly. 1972- . Focus on the American presidency.

Public Administration Review. 1940- . Focus on municipal, state, and federal management issues.

Public Opinion Quarterly. 1937-   All aspects of public opinion and polling.

Public Policy. 1953- . Articles on public policy formulation.

Publius: The Journal of Federalism. 1971- . Intergovernmental relations in federal systems; multidisciplinary articles.

Science and Society. 1936- . Journal of Marxist thought and analysis.

Terrorism: An International Journal. 1977- . Devoted to the study of terrorism.

Urban Affairs Quarterly. 1965- . Interdisciplinary articles on urban affairs.

World Politics. 1948- . Current international affairs articles.

Major Journals in Related Disciplines

American Economic Review. 1911- . Major economics journal.

American Journal of Sociology. 1895- . Wide-ranging coverage of topics in sociology and related fields.

American Psychologist. 1946- . Official journal of the American Psychological Association; current issues in psychology.

American Sociological Review. 1936- . Official journal of the American Sociological Association; general articles in the field of sociology.

JAPA: Journal of the American Planning Association. 1925- . Major sources of scholarship on matters relating to planning and public policy.

Resources for Feminist Research. 1971- . International journal with research articles and substantive bibliographic information.

Indexes, Bibliographies, and Abstracts

A literature search will also use the information contained in indexes, bibliographies, and collections of abstracts. There are numerous indexes to periodical literature, books, and government publications. Some are quite comprehensive, others are more selective. It is a good idea to check the description of a particular index—usually contained in the front of the index—before using it.

Unfortunately, there is a time lag between publication of a periodical or book and its entry in an index. However, you may discover that articles of interest are concentrated among a few journals. To identify articles related to your topic that have not yet been indexed, skim the table of contents of the latest issues of these journals.

The first time you conduct a comprehensive literature search, you may be overwhelmed by the number of citations you discover. Managing them systematically may present a major problem. It may help to put each relevant citation on a separate 3 x 5 index card. If the citation proves to be useful, then complete bibliographic information can be entered later on the card in the form you will be using for your bibliography. These cards can be sorted according to various needs. This method preserves the fruits of a literature search in a form that will be useful to you, and it saves the step of writing the citation information onto a list and then transferring it to a card.

After you have located a number of sources pertinent to your research project, you will want to become familiar with this literature in the most efficient way possible. Each researcher develops a strategy best suited to the situation at hand, but we offer here three suggestions. First, locate the most important and relevant research reports immediately and concentrate on them rather than trying to read all of the numerous research reports you have discovered, some of which are of only peripheral concern. Abstracts are helpful here. Abstracts are short summaries of the contents of books and articles. These will aid in identifying those sources most relevant to your topic and improve the efficiency of your literature review. Collections of abstracts are included in our list of indexes and bibliographies.

Second, start with the most recent publications. They will contain references to past literature. Even when the content of past work is not discussed, repeated reference to a work will indicate that it is considered by many to be important. Thus you should probably review the work early on in your review.

A final strategy is to take a number of works that you know are directly related to your topic. Using the citation index of the *Social Sciences Citation Index,* locate the author and work. Below this entry will be a list of all subsequent publications that have referenced the work. These publications are likely to be closely related to your topic as well. The number of times a work is cited by others is a rough indication of its significance (or controversiality). This may guide your decisions about which works to read first.

The following is a list of indexes, bibliographies, and collections of abstracts and other sources of use to political science researchers conducting a literature search. Although each source is briefly described, you will ultimately be the judge of whether the work is a useful source for your own literature review.

ABC Pol Sci: A Bibliography of Contents. 1969- . Timely index with tables of contents of about 300 international journals in their original language in the fields of political science, sociology, economics, policy studies, and law. Author, title, and subject indexes. Updated quarterly.

America: History and Life. 1964- . Abstracts and citations of articles on U.S. and Canadian history from prehistory to present. Volume 0 includes abstracts from *Historical Abstracts,* 1954-65. Updated quarterly.

Combined Retrospective Index to Scholarly Journals in Political Science. 1886-1974. An index of articles from 531 journals in history, political science, and sociology. Arranged by subject. Also includes author index.

Current Contents/Social and Behavioral Science. 1974- . Weekly index with tables of contents of journals arranged by broad discipline headings. Good for searching for recent articles. Includes author and title word index.

Current Law Index. 1980- . Monthly index of some 700 periodicals.

Dissertation Abstracts International: Humanities and Social Sciences. 1938- . Monthly compilation of abstracts of doctoral dissertations from cooperating U.S., Canadian, and European institutions. Formerly called *Dissertation Abstracts and Microfilm Abstracts.* Change in title reflects increased coverage.

Index to Legal Periodicals. 1908- . Monthly index with annual cumulation.

Index to Periodical Articles Related to Law. 1958- . Quarterly index of journals not covered by *Current Law Index* or *Index to Legal Periodicals.* Therefore does not cover law journals or directly law-related publications.

Index to U.S. Government Periodicals. 1970- . Quarterly index of approximately 200 out of more than 2,000 government periodicals.

International Bibliography of the Social Sciences-Political Science. 1953- . Covers international journals in political science, updated yearly.

Magazine Index. January 1970- . Microfilm index, updated monthly, of approximately 400 magazine titles.

Monthly Catalog of United States Government Publications. 1895- . Most complete index to U.S. government publications.

Public Affairs Information Service Bulletin. 1915- . Biweekly index of policy-oriented literature. Includes periodicals, books, and government documents.

Public Affairs Information Service Bulletin: Foreign Language Index. 1972- . Foreign language counterpart of *PAIS Bulletin,* updated quarterly.

Readers' Guide to Periodical Literature. 1900- . Semimonthly index of approximately 200 popular newsstand periodicals.

Sage Public Administration Abstracts. 1974- . Quarterly index of articles, books, government publications, pamphlets, and so on. International in scope.

Sage Urban Studies Abstracts. 1973- . Quarterly collection of articles international in scope. No cumulative indexes.

Social Sciences Citation Index. 1973- . An index, updated three times a
  year, of 2,000 journals. Subject, source, and citation indexes.
Social Sciences Index. 1974- . Quarterly index of approximately 300
  frequently used journals in the social sciences.
Sociological Abstracts. 1953- . Extensive coverage of publications in
  and related to sociology. Supplements include papers presented at
  sociological meetings, updated five times a year.
Women Studies Abstracts. 1972- . Updated quarterly.
Universal Reference System: Political Science Series. 1969- . Annual
  supplements commence in 1969. A ten-volume set arranged by broad
  topic headings indexes material prior to 1969. Includes abstracts.
Urban Affairs Abstracts. 1971- . Updated weekly with semiannual and
  annual cumulations.
USPD, United States Political Science Documents. 1975- . Indexes
  and abstracts from political science journals; updated yearly.

Compact Disc Databases

Sociofile. 1974- . Compact disc equivalent to *Sociological Abstracts.*
Auto-Graphics Government Documents Catalog System. 1976- . An
  index to all government documents cataloged by the Government
  Printing Office since June 1976. Compact disc equivalent to *Monthly
  Catalog.*
PAIS. 1972- . Compact disc incorporates the *Public Affairs Informa-
  tion Service Bulletin* and the *PAIS Foreign Language Index.*

Newspaper Indexes

Newspaper articles may be a source of background information as
well as of explanations and hypotheses about politics. These major
newspapers have indexes:

Christian Science Monitor

New York Times

Times (London)

Wall Street Journal

Washington Post

There is also a microfilm index, the *National Newspaper Index,* that
indexes since January 1979 the *Christian Science Monitor,* the *New York
Times,* and the *Wall Street Journal.* The *Washington Post* was added in
September 1982 and the *Los Angeles Times* in October 1982. Your
library may also have an on-line or compact disc computer newspaper
index.

Book Reviews

You may find it helpful to know how others have evaluated key books related to your research topic. Reviewers often critique the books, compare them with other works in the field, and offer interpretations and explanations that differ from those of the author.

Book Review Digest. 1905- .
Book Review Index. 1965- .
Combined Retrospective Index to Book Reviews in Scholarly Journals. 1886-1974.
Current Book Review Citations. 1976- . Monthly index to book reviews published in more than 1,200 periodicals.
Perspective. 1972- . Monthly review of new books.
Political Science Reviewer. 1971- .

Conference Proceedings

Frequently research is presented at professional conferences before it is published in a professional journal. Thus if you want to be informed up to the minute or if a research topic is quite new, it may be worthwhile to investigate papers given at professional conferences.

The *Index to Social Sciences & Humanities Proceedings* (1979-) indexes published proceedings. However, the proceedings of the annual meetings of the American Political Science Association (APSA) and regional political science associations have not been published. Summer issues of the APSA's *PS* contain the preliminary program for the forthcoming annual meeting. The program lists authors and paper titles. The *International Studies Newsletter* publishes preliminary programs for International Studies Association meetings. Copies of programs for other political science and related conferences (frequently announced in *PS*) may be obtained from the sponsoring organization. Abstracts for some fields, for example *Sociological Abstracts,* include papers presented at conferences. Once promising papers presented at professional conferences have been located, copies of the papers may usually be obtained by writing to the authors directly.

Conclusion

No matter what the original purpose of your literature search, it should be thorough. In your research report you should discuss those sources that provide explanations for the phenomena you are studying and that support the plausibility of your hypotheses. You should also discuss how your research relates to other research and use the existing literature to document the significance of your research. An example of a literature review is contained in the research report in Chapter 14.

Notes

1. Sidney Tarrow, "The Urban-Rural Cleavage in Political Involvement: The Case of France," *American Political Science Review* 65 (June 1971): 341-357.
2. Angus Campbell, Gerald Gurin, and Warren E. Miller, *The Voter Decides* (Evanston, Ill.: Row, Peterson, 1959), 187.
3. David Easton and Jack Dennis, "The Child's Acquisition of Regime Norms: Political Efficacy," *American Political Science Review* 61 (March 1967): 26.
4. Robert Weissberg, *Political Learning, Political Choice and Democratic Citizenship* (Englewood Cliffs, N.J.: Prentice-Hall, 1974), 470.
5. Donald R. Matthews and James W. Prothro, *Negroes and the New Southern Politics* (New York: Harcourt, Brace & World, 1966), 276.
6. Jerome D. Becker and Ivan L. Preston, "Media Usage and Political Activity," *Journalism Quarterly* 46 (Spring 1969): 130.
7. Arthur H. Miller, Edie N. Goldenberg, and Lutz Erbring, "Type-Set Politics: Impacts of Newspapers on Public Confidence," *American Political Science Review* 73 (March 1979): 67.
8. A source of much of the commentary in this chapter on journals, indexes, bibliographies, and abstracts was Bill Katz and Linda Sternberg Katz, *Magazines for Libraries,* 6th ed. (New York: R. R. Bowker, 1989). Appreciation also goes to Margaret G. Bronner, reference librarian at the University of Delaware, for her assistance in compiling this information and to Caroline Tibbetts, reference librarian at the University of Delaware, for her assistance in updating this information for the second edition.

Exercises

1. Using the citation index of the 1989 *Social Sciences Citation Index,* determine the number of times R. Shep Melnick's book, *Regulation and the Courts: The Case of the Clean Air Act,* has been cited. Then use the source index to obtain complete information on the first source that cites the book.

2. How many issues of *Legislative Studies Quarterly* are cited in *ABC Pol Sci* 1989? Give the year, volume, and issue number for each issue. Give the name and author of the first article in the first issue cited.

3. Using the 1989 subject index of the *Social Sciences Index,* determine the number of sources listed for one of the following topics: budget deficits, global warming, glasnost, state supreme courts.

Suggested Reading

Cooper, Harris M. *Integrating Research: A Guide for Literature Reviews,* 2d ed. Beverly Hills, Calif.: Sage, 1989.

CHAPTER 7

Sampling

This chapter examines a decision that all researchers have to make sooner or later: how to select observations to evaluate a proposed hypothesis. Whatever the hypothesis under consideration, a researcher must decide what observations are appropriate for testing it. Furthermore, researchers must decide whether they will measure the concepts in question for all or for only some of the pertinent observations. If data are collected on only some of the observations, then care must be taken to ensure that the observations selected are appropriate for the inquiry. We will illustrate the nature of this choice by returning to our examples of political science research. Recall that Segal and Cover were interested in the relationship between the ideological values of U.S. Supreme Court justices and their votes. The unit of analysis was the justice, and their votes on cases and their ideological outlook were the variables measured. The researchers had to decide whether to perform this measurement (that is, collect the data) for all Supreme Court justices or for only some of the justices. They chose to collect data for only some of the justices: all justices from Earl Warren to Anthony Kennedy. They also chose to limit their analysis to the justices' votes on civil liberties cases.

In their study of the relationship between the time a leader is in office and the leader's risk of losing office, the unit of analysis was a leader of a nation with no legal limit on length of term in office. Henry Bienen and Nicolas van de Walle chose to limit their study to African leaders. They examined all postindependence leaders of all Organization of African Unity member states. They collected information on the characteristics of leaders and of countries.

Page and Shapiro were interested in the responsiveness of government policy to citizens' preferences. To find cases of significant changes in Americans' policy preferences, they sorted through hundreds of surveys that were conducted between 1935 and 1979 by three major survey organizations using national samples. They found 609 questions that were repeated in identical form at two or more points in time and found 357 instances of significant changes in citizens' policy preferences.

In order to test his theory of patterned land inequality, Midlarsky selected only those nations to which his theory relating land inequality and political violence was intended to apply and for which appropriate data were available. Finally, Gary Jacobson was interested in the relationship between campaign spending and vote totals for congressional candidates. He, too, had to decide whether to measure these phenomena for all congressional candidates or for only some. He chose to collect data for all candidates for the U.S. Congress (but only in certain years).

In the cases of Page and Shapiro, Midlarsky, and Jacobson, then, the researchers decided to collect data on all of the observations covered by the hypothesis. This is called the *population* of cases. In the cases of Bienen and van De Walle and Segal and Cover, however, the researchers decided to collect data on only some of the pertinent observations. In this case, a *sample* of observations was taken. In the remainder of this chapter we will discuss the differences between a population and a sample and the numerous ways in which a sample may be chosen.

Population or Sample?

A researcher's decision whether to collect data for a population or for a sample is usually made on practical grounds. If time, money, and other costs were not considerations, it would almost always be better to collect data for a population. However, since research is costly, researchers must weigh the advantages and disadvantages of collecting data on a sample. The advantages of taking a sample are usually savings in time and in money. The disadvantages are that the researcher's information based on a sample usually is less accurate than it would be were data on the entire population collected. In political research, investigators often collect data on a sample if the population is large or difficult to observe. For example, finding and paying enough qualified interviewers to collect data on every adult in the United States for testing a hypothesis about adult political behavior would pose quite a problem. Substituting inexperienced, less expensive interviewers would increase the chances of making mistakes in asking questions and recording answers.[1] Also such a survey would take a very long time to complete. In the meantime, unanticipated events could cause the responses of persons interviewed late in the process to differ from the responses of those interviewed earlier. Thus the cost of such an endeavor would be prohibitive and the validity of the data collected would be questionable.

Consider another example of the decision whether to collect data on a population or on a sample. One researcher wanted to test some hypotheses regarding the content of televised political campaign commercials. This would require collecting data on the content of commercials, the unit of analysis in this case. Clearly, from the standpoint of accuracy, it would be preferable to have data on the population of televised commercials (in other words, to have available for measurement every campaign commercial ever aired on television). However, data collection on the population is simply impossible. No such collection exists anywhere, nor does anyone know how many commercials have been televised across the country in the last thirty years. Consequently, the researcher relied on a sample of commercials to test his hypotheses—a decision that was practical, necessary, and less costly, but also likely to yield a less accurate result.[2] Thus for reasons of necessity and convenience, political science researchers often collect data on a sample of observations. In fact, public opinion and voting behavior researchers *always* rely on samples. This means, however, that they must know how to select good samples and must appreciate the implications of relying on samples for testing hypotheses if they want to be able to claim that their findings for the sample accurately reflect what they would find if they were to test the hypothesis on the whole population.

The Basics of Sampling

A sample is simply a subset of a larger population. If the sample is selected properly, the information collected about the sample may be used to make statements about the whole population. Since sampling is always used in public opinion surveys, it is often thought of in connection with that type of data. However, issues of sampling arise whenever a researcher takes measurements on a subset of those observations covered by the hypothesis being tested. Several different types of samples will be described in this chapter. Before we discuss various sampling procedures, it will be helpful to review some terms commonly used in discussions of sampling.[3]

An *element* is the entity about which a researcher collects information or the unit of analysis in a research project. Elements in political science research are often individuals, but they also can be states, cities, agencies, countries, campaign advertisements, political speeches, social or professional organizations, crimes, or legislatures.

The term *population* refers to elements in the aggregate. A population is the collection of elements of interest to a researcher. For example, a population may consist of all campaign speeches given by major candidates for president in the last four presidential elections. Notice that the description of the population should be fairly specific. You may refer to presidential campaign speeches as the focus of your research, but at some point you should make clear which presidential campaign speeches are included in the population.

For reasons that we will discuss shortly, a population may be *stratified*—that is, subdivided or broken up into groups of similar elements or *strata* before a sample is drawn. For example, you may divide the population of presidential campaign speeches in the last four presidential elections into four strata, each stratum containing speeches from one of the four presidential elections in the study. In a study of students' attitudes, particularly at a university, the student body may be stratified in terms of their class, major, and grade-point average. The strata that are chosen are usually characteristics or attributes thought to be related to the dependent variables under study.

The population from which a sample is actually drawn is called a *sampling frame*. Technically speaking, all elements that are part of the population defined to be of interest to the research question should be part of the sampling frame. If they are not, any data collected may not be representative of the population studied. Often, however, sampling frames are incomplete, as the following example illustrates. Suppose community opinion about snow removal is evaluated by interviewing every fifth adult entering a local supermarket. The sampling frame would consist of all adults entering the supermarket while the researcher was standing outside. This sampling frame could hardly be construed as including all adult members of the community unless all adult members of the community made a trip to the supermarket when the researcher was there. (In a few communities this might be a valid assumption.) Furthermore, use of such a sampling frame would probably introduce bias in survey results. Perhaps many of the people who stayed at home rather than going to the supermarket considered the trip too hazardous because of poor snow removal. Therefore, the closer the sampling frame is to the target population, the better.

Sometimes lists of elements exist that constitute the sampling frame. For example, a university may have a list of all students, or the Conference of Mayors may have a list of current mayors of cities with 500,000 residents or more. The existence of a list may be enticing to a researcher since it removes the need to create one from scratch. But lists may represent an inappropriate sampling frame if they are out of date, incorrect, or do not really correspond to the population of interest. A common example would be if a researcher used a telephone directory as the sampling frame for interviewing sample households within the service area. Households with unlisted numbers would be missed, some numbers would no longer be working, and recently assigned numbers would not be included. Consequently, the telephone book would constitute an inaccurate sampling frame for the population in that area. Researchers should carefully check their sampling frames for potential omissions or erroneously included elements. Consumers of research should also carefully examine sampling frames to see that they match the populations researchers claim to be studying.

A famous example of a poll that relied on an incomplete sampling frame is the *Literary Digest* poll of 1936. It predicted that the winner of the presidential election would be Alf Landon, not Franklin D. Roosevelt. This poll imprudently relied on a sample drawn from telephone directories and automobile registration lists. At that time telephone and automobile ownership were not as widespread as they are today. Thus the sampling frame overrepresented the wealthy.[4] The problem was compounded by the fact that in the midst of the Depression an unprecedented number of poor people voted, and they voted overwhelmingly for Roosevelt.

In many instances a list of the population may not exist or it may not be feasible to create a list of all elements. It may be possible, however, to create a list of *groups*. Then the researcher could sample from among the groups and enumerate the elements only in the selected groups. In this case the initial sampling frame would consist of a list of groups, not elements.

For example, suppose you wanted to collect data on the attitudes and behavior of civic and social service volunteers in a large metropolitan area. Rather than initially developing a list of all such volunteers—a laborious and time-consuming task—you could develop a list of all organizations known to have volunteers. Next a subset of these organizations could be selected and then a list of volunteers secured for only this subset, hence avoiding listing the volunteers in the nonselected organizations.

The *sampling unit* is the entity listed in a sampling frame. In simple cases the sampling unit is the same as an element. In more complicated sampling designs it may be a collection of elements.

Types of Samples

Researchers make a basic distinction among types of samples according to the amount of control over *sample bias* they provide. We mentioned earlier that political scientists often select a sample, collect information about the sample, and then use that information to talk about the population from which the sample was drawn. In other words, they make inferences about the whole population from what they know about a smaller group. If a sampling frame is incomplete or inappropriate, the sample will be unrepresentative of the population of interest to the researcher. But sample bias may also be caused by a biased selection of elements, even if the sampling frame is a complete and accurate list of elements.

Suppose that in the survey of opinion on snow removal every adult in the community did enter the supermarket while the researcher was there. And suppose that instead of selecting every fifth adult who entered, the researcher avoided individuals who appeared in a hurry or in a poor humor (perhaps because of snowy roads). The researcher's sample could easily be biased, then, and not representative of public opinion in that community.

Because of the concern over sample bias it is important to distinguish between two basic types of samples: probability and nonprobability samples. A *probability sample* is simply a sample for which each element in the total population has a known probability of being selected. This allows a researcher to calculate how accurately the sample reflects the population from which it is drawn. A *nonprobability sample* is a sample for which each element in the population has an unknown probability of being selected, thus preventing the calculation of how accurate the sample is. When possible, probability samples are preferred to nonprobability samples.

In this section different types of probability samples will be considered: simple random samples, systematic samples, stratified samples (both proportionate and disproportionate), cluster samples, and telephone samples. We then will discuss nonprobability samples and the situations in which they are used.

Simple Random Samples

In a random sample, each element and combination of elements must have an equal chance of being selected. A list of all the elements in the population must be available, and a method of selecting those elements must be used that ensures that each element has an equal chance of being selected.[5] Two common ways of selecting a simple random sample will be reviewed so that you can see how elements are given an equal chance of selection.

One way of selecting elements at random from a list is by assigning a number to each element and using a *random numbers table* to select numbers. A portion of a random numbers table is shown in Table 7-1.

If we have a population of 1,507 elements and wish to draw a sample of 150, we can select any four adjacent columns on the random numbers table and look down those columns of numbers. Each time a number between 0001 and 1,507 appears, that element is selected. If a number

Table 7-1 Portion of a Random Numbers Table

37	52	35	15	80
07	99	95	64	06
21	28	31	42	72
10	16	69	93	08
00	84	65	56	29

Source: Hypothetical data.

appears more than once, that number is ignored after the first time, and we simply go on to another number on the random numbers table. (This is called sampling without replacement.) If we start with the first four columns in Table 7-1 and go down the columns, elements 0799, 1,016, and 0084 would be included. As long as we do not deliberately look for a certain number, we may start anywhere and use any system to move through the table. Random numbers may be generated by computer programs as well. It is not acceptable to generate four-digit numbers in one's head, however, since these are likely to be biased in some way.

The second way of selecting a random sample is with the *lot* method. In this method all the elements in the population are tossed in a hat (or some analogous procedure), and elements are randomly drawn out until the desired sample size has been reached. This procedure requires that the elements "in the hat" are continuously and thoroughly mixed so that each element has an equal chance of being selected. This procedure can be quite cumbersome when the population size is large. It does, however, eliminate the necessity of assigning a number to each element in the sampling frame.

Whichever method of selection is used, simple random sampling requires a list of the total population. For example, a random sample of members of Congress could be drawn from a list of all 100 senators and 435 representatives. A random sample of countries could be chosen from a list of all of the countries in the world. A random sample of American cities with more than 50,000 people could be selected from a list of all such cities in the United States. In other words, whenever an accurate and complete list of the target population is available and is of manageable size, a simple random sample can usually be drawn quite easily from that list.

Systematic Samples

Systematic sampling, an alternative to simple random sampling, also requires a list of the target population. Assigning numbers to all elements in a list and then using a random numbers table to select elements may be a cumbersome procedure. But in systematic sampling, elements are chosen off the list systematically rather than randomly. That is, every *j*th element on the list is selected where j is the number that will result in the desired number of elements being selected; j is called the *sampling interval*.

For example, suppose we wanted to draw a sample of 100 names from a list of all 5,000 students attending a particular college. If we were going to use systematic sampling, we would first calculate the *sampling interval* by dividing the number of elements in the list by the sample size. In this case dividing the list of 5,000 names by the desired sample size of 100, we would get a sampling interval of 50. Then we would systematically go through the list and select every fiftieth student (hence selecting 100 names). To determine where on the list to start, a number between 1 and 50 is selected at random using a random numbers table. (This is called a *random start*.) Thus if the number 31 is randomly selected, students 31, 81, and 131 would be included in the sample.

Systematic sampling is very useful when dealing with a long list of population elements. It is often used in product testing. Suppose you have been given the job of ensuring that a firm's tuna fish cans are properly sealed before they are delivered to grocery stores. And assume that your resources permit you to test only a sample of tuna fish cans rather than the entire population of tuna fish cans. It would be much easier to systematically select every jth tuna fish can as it rolls off the assembly line than to collect all the cans in one place and randomly select some of them for testing.

Despite its advantages, systematic sampling may result in a biased sample in two situations.[6] One occurs if elements on the list have been ranked according to a characteristic. In that situation the position of the random start will affect the average value of the characteristic for the sample. For example, if students were ranked from the lowest to the highest grade-point average, a systematic sample with students 1, 51, and 101 would have a lower grade-point average than a sample with students 50, 100, and 150. Each sample would yield a grade-point average that presents a biased picture of the student population.

The second situation that may lead to bias occurs if the list contains a pattern that corresponds to the sampling interval. Suppose you were conducting a study of the attitudes of children from large families and you were working with a list where the children in each family were listed by age. If the families included in the list all had six children and your sampling interval was 6 (or any multiple of 6), then systematic sampling would result in a sample of children who were all in the same position among their siblings. If attitudes varied with birth order, then your findings would be biased.

A survey of soldiers conducted during World War II is a good example of a case in which a pattern in the list used as the sampling frame interfered with the selection of a systematic sample.[7] The list of soldiers was arranged by squad, with each squad roster arranged by rank. The sampling interval and squad size were both 10. Consequently, the sample consisted of all persons who held the same rank, in this case squad sergeant. Clearly, sergeants might not be representative of all soldiers serving in World War II.

Stratified Samples

Stratified sampling takes advantage of the principle that the more homogeneous the population, the easier it is to select from it a representative sample. Also if a population is relatively homogeneous, the size of the sample needed to produce a given degree of accuracy will be smaller than for a heterogeneous population. In stratified sampling, sampling units are divided into strata with each unit appearing in only one stratum. Then a simple random sample or systematic sample is taken from each stratum.

Proportionate Sampling. Let's assume we have a total population of 500 colored balls: 50 each of red, yellow, orange, and green balls and 100 each of blue, black, and white balls. We wish to draw a sample of 100 balls. To ensure a sample with each color represented in proportion to its presence in the population, we would first stratify the balls according to color. To determine the number of balls to sample from each stratum, we calculate the *sampling fraction,* which is the size of the desired sample divided by the size of the population. In this example the sampling fraction is 100/500 or one-fifth of the balls. Therefore we must sample one-fifth of all the balls in each stratum.

Since there are 50 red balls, we want one-fifth or 10 red balls. We could select these 10 red balls at random or select every fifth ball with a random start between 1 and 5. If we followed this procedure for each color, we would end up with a sample of 10 each of red, yellow, orange, and green balls and 20 each of blue, black, and white balls. Note that if we select a simple random sample of 100 balls, there is a finite chance (albeit slight) that all 100 balls will be blue or black or white. Stratified sampling guarantees that this cannot happen, and that is why stratified sampling results in a more representative sample.

Systematic sampling of an entire stratified list, rather than sampling from each stratum will yield a sample in which each stratum's representation is roughly proportional to its representation in the population. Some deviation from proportional representation will occur, depending on the sampling interval, the random start, and the number of sampling units in a stratum.

In selecting characteristics on which to stratify a list, you should choose characteristics that are expected to be related to or affect the dependent variables in your study. If you are attempting to measure the average income of households in a city, for example, you might stratify the list of households by education, sex, or race of household head. Because income may vary by education, sex, or race, you would want to make sure that the sample is representative with respect to these factors. Otherwise the sample estimate of average household income might be biased.

If you were selecting a sample of members of Congress to interview, you might want to divide the list of members into strata consisting of the two major parties, or the length of congressional service, or both. This would ensure that your sample accurately reflected the distribution of party and seniority in Congress. Or if you were selecting a sample of television news stories to analyze, you might want to divide the population of news stories into three strata based on the network of origin to ensure that your sample contained an equal number of stories from NBC, CBS, and ABC.

Some lists may be inherently stratified. Telephone directories are stratified to a degree by ethnic groups since certain last names are associated with particular ethnic groups. Lists of social security numbers arranged consecutively are stratified by geographical area since numbers are assigned based on the applicant's place of residence.

Disproportionate Sampling. In the examples of stratified sampling we have considered so far, we assured ourselves of a more representative sample in which each stratum was represented in proportion to its size in the population. There may be occasions, however, when we wish to take a disproportionate sample.[8]

For example, suppose we are conducting a survey of 200 students at a college, and there are 500 liberal arts majors, 100 engineering majors, and 200 business majors, for a total of 800 students at the college. If we sampled from each major (the strata) in proportion to its size, we would have 125 liberal arts majors, 25 engineering majors, and 50 business majors. If we wished to analyze the student population as a whole, this would be an acceptable sample. But if we wished to investigate some questions by looking at students in each major separately, we would find that 25 engineering students was too small a sample for statistical analysis.

To get around this problem we could sample disproportionately—for example, 100 liberal arts majors, 50 engineering students, and 50 business majors. Then we would have enough engineering students for separate analyses. The problem now becomes evaluating the student population as a whole since our sample is biased due to an undersampling of liberal arts majors and an oversampling of engineering majors. Suppose engineering students have high grade-point averages. Our sample estimate of the student body's grade-point average would be biased upward because we have oversampled engineering students. Therefore, when we wish to analyze the total sample, not just a major, we need some method of adjusting our sample so that each major is represented in proportion to its real representation in the total student population.[9]

Table 7-2 shows the proportion of the population of each major and the mean grade-point average (GPA) for each group in the sample. To calculate an unbiased estimate of the overall mean GPA for the college, we would multiply the mean GPA for each major by the proportion or weighting factor.[10] Thus the mean GPA would be

$$.625(2.5) + .125(3.3) + .25(2.7) = 2.65$$

Disproportionate stratified samples allow a researcher to represent more accurately the elements in each stratum and ensure that the overall sample is an accurate representation of important strata within the target population. This is done by weighting the data from each stratum when the sample is used to estimate characteristics of the target population. Of course, to accomplish disproportionate stratified sampling, the proportion of each stratum in the target population must be known.

Cluster Samples

Thus far we have considered examples in which a list of elements in the sampling frame existed. There are, however, situations where a sample is needed but no list of elements exists and to create one would be prohibitively expensive. Since only some of the elements are to be included in the sample, it is unnecessary to be able to list all elements. Cluster sampling is used to address the problem of having no list of the elements in the target population. In cluster sampling, groups or clusters of elements are identified and listed. Next a sample is drawn from this list of sampling units. Then for the sampled units only, elements are identified and sampled. For example, let's take an opinion poll of 1,000 persons in a city. Since there is no complete list of city residents, we might begin by obtaining a map of the city and identifying and listing all blocks. This list of blocks becomes the sampling frame from which a number of blocks are sampled at random or systematically. Next we would go to the selected blocks and list all the dwelling units in those blocks. Then a sample of dwelling units would be drawn from each block. Finally, the households in the sampled dwellings would be contacted, and someone in each household would be interviewed for the opinion poll. Suppose there are 500 blocks, and from these 500 blocks 25 are chosen at random. On these 25 blocks, 4,000 dwelling units or households are identified. One-quarter of these households will be contacted because a sample of 1,000 individuals is desired. These 1,000 households could be selected with a random sample or a systematic sample.

Table 7-2 Stratified Sample of Student Majors

	Liberal Arts	*Engineering*	*Business*	*Total*
Number of students	500	100	200	800
Proportion or weight	.625	.125	.25	1.00
Size of sample	100	50	50	200
Sample mean grade-point average	2.5	3.3	2.7	

Source: Hypothetical data.

Note that even though we did not know the number of households ahead of time, each household is given an equal chance of being selected. This probability is equal to the probability of one's block being selected times the probability of one's household being selected or 25/500 x 1000/4000 = 1/80. Thus cluster sampling conforms to the requirements of a probability sample.

Our example involved taking only two samples or levels (the city block and the household). Some cluster samples involve many levels or stages and thus many samples. For example, in a national opinion poll the researcher might list and sample states, list and sample counties within states, list and sample municipalities within counties, list and sample census tracts within municipalities, list and sample blocks within census tracts, and finally list and sample households—a total of six stages.

Cluster sampling allows researchers to get around the problem of acquiring a list of elements in the target population. Cluster sampling also reduces fieldwork costs because it produces respondents who are close together. For example, in a national opinion poll respondents will not come from every state. This reduces travel and administrative costs.

A drawback to cluster sampling is that there is more imprecision. Sampling error occurs at each stage of the cluster sample. For example, a sample of states will not be totally representative of all states, a sample of counties will not be totally representative of all counties, and so on. The sampling error at each level must be added together to arrive at the total sampling error for a cluster sample.

In cluster sampling, the researcher must decide how many elements to select from each cluster. In the previous example, the researcher could have selected two individuals from each of the 500 blocks (hence requiring no selection of blocks), or 1,000 individuals from one of the blocks (hence making the selection of the particular block terribly important), or some other combination in between (40 individuals from 25 blocks, 25 individuals from 40 blocks, and so on). But how does the researcher decide how many units to sample at each stage?

We know that samples are more accurate when drawn from homogeneous populations. Generally, elements within a group are more similar than are elements from two different groups. Thus households on the same block are more likely to resemble each other than households on different blocks. Sample size can be smaller for homogeneous populations than for heterogeneous populations and still be as accurate. (If a population is totally homogeneous, a sample of one element will be accurate). Therefore, sampling error could be reduced by selecting many blocks but interviewing only a few households from each block. Following this reasoning to the extreme, we could select all 500 blocks and sample two households from each block. This, however, would be very expensive since every household in the city would have to be identified and listed, which defeats the purpose of a cluster sample. The desire to maximize the accuracy of a sample must be balanced by the need to reduce the time and cost of creating a sampling frame—a major advantage of cluster sampling. Stratification of clusters can reduce sampling error. States can be grouped by region, census tracts by average income, and so forth.

Systematic, stratified (both proportionate and disproportionate), and cluster samples are acceptable and often more practical alternatives to the simple random sample. In each case the probability of a particular element being selected is known, and consequently the accuracy of the sample can be determined. The type of sample chosen depends upon the resources a researcher has available and the availability of an accurate and comprehensive list of a well-defined target population.

Telephone Samples

Telephone surveys are becoming a common sample survey practice. As we have mentioned, telephone directories are generally incomplete sampling frames. However, there is quite a bit of debate about how inaccurate they are and whether it is always advisable to develop a different sampling frame.[11] A procedure called *random digit dialing* (RDD) can be used to contact a sample of all telephone owners, whether they have listed numbers or not.[12] However, keep in mind that not all households have telephones. Therefore a sampling frame consisting of randomly generated telephone numbers is still an incomplete listing of households. It is estimated that 90 to 98 percent of all households have telephones.[13] Therefore if the survey population is *all* households in the United States, a telephone sample will not be entirely satisfactory.

Nonprobability Samples

Probability samples are usually preferable to nonprobability samples because they represent fairly accurately a large population, and it is possible to calculate how accurate an estimate the sample is of that population. However, in some situations probability sampling may be too expensive to justify (in exploratory research, for example), or the target population may be too ill-defined to permit probability sampling (this was the case with the television commercials example discussed earlier). Researchers may feel that they can learn more by studying carefully selected and perhaps unusual cases than by studying representative ones. A brief description follows of some of the types of nonprobability samples.

With *purposive* or *judgmental samples* a researcher exercises considerable discretion over what observations to include in the data collection. Here the goal is more typically to study a diverse and usually limited number of observations than to study a sample representative of a larger target population. Richard Fenno's *Home Style,* which describes the behavior of eighteen incumbent representatives, is an example of research based on a purposive sample.[14] Likewise, a study of journalists that concentrated on the most prominent journalists in Washington or New York would be a purposive rather than a representative sample of all journalists.

In *convenience* or *haphazard samples,* elements are included because they are convenient or easy for a researcher to select. A public opinion sample in which interviewers haphazardly select whomever they wish is this type of sample. A sample of campaign commercials that consists of those advertisements that a researcher is able to acquire is also this type. A study of the personalities of politicians dependent upon those who have sought psychoanalysis is also a convenience sample, as is any public opinion survey consisting of those who volunteer their opinions. Convenience samples are most appropriate when the research is exploratory or when a target population is impossible to define or locate. But like other nonprobability samples, convenience samples do not provide accurate estimates of the attributes of target populations.

In *quota sampling,* elements are sampled in proportion to their representation in the population, and thus it is similar to proportionate stratified sampling. The difference between quota and stratified sampling is that the elements in the quota sample are not chosen in a probabilistic manner. Instead they are chosen in a purposive or haphazard or convenient fashion until the appropriate number of each type of element (quota) has been found. Because of the lack of probability sampling of elements, quota samples are usually biased estimates of the target population. Even more important, it is impossible to calculate the accuracy of a quota sample.

A researcher who decided to conduct a public opinion survey of 550 women and 450 men and who instructed his interviewers to select whomever they pleased until these quotas were reached would be drawing a quota sample. A famous example of an error-ridden quota sample is the one in 1948 by Gallup and other pollsters that predicted that Thomas Dewey would defeat Harry Truman for president.[15]

In *snowball sampling,* respondents are used to identify other persons who might qualify for inclusion in the sample.[16] These people are then interviewed and asked to supply appropriate names for further interviewing. This process is continued until enough persons are interviewed to satisfy the researcher's needs. Snowball sampling is particularly useful to study a relatively select or rare population such as draft evaders, campaign contributors, political protesters, or even home gardeners who use sewage sludge on their gardens—a group estimated to constitute only 3 percent to 4 percent of households.[17]

We have discussed the various types of samples that political science researchers use in their data collection. Samples allow researchers to save time, money, and other costs. However, this benefit is a mixed blessing, for by avoiding these costs researchers must rely on information that is less accurate than if they had collected data on the entire target population. Now we will consider the type of information that samples provide.

Sample Information

At best, samples provide us with estimates of attributes of, or relationships within, the target population. For example, a finding that 30 percent of a random sample of members of Congress did not accept campaign contributions from political action committees does not mean that exactly 30 percent of all members refused such contributions; it means that approximately 30 percent refused them. In other words, researchers sacrifice some precision of information whenever they decide to rely on samples for their empirical observations. How much precision is lost depends on how the sample has been drawn. The accuracy of the estimates gleaned from sample data can be calculated for probability samples but not for nonprobability samples. The accuracy of these sample estimates for probability samples is expressed in terms of what are known as the *margin of error* and the *confidence level.*

When a researcher measures some attribute in a sample, the result of that measurement is called the *sample statistic.* However, the researcher is usually not interested in the measurement of that attribute for the sample only but in the incidence of the attribute in the target population (called the *population parameter*). The sample statistic provides the basis for estimating the incidence of the attribute of interest in the target population. Around the sample statistic is placed a mathematically calculated range (the margin of error) within which the population parameter is likely to fall.

For example, suppose a researcher is interested in the proportion of Americans of voting age who believe the United States should have sent troops to Saudi Arabia. A cluster sample is drawn, and it is discovered that 40 percent of the respondents in the sample think that the troops should have been sent. This 40 percent (the sample statistic) is only an estimate of the attitudes of the target population (the population parameter). Around this 40 percent a margin of error will be calculated mathematically, and that range will constitute the estimate of the population parameter. If the margin of error were ±3 percent, then the sample result would provide an estimate that somewhere between 37 percent and 43 percent of the target population believes that U.S. troops should have been committed to Saudi Arabia. The sample information cannot tell us exactly where, within the range defined by the margin of error, the population parameter exists.

Associated with the margin of error is the *confidence level.* This number, also mathematically calculated for probability samples, indicates the degree of certainty that the population parameter falls within the margin of error. A certainty level of 95 percent is the convention used by social science researchers; this indicates 95 percent certainty that the population parameter falls within the margin of error of the sample statistic. It also means that there is a 5 percent chance that the population parameter falls outside the margin of error. Most researchers find 95-to-5 odds acceptable.

Sampling Error

The margin of error and the confidence level together constitute *sampling error.* They are mathematically related so that the calculation of one determines the calculation of the other. Thus sampling error is expressed in this way: "With 95 percent certainty the target population is within ±3 percentage points (or whatever) of the sample."

Ideally, sample estimates of the target population are as accurate and precise as possible. The margin of error should be small and the confidence level high. However, the only way to eliminate sampling error entirely is to collect data from the whole target population (in other words, not rely on a sample at all). Sampling error is the price researchers pay for reducing the costs involved in measuring some attribute of the target population.

You may have seen reports of sample-based information that imply that the sample results are precise estimates of the target population. During election campaigns, for example, newspaper headlines may declare: "Bush Leads Dukakis, 60% to 40%." Such reports are misleading and erroneous. No probability sample can produce precise estimates of the national voting-age population. Although the results for the cluster sample may have been 60 percent to 40 percent, the estimate of presidential preferences in the target population is always subject to some sampling error.

Error is possible whenever a researcher relies on a sample. For example, any measurements of attributes in samples of members of Congress, convention delegates, census tracts, or nation-states are estimates of the target population of members, convention delegates, census tracts, or nation-states, and therefore are subject to sampling error. Sampling error is not applicable only to public opinion surveys.

The most important factor in the sampling error of probability samples is the size of the sample. The larger the sample, the smaller the sampling error. However, there is an exponential rather than a linear relationship between sample size and sampling error. For example, to cut sampling error in half, the sample size must be quadrupled. This means that researchers must balance the costs of increasing sample size with the size of the sampling error they are willing to tolerate. Table 7-3 shows the relationship between sample size and the margin of error for Gallup Poll-type samples.

Sampling error is also dependent on the type of sample drawn. For a given sample size, a simple random sample provides a more accurate estimate of the target (that is, a smaller margin of error) than a cluster sample does. Sampling error is also smaller for an attribute that is shared by almost all elements in the sample than for an attribute that is distributed across half the sample elements.

Finally, sampling error is reduced if the sample is a significant proportion of the target population (called the *sampling fraction*). However, this does not pertain unless the sample represents more than one-fourth of the target population, so the effect of the sampling fraction on sampling error is usually minuscule.

Of all the factors that reduce sampling error, sample size is usually the easiest for researchers to control. But in research based on public opinion surveys, increasing sample size may be too costly. Public opinion researchers usually draw samples of 1,500 to 2,000 people (regardless of the size of the target population). This yields a margin of error (about ± 3 percent) and a confidence level (95 percent) at a cost that is within reach for at least some survey organizations. Reducing the sampling error appreciably in this kind of research would mean incurring costs that are prohibitive for most researchers.

Conclusion

In this chapter we have discussed what it means to select a sample out of a target population, the various types of samples that political scientists use, and the kind of information that a sample yields. The

Table 7-3   The Relationship between Sample Size and Sampling Error

Sample Size	Confidence Interval
4,000	± 2%
1,500	± 3
1,000	± 4
600	± 5
400	± 6
200	± 8
100	±11

Source: Charles W. Roll, Jr., and Albert H. Cantril, *Polls: Their Use and Misuse in Politics,* 72. Copyright © 1972 by Basic Books, Inc. Reprinted by permission of the publisher.

Note: This table is based on a 95 percent confidence level and is derived from experience with Gallup Poll samples.

following guidelines may help researchers who are deciding whether to rely on a sample and students evaluating research based on a sample.

1. If cost is not a major consideration and the validity of one's measures will not suffer, it is generally better to collect data for one's target population than for a sample thereof.
2. If cost or validity considerations dictate that a sample be drawn, a probability sample is usually preferable to a nonprobability sample. It is only for probability samples that the accuracy of sample estimates can be determined. If the desire to accurately represent a target population is not a major concern or is impossible to achieve, then a nonprobability sample may be used.
3. Remember that probability samples yield estimates of the target population. All samples are subject to sampling error; no sample, no matter how well drawn, can provide an exact measurement of an attribute of, or relationship within, the target population.
4. Finally, keep in mind that the accuracy of sample estimates is expressed in terms of the margin of error and the confidence level. Sampling error is dependent mainly on sample size, but it is also somewhat dependent on the distribution of the attribute being measured, the type of probability sample, and the sampling fraction.

   In the next chapter we will discuss in more detail one type of data collection procedure involving sampling—the public opinion survey. In Chapter 11 we will illustrate how to calculate sampling error mathematically.

Notes

1. Earl R. Babbie, *Survey Research Methods* (Belmont, Calif.: Wadsworth, 1973), 74.
2. Richard A. Joslyn, *Mass Media and Elections* (Reading, Mass.: Addison-Wesley, 1984).
3. This discussion of terms used in sampling is drawn primarily from Babbie, *Survey Research Methods*, 79-81.
4. Ibid., 74-75.
5. Strictly speaking, to ensure an equal chance of selection, *replacement* is required; that is, putting each selected element back on the list before the next element is selected. In *simple* random sampling, however, elements are selected without replacement. This means that on each successive draw, the probability of an element's being selected increases because there are fewer and fewer elements remaining. But for each draw the probability of being selected is equal among the remaining elements. If the sample size is less than one-fifth the size of the population, the slight deviation from strict random sampling caused by sampling without replacement is acceptable. See Hubert M. Blalock, Jr., *Social Statistics*, 2d ed., (New York: McGraw-Hill, 1972), 513-514.
6. Ibid., 515.
7. Babbie, *Survey Research Methods*, 93.
8. There are two reasons for disproportionate sampling, in addition to obtaining enough cases for statistical analysis of subgroups: the high cost of sampling some strata and differences in the heterogeneity of some strata, with resulting differences in sampling error. A researcher might want to minimize sampling where it was costly and increase sampling from heterogeneous strata while decreasing it from homogeneous strata. See Blalock, *Social Statistics*, 518-519.
9. Ibid., 521-522.
10. We could have obtained the same results by multiplying the GPA of each student by the weighting factor associated with the student's major and then calculating the mean GPA for the whole sample.
11. C. L. Rich, "Is Random Digit Dialing Really Necessary?" *Journal of Marketing Research* 14 (August 1977): 300-305.
12. For various methods of RDD, see E. L. Landon, Jr., and S. K. Banks, "Relative Efficiency and Bias of Plus-One Telephone Sampling," *Journal of Marketing Research* 14 (August 1977): 294-299; K. M. Cummings, "Random Digit Dialing: A Sampling Technique for Telephone Surveys," *Public Opinion Quarterly* 43 (Summer 1979): 233-244; R. M. Groves and R. L. Kahn, *Surveys by Telephone* (New York: Academic Press, 1979); and J. Waksberg, "Sampling Methods for Random Digit Dialing," *Journal of the American Statistical Association* 73 (March 1978): 40-46.
13. James H. Frey, *Survey Research by Telephone* (Beverly Hills, Calif.: Sage, 1983), 22.
14. Richard F. Fenno, Jr., *Home Style: House Members in Their Districts* (Boston: Little, Brown, 1978).
15. Babbie, *Survey Research Methods*, 75.
16. Snowball sampling is generally considered to be a nonprobability sampling technique, although strategies have been developed to achieve a probability sample with this method. See Kenneth D. Bailey, *Methods of Social Research* (New York: Free Press, 1978), 83.

17. J. W. Bergsten and S. A. Pierson, "Telephone Screening for Rare Characteristics Using Multiplicity Counting Rules," *1982 Proceedings of the American Statistical Association Section on Survey Research Methods,* 145-150.

Terms Introduced

Cluster sample. A probability sample used when no list of elements exists. The sampling frame initially consists of clusters of elements.

Confidence level. The probability that the population parameter actually falls within the margin of error of a sample statistic.

Convenience sample. A nonprobability sample in which the selection of elements is determined by the researcher's convenience.

Disproportionate sample. A stratified sample in which elements sharing a characteristic are underrepresented or overrepresented in a sample.

Element. Entity about which information is collected, or the unit of analysis.

Margin of error. The range around a sample statistic within which the population parameter is likely to fall.

Nonprobability sample. A sample for which each element in the total population has an unknown probability of being selected.

Population. All of the cases or observations covered by a hypothesis; all the units of analysis to which a hypothesis applies.

Population parameter. The incidence of a characteristic or attribute in a population (not a sample).

Probability sample. A sample for which each element in the total population has a known probability of being selected.

Purposive or judgmental sample. A nonprobability sample in which a researcher uses discretion in selecting elements for observation.

Quota sample. A nonprobability sample in which elements are sampled in proportion to their representation in the population.

Random digit dialing. A procedure used to improve the representativeness of telephone samples by giving listed and unlisted numbers a chance of selection.

Random numbers table. A list of random numbers.

Random start. Selection of a number at random to determine where to start selecting elements in a systematic sample.

Sample. A subset of all the observations or cases covered by a hypothesis; a portion of a population.

Sample bias. The bias that occurs whenever some elements of a population are systematically excluded from a sample. It is usually due to an incomplete sampling frame or a nonprobability method of selecting elements.

Sample statistic. The estimate of a characteristic or attribute in a sample.

Sampling error. The confidence level and the margin of error taken together.

Sampling fraction. The proportion of the population included in a sample.

Sampling frame. The population from which a sample is drawn. Ideally it is the same as the total population of interest to a study.

Sampling interval. The number of elements in a sampling frame divided by the desired sample size.

Sampling unit. The entity listed in a sampling frame. It may be the same as an element, or it may be a group or cluster of elements.

Simple random sample. A probability sample in which each element has an equal chance of being selected.

Snowball sample. A sample in which respondents are asked to identify additional members of a population.
Stratified sample. A probability sample in which elements sharing one or more characteristics are grouped, and elements are selected from each group in proportion to the group's representation in the total population.
Stratum. A subgroup of a population that shares one or more characteristics.
Systematic sample. A probability sample in which elements are selected from a list at predetermined intervals.
Weighting factor. A mathematical factor used to make a disproportionate sample representative.

Exercises

1. If there are 5,000 elements in a sampling frame and a simple random sample of 200 elements is taken, what is the chance of an element being included in the sample? What is this chance called?

2. If a systematic sample of 250 elements is taken from a sampling frame of 2,000 elements, what is the sampling interval? How would one decide where to start?

3. Suppose you are drawing a sample of state legislative candidates running in several nearby states. You would like your sample to be representative of incumbents and challengers and of both parties. You determine that there are 350 incumbent Republicans, 300 Democratic challengers, 250 incumbent Democrats, and 210 Republican challengers. Your sample size is 100. How many of each group of candidates must you sample?

4. A researcher has collected data on voter turnout rates for city council elections in a sample of cities. To analyze her data by region, she found it necessary to oversample in some regions. Now she would like to calculate the overall mean turnout for her sample as a whole. Based on the information below, complete the table and calculate the overall mean turnout rate for the sample.

City Council Election Voter Turnout

	South	Northeast	Midwest	West	Total
Number of cities	200	300	400	100	1,000
Proportion					1.00
Size of sample	50	50	50	50	200
Mean percent turnout	18.5	22.0	25.0	21.0	

5. Suppose a cluster sample has been taken for a study of the contents of editorials in newspapers with a daily circulation of at least 10,000. First a sample of 25 states was taken. Then within the selected states, all the newspapers meeting the qualifications were listed for a total of 500 newspapers. Then a sample of 100 newspapers was selected. What is the probability of a newspaper being included in the study?

6. A research project has been established to investigate the potential for increased support by voluntary service organizations for social service activities. Increased private support for these activities is being sought because governmental programs have been cut drastically due to a severe state budget shortfall.

A survey of members is planned to investigate members' perceptions of the need for certain programs and their willingness to devote their organization's resources to these programs. It is estimated that there are 1,000 local organizations across the state and about 500,000 members. A sample size of 500 has been decided. How would you go about selecting a probability sample? Explain your decision.

Suggested Readings

Backstrom, Charles H., and Gerald Hursh-Cesar. *Survey Research,* 2d ed. New York: Wiley, 1981.

Blalock, Hubert M., Jr. *Social Statistics,* 2d ed. New York: McGraw-Hill, 1972.

Groves, Robert M., and Robert L. Kahn. *Surveys by Telephone.* New York: Academic Press, 1979.

Kalton, Graham. *Introduction to Survey Sampling.* Beverly Hills, Calif.: Sage, 1983.

CHAPTER 8

Making Empirical Observations: Survey Research and Elite Interviewing

In the preceding chapters we have discussed the nature of scientific explanation and the initial stages of a social science research project: formulating testable hypotheses, selecting a suitable research design, and conducting background research. The difficulties associated with measuring political phenomena and with sampling techniques also have been described. In this and the next two chapters we address the task of making the empirical observations with which to implement our research design and test our hypotheses. This is what is generally called the *data collection* stage of a research project.

We have said that empirical observations are necessary to test the hypotheses that we have devised, but so far we have not explained how those observations are made and what the implications are of making the observations in particular ways. Political scientists tend to use three broad types of observations or data, depending on the phenomena they are interested in studying.

Types of Data and Collection Techniques

Interview data, the subject of this chapter, are data derived from written or verbal questioning of some group of respondents. This type of data collection may involve interviewing a representative cross-section of the national adult population or a select group of political actors, such as committee chairs in Congress. It may involve face-to-face interviews or interviews conducted over the phone or through the mail. It may involve highly structured interviews in which a questionnaire is closely followed or a less structured, open-ended discussion. Regardless of the particular type of interview setting, however, the essentials of the data collection method are the same: the data come from responses to verbal or written cues of the researcher and the respondent knows these responses are being recorded.

Sometimes researchers do not design and conduct the interview process themselves. Rather they rely on survey organizations that conduct the interviews and supply the data to researchers who analyze them. Secondary analysis of existing surveys is less expensive and can save time, but existing survey data may not fit a researcher's needs well because of the wording of questions, the date of the survey, or the population surveyed. Gaining access to individual survey returns, not just aggregated responses, may be difficult. Surveys conducted by private organizations may not be available at all. Major survey archives include the following:

> Behavioral Sciences Laboratory, University of Cincinnati, Cincinnati, OH 45221
>
> Data and Program Library Service, University of Wisconsin, 4451 Social Science Building, Madison, WI 53706
>
> Institute for Research in Social Science, Manning Hall, University of North Carolina, Chapel Hill, NC 27514
>
> Inter-University Consortium for Political and Social Research, University of Michigan, Ann Arbor, MI 48106
>
> National Opinion Research Center, University of Chicago, 1155 East 60th Street, Chicago, IL 60637
>
> Roper Center, University of Connecticut, Storrs, CT 06268
>
> Survey Research Center, University of California, Berkeley, Calif. 94720.[1]

In addition to interview data, political scientists rely heavily on data that exist in various archival records. In this type of data collection, known as *document analysis* (the subject of Chapter 9), researchers rely on the recordkeeping activities of government agencies, private institutes, interest groups, media organizations, and even private citizens. Some of this data may be based on interviews, but it is in summary form. For example, unemployment statistics are derived from the Census Bureau's Current Population Survey, a household survey conducted each month. What sets document analysis apart from other data collection methods is that the researcher is usually not the original collector of the data and the original reason for the collection of the data may not have been to further a scientific research project. The recordkeepers are usually unaware of how the data they collect will ultimately be used, and the phenomena they record are not generally the personal beliefs and attitudes collected through interviews.

Finally, data may be collected through *direct observation,* which will be discussed in more detail in Chapter 10. In this type of data collection the researcher collects data on political behavior by observing either the behavior itself or some physical trace of the behavior. Unlike interviewing, this method of data collection does not rely on people's verbal responses to verbal stimuli presented by the researcher. Furthermore, those whose behavior is being directly observed may be unaware that they are being observed or may not know why.

A political scientist's choice of a data collection method depends upon a number of factors. One important consideration is the *validity* of the measurements that a particular method will permit. For example, a researcher who wants to measure the crime rate of different cities may feel that the crime rates reported by local police departments to the FBI are not sufficiently accurate to support a research project. The researcher may be concerned that some departments overreport and some underreport various criminal acts, hence rendering that method of collecting data and measuring the crime rate unacceptable. Therefore, the researcher may decide that a more accurate indication of the crime rate can be secured by interviewing a sample of citizens in different cities and asking them how much crime they have experienced themselves.

A political scientist is also influenced by the *reactivity* of a data collection method—the effect of the data collection itself on the phenomena being observed. When people know their behavior is being observed and know or can guess the purpose of the observation, they may alter their behavior. As a result, the observed behavior may be an unnatural reaction to the process of being observed. People may be reluctant, for example, to admit to an interviewer that they are anti-Semitic or have failed to vote in an election. For this reason many researchers prefer unobtrusive or nonreactive measures of political behavior because they believe that the resulting data are more natural or real.

The *population* covered by a data collection method is another important consideration for a researcher. The population determines whose behavior is observed. One type of data may be available for only a few people, while another type may permit more numerous, interesting, and worthwhile comparisons. A researcher studying the behavior of political consultants, for example, may decide that relying on the published memoirs of a handful of consultants will not adequately cover the population of consultants (not to mention the validity problems of the data) and that it would be better to seek out a broad cross-section of consultants and interview them. Or a researcher interested in political corruption might decide that interviewing a broad cross-section of politicians charged with various corrupt practices is not feasible and that data (of a different kind) could be obtained for a more diverse set of corrupt acts from accounts published in the mass media.

Finally, *cost* and *availability* are crucial elements in the choice of a data collection technique. Some types of data collection are simply more expensive than others, and some types of observations are more readily made than others. Large-scale interviewing, for example, is very expensive and time-consuming, and the types of questions that can be asked and behaviors that can be observed are limited. Data from archival records are usually much less expensive since the recordkeeping entity has borne most of the cost of collecting and publishing the data. With the increased use of computers, many organizations are systematically collecting data of interest to researchers. The disadvantage, however, is that because the data are not under the researcher's control they must be made available by the recordkeeping organization, which can refuse a researcher's request or take a long time filling it. Finally, direct observation can be time-consuming (if the researcher does it) or expensive (if the researcher pays others to do it). And again there are physical, legal, and ethical limits to what can be observed.

After weighing the importance of each of the above factors, the researchers select a particular method or methods of data collection. Often practical considerations (such as cost and availability) necessitate the use of data that are suspect on other grounds (such as validity and reactivity). If possible, it is preferable to use different data collection methods and cross-check the results.

In this and the following two chapters, the relative advantages and disadvantages of each of the major data collection methods will be examined with respect to the factors of validity, reactivity, population coverage, cost, and availability. We begin here with a discussion of the information political scientists garner from written polls and oral interviews.

Survey Research

Survey research or opinion polling is one of the most familiar research methods. Scarcely a day goes by in which we are not told the results of one poll or another. There are presidential performance and popularity polls. Businesses use polling to determine satisfaction with products and services. Nonprofit organizations conduct polls to find out about their public image and how to increase contributions. Candidates for public office use polls to help map campaign strategies; polls tell them what appeals to make to constituents, what issues to stress, and which matters to avoid. Interest groups conduct public opinion polls to determine public support for their issue positions. Public officials use surveys to evaluate the effectiveness of the programs they administer or to learn more about problems in the population that need to be addressed by new or different programs. More recently developed uses for surveys are in the legal area. For example, surveys of community members may be conducted to determine what proportion of the community has heard about a major criminal case and has developed opinions about the defendant. This information is used by judges to determine the need for a change in venue for the trial.[2] Surveys also are used in measuring deceptive advertising and trademark infringement, and in selecting juries.[3] Social scientists also use surveys to explore and test theories about human beliefs and activities.

As the use of surveys as a research method has grown, so has the amount of research on the method itself increased. This research is concerned with the validity and reliability of survey results and the costs of survey research. We now know more about many aspects of survey research than was known when the method was first used, much to the benefit of researchers and consumers of survey research.

To construct a good questionnaire, a researcher must write well-worded questions, choose the appropriate type of question (closed- or open-ended), and place questions in the appropriate order. A clearly defined research purpose and well-developed hypotheses will help eliminate unnecessary questions, thereby reducing respondent effort and survey costs. A well constructed questionnaire is easy for both the interviewer and the respondent to follow, resulting in correctly administered and completed interviews.

We will begin our review of the survey research method by discussing how to construct a survey instrument or questionnaire. We will then discuss surveys by mail, telephone, and personal interview, rating their relative advantages and disadvantages, and review issues of particular importance to the application of each. Finally we will conclude with a discussion of the special difficulties involved in interviewing elite respondents.

Question Wording

The goal of survey research is to measure accurately people's attitudes, beliefs, and behavior by asking them questions. Success greatly depends on the quality of the questions. Good questions prompt accurate answers; poor questions provide inappropriate stimuli and result in unreliable or inaccurate responses. When writing questions, researchers should avoid double-barreled, ambiguous, vague, or leading questions and should use appropriate vocabulary. Failure to do so may result in uncompleted questionnaires by frustrated or offended respondents and meaningless data for the researcher.

Double-barreled questions are really two questions in one, such as "Do you agree with the statement that the Soviet Union is ahead of the United States in the arms race and that the United States should increase defense spending?" How does a person answer who believes that the Soviets are superior in military capacity, but does not wish an increase in defense spending? And how does the researcher interpret an answer to such a question? The researcher does not know whether the respondent meant for his or her answer to apply to both components or whether one component was given precedence over the other.

Despite a conscious effort by researchers to define and clarify concepts, words with multiple meanings or interpretations may creep into questions. An example of an ambiguous question is "What is your income?" Is the question asking for family income or just the personal income of the respondent? Is the question asking for earned income (salary or wages), or should interest and stock dividends be included? Similarly, the question "Do you prefer Brand A or Brand B?" is ambiguous. Is the respondent telling us which brand is purchased or which brand would be purchased if there were no price difference between the brands?

Ambiguity may also result from using the word *he*. Are respondents to assume that *he* is being used generically to refer both to males and females or to males only? If a respondent interprets the question as applying only to males and would respond differently for females, it would be a mistake for the researcher to conclude that the response applies to all people.[4]

After the 1976 debate between presidential contenders Jimmy Carter and Gerald Ford, respondents to one poll were asked to rate the performance of the two debaters as good, bad, or indifferent. This vague question confused respondents, who then asked whether the ratings were to be made (1) by comparing the debate with other, unspecified, political debates that they had witnessed; (2) by comparing the debate with the one between John F. Kennedy and Richard Nixon; (3) by comparing Carter and Ford with each other; or (4) by measuring the candidates against the respondent's predebate expectations. Respondents were also unsure whether performance meant style, substance, or something else.[5]

As we have seen, poorly worded questions may be double-barreled, ambiguous, or vague. They also may lead the respondent to choose a particular response because the question indicates that the researcher expects it. The leading question "Don't you think that global warming is a serious environmental problem?" implies that to think otherwise would be unusual. Choice of words may also lead respondents. Research has shown that people are more willing to help "the needy" than those "on welfare." Asking people if they favor socialized medicine rather than national health insurance is bound to decrease affirmative responses. Moreover, linking personalities or institutions to issues can affect responses. For example, whether or not a person liked the governor would affect responses to the question, "Would you say that Governor Burnett's program for promoting economic development has been very effective, fairly effective, not too effective, or not effective at all?"[6] There are numerous additional ways of leading the respondent, such as by characterizing one response as the preference of others, and thereby creating an atmosphere that is anything but neutral.[7]

Polls conducted by political organizations and politicians often include leading questions. For example, a 1980 poll for the Republican National Committee asked: "Recently the Soviet armed forces openly invaded the independent country of Afghanistan. Do you think the U.S. should supply military equipment to the rebel freedom fighters?"[8] Before accepting any interpretation of survey responses, check the full text of a question to make sure that it is neither leading nor biased.

As Margrit Eichler demonstrates, gender bias may occur if, for example, respondents are asked to agree or disagree with the statement "It is generally better to have a man at the head of a department composed of both men and women employees." This wording does not make it possible for a respondent to indicate that a woman as head is preferable. It would be better to rephrase the statement "What do you think is generally better: To have a woman or a man at the head of a department that is composed of both men and women employees?" and to give respondents the opportunity to indicate a man is better, a woman is better, or there is no difference.[9]

Use of inappropriate wording is another mistake often made by researchers. Technical words, slang, and unusual vocabulary should be avoided since their meaning may be misinterpreted by respondents. Questions including words with several meanings will result in ambiguous answers. For example, the answer to the question "How much bread do you have?" depends on whether the respondent thinks of bread as coming in loaves or dollar bills.

In cross-cultural research the use of appropriate wording is especially important. For researchers to compare answers across cultures, questions should be equivalent in meaning. For example, the question "Are you interested in politics?" may be interpreted as "Do you vote in elections?" or "Do you belong to a political party?" The interpretation would depend on the country or culture of the respondent.

Questions also should be personal and relevant to the respondent. For example in a questionnaire on abortion, the question "Have you ever had an abortion?" could be changed to "Have you [your wife, girlfriend] ever had an abortion?" This will permit the researcher to include the responses of men as well as women.

Questions should also be worded and selected for the research purpose and survey population at hand. This does not mean, however, that every researcher must formulate questions anew, as Seymour Sudman and Norman Bradburn point out.[10] They advise researchers to review questions asked by others. Copies of questionnaires are included in book-length research reports or may be obtained by writing to the authors of journal articles. The following general sources include survey questions:

New York Times Index (for CBS News/*New York Times* polls)

The Gallup Poll: Public Opinion, 1935-1971 (Gallup, 1972) and *The Gallup Poll: Public Opinion, 1972-1977* (Gallup, 1978) with annual updates from 1979 to the present

General Social Surveys, 1972-1990: Cumulative Codebook (National Opinion Research Center, 1990)

Index to International Public Opinion, 1978-1979 (Hastings & Hastings, 1980)

Measures of Political Attitudes (Robinson, Ruse, & Head, 1968)

Public Opinion (opinion roundup section)

Public Opinion Quarterly (polls section)

Survey Data for Trend Analysis: An Index to Repeated Questions in U.S. National Surveys (Roper Public Opinion Research Center, 1974).[11]

Using existing questions has numerous benefits for the researcher. Replication and the ability to compare research results with previous research is an important aspect of accumulating scientific knowledge. Repeated use of questions in similar contexts with similar results indicates reliability of measurement. Repeated use also may allow estimates of trends.[12] Before using a question, a researcher should find out whether permission is needed; usually it is not.

Attention to these basic guidelines for question wording increases the probability that respondents will interpret a question consistently and as intended, yielding reliable and valid responses.

Question Type

The form or type of question as well as its specific wording is important. There are two basic types of questions: closed-ended and open-ended. Closed-ended questions provide the respondent with responses from which to choose. "Do you agree or disagree with the statement that the government ought to do more to help farmers?" and "Do you think that penalties for drunk driving are too severe, too lenient, or just about right?" are two examples of closed-ended questions.

A variation of the closed-ended question is a question with multiple choices for the respondent to accept or reject. A question with multiple choices is really a series of closed-ended questions. Consider the following example: "Numerous strategies have been proposed concerning the federal budget deficit. Please indicate whether you find the following alternatives acceptable or unacceptable: raise income taxes, adopt a national sales tax, reduce military spending, reduce spending on domestic programs."

In an open-ended question, the respondent is not provided with any answers from which to choose. The respondent or interviewer writes down the answer. Examples of open-ended questions are: "What do you think is the biggest problem facing the country today?" and "Is there anything you particularly like about Candidate A?"

Closed-ended Questions: Advantages and Disadvantages. The main advantage of a closed-ended question is that it is easy to answer and takes little time. Also the answers can be precoded (that is, assigned a number) and the code then easily transferred from the questionnaire to a computer. Another advantage is that answers are easy to compare since all responses fall into a fixed number of predetermined categories. These advantages aid in the quick statistical analysis of data. In open-ended questions, on the other hand, the researcher must read each answer, decide which answers are equivalent, decide how many categories or different types of answers to code, and assign codes before the data can be computerized.

Another advantage of closed-ended questions over open-ended ones is that respondents are usually willing to respond on personal or sensitive topics (for example, income, age, frequency of sexual activity, or political views) by choosing a category rather than stating the actual answer. This is especially true if the answer categories include ranges. Finally, closed-ended questions may help clarify the question for the respondent, thus avoiding misinterpretations of the question and unusable answers for the researcher.

Critics of closed-ended questions charge that they force a respondent to choose an answer category that may not accurately represent his or her position. Therefore, the response has less meaning and is less useful to the researcher. Also closed-ended questions often are phrased so that a respondent must choose between two alternatives or state which one is preferred. This may result in an oversimplified and distorted picture of public opinion. A closed-ended question allowing multiple choices does not force a respondent to choose simply between alternatives. The information produced by the question indicates which choices are acceptable to a majority of respondents. This knowledge may be much more useful to policy makers in fashioning a policy that is acceptable to most people.

Just as the wording of a question may influence responses, so may the wording of response choices. Changes in the wording of question responses can result in different response distributions. An example of this problem is a question concerning troop withdrawal from Vietnam.[13] A June 1969 Gallup Poll question asked:

> President Nixon has ordered the withdrawal of 25,000 United States troops from Vietnam in the next three months. How do you feel about this—do you think troops should be withdrawn at a faster rate or a slower rate?

The answer "same as now" was not presented but was accepted if given. The response distribution was: faster, 42 percent; same as now, 29 percent; slower, 16 percent; no opinion, 13 percent. Compare the responses with those to a September-October 1969 Harris Poll. Respondents were asked:

> In general, do you feel the pace at which the president is withdrawing troops is too fast, too slow, or about right?

Responses to this question were: too slow, 28 percent; about right, 49 percent; too fast, 6 percent; no opinion, 18 percent.

Thus, depending on the question, support for presidential plans varied from 29 percent to 49 percent. This clearly shows the effect of question wording. The difference in response is a result of whether respondents were directly given the choice of agreeing with presidential policy or had to mention such a response spontaneously.

Response categories may also contain leading or biased language and may not provide respondents with equal opportunities to agree or disagree. Response distributions may also be affected by whether a question asks the respondent to agree or disagree with a single substantive statement or offers the respondent two substantive choices. An example of a one-sided question is:

> Do you agree or disagree with the idea that the government should see to it that every person has a job and a good standard of living?

The two-sided question is:

> Do you think that the government should see to it that every person has a job and a good standard of living, or should it let each person get ahead on his or her own?

With a single-sided question there is a tendency for a larger percentage of respondents to agree with the statement given. Forty-four percent of the respondents to the single-sided question agreed that the government should guarantee employment, while only 30.3 percent of the respondents given the two-sided question chose this position.[14] It has also been found that presenting two substantive choices reduces the proportion of respondents who give no opinion.[15]

Closed-ended questions may provide inappropriate choices, thus leading many respondents not to answer or to choose the "other" category. Unless space is provided to explain "other" (which then makes the question resemble an open-ended one), it is anybody's guess what "other" means. Another problem is that errors may enter into the data if the wrong response code is marked. With no written answer, inadvertent errors cannot be checked. A problem also arises with questions having a great many possible answers. It is time consuming to have an interviewer read a long list of fixed responses that the respondent may forget. A solution to this problem is to use a *response card*. Responses are typed on a card that is handed to the respondent to read and choose from.

Open-ended Questions: Advantages and Disadvantages. Unstructured, free-response questions allow respondents to state what they know and think. They are not forced to choose between fixed responses that do not apply. Open-ended questions allow the respondent to tell the researcher how he or she defines a complex issue or concept. As one survey researcher in favor of open-ended questions points out, "Presumably, although this is often forgotten, the main purpose of an interview, the most important goal of the entire survey profession, is to let the respondent have his say, to let him tell the researcher what he means, not vice versa. If we do not let the respondent have his say, why bother to interview him at all?" [16]

Sometimes researchers are unable to specify in advance all possible responses to a question. In this situation, an open-ended question is appropriate. Open-ended questions are also appropriate if the researcher is trying to test the knowledge of respondents. Respondents are better able to *recognize* names of candidates in a closed-ended question (that is, pick the candidates from a list of names) than they are able to *recall* names in response to an open-ended question about candidates. Using only one question or the other would yield an incomplete picture of citizens' awareness of candidates.

Paradoxically, a disadvantage of the open-ended question is that respondents may respond too much or too little. Some may reply at great length about an issue—a time-consuming and costly problem for the researcher. If open-ended questions are included on mailed surveys, some respondents with poor writing skills may not answer. This may bias responses. Thus the use of open-ended questions depends upon the type of survey. Another problem is that interviewers may err in recording a respondent's answer. Recording answers verbatim is tedious. Furthermore, unstructured answers may be difficult to code, interpretations of answers may vary (affecting the reliability of data), and processing answers may become time consuming and costly. For these reasons, open-ended questions are often avoided—although unnecessarily, in Patricia Labaw's opinion:

> I believe that coding costs have now been transferred into data-processing costs. To substitute for open questions, researchers lengthen their questionnaires with endless lists of multiple choice and agree/disagree statements, which are then handled by sophisticated data-processing analytical techniques to try to massage some pattern or meaning out of the huge mass of precoded and punched data. I have found that a well-written open-ended question can eliminate the need for several closed questions, and that subsequent data analysis becomes clear and easy compared to the obfuscation provided by data massaging. [17]

Question Order

The order in which questions are presented to respondents may influence the reliability and validity of answers. In ordering questions, the researcher should consider the impact on the respondent of the previous question, the likelihood of the respondent's completing the questionnaire, and the need to select out groups of respondents for certain questions. In many ways, answering a survey is a learning situation, and previous questions can be expected to influence subsequent answers. This presents problems as well as opportunities for the researcher.

The first several questions are usually designed to break the ice. They are general questions that are easy to answer. Complex, specific questions may cause respondents to terminate an interview or not complete a questionnaire because they think it will be too hard. Questions on personal or sensitive topics usually are left to the end. Otherwise some respondents may suspect that the purpose of the survey is to check up on them rather than to find out public attitudes and activities in general. In some cases, however, it may be important to collect demographic information first. In a study of attitudes toward abortion, one researcher used demographic information to infer the responses of those who terminated the interview. She found that older, low-income women were most likely to terminate the interview on the abortion section. Since their group matched those who completed the interviews and who were strongly opposed to abortion, she concluded that termination expressed opposition to abortion.[18]

One problem to avoid is known as a *response set* or *straight-line responding*. A response set may occur when there is a series of questions with the same answer choices. A person finding himself "agreeing" with the first several statements may skim over subsequent statements and also check "agree." This is likely to happen if statements are on related topics. To avoid the response set phenomenon, statements should be worded so that the respondent may agree with the first, disagree with the second, and so on. This way the respondent is forced to read each statement carefully before responding.

Additional *question-order effects* include saliency, redundancy, consistency, and fatigue.[19] *Saliency* is the effect that specific mention of an issue in a survey may have in causing a respondent to mention the issue in connection with a later question: the earlier question brings the issue forward in the respondent's mind. For example, a researcher should not be surprised if respondents mention crime as a problem in response to a general question on problems affecting their community if the survey had earlier asked them about crime in the community. *Redundancy* is the reverse of saliency. Some respondents, unwilling to repeat themselves, may not say crime is a problem in response to the general query if earlier they had indicated that crime was a problem. Respondents may also strive to appear *consistent*. An answer to a question may be constrained by an answer given earlier. Finally, *fatigue* may cause respondents to give perfunctory answers to questions late in the survey. In lengthy questionnaires, response set problems often arise due to fatigue.[20]

Lee Sigelman has explored the effects of question order in presidential popularity polls.[21] He found that placing the presidential popularity item early in the survey elicited more "no opinion" answers than occurred when it was asked toward the end of the interview. This is explained by the tendency of respondents to respond in a safe or socially desirable way early in an interview before their critical faculties have been fully engaged and before they begin to trust the interviewer. Since presidential popularity is measured in terms of all Gallup Poll respondents, including those with no opinions, the percentage of people approving or disapproving of a president will be deflated by early placement of the question.

Another study tested the assumption that specific questions create a saliency effect that influences answers to more general questions.[22] People were found to express significantly more interest in politics and religion when these questions followed specific questions on political and religious matters. However, respondents' evaluations of the seriousness of energy and economic problems were not affected by previous questions about these problems. Perhaps interest is more easily influenced by question order than is evaluation because evaluation questions require more discriminating, concrete responses than do interest questions. The study also suggests that if specific questions about behavior are asked first, they give respondents concrete, behavioral references for answering later on a related, more general question.[23] For example, the answer to "How actively do you engage in sports?" may depend on whether the respondent had first been asked about participation in a number of specific sporting activities.

The learning that takes place during an interview may be an important aspect of the research being conducted. The researcher may intentionally use this process to find out more about the respondent's attitudes and potential behavior. Labaw refers to this as "leading" the respondent and notes it is used "to duplicate the effects of information, communication and education on the respondent in real life."[24] The extent of a respondent's approval or opposition to an issue may be clarified as the interviewer introduces new information about the issue.

In some cases such education *must* be done to elicit needed information on public opinion. For example, one study set out to evaluate public opinion on ethical issues in biomedical research.[25] Because the public is generally uninformed about the issues, some way had to be devised to enable respondents to make meaningful judgments. The researchers developed a procedure of presenting "research vignettes." Each vignette described or illustrated a dilemma actually encountered in biomedical research. A series of questions asking respondents to make ethical judgments followed each vignette. Such a procedure was felt to provide an appropriate decision-making framework for meaningful, spontaneous answers and a standard stimulus for respondents. A majority of persons were able to express meaningful and consistent opinions, even those with less than a high school education.

If there is no specific reason for placing questions in a particular order, researchers may vary questions randomly to control question order bias. Computerized word processing of questionnaires makes this an easier task.[26]

Question order also becomes an important consideration when the researcher wants to sort respondents into subgroups and direct these subgroups to different parts of the questionnaire using branching questions. This is called *routing respondents*. For example, a marketing survey on new car purchases may sort people into several groups: one that has bought a car in the past year, one that is contemplating buying a car in the next year, and one that is not anticipating buying a car in the foreseeable future. For each group a different set of questions about automobile purchasing may be appropriate. Questions that sort people into different groups are called *filters*, a valuable tool to prevent the uninformed from answering questions. For example, respondents in the 1980 National Election Study were given a list of presidential candidates and asked to mark those names they had never heard of or didn't know much about. Respondents were then asked questions only about those names that they hadn't marked.

Branching questions increase chances for interviewer and respondent error.[27] Questions to be answered by all respondents may be missed. However, careful attention to questionnaire layout, clear instructions to interviewer and respondent, and well-ordered questions will minimize the possibility of confusion and lost or inappropriate information.

Questionnaire Design

The term *questionnaire design* refers to the physical layout and packaging of the questionnaire. An important goal of questionnaire design is to make the questionnaire attractive and easy for the interviewer and respondent to follow. Good design increases the likelihood that the questionnaire will be completed properly. Design may also make the transfer of data from the questionnaire to the computer easier.

Design considerations are most important for mailed questionnaires. First, the researcher must make a favorable impression based almost entirely on the questionnaire materials mailed to the respondent. Second, because there is no interviewer present to explain the questionnaire to the respondent, a mailed questionnaire must be self-explanatory. Poor design increases respondent error and nonresponse. Whereas telephone and personal interviewers can and should familiarize themselves with questionnaires before administering them to a respondent, the recipient of a mailed questionnaire cannot be expected to spend much time trying to figure out a poorly designed form.

Mailed Questionnaires and Telephone and Personal Interviews

Now that we have considered basic aspects of survey instrument construction, let us turn our attention to the three major ways of administering surveys. In a mailed survey, questionnaires are mailed to the respondent to be filled out at his or her convenience without the presence of the researcher or interviewer. In the telephone and personal interviews, an interviewer asks the respondent questions and records answers. Until recently, survey research connoted personal interviews: telephone and mailed surveys were considered inferior. Now, however, some consider telephone and mailed surveys superior to the personal interview in certain situations.

The three types of surveys will be compared with respect to response rate, population coverage, response quality, and cost and administrative requirements. These four factors account for much of the debate and research on the relative merits of the survey types. As Floyd Fowler points out, researchers may be able to combine mail, telephone, and personal interviews in a research project in order to take advantage of the particular strengths of each type.[28] Often researchers must make compromises in choosing a survey instrument. As Don Dillman notes, "The use of any of the three [types] requires accepting less of certain qualities to achieve others, the desirability of which cannot be isolated from a consideration of the survey topic and the population to be studied."[29]

Response Rate. Response rate refers to the proportion of persons selected for participation in a survey who actually participate. If this proportion is low, either because persons cannot be reached or because they refuse to participate, the ability to make statistical inferences for the population being studied may be limited. Also those who do participate may differ systematically from those who do not, thereby biasing survey results. Increasing the size of the survey sample to compensate for low response rates may increase costs.

At one time, response rates were clearly superior for personal interview surveys of the general population than for other types of surveys. Response rates of 80 percent to 85 percent were often required for federally funded surveys.[30] Higher response rates were not uncommon. By the 1970s, however, response rates for personal interview surveys declined. In 1979, it was reported that in "the central cities of large metropolitan areas the final proportion of respondents that are located *and* consent to an interview is declining to a rate sometimes close to 50 percent." [31]

In general, the decrease in response rates for personal interview surveys has been attributed to both an increased difficulty in contacting respondents and an increased reluctance among the population to participate in surveys. There are more households now in which all adults work outside the home, which makes it difficult for interviewers to get responses. In large cities, nonresponse is due to a number of additional factors: respondents are less likely to be home and are more likely to speak foreign languages; interviewers are less likely to enter neighborhoods after dark; and security arrangements in multiple-unit apartment buildings make it difficult for interviewers to reach potential respondents. Because of poor working conditions, it is hard to find skilled and experienced interviewers to work in large cities. In smaller cities and towns, people also have shown an increased tendency to refuse to participate in surveys.[32]

Higher refusal rates may be due to greater distrust of strangers and fear of crime as well as to the increased number of polls. For example, in one study of respondents' attitudes toward surveys, about one-third did not believe that survey participation benefited the respondent or influenced government.[33] An equal number thought that too many surveys were conducted and that too many personal questions were asked. Some survey researchers feared that the National Privacy Act, which requires researchers to inform respondents that their participation is voluntary, would lead to more refusals. However, one study found that privacy concerns and past survey experience were more frequent reasons for refusals than reminders of the voluntary nature of participation.[34]

Some of these findings about why people do not participate in personal interview surveys raise the possibility that survey research of all types may become increasingly difficult. The effect of increased nonresponse has been to reduce the advantage of the personal interview over mailed and telephone surveys. In fact, response rates rivaling those for personal interviews have been achieved by Don Dillman using his "total design method" for mail and telephone surveys.[35] He concludes that the chance someone will agree to be surveyed is best for the personal interview. Telephone interviews are a close second, followed by mailed surveys. Other research comparing response rates of telephone and personal interview surveys have found little difference.[36]

It is often thought that personal interviews can obtain higher response rates because the interviewer can ask neighbors the best time to contact a respondent who is not at home, thus making return visits more efficient and effective. But repeated efforts by interviewers to contact respondents in person are expensive. Much less expensive are repeated telephone calls, even long distance ones, if special telephone services like WATS lines are used.

Two norms of telephone usage contribute to success in contacting respondents and completing telephone interviews.[37] First, most people feel compelled to answer the phone when it rings. A telephone call represents the potential for a positive social exchange. With the advent of telephone solicitation and surveys, this norm may be revised, however. A potential obstacle to telephone surveys is something called *common channel interoffice signaling* (CCIS).[38] Developed in response to junk phone calls, this system permits a person to know the origin of an incoming call, and it can be used to screen and redirect unwanted calls. If CCIS becomes more widely available, telephone surveys may become more difficult to conduct.

A second norm of telephone usage is that the initiator should terminate the call. This norm gives the interviewer the opportunity to introduce himself or herself. And in a telephone interview the introductory statement is crucial. Because the respondent lacks any visual cues about the caller, there is uncertainty and distrust. Unless the caller can quickly alleviate the respondent's discomfort, the norm of caller termination may be short lived, and the respondent may hang up. For this reason telephone interviews are more likely to be terminated before completion than personal interviews. It is harder to ask the interviewer to leave than it is to hang up the phone. One advantage of mailed surveys is that designated respondents who have changed their address may still be reached since the postal service forwards mail for about a year; it is not as easy in phone surveys to track down persons who have moved. In personal and telephone interviews it is also harder to change the minds of those who initially refuse to be interviewed since personal contact is involved and respondents may view repeated requests as harassment. Mailed recontacts are less personal.[39]

Because of the importance attached to high response rates, much research on how to achieve them has been conducted. For example, an introductory letter sent prior to a telephone interview was found to reduce refusal rates.[40] In fact, as a result there may be no significant difference in response rates between telephone and personal surveys.[41] Researchers have also investigated the best times to find people at home. One study found that for telephone interviews, evening hours are best (6:00 to 6:59 especially), with little variation by day (weekends excluded).[42] Another study concluded that the best times for finding someone at home were late afternoon and early evening during weekdays; Saturday until four in the afternoon was the best day overall.[43]

Since mailed surveys usually have the poorest response rates, many researchers have investigated ways to increase responses to them.[44] Incentives (money, pens, and other token gifts) have been found to be effective, and prepaid incentives are better than promised incentives. Follow-up, prior contact, type of postage, sponsorship, and title of the person who signs the accompanying letter are also important factors in improving response rates. A telephone call prior to mailing a survey may increase response rates by alerting a respondent to its arrival. Telephone calls also are a quick method of reminding respondents to complete and return questionnaires. Good follow-up procedures allow a researcher to distinguish between respondents who have replied and those who have not without violating the anonymity of respondents' answers.[45] Generally, mailed surveys work best when the population is highly literate and interested in the research problem.[46]

In sum, response rates are an important consideration in survey research. When evaluating research findings based on survey research, you should check the response rate and what measures, if any, were taken to increase it. Should you ever conduct a survey of your own, there is a wealth of information that will help you to achieve adequate response rates.

Representativeness of Respondents. Bias can enter survey results either through the initial selection of respondents or through incomplete participation of those selected. In each of the survey methods, these problems arise to varying degrees. If all members of a population can be listed, there is an equal opportunity for all members to be included in the sample. This is rarely the case, however. Personal interviews based on area probability sampling that gives each household an equal chance of being selected are likely to be more representative than mailed or telephone surveys based on published lists, which are often incomplete. *Random digit dialing* (the use of randomly generated telephone numbers instead of telephone directories) and correcting for households with more than one number has improved the representativeness of telephone samples. Thus people who have unlisted numbers or new numbers may be included in the sample. Otherwise a telephone survey may be biased by the exclusion of these households. Estimates of the number of households in the United States that do not have phones vary from 10 percent to 2 percent, while only about 5 percent of the dwelling units are missed with personal interview sampling procedures.[47]

Sometimes researchers make substitutions if respondents cannot or will not participate. Substituting another member of a household may bias results if the survey specifically asks about the respondent rather than the respondent's household. Substituting another household from the same block for personal surveys is better than substituting another telephone number since city blocks tend to be homogeneous whereas there is no way to estimate the similarity of households reached by telephone. Substitution of respondents in mailed surveys may pose a special problem. The researcher cannot control whether the intended respondent or another member of the household completed the questionnaire. The extent of bias thus introduced by substitution of respondents depends on the nature of the survey.

As mentioned earlier, one of the major reasons for concern over response rates is the possibility that those who do not respond will differ from those who do.[48] There is ample evidence that those who refuse to participate differ from those who respond. Blacks have been found more likely to refuse telephone interviews.[49] Refusals are also more common among older, middle-class persons, urban residents, and westerners.[50] For personal and telephone interviews, techniques to randomly select a member of the household to participate in the survey are often used. They may not result in perfect random selection of respondents, however. One method, the Troldahl-Carter method, bases selection on the number of adult males living at the address. Some females living alone feel threatened by this question, though, and refuse to participate. The next-birthday method, which selects the adult having the next birthday, results in fewer refusals and therefore less bias in selecting households.[51]

The amount of bias introduced by nonresponse due to refusal or unavailability varies depending on the purpose of the study and the explanatory factors stressed by the research. For example, if urbanization was a key explanatory variable and refusals were concentrated in urban areas, the study could misrepresent respondents from urban areas because the urban respondents who agreed to participate could differ systematically from those who refused. The personal interview provides the best direct opportunity to judge the characteristics of refusers and estimate whether their refusal will bias the survey.[52]

Response Quality. The opportunities to obtain quality responses differ according to the type of survey used. Mailed surveys may have an advantage in obtaining truthful answers to threatening or embarrassing questions. Anonymity can be assured and answers given in private. A mailed survey also gives the respondent enough time to finish when it is convenient; this enables the respondent to check records to provide accurate information, something that is harder to arrange for in telephone and personal interviews.

Disadvantages to the mailed survey include problems with open-ended questions. Some respondents may lack writing skills or find answering at length a burden. There is no interviewer present to probe for more information or to clear up confusion over complex or baffling questions. Further drawbacks to mailed surveys include limits to the

188 Political Science Research Methods

length, the researcher's inability to control the sequence in which the respondent answers questions and to motivate the respondent to answer tedious or boring questions, and the lack of control over who else may contribute to or influence answers.

Personal and telephone interviews share many advantages and disadvantages with respect to obtaining quality responses, although there are also some important differences. Several of the advantages of personal and telephone interviews over mailed surveys stem from the presence of an interviewer. As noted earlier, an interviewer may lead to better quality data by explaining questions, by probing for more information to open-ended questions, and by making observations about the respondent and his or her environment (for example, for a personal interview, quality of furnishings and housing as an indicator of income; for a telephone interview, amount of background noise that might affect the respondent's concentration).

In a personal interview, the interviewer may note that another household member is influencing a respondent's answers and take steps to avoid it. Influence by others is generally not a problem with telephone interviews since only the respondent hears the questions. One response quality problem that does occur with telephone interviews is that the respondent may not be giving the interviewer his or her undivided attention. This may be difficult for the interviewer to detect and correct.

Interviewers are expected to motivate the respondents. Generally it has been thought that warm, friendly interviewers who develop a good rapport with respondents motivate them to give quality answers and to complete the survey. Yet some research has begun to question the importance of rapport.[53] Friendly, neutral, "rapport-style" interviews in which interviewers give only positive feedback no matter what the response may not be good enough, especially if the questions involve difficult reporting tasks. Feedback that is both positive ("yes, that's the kind of information we want") and negative ("that's only two things") may improve response quality. Interviewers also may need to instruct respondents about how to give complete and accurate information. This more businesslike, task-oriented style has been found to lead to better reporting than the rapport-style interview.[54]

Interviewer style appears to make less difference in telephone interviews, perhaps because of the lack of visual cues for the respondent to judge the interviewer's sincerity.[55] Even something as simple as intonation, however, may affect data quality: interviewers whose voices go up rather than down at the end of a question appear to motivate a respondent's interest in reporting.[56]

Despite the advantages of interviewers in improving response quality, the interviewer-respondent interaction may bias a respondent's answers. The interviewer may give a respondent the impression that certain answers are expected or right. For example, interviewers who anticipate difficulties in persuading respondents to respond or to report sensitive behavior have been found to obtain lower response and reporting rates.[57] The age, sex, or race of the interviewer may affect the respondent's willingness to give honest answers. For example, on racial questions, respondents interviewed by a member of another race have been found to be more deferential to the interviewer (that is, try harder not to cause offense) than those interviewed by a member of their own race.[58] Education has an impact on race-of-interviewer effects: less educated blacks are more deferential than better educated blacks and better educated whites more deferential than less educated whites.[59]

Interviewer bias may have a larger impact on telephone surveys than on mailed surveys.[60] The efficiency of telephone interviewing requires fewer interviewers to complete the same number of interviews as compared to personal interviews. Also telephone interviewers, even for national surveys, do not need to be geographically dispersed, so that the same interviewers can be used for a greater number of interviews. Centralization of telephone interviewing operations, however, allows closer supervision and monitoring of interviewers, making it easier to identify and control interviewer problems. For both personal and telephone interviewers, interview training and practice is an essential part of the research process.

A number of studies have compared response quality for personal and telephone interviews. One expected difference is in answers to open-ended questions. Telephone interviewers lack visual cues for probing. Thus telephone interviews tend to be quickly paced; pausing to see if the respondent adds more to an answer is more awkward on the telephone than in person. Research findings, however, have been mixed. One study found that shorter answers were given to open-ended questions in telephone interviews, especially among respondents who typically give complete and detailed responses; another study found no differences between personal and telephone interviews in the number of responses to open-ended questions.[61] Asking an open-ended question early in a telephone survey helps to relax the respondent, reduce the pace of the interview, and ensure that the respondent is thinking about his or her answers.[62]

Response quality for telephone interviews may be lowered because of the difficulty of asking complex questions or questions with many response categories over the phone. Research has found more acquiescence, evasiveness, and extremeness in telephone survey responses than in personal survey responses. In addition, phone respondents give more contradictory answers to checklist items and are less likely to admit to problems.[63] This finding contradicts the expectation that telephone interviews result in more accurate answers to sensitive questions due to reduced personal contact.

As we mentioned earlier, one advantage attributed to mailed questionnaires is greater privacy for the respondent in answering sensitive questions. Consequently, researchers using personal and telephone interviews have developed a number of techniques to obtain more accurate data on sensitive topics.[64] Many of these techniques depend on proper wording. For example, when asking questions about socially desirable behavior, a casual approach reduces the threat by lessening the perceived importance of the topic. The question "Did you happen to read any books this past month?" will likely result in more accurate answers than "What books did you read last month?" Giving respondents reasons for not doing something perceived as socially desirable also reduces threat and may cut down on overreporting.

A very different approach to the problem of obtaining accurate answers to sensitive questions is the *randomized response technique* (RRT).[65] This technique may reduce the disadvantage of personal and telephone interviews for asking sensitive questions. RRT is designed to allow respondents to answer sensitive questions truthfully without the interviewer knowing the question being answered. For example, the interviewer gives the respondent a card with two questions, one sensitive and one nonsensitive. A device such as a coin or a box with two colors of beads is used to randomly determine which question the respondent will answer. If a coin is used, the respondent will be instructed to answer one question if the tossed coin is a heads and the other if tails shows up. The respondent flips the coin, and without showing the interviewer the outcome of the toss, answers the appropriate question. To calculate the proportion of yes answers to the sensitive question, the expected proportion of yes answers to the nonsensitive question must be known. Thus the nonsensitive question could be "Were you born in July?" Assuming that birthdays are distributed equally among the months, one-twelfth of the respondents would be expected to say yes to the nonsensitive question. Or the proportion of persons exhibiting the nonsensitive behavior could be estimated by asking a sample population a direct question about the nonsensitive behavior.[66] The proportion of respondents answering yes to the sensitive question can be calculated using the formula:

$$R_{yes} = P(S_{yes}) + (1 - P)(N_{yes}) \qquad (8.1)$$

Where

R_{yes} = probability of obtaining yes answer to random question
P = probability of respondent choosing sensitive question
$1 - P$ = probability of respondent choosing nonsensitive question
S_{yes} = proportion of respondents exhibiting sensitive behavior
N_{yes} = proportion of respondents exhibiting nonsensitive behavior

Continued

Therefore

$$S_{yes} = \frac{R_{yes} - (1 - P)(N_{yes})}{P}$$

Let's assume that out of 1,000 respondents, we get 500 "yes" responses and that we have estimates showing that 80 percent of our sample should answer "yes" to the nonsensitive question. If a balanced coin is used, P equals .5. Making the substitutions, we get

$$S_{yes} = \frac{500/1000 - (1 - .5)(.80)}{.5} = \frac{.5 - .5(.80)}{.5} = .20 \text{ or } 20\% \qquad (8.2)$$

The accuracy of RRT depends on the assumption that a respondent will answer both the sensitive and nonsensitive questions truthfully. The success in obtaining accurate information depends on the respondent's ability to understand the method and follow instructions and his or her belief that the random-choice device is not rigged.[67] The technique seems to work better when the nonsensitive question deals with a socially positive activity, thus further reducing the stigma attached to a "yes" response.[68]

Research has found RRT superior to other methods of asking threatening questions, such as having the respondent answer a direct question and return it in a sealed envelope.[69] For example, use of RRT produced higher estimates of abortion than previous measures.[70] RRT can be used for telephone as well as personal interviews. Random-choice devices can be supplied by the respondent—thus eliminating suspicion that the device is fixed—or they can be mailed by the researcher to the respondent.[71]

Cost and Administrative Requirements. When deciding between personal interviews, telephone interviews, and mailed surveys, cost and administrative considerations are important. Among the factors determining survey costs are the amount of professional time required for questionnaire design, the length of the questionnaire, the geographic dispersion of the sample, callback procedures, respondent selection rules, and availability of trained staff.[72]

Personal interview surveys are the most expensive due to the cost of hiring experienced, well-qualified interviewers who are willing to tolerate working conditions that are becoming less attractive. National surveys also incur greater administrative costs. Regional supervisory personnel must be hired and survey instruments mailed back and forth between the researcher and interviewers. While mailed surveys are thought to be less expensive than telephone surveys, Fowler argues that the cost of properly executed mail surveys is likely to be very similar to that of telephone surveys.[73]

Compared with personal interview surveys, telephone surveys have numerous administrative advantages.[74] Despite the cost of long-distance calls, centralization of survey administration is advantageous. Training of telephone interviewers is easier, and flexible working hours are attractive. But the real advantages to telephone survey administration begin after interviewing starts. Greater supervision of interviewers and quick feedback to them is possible. Also interviewers can easily inform researchers of any problems they encounter with the survey. Coders can begin coding data immediately. If they discover any errors, they can inform interviewers before a large problem emerges. With proper facilities, interviewers may be able to code respondents' answers directly on computer terminals. In some cases, the whole interview schedule may be computerized, with questions and responses displayed on a screen in front of the interviewer. These are known as *computer assisted telephone interviews.* The development of computer and telephone technologies gives telephone surveys a significant time advantage over personal interviews and mailed surveys. Telephone interviews may be completed and data analyzed almost immediately.[75]

As researchers and research organizations gain experience in telephone surveys, further developments are likely to occur that will reduce the cost of this method. For example, advances continue to be made in improving the efficiency of random digit dialing.[76] The efficiency of telephone surveys was also improved by a study that found that almost 97 percent of households are reached with four rings and more than 99 percent with five rings; extra rings waste time and money.[77]

Telephone surveys are particularly good for situations in which statistically rare subgroups must be reached or estimated. For example, a telephone survey was used to estimate the disabled population in an area (the only problem being that the hearing impaired were underestimated).[78] A large sample was required to obtain enough disabled persons for the survey. Where large samples are required, telephone surveys are one-half to one-third the cost of personal interviews.[79] Telephone interviews cut down on the cost of screening the population. In some cases telephone surveys may be used to locate appropriate households, and then the survey itself may be completed by personal interview. Telephone surveys are also best if the research must be conducted in a short period of time. Personal surveys are not as fast, and mail surveys are quite slow.

The type of survey chosen by a researcher will depend on the population to be reached, response quality issues, representativeness of completed interviews, and cost and time factors. No one type of survey is superior in all situations. Sometimes a single factor may dictate the type of survey to be used. In other situations the choice will be less clear cut. In many situations researchers will communicate with respondents by mail, by telephone, and in person to ensure that data collection results in a high response rate and quality responses from a representative group of respondents.

Elite Interviewing

Elite interviewing is a special form of the personal interview. In his classic book *Elite and Specialized Interviewing*, Lewis Dexter defines an elite as anyone "who in terms of the current purposes of the interviewer is given special, nonstandardized treatment." [80]

Elite interviews usually differ substantially from the highly structured, standardized format of survey research discussed earlier.[81] There are a number of reasons for this difference. First, a researcher may lack sufficient understanding of events to be able to design an effective, structured survey instrument. The only way for researchers to learn about certain events is to interview participants or eyewitnesses directly. Second, a researcher is usually especially interested in an elite interviewee's own interpretation of events or issues and does not want to lose the valuable information that an elite "insider" may possess by constraining responses. As one researcher put it, "A less structured format is relatively exploratory and stresses subject rather than researcher definitions of a problem." [82]

Finally, elite interviewees may resent being asked to respond to a standardized set of questions. In her study of Nobel laureates, for example, Harriet Zuckerman found that her subjects soon detected standardized questions. Because these were people used to being treated as individuals with minds of their own, they resented "being encased in the straightjacket of standardized questions." [83] Therefore, those who interview elites often vary the order in which topics are broached and the exact form of questions asked from interview to interview. Eliciting valid information from elites may require variability in approaches.[84]

Elite interviewing is not as simple as lining up a few interviews and chatting for a while. Researchers using elite interviews must consider numerous logistical and methodological questions. Advance preparation is extremely important. The researcher should study all available documentation of events and pertinent biographical material before interviewing elites.

Advance preparation serves many purposes. First, it saves the interviewee's time by eliminating questions that can be answered elsewhere. The researcher may ask the interviewee, however, to verify the accuracy of the information obtained from other sources. Second, it gives the researcher a basis for deciding what questions to ask and in what order. Third, advance preparation helps the researcher interpret and understand the significance of what is being said, to recognize a remark that sheds new light on a topic, and to catch inconsistencies between the interviewee's version and other versions of events. Fourth, it impresses the interviewee with the researcher's serious interest in the topic. At no time, however, should the researcher dominate the conversation to show off his or her knowledge. Finally, good preparation buoys the confidence of the novice researcher interviewing important people.

The ground rules that will apply to what is said in an interview should be made clear at the start.[85] When the interview is requested and at the beginning of the interview itself, the researcher should mention whether confidentiality is desired. If he or she promises confidentiality, the researcher should be careful not to reveal a person's identity in written descriptions. A touchy problem in confidentiality may arise if questions are based on previous interviews. It may be possible for an interviewee to guess the identity of the person whose comments must have prompted a particular question.

A researcher may desire and promise confidentiality in the hope that the interviewee will be more candid.[86] Interviewees may request confidentiality if they fear they may reveal something damaging to themselves or to others. Some persons may want to approve anything written based on what they have said. In any event, it often is beneficial to the researcher to give interviewees a chance to review what has been written about them and the opportunity to clarify and expand on what they said. Sometimes a researcher and interviewee may disagree over the content or interpretation of the interview. If the researcher has agreed to let an interviewee have final say on the use of an interview, the agreement should be honored. Otherwise the decision is the researcher's—to be made in light of the need of the researcher and those who follow for future access to elites.

Sometimes gaining access to elites is difficult. They may want further information about the purpose of the research or need to be convinced of the professionalism of the researcher. Important people often have "gatekeepers" who limit access to them. It is advisable to obtain references from people who are known to potential interviewees. Sometimes a person who has already been interviewed will assist a researcher in gaining access to other elites.

Two researchers encountered particular access problems in their study of the 1981 outbreaks of civil disorder in several British cities when they attempted to interview community activists.[87] These activists, whom the researchers termed the "counter-elite" or the "threatened elite," were reluctant to cooperate, even hostile. They feared that the findings might be abused, that the research was for the benefit of the establishment and part of a system of oppression, and that cooperation would jeopardize their standing in their community. Unlike conventional elites, they did not assume that social science research was useful.

Whom to interview first is a difficult decision for a researcher. Interviewing first the persons of lesser importance in an event or lower rank in an organization allows a researcher to become familiar with special terminology used by an elite group and more knowledgeable about a topic before interviewing key elites. It also may bolster a researcher's experience and confidence. Lower level personnel may be more candid and revealing about events because they are able to observe major participants and have less personal involvement. On the other hand, talking to superiors first may indicate to subordinates that being interviewed is permissible. Moreover, interviewing key elites first may provide a researcher with important information early on and make subsequent interviewing more efficient. Other factors, such as age of respondents, availability, and convenience, may also affect interview order.

A tape recorder or handwritten notes may be used to record an interview. There are numerous factors to consider in choosing between the two methods. Tape recording allows the researcher to think about what the interviewee is saying, to check notes, and to formulate follow-up questions. If the recording is clear, it removes the possibility of error about what is said. Disadvantages include the fact that everything is recorded. The material must then be transcribed (an expense) and read before useful data are at hand. Much of what is transcribed will not be useful—a problem of elite interviewing in general. A tape recorder may make some interviewees uncomfortable, and they may not be candid even if promised confidentiality; there can be no denying what is recorded. Sometimes the researcher will be unfamiliar with recording equipment and appear awkward.

Many researchers rely on handwritten notes taken during an interview. It is very important to write up interviews in more complete form soon after the interview, while it is still fresh in the researcher's mind. Typically this takes much longer than the interview itself, so enough time should be allotted. Only a few interviews should be scheduled in one day; after two or three, the researcher may not be able to distinctly recollect individual conversations.

How researchers go about conducting interviews will vary by topic, by researcher, and by respondent. Although elite interviews are usually not rigidly structured, researchers still may choose to exercise control and direction in an interview. Many researchers conduct what is called a *semistructured* or *focused interview*. They prepare an interview guide, including topics, questions, and the order in which they should be raised. Sometimes alternative forms of questions may be prepared. Generally the more exploratory the purpose of the research, the less topic control exercised by the researcher. Researchers who desire information about specific topics should communicate this need to the person being interviewed and exercise enough control over the interview to keep it on track.

Elite interviewing is difficult work. A researcher must listen, observe nonverbal behavior, think, and take notes all at the same time. Maintaining appropriate interpersonal relations is also required. A good rapport between the researcher and interviewee facilitates the flow of information, although it may be difficult to establish. For example, Zuckerman relates that one Nobel laureate she interviewed sat about four feet from her in a chair with rollers. By the end of the interview he had moved an additional ten feet away.

How aggressive should a researcher be in questioning elites? This question is often debated. Although aggressive questioning may yield more information and allow the researcher to ferret out misinformation, it also may alienate or irritate the interviewee. Zuckerman used the tactic of rephrasing the interviewee's comments in extreme form to elicit further details. In some cases the Nobel laureates expressed irritation that she had not understood what they had already said.[88]

Establishing the meaningfulness and validity of the data collected through elite interviewing is very important. Interview data may be biased by the questions and actions of the interviewer. Interviewees may give evasive or untruthful answers. As noted earlier, advance preparation may help an interviewer recognize remarks that differ from established fact. The validity of an interviewee's statements also may be determined by examining their plausibility, checking for internal consistency, and corroborating them with other interviewees. John Dean and William Whyte argue that a researcher should understand an interviewee's mental set and how it might affect his or her perception and interpretation of events.[89] Raymond Gordon stresses the value of being able to empathize with interviewees to understand the meaning of what they are saying.[90] Lewis Dexter warns that interviewing should be used only if "interviewers have enough relevant background to be sure that they can make sense out of interview conversations or unless there is reasonable hope of being able to ... learn what is meaningful and significant to ask." [91]

Conclusion

This chapter has introduced three main types of data—interview data, archival records, and data collected through direct observation—and discussed the two principal types of interviews—survey research and elite interviewing. Whether the interview is conducted over the phone, through the mail, or in person, the researcher attempts to elicit information that is accurate and informative. This goal is advanced by being attentive to how question wording, question type, question order, and questionnaire design affect the responses of those interviewed. The choice of an in-person, telephone, or mailed survey can also affect the quality of the data collected. Interviews of elite populations require attention to a special set of issues and generally result in a less structured type of interview. Although you may never be in a position to conduct a survey of your own, the information in this chapter should help you evaluate the survey research of others. Polls, surveys, and interview data have become so prevalent in American life that an awareness of the decisions made and problems encountered by survey researchers is necessary for rendering an independent judgment of survey results.

Notes

1. Norman M. Bradburn and Seymour Sudman, *Polls and Surveys: Understanding What They Tell Us* (San Francisco: Jossey-Bass, 1988), 62.
2. Ibid., 59.
3. Ibid., 60.
4. Margrit Eichler, *Nonsexist Research Methods: A Practical Guide* (Winchester, Mass: Allen & Unwin, Inc., 1988), 51-52.
5. Doris A. Graber, "Problems in Measuring Audience Effects of the 1976 Debate," in George F. Bishop, Robert G. Meadow, and Marilyn Jackson-Beeck, eds., *The Presidential Debates: Media, Electoral and Policy Perspectives* (New York: Praeger, 1978), 116.
6. Charles H. Backstrom and Gerald Hursh-Cesar, *Survey Research*, 2d ed. (New York: Wiley, 1981), 142, 146.
7. Ibid., 141.
8. Republican National Committee, *1980 Official Republican Poll on U.S. Defense and Foreign Policy.*
9. Eichler, *Nonsexist Research Methods*, 43-44.
10. Seymour Sudman and Norman M. Bradburn, *Asking Questions: A Practical Guide to Questionnaire Design* (San Francisco: Jossey-Bass, 1982), 15.
11. Ibid., 16-17; updated by the authors.
12. Ibid., 16.
13. John P. Dean and William Foote Whyte, "How Do You Know if the Informant Is Telling the Truth?" in Lewis Anthony Dexter, *Elite and Specialized Interviewing* (Evanston, Ill.: Northwestern University Press, 1970), 127.
14. Raymond L. Gordon, *Interviewing: Strategy, Techniques, and Tactics* (Homewood, Ill.: Dorsey, 1969), 18.
15. Dexter, *Elite and Specialized Interviewing*, 17.
16. Patricia J. Labaw, *Advanced Questionnaire Design* (Cambridge, Mass.: Abt Books, 1980), 132.
17. Ibid., 132-133.
18. Ibid., 117.
19. Norman M. Bradburn and W. M. Mason, "The Effect of Question Order on Responses," *Journal of Marketing Research* 1 (1964): 57-64.
20. A. Regula Herzog and Jerald G. Bachman, "Effects of Questionnaire Length on Response Quality," *Public Opinion Quarterly* 45 (1981): 549-559.
21. Lee Sigelman, "Question-Order Effects on Presidential Popularity," *Public Opinion Quarterly* 45 (1981): 199-207.
22. Sam G. MacFarland, "Effects of Question Order on Survey Responses," *Public Opinion Quarterly* 45 (1981): 208-215.
23. Ibid., 213, 214.

24. Labaw, *Advanced Questionnaire Design*, 122.
25. Glen D. Mellinger, Carol L. Huffine, and Mitchell B. Balter, "Assessing Comprehension in a Survey of Public Reactions to Complex Issues," *Public Opinion Quarterly* 46 (1982): 97-109.
26. William D. Perrault, Jr., "Controlling Order-Effect Bias," *Public Opinion Quarterly* 39 (1975): 544-551.
27. Donald J. Messmer and Daniel T. Seymour, "The Effects of Branching on Item Nonresponse," *Public Opinion Quarterly* 46 (1982): 270-277.
28. Floyd J. Fowler, *Survey Research Methods*, rev. ed. (Newbury Park, Calif: Sage, 1988), 61.
29. Don A. Dillman, *Mail and Telephone Surveys: The Total Design Method* (New York: Wiley, 1978), 40.
30. Earl R. Babbie, *Survey Research Methods* (Belmont, Calif.: Wadsworth, 1973), 171.
31. Robert M. Groves and Robert L. Kahn, *Surveys by Telephone: A National Comparison with Personal Interviews* (New York: Academic, 1979), 3.
32. Charlotte G. Steeh, "Trends in Nonresponse Rates, 1952-1979," *Public Opinion Quarterly* 45 (1981): 40-57.
33. Laure M. Sharp and Joanne Frankel, "Respondent Burden: A Test of Some Common Assumptions," *Public Opinion Quarterly* 47 (1983): 36-53.
34. Theresa J. DeMaio, "Refusals: Who, Where and Why," *Public Opinion Quarterly* 44 (1980): 223-233.
35. Dillman, *Mail and Telephone Surveys*.
36. See Theresa F. Rogers, "Interviews by Telephone and in Person: Quality of Responses and Field Performance," *Public Opinion Quarterly* 39 (1975): 51-64; and Groves and Kahn, *Surveys by Telephone*. Response rates are affected by different methods of calculating rates for the three types of surveys. For example, nonreachable and ineligible persons may be dropped from the total survey population for telephone and personal interviews before response rates are calculated. Response rates to mailed surveys are depressed because all nonresponses are assumed to be refusals, not ineligibles or nonreachables. Telephone response rates may be depressed if nonworking but ringing numbers are treated as nonreachable but eligible respondents. Telephone companies vary in their willingness to identify working numbers. If noneligibility is likely to be a problem in a mailed survey, ineligibles should be asked to return the questionnaire anyway so that they can be identified and distinguished from refusals.
37. James H. Frey, *Survey Research by Telephone* (Beverly Hills, Calif.: Sage, 1983), 15-16.
38. Ibid., 175.
39. Herschel Shosteck and William R. Fairweather, "Physician Response Rates to Mail and Personal Interview Surveys," *Public Opinion Quarterly* 43 (1979): 206-217.
40. Don A. Dillman, Jean Gorton Gallegos, and James H. Frey, "Reducing Refusal Rates for Telephone Interviews," *Public Opinion Quarterly* 40 (1976): 66-78.
41. Fowler, *Survey Research Methods*, 67.
42. Gideon Vigderhous, "Scheduling Telephone Interviews: A Study of Seasonal Patterns," *Public Opinion Quarterly* 45 (1981): 250-259.
43. M. F. Weeks et al., "Optimal Times to Contact Sample Households," *Public Opinion Quarterly* 44 (1980): 101-114.
44. See J. Scott Armstrong, "Monetary Incentive in Mail Surveys," *Public*

Opinion Quarterly 39 (1975): 111-116; Arnold S. Linsky, "Stimulating Responses to Mailed Questionnaires: A Review," *Public Opinion Quarterly* 39 (1975): 82-101; James R. Chromy and Daniel G. Horvitz, "The Use of Monetary Incentives in National Assessment Households Survey," *Journal of the American Statistical Association* 73 (1978): 473-478; Thomas A. Heberlein and Robert Baumgartner, "Factors Affecting Response Rates to Mailed Questionnaires," *American Sociological Review* 43 (1978): 447-462; R. Kenneth Godwin, "The Consequences of Large Monetary Incentives in Mail Surveys of Elites," *Public Opinion Quarterly* 43 (1979): 378-387; Kent L. Tedin and C. Richard Hofstetter, "The Effect of Cost and Importance Factors on the Return Date for Single and Multiple Mailings," *Public Opinion Quarterly* 46 (1982): 122-128; Anton J. Nederhof, "The Effects of Material Incentives in Mail Surveys: Two Studies," *Public Opinion Quarterly* 47 (1983): 103-111; Charles D. Schewe and Norman G. Cournoyer, "Prepaid vs. Promised Monetary Incentives to Questionnaire Response: Further Evidence," *Public Opinion Quarterly* 40 (1976): 105-107; James R. Henley, Jr., "Response Rate to Mail Questionnaire with a Return Deadline," *Public Opinion Quarterly* 40 (1976): 374-375; Thomas A. Heberlein and Robert Baumgartner, "Is a Questionnaire Necessary in a Second Mailing?" *Public Opinion Quarterly* 45 (1981): 102-108; and Wesley H. Jones, "Generalized Mail Survey Inducement Methods: Population Interactions with Anonymity and Sponsorship," *Public Opinion Quarterly* 43 (1979): 102-111.

45. For detailed instructions on improving the response rate to mailed surveys, see Dillman, *Mail and Telephone Surveys.*

46. Fowler, *Survey Research Methods,* 63.

47. Groves and Kahn, *Surveys by Telephone,* 214; Frey, *Survey Research by Telephone.* 22.

48. For research estimating amount of bias introduced by nonresponse due to unavailability or refusal, see F. L. Filion, "Estimating Bias Due to Nonresponse in Mail Surveys," *Public Opinion Quarterly* 39 (1975): 482-492; Michael J. O'Neil, "Estimating the Nonresponse Bias Due to Refusals in Telephone Surveys," *Public Opinion Quarterly* 43 (1979): 218-232; and Arthur L. Stinchcombe, Calvin Jones, and Paul Sheatsley, "Nonresponse Bias for Attitude Questions," *Public Opinion Quarterly* 45 (1981): 359-375.

49. Carol S. Aneshensel et al., "Measuring Depression in the Community: A Comparison of Telephone and Personal Interviews," *Public Opinion Quarterly* 46 (1982): 110-121.

50. DeMaio, "Refusals," 223-233; and Steeh, "Trends in Nonresponse Rates," 40-57.

51. Charles T. Salmon and John Spicer Nichols, "The Next-Birthday Method of Respondent Selection," *Public Opinion Quarterly* 47 (1983): 270-276.

52. Dillman, *Mail and Telephone Surveys.*

53. See Willis J. Goudy and Harry R. Potter, "Interview Rapport: Demise of a Concept," *Public Opinion Quarterly* 39 (1975): 529-543; and Charles F. Cannell, Peter V. Miller and Lois Oksenberg, "Research on Interviewing Techniques," in Samuel Leinhardt, ed., *Sociological Methodology 1981* (San Francisco: Jossey-Bass, 1981), 389-437.

54. Rogers, "Interviews by Telephone and in Person," 51-65.

55. Ibid.; and Peter V. Miller and Charles F. Cannell, "A Study of Experimental Techniques for Telephone Interviewing," *Public Opinion Quarterly* 46 (1982): 250-269.

56. Arpad Barath and Charles F. Cannell, "Effect of Interviewer's Voice Intona-

tion," *Public Opinion Quarterly* 40 (1976): 370-373.
57. Eleanor Singer, Martin R. Frankel, and Marc B. Glassman, "The Effect of Interviewer Characteristics and Expectations on Response," *Public Opinion Quarterly* 47 (1983): 68-83; and Eleanor Singer and Luane Kohnke-Aguirre, "Interviewer Expectation Effects: A Replication and Extension," *Public Opinion Quarterly* 43 (1979): 245-260.
58. Patrick R. Cotter, Jeffrey Cohen, and Philip B. Coulter, "Race-of-Interviewer Effects in Telephone Interviews," *Public Opinion Quarterly* 46 (1982): 278-284; and Bruce A. Campbell, "Race of Interviewer Effects among Southern Adolescents," *Public Opinion Quarterly* 45 (1981): 231-244.
59. Shirley Hatchett and Howard Schuman, "White Respondents and Race-of-Interviewer Effects," *Public Opinion Quarterly* 39 (1975): 523-528; and Michael F. Weeks and R. Paul Moore, "Ethnicity of Interviewer Effects on Ethnic Respondents," *Public Opinion Quarterly* 45 (1981): 245-249.
60. See Singer, Frankel, and Glassman, "The Effect of Interviewer Characteristics and Expectations on Response"; Groves and Kahn, *Surveys by Telephone;* Dillman, *Mail and Telephone Surveys;* and John Freeman and Edgar W. Butler, "Some Sources of Interviewer Variance in Surveys," *Public Opinion Quarterly* 40 (1976): 79-91.
61. See Groves and Kahn, *Surveys by Telephone;* and Lawrence A. Jordan, Alfred C. Marcus, and Leo G. Reeder, "Response Styles in Telephone and Household Interviewing," *Public Opinion Quarterly* 44 (1980): 210-222.
62. Dillman, *Mail and Telephone Surveys.*
63. Jordan, Marcus, and Reeder, "Response Styles"; and Groves and Kahn, *Surveys by Telephone.* See also Rogers, "Interviews by Telephone and in Person."
64. For example, see Sudman and Bradburn, *Asking Questions,* 55-86; and Jerald G. Bachman and Patrick M. O'Malley, "When Four Months Equal a Year: Inconsistencies in Student Reports of Drug Use," *Public Opinion Quarterly* 45 (1981): 542.
65. RRT was first proposed by S. L. Warner in "Randomized Response," *Journal of the American Statistical Association* 60 (1965): 63-69.
66. S. M. Zdep and Isabelle N. Rhodes, "Making the Randomized Response Technique Work," *Public Opinion Quarterly* 40 (1976): 531-537.
67. Frederick Wiseman, Mark Moriarty, and Marianne Schafer, "Estimating Public Opinion with the Randomized Response Model," *Public Opinion Quarterly* 39 (1975): 507-513.
68. Zdep and Rhodes, "Making the Randomized Response Technique Work."
69. Ibid.
70. Iris M. Shimizu and Gordon Scott Bonham, "Randomized Response Technique in a National Survey," *Journal of the American Statistical Association* 73 (1978): 35-39.
71. Robert G. Orwin and Robert F. Boruch, "RRT Meets RDD: Statistical Strategies for Assuring Response Privacy in Telephone Surveys," *Public Opinion Quarterly* 46 (1982): 560-571.
72. Fowler, *Survey Research Methods,* 68.
73. Ibid.
74. Groves and Kahn, *Surveys by Telephone;* and Frey, *Survey Research by Telephone.*
75. Frey, *Survey Research by Telephone,* 24-25.
76. Joseph Waksberg, "Sampling Methods for Random Digit Dialing," *Journal of the American Statistical Association* 73 (1978): 40-46; and K. Michael

Cummings, "Random Digit Dialing: A Sampling Technique for Telephone Surveys," *Public Opinion Quarterly* 43 (1979): 233-244.

77. Raymond J. Smead and James Wilcox, "Ring Policy in Telephone Surveys," *Public Opinion Quarterly* 44 (1980): 115-116.

78. Howard E. Freeman et al., "Telephone Sampling Bias in Surveying Disability," *Public Opinion Quarterly* 46 (1982): 392-407.

79. Ibid.

80. Dexter, *Elite and Specialized Interviewing*, 5.

81. There are exceptions to this general rule, however. See John Kessel, *The Domestic Presidency* (Belmont, Calif.: Duxbury, 1975). Kessel administered a highly structured survey instrument to Richard Nixon's Domestic Council staff.

82. Joseph A. Pika, "Interviewing Presidential Aides: A Political Scientist's Perspective," in George C. Edwards III and Stephen J. Wayne, eds., *Studying the Presidency* (Knoxville: University of Tennessee Press, 1982), 282.

83. Harriet Zuckerman, "Interviewing an Ultra-Elite," *Public Opinion Quarterly* 36 (1972): 167.

84. Gordon, *Interviewing*, 49-50.

85. Dom Bonafede, "Interviewing Presidential Aides: A Journalist's Perspective" in *Studying the Presidency*, 269.

86. Richard F. Fenno, Jr., *Home Style: House Members in Their Districts* (Boston: Little, Brown, 1978), 280.

87. Margaret Wagstaffe and George Moyser, "The Threatened Elite: Studying Leaders in an Urban Community," in George Moyser and Margaret Wagstaffe, eds., *Research Methods for Elite Studies* (London: Allen & Unwin, 1987), 186-188.

88. Zuckerman, "Interviewing an Ultra-Elite," 174.

89. Dean and Whyte, "How Do You Know if the Informant Is Telling the Truth?" 127.

90. Gordon, *Interviewing*, 18.

91. Dexter, *Elite and Specialized Interviewing*, 17.

Terms Introduced

Ambiguous question. A question containing a concept that is not clearly defined.

Closed-ended question. A question with response alternatives provided.

Direct observation. A data collection method in which the researcher directly observes a behavior or physical traces of the behavior.

Document analysis. Data collection based on records kept by institutions or individuals.

Double-barreled question. A question that is really two questions in one.

Elite interviewing. Interviewing respondents in a nonstandardized, individualized manner.

Filter question. A question used to screen respondents so that subsequent questions will be asked only of certain respondents for whom the questions are appropriate.

Focused interview. A semistructured or flexible interview schedule used when interviewing elites.

Interview data. Observations derived from written or verbal questioning of the respondent by the researcher.

Interviewer bias. The interviewer's influence on the respondent's answers; an example of reactivity.

Leading question. A question that leads the respondent to choose a particular response.

Mailed questionnaire. A survey instrument mailed to the respondent for completion and return.

Open-ended question. A question with no response alternatives provided for the respondent.

Personal interview. Face-to-face questioning of the respondent.

Question order effect. The effect on responses of question placement within a questionnaire.

Questionnaire design. The physical layout and packaging of a questionnaire.

Randomized response technique (RRT). A method of obtaining accurate answers to sensitive questions that protects the respondent's privacy.

Reactivity. The effect of data collection on the phenomenon being observed.

Response quality. The extent to which responses provide accurate and complete information.

Response rate. The proportion of respondents selected for participation in a survey who actually participate.

Response set. The pattern of responding to a series of questions in a similar fashion without careful reading of each question.

Single-sided question. A question with only one substantive alternative provided for the respondent.

Survey instrument. The schedule of questions to be asked of the respondent.

Survey research. Research based on the interview method of data collection.

Telephone interview. The questioning of the respondent via telephone.

Termination. The respondent's refusal to finish the interview.

Two-sided question. A question with two substantive alternatives provided for the respondent.

Unobtrusive measure. A measure of a phenomenon that does not involve reaction to measurement.

Suggested Readings

Aberbach, Joel D., James D. Chesney, and Bert A. Rockman. "Exploring Elite Political Attitudes: Some Methodological Lessons." *Political Methodology* 2 (1975): 1-27.

Backstrom, Charles H., and Gerald Hursh-Cesar. *Survey Research.* 2d ed. New York: Wiley, 1981.

Converse, Jean M., and Howard Schuman. *Conversations at Random: Survey Research as Interviewers See It.* New York: Wiley, 1974.

Dillman, Don A. *Mail and Telephone Surveys: The Total Design Method.* New York: Wiley, 1978.

Fowler, Floyd J., Jr., *Survey Research Methods.* Rev. ed. Beverly Hills, Calif.: Sage, 1988.

Frey, James H. *Research by Telephone.* 2d ed. Beverly Hills, Calif.: Sage, 1989.

Groves, Robert M. *Survey Errors and Survey Costs.* New York: Wiley, 1989.

Groves, Robert M., and Robert L. Kahn. *Surveys by Telephone: A National*

Comparison with Personal Interviews. New York: Academic, 1979.

Labaw, Patricia J. *Advanced Questionnaire Design.* Cambridge, Mass.: Abt Books, 1980.

Payne, Stanley. *The Art of Asking Questions.* Princeton, N.J.: Princeton University Press, 1971.

Sudman, Seymour, and Norman M. Bradburn. *Asking Questions: A Practical Guide to Questionnaire Design.* San Francisco: Jossey-Bass, 1982.

CHAPTER 9

Document Analysis:
Using the Written Record

Political scientists have three main methods of collecting the data they need to test their hypotheses: *interviewing, document analysis,* and *observation.* Of these, interviewing and document analysis are the most frequently used. In the last chapter we discussed interviewing techniques; here we will describe how empirical observations can be made using written documents, records, and personal materials.

Political scientists turn to the written record when the political phenomena that interest them cannot be measured through personal interviews, with questionnaires, or by direct observation. For example, interviewing and observation are of limited utility to researchers interested in large-scale collective behavior (such as civil unrest and the budget allocations of national governments), or in phenomena that are distant in time (Supreme Court decisions during the Civil War) or space (defense spending by different countries).

The political phenomena that have been observed through written records are many and varied—for example, judicial decisions concerning the free exercise of religion, voter turnout rates in gubernatorial elections, the change over time in Soviet military expenditures, and the incidence of political corruption in the People's Republic of China.[1] Of the examples of political science research described in Chapter 1 and referred to throughout this book, Jacobson's study of campaign expenditures by congressional candidates, Midlarsky's analysis of the effect of land inequality on political violence, and Segal and Cover's investigation of the behavior of Supreme Court justices all depended upon written records for the measurement of important political concepts.[2] Not all portions of the written record are equally useful to political scientists. This chapter will discuss the major components of the written record of interest to political scientists and how they are used to measure significant political phenomena.

Types of Written Records

Some written records are ongoing and cover an extensive period of time; others are more episodic. Some are produced by public organizations at taxpayers' expense; others are produced by business concerns or by private citizens. Some are carefully preserved and indexed; other records are written and forgotten. In this section we will discuss two types of written records: the episodic record and the running record.

The Episodic Record

Records that are not part of an ongoing, systematic record-keeping program but are produced and preserved in a more casual, personal, and accidental manner are called *episodic records*. Good examples are personal diaries, memoirs, manuscripts, correspondence, and autobiographies; biographical sketches and other biographical materials; the temporary records of organizations; and media of temporary existence, such as brochures, posters, and pamphlets. The episodic record is of particular importance to political historians since much of their subject matter can be studied only through these data.

To use written records, researchers must, first, gain access to the materials, and second, code and analyze them. In the case of the episodic record, gaining access is sometimes particularly difficult.[3] Locating suitable materials can easily be the most time-consuming aspect of the whole data collection exercise, as the following example illustrates.

Historian Sandra Frances Van Burkleo became interested in Kentucky politicians' response to the financial panic of 1819. In particular, she wanted to find out how the panic altered banking practices and land law, the relationship between Kentucky and Virginia, and Kentucky's view of the judiciary. Her research led her to consult historical documents in four Kentucky archives—a quest that points out the difficulties and opportunities presented by the episodic record.

> At my first stop ... I reviewed legislative journals and statute books while trying to learn something about the contents of several steel warehouses. A glance at the finding aids, prepared years before and patched together by untrained personnel, suggested inaccuracy— especially because so much was stacked in packing crates. Through conversations, I gradually gained familiarity with the repository's criteria for collecting materials, and gathered clues about the crates' contents. ...
> I also discovered several hundred bound volumes of banking

records—unrecorded in any manuscript guide—and was given a preliminary inventory, which was only partly accurate: size was recorded properly, while substance was not. "Record books," for example, variously meant ledgers, minute books, and miscellaneous volumes. . . .

The staff granted me permission to photocopy. I spent two weeks reading, selecting pages, making lists and cross references, and expanding the search into hinterland branch records as clues emerged— only to learn that archival policy had changed. Photocopying of selections was disallowed. I could choose between staff microfilming of selections at a steep price, or using the cameras myself for much less cost, provided that I filmed whole volumes rather than selected pages and left the master behind. I tried to remain calm, donned a technician's coat, and found myself behind sophisticated microfilming equipment under hot floodlights in a dank warehouse. Two weeks later, I had filmed over 10,000 pages, garnered prints, finished other research, and moved on to another repository. . . .

My second stop was a state historical society, where I was greeted by friendly volunteers, a classically southern librarian, and a small horde of genealogists. . . . At night, I studied names in local histories; by day, I searched collections. Soon, a network of kin and business associates appeared. . . .

I gained permission to use the original governor's papers and saw that the inventory had been prepared in the 1940s by a volunteer. Nobody knew anything about her. But whole boxes were missing and the numbers of bundles inside boxes did not tally with the inventory. . . .

Finally, I discovered, through a volunteer, that the "storeroom" held material that nobody had ever used. Why not, I asked? She didn't know. I was granted permission to roam in the mysterious "storeroom"—a place reminiscent of another small room in a Carolina library called "the coffin." There were cobwebs, boxes, and old books buried beneath boxes. I lifted, gently moved, and dug. There was an unlabeled register of monies received by the treasury, linked to landholdings in ways that were not clear, and the volume had not been indexed because it lacked a title page. I found five amazing minute books, kept by the Senate clerk during five sessions after 1821—but in a curious shorthand, complete with splendid caricatures of Senate speakers in the margins. . . . I quickly photocopied them. These volumes were a reasonable substitute for long-lost legislative proceedings, providing I could penetrate the shorthand system. They listed individual votes on bills; they summarized speeches. In my hotel room, I read about early American shorthand and eventually deciphered the clerk's alphabetic coding.

At a third repository, located at a state university, another two days were given over to conversation with staff and to generalized poking and digging in finding aids. Again, I wanted to learn something about criteria for collecting, the degree of bibliographic control, the quality of calendars and descriptive inventories. And I hoped to locate someone familiar with the contents of three huge family paper collections which had never been inventoried formally. I found a junior staff member who had processed two of the collections, and had been curious enough to absorb and jot down some of the contents. She was thoughtful and meticulous. I trusted her notes and memory, and eliminated considerable searching. . . .

I had been gone well over two months, and it was clear that I would not be able to visit both repositories remaining on my list. Already I was reduced to two meals a day. I aborted a plan to drive to a small western college in order to survey three family paper collections, fragments of which had been explored in the state historical society and had proved irrelevant, and decided to concentrate remaining resources upon a private historical society in Louisville. . . .

My weeks at this final archive were the most instructive of all. The society was underbudgeted and understaffed—an increasingly typical archival condition, but the staff was dedicated. And they chose to befriend me. Over lunch, I heard horror stories (very like those told elsewhere) about visiting scholars—the "loot and pillage" variety who storm a repository with pockets filled with dimes for photocopying, and who leave without acknowledging a debt; dependent scholars who expect curatorial workers to conduct research *for* them; lethargic historians who, when confronted with hundreds of relevant entries in a card catalog, simply leave; or gratuitous visitors who view archivists as failed historians or bright clerks. The staff habitually responded in kind, usually by refusing to volunteer information.[4]

As Van Burkleo's saga suggests, locating episodic records can be a time-consuming and frustrating task yet a rewarding one as well.

Researchers generally use episodic records to illustrate phenomena rather than as the basis for numerical measures. Consequently, quotations and other excerpts from research materials are often used as evidence for a thesis or hypothesis.

Over the years, social scientists have conducted some exceptionally interesting and imaginative studies of political phenomena based on the episodic record. We will describe three particular studies that used the episodic record to illuminate an important political phenomenon.

Deviance in the Massachusetts Bay Colony. Twenty-five years ago sociologist Kai Erikson studied deviance in the Puritans' Massachusetts Bay Colony during the seventeenth century.[5] He was interested in the process by which communities decide what constitutes deviant behavior. In particular, he wished to test the idea that communities alter their definitions of deviance over time and use deviant behavior to reaffirm and establish the boundaries of acceptable behavior. Contrary to the conventional view that deviant behavior is uniformly harmful, Erikson believed that the identification of and reaction to deviant behavior can serve a useful social purpose for a community.

Obviously, no one is still alive who could be interviewed about the Puritan form of justice in the colony. Consequently, Erikson had to search existing historical documents for evidence relating to his thesis. He found two main collections germane to his inquiry: *The Records of the Governor and Company of the Massachusetts Bay in New England* and *The Records and Files of the Quarterly Courts of Essex County, Massachusetts, 1636-1682.*[6] With these documents Erikson was able to weave together a fascinating tale of crime and punishment, Puritan style, during the mid-1600s.

Erikson's primary concern was with the identification of acts judged deviant in the Massachusetts Bay Colony. From the records of the Essex County courts he was able to collect information on all 1,954 convictions reached between 1651 and 1680. These data allowed Erikson to investigate the frequency of criminal behavior and to calculate a crude crime rate for the Bay Colony during this period.

Erikson's analysis of the historical records was not altogether straightforward. For example, he discovered that the Puritans were extremely casual about how they spelled people's names. One man named Francis Usselton made many appearances before the Essex County Court, and his name was spelled at least fourteen different ways in the court's records. This did not present insurmountable difficulties in his case because his name was so distinctive. However, Erikson had a more difficult time deciding whether Edwin and Edward Batter were the same man and whether "the George Hampton who stole a chicken in 1649" was "the same man as the George Hampden who was found drunk in 1651."[7]

A second problem with the Puritans' record keeping was that they often passed the same name from generation to generation. Hence it was sometimes unclear whether two crimes twenty years apart were committed by the same person or by a father and a son. Between 1656 and 1681, for example, John Brown was convicted of seven offenses. However, since John Brown's father and grandfather were also named John Brown, it was unclear who committed which crimes.

Despite these difficulties, Erikson's research is a testimonial to the ability of historical records to address important contemporary issues. Without the foresight of those who preserved and printed these records, an important aspect of life in Puritan New England would have been measurably more difficult to piece together.

Economics and the U.S. Constitution. In 1913 historian Charles Beard published a book about the U.S. Constitution in which he made imaginative use of the episodic record.[8] Beard's thesis was that economic interests prompted the movement to frame the Constitution. He reasoned that if he could show that the framers and pro-Constitution groups were familiar with the economic benefits that would ensue upon ratification of the Constitution, then he would be able to argue that economic considerations were central to the Constitution debate. If, in addition, he could show that the framers themselves benefited economically from the system of government established by the Constitution, the case would be that much stronger. This thesis, which has stimulated a good deal of controversy in the intervening years, was tested by Beard with a variety of data from the episodic record.

The first body of evidence presented by Beard measured the property holdings of those present at the 1787 Constitutional Convention. These measures, which Beard admits are distressingly incomplete, are derived largely from six different types of sources: biographical materials, such as James Herring's multivolume *National Portrait Gallery*, and the *National Encyclopedia of Biography;* census materials, in particular the 1790 census of heads of families, which showed the number of slaves owned by some of the framers; U.S. Treasury records, including ledger books containing lists of securities; records of individual state loan offices; records concerning the histories of certain businesses, such as the *History of the Bank of North America*, and the *History of the Insurance Company of North America;* and collections of personal papers stored in the Library of Congress.

From these written records Beard was able to discover the occupations, land holdings, number of slaves, securities, and mercantile interests of the framers. This allowed him to establish a plausible case that the framers were not economically disinterested when they met in Philadelphia to "revise" the Articles of Confederation.

Beard coupled his inventory of the framers' personal wealth with a second body of evidence concerning their political views. His objective was to demonstrate that the framers realized and discussed the economic implications of the Constitution and the new system of government. By using the existing minutes of the debate at the convention, the personal correspondence and writings of some of the framers, and the *Federalist Papers* by James Madison, Alexander Hamilton, and John Jay—which were written to persuade people to vote for the Constitution—Beard was able to demonstrate that the framers were concerned about, and cognizant of, the economic implications of the Constitution they wrote.

A third body of evidence allowed Beard to analyze the distribution of the vote for and against the Constitution. Where the data permitted, Beard measured the geographical distribution of the popular vote in favor of ratification and compared this with information about the economic interests of different geographical areas in each of the states. He also attempted to measure the personal wealth of those present at the state ratification conventions and then related those measures to the vote on the Constitution. These data were gleaned from the financial records of the individual states, the U.S. Treasury Department, and historical accounts of the ratification process in the states.

Through this painstaking and time-consuming reading of the historical record, Beard constructed a persuasive (although not necessarily proven) case for his conclusion that "the movement for the Constitution of the United States was originated and carried through principally by four groups of personalty interests which had been adversely affected under the Articles of Confederation: money, public securities, manufactures, and trade and shipping." [9]

Presidential Personality. A third example of the use of the episodic record may be found in James David Barber's *The Presidential Character.* Because of the importance of the presidency in the American political system and the extent to which that institution is shaped by its sole occupant, Barber was interested in understanding the personalities of the individuals who have occupied the office during the twentieth century. Although he no doubt would have preferred to observe directly the behavior of the fourteen presidents who held office between 1908 and 1984, he was forced instead to rely on the available written materials about them.

For Barber, discerning a president's personality means understanding his style, world view, and character. Style is *"the President's habitual way of performing his three political roles: rhetoric, personal relations, and homework."* A president's world view is measured by his *"primary, politically relevant beliefs, particularly his conceptions of social causality, human nature, and the central moral conflicts of the time."* And character *"is the way the President orients himself toward life."* Barber believes that a president's style, character, and world view "fit together in a dynamic package understandable in psychological terms" and that this personality "is an important shaper of his Presidential behavior on nontrivial matters." But how is one to measure the style, character, and world view of presidents who are dead or who will not permit a political psychologist access to their thoughts and deeds? This is an especially troublesome question when one believes, as Barber does, that "the best way to predict a President's character, world view, and style is to see how they were put together in the first place . . . in his early life, culminating in his first independent political success." [10]

Barber's solution to this problem was to use available materials on the twentieth-century presidents, including biographies, memoirs, diaries, speeches, and, in the case of Richard Nixon, tape recordings of presidential conversations. Barber did not use all the available biographical materials. For example, he "steered clear of obvious puff jobs put out in campaigns and of the quickie exposés composed to destroy reputations." [11] He quotes frequently from the biographical materials as he builds his case that a particular president was one of four basic personality types. Had these materials been unavailable or of questionable accuracy (a possibility that Barber glosses over in a single paragraph), measuring presidential personalities would have been a good deal more difficult, if not impossible.

Barber's analysis of the presidential personality is exclusively qualitative; there is not one table or graph in the book. He uses the biographical material to categorize each president as one of four personality types and to show that the presidents with similar personalities exhibited similar behavioral patterns when in office. In brief, Barber uses two dimensions—activity-passivity (how much energy does the man invest in his presidency?) and positive-negative affect (how does he feel about what he does?)—to define the four types of presidential personality (Table 9-1).

Barber's research is a provocative and imaginative example of the use of the episodic record—in this case, biographical material—as evidence for a series of generalizations about presidential personality. Although Barber does not empirically test his hypotheses in the ways that we have been discussing in this book, he does accumulate a body of evidence in support of his assertions and present his evidence in such a way that the reader can evaluate how persuasive it is.[12]

The Running Record

Unlike the episodic record, the running record is more likely to be produced by organizations than by private citizens; it is carefully stored and easily accessed; and it is available for long periods of time. The portion of the running record that is concerned with political phenomena is extensive and growing. The data collection and reporting efforts of the U.S. government alone are impressive, and if one adds to that the written records collected and preserved by state and local governments, interest groups, publishing houses, research institutes, and commercial concerns, the quantity of politically relevant written records increases quickly. Reports of the U.S. government, for example, now cover everything from electoral votes to electrical rates, taxes to taxi cabs, and, in summary form, fill one thousand pages in the *Statistical Abstract of the United States,* published annually by the U.S. Bureau of the Census.

In this section we will summarize the main types of running records of interest to political scientists.

Election Returns. Election returns have been collected, tabulated, and published for almost 200 years. They are available for most federal offices and some statewide offices at the state and county levels. Commonly used sources of such data are the *America Votes* series (published biennially since 1956 by the Elections Research Center and Congressional Quarterly) and the Inter-University Consortium for Political and Social Research (ICPSR) at the University of Michigan.

Congressional Voting. Votes of members of the U.S. Congress since 1789 are available from the ICPSR. Congressional roll call votes

Table 9-1 Presidential Personality Types

Positive-Negative Affect	Activity-Passivity	
	Active	Passive
Positive	Franklin D. Roosevelt Harry S. Truman John F. Kennedy Gerald Ford Jimmy Carter	William Howard Taft Warren Harding Ronald Reagan
Negative	Woodrow Wilson Herbert Hoover Lyndon Johnson Richard Nixon	Calvin Coolidge Dwight Eisenhower

Source: This table is based on data found in James David Barber, *The Presidential Character,* 3d ed. (Englewood Cliffs, N.J.: Prentice-Hall, 1985).

since 1945 and a plethora of other records concerning individual members of Congress (presidential support scores and party support scores, for example) are published annually in the *Congressional Quarterly Almanac. Politics in America,* published biennially by Congressional Quarterly since 1972, contains more detailed information on individual members, including data on each member's district or state, political career, and voting record, as rated by a variety of interest groups.

Judicial Decisions. Summaries of all state and federal judicial decisions are reported in the *Decennial Digest* (published by West Publishing Co.) and the text of all Supreme Court decisions may be found in *United States Reports,* published by the U.S. Government Printing Office. In addition, the ICPSR has information on the votes cast in the 4,573 cases decided by the U.S. Supreme Court between 1946 and 1969. The ICPSR also has more limited collections of data on topics such as civil and criminal federal court cases (1962-1963), plea bargaining in felony cases in Alaska (1974-1976), state criminal court cases (1962), and U.S. Supreme Court certiorari decisions (1947-1956).

Governmental Policy. For information on public policy, researchers have a wide variety of sources. The laws passed each year by the federal government are summarized in the *Congressional Quarterly Almanac* and cited in full in the *United States Statutes at Large.* Data on federal expenditures are included in the *Congressional Quarterly Almanac* as well as the *Statistical Abstract of the United States.* Measures of public policy at the state and local levels may be found in the

Book of the States (published biennially by the Council of State Governments), the *County and City Data Book* (published by the U.S. Bureau of the Census), the *Statistical Abstract of the United States,* and the U.S. Census Bureau's *Annual Survey of Governments.*

The ICPSR also has useful data describing government policy at the national, state, and local levels. *Annual Time Series Statistics for the U.S.* describes federal expenditures by various departments, agencies, and commissions from 1929 to 1968. Four separate studies contain information on state policy making and governmental expenditures; one covers 1950 to 1964, one provides data at decennial points from 1890 to 1960, one covers 1956 to 1965, and one has select data from the nineteenth and twentieth centuries. At the local level, ICPSR has data for 676 incorporated urban places with populations of 25,000 or more during the 1960s and other data since 1960 for 130 incorporated cities with populations greater than 100,000.

The *Statistical Abstract of the United States* is a treasure trove of data on American society. It contains summaries of all of the major data collection efforts of the national government. Between its covers you will find information on health care expenditures, drug use, crime and victimization rates, numbers of arrests and prisoners, air quality, weather, environmental control expenditures, leisure time activities, state and local government finances, federal government personnel and expenditures, veterans' benefits, unemployment, occupational injury rates, the consumer price index, banking and publishing activities, number of foreign-owned U.S. firms, energy production and consumption, transportation revenues, motor vehicle accidents, crop production, housing construction, public housing, department store sales, foreign assistance, and exports and imports. Such a publication is truly an archival researcher's delight! Another useful guide to government records is Andrew Hacker's *U/S: A Statistical Portrait.*[13]

Crime Statistics. One particular area of American life that has generated a huge record-keeping enterprise is the criminal justice system. Some crime data may be found in the *Statistical Abstract.* The ICPSR also has data describing many aspects of crime and the criminal justice system. These include the following:

The FBI's *Uniform Crime Report* (data from 1966 to 1976 on the seven index crimes—murder, forcible rape, robbery, aggravated assault, burglary, larceny-theft, and motor vehicle theft)

National Crime Surveys (victimization data, 1972-1980)

National Jail Census (data on local jails, 1970, 1972, 1978)

Census of Correctional Facilities (1974 and 1979)

Survey of Jail Inmates (1972 and 1978)

Criminal Case Processing in Metropolitan Courts (1976)
Pretrial Release Practices in the U.S. (1976-1978)
Expenditure and Employment Data for the Criminal Justice System
(1971-1979).

Campaign Spending. For decades, political scientists have been interested in the role of money in election campaigns. However, it is only within the past twenty years that reliable and comprehensive data on campaign spending have been available to researchers. As a result of the Federal Election Campaign Act of 1971, a federal agency—the Federal Election Commission—was established and given the responsibility of collecting data on the fund-raising and campaign spending practices of candidates for federal elective office. Political scientists now have a rich new source of archival data on a consequential area of political life. In fact, it is this source of data that allowed Gary Jacobson to analyze the relationship between the campaign expenditures and vote totals of candidates for the U.S. Congress.[14]

Speeches. There is also an ongoing written record of the public statements of politicians. Presidential campaign speeches, for example, are contained in a variety of publications, including those published by individual candidates (such as *Nixon Speaks Out,* published by the Nixon-Agnew Campaign Committee) and those published for every president (such as *Public Papers of the Presidents of the United States,* published annually by the U.S. Government Office of the Federal Register). Presidential debate transcripts for 1960, 1976, 1980, and 1984 are also available.[15]

Speeches given on the floor of the U.S. Congress are recorded in the *Congressional Record,* although since members are allowed to excise, revise, and add to what they actually said this record is not completely accurate. *National Party Platforms,* published by the University of Illinois Press, contains a collection of the documents put together every four years since 1840 by the American political parties.

Mass Media Materials. The output of news organizations is a running record of daily events and public affairs. The types of stories written, the political issues and personalities covered, the photographs taken, and the opinions expressed may all be considered as a written record of our political and social life. Recall that Segal and Cover's study of the relationship between the personal ideology and judicial decisions of Supreme Court justices relied on published newspaper editorials for the measure of political ideology.[16]

In the past, the running news record was difficult to use simply because it was so massive, disorganized, and hard to retrieve, yet now with the development of newspaper and television indices a sizable portion of the news is both enduring and readily accessible. The *New*

York Times has been indexed since 1851, the *Wall Street Journal* since 1957, the *Christian Science Monitor* since 1960, and the *Washington Post* since 1971.

Local libraries often have extensive collections of local newspapers. The Philadelphia Free Library, for example, has preserved the *Philadelphia Inquirer* since 1860, the *Evening-Bulletin* for 1847-1982, the *Public Ledger* for 1836-1934, and the *North American* for 1839-1925 (the last three papers went out of business in 1982, 1934, and 1925, respectively).

If a researcher is interested in a phenomenon that can be measured using newspaper content, the running news record is well preserved and extensive. But the running record for broadcast news is less satisfactory. Television network news coverage has been preserved and indexed only since 1968. And, as far as we know, there is no archive or collection of radio news or local television news that can be used by researchers.

Foreign Affairs. Researchers interested in comparative politics and international relations have collected a variety of data on an array of subjects, including the socioeconomic and political attributes of nations; instances of political dissent, conflicts, or violence within different nations; events of conflict and cooperation between nations; trade and arms transfers between nations; and defense expenditures and use of military force by nations. These data represent a rich and readily accessible archival source of observations that would be time consuming and difficult to collect oneself. Midlarsky's research on the relationship between land inequality and political violence, for example, was facilitated by the availability of data on both the distribution of land ownership and the number of deaths due to political violence in a number of countries.[17]

Biographical Data. Finally, biographical data are part of the running record. Using biographical publications such as *Who's Who in America* and the *Social Register*, researchers have been able to trace the origins and relationships among people in various positions of power and influence and to contrast different types of elite groups.[18] The ICPSR has biographical data on higher echelon federal executive appointees (1932-1965), arms control bureaucrats, higher civil servants in American federal agencies (1963), state and federal supreme court judges (1955), U.S. Supreme Court justices (1789-1958), members of the Congress of the Confederate States of America (1862-1865), and members of the U.S. Congress (1789-1980). Biographical data also exist on selected foreign elites. The ICPSR has data on political elites in Eastern Europe (1971), Kenya (1966-1967), Tanzania (1964-1968), the Soviet Union (1966), France and Germany (1964), Brazil (1960), and Uganda (1964-1968).

The Running Record and Episodic Record Compared

There are three primary advantages to using the running record over the episodic record. The first is cost, in terms of both time and money. Since the costs of collecting, tabulating, storing, and reporting the data in the running record are generally borne by the record keepers themselves, political scientists are usually able to use these data very inexpensively. In contrast to the time-consuming and expensive research of the episodic record described earlier by the historian interested in early nineteenth-century Kentucky, researchers can often use the data stored in the running record by photocopying a few pages of a reference book, purchasing a government report, or acquiring a computer tape. In fact, the recent expansion of the data collection and record-keeping activities of the national government has been a financial boon to social scientists of all types.

A second, related advantage is the accessibility of the running record. Instead of searching packing crates, deteriorated ledgers, and musty storerooms, as users of the episodic record often do, users of the running record more often handle reference books, government publications, computer printouts, and computer tapes. Many political science research projects have been completed with only the data stored in the reference books and government documents of a decent research library.

A third advantage of the running record is that by definition it covers a more extensive period of time than the episodic record does. This permits the type of longitudinal analysis and before-and-after research designs discussed in Chapter 5. Although the episodic record helps explain the origins of and reasons for a particular event, episode, or period, the running record allows the measurement of political phenomena over time.

The running record is not without its defects, however. One is that a researcher is at the mercy of the data collection practices and procedures of the record-keeping organizations themselves. Researchers are rarely in a position to influence record-keeping practices; they must rely instead on what organizations such as the U.S. Census Bureau, Federal Election Commission, and the Roper Center for Public Opinion Research decide to do. There is often a tradeoff between ease of access and researcher influence over the measurements that are made.

Another related disadvantage of the running record is that some organizations are not willing to share their raw data with researchers. The processed data that they do release may reflect calculations, categorizations, and aggregations that are inaccurate or uninformative.

Finally, it is sometimes difficult for researchers to find out exactly what the record-keeping practices of some organizations are. Unless the organization publishes a description of its procedures, a researcher may not know what decisions have guided the record-keeping process. This can be a special problem when these practices change, altering in an unknown way the measurements reported.

Although the running record has its disadvantages, often political scientists must rely on it if they wish to do any empirical research on a particular topic. For years, for example, the only reasonable way of conducting research on crime in the United States was to use the *Uniform Crime Report* (UCR) of the Federal Bureau of Investigation. To illustrate some of the problems with using written records, we conclude this section with a description of the *Uniform Crime Report,* one of the longest and most often used portions of the running record.

The Uniform Crime Report

First issued in 1930, the *Uniform Crime Report* is the only enduring, national compilation of statistics on crime in the United States; consequently it has become the basis for numerous research reports on crime and police behavior. In recent years, however, the accuracy and precision of the measures reported in the UCR have been called into question and the report has been criticized by many of its users.

The FBI's measure of criminal activity is based on the reports it receives from thousands of law enforcement agencies across the country. State and local police departments voluntarily submit these reports; the FBI has never been given the power to enforce participation. Each police agency must bear the cost and responsibility of providing the information, although the FBI does provide instructions and assistance to participating police departments. The FBI's intent, then, is to produce a report representing the *population* of police departments; no sampling is done.

Police departments are asked to report two types of information: the number of criminal acts of seven different kinds that come to their attention ("Part I" crimes) and the number of arrests that they make for many other types of crimes ("Part II" crimes). Part I crimes include criminal homicide, forcible rape, robbery, aggravated assault, burglary, larceny, and auto theft. Part II crimes include other assaults; forgery and counterfeiting; embezzlement and fraud; buying, receiving, or possessing stolen property; carrying or possessing weapons; prostitution and commercialized vice; sex offenses; offenses against the family and children; violations of narcotic drug laws; violations of liquor laws; drunkenness; disorderly conduct; vagrancy; gambling; driving while intoxicated; violation of road and driving laws; parking violations; other violations of traffic and motor vehicle laws; all other offenses; and suspicion.[19] Trends in crime over time are reported, as well as rates of crimes per 100,000 people.

In this section we will discuss the flaws in the UCR that have led to questionable measures of criminal activity in the United States. The most obvious problem is that not all crimes are reported to the police and therefore are never included in the UCR.[20] There are many reasons why victims do not report a crime: they may be unable to do so (for example, they may have been murdered), they may fear reprisal by the accused, they may think that nothing will be done by the police, they may wish to hide their own participation in criminal activity, they may consider their losses too minor to justify the inconvenience, they may be reluctant to publicize their victimization, and they may be able to secure compensation from other sources (for example, from an insurance company).[21] Many crimes are reported elsewhere: to military officials, prosecutors, and regulatory agencies with judicial power, such as the Securities and Exchange Commission. Violations of federal laws, misrepresentation in advertising, restraints of trade, and manipulation of prices and markets are not the kinds of crimes reported to state and local police forces.

Moreover, the police themselves may neglect, either by accident or intention, to report crimes to headquarters or to the FBI. Manpower is often scarce, records poorly kept, and employees incompetent and inefficient. In addition, the police may try to protect the reputation of their co-workers, superiors, precincts, and municipality by failing to report criminal acts. If they know that the UCR statistics are going to be used to compare the safety of their city with that of another, they may be tempted to underreport crime.[22] Who wants to be a policeman in the city dubbed "the murder capital of the world"?

Another problem with the UCR is that Part II crimes are included only if an arrest is made. This is because it is known that many Part II crimes are never reported to the police, thus making UCR reports of these crimes even less reliable than they are for Part I crimes.[23]

Just as some crimes go unreported, some crimes are reported that never took place. After all, the courts, not the victim, decide that someone is guilty of committing a crime. Yet the UCR assumes that any criminal act reported to the police did, in fact, happen, regardless of the eventual disposition of the case. Crimes may be overreported, then, as well as underreported.[24]

The FBI asks that crimes be reported in one of twenty-seven categories—seven Part I crimes, twenty Part II crimes. The behavior that constitutes each of these crimes, however, varies widely across the many police departments represented in the UCR. Assault and larceny are often used as substitutes for robbery, for example, and there is tremendous variation in what constitutes drunkenness, disorderly conduct, prostitution, vagrancy, assault and battery, and aggravated assault.[25] An act committed by a minority youth in a center city precinct may be considered criminal, whereas the same act committed by a white youth in a privileged suburban community might simply engender a stern warning and a free ride home.[26] Yet there is no way that the FBI can force state and local police departments to maintain uniformity in either law or practice. As long as individual state and local legislatures are the ones defining crimes and state and local police are the ones enforcing these laws, there will be no uniformity in how criminal acts are reported.[27]

By the late 1960s, most police departments had joined the UCR system, amounting to coverage of areas containing 96 percent of the U.S. population.[28] In earlier years, however, the rate of participation was much lower, and there were no crime statistics for large areas of the country. Thus UCR measures of over-time trends, if not based on identical reporting areas, are suspect.

One criminal incident may involve the breaking of several laws. Yet the FBI has decided that the UCR should reflect only the most serious offense in a multiple-offense episode. For example, if someone breaks into a home, steals $300 worth of jewels, kills an occupant, injures a bystander, and steals a car with which to make an escape, only the murder will be recorded. Obviously this systematically underestimates the number of criminal acts committed or laws broken.[29]

Beginning in 1958, the UCR included an "index" of criminal activity calculated by summing the Part I crimes reported. The rationale for calculating such an index was that Part I crimes are the most serious and the most likely to be reported to the police.[30]

The crime index has been the subject of two major criticisms. First, by excluding Part II crimes, the index does not reflect many crimes that are serious and cause major physical harm (such as arson, kidnapping, and assault and battery) or substantial financial loss and property damage (such as embezzlement, malicious mischief, and disorderly conduct). Second, by summing the number of Part I crimes, the index effectively treats each crime, regardless of its type, equally. A murder counts the same as an auto theft in calculating the crime index. Since the FBI believes that the seven Part I crimes may be rank-ordered in terms of severity, the equally weighted index would seem to be inconsistent with the FBI's own approach to the measurement of crime.[31]

In short, one must be careful about the inferences drawn from the crime index. The index does not represent all crime, or all crimes reported to the police, or even all serious crimes reported to the police. Nor do changes in the crime index necessarily mean that crime has become any more or less serious. Since the index is composed of many very different kinds of crime but not all crimes, exactly what it does measure is unclear.

As we have seen, the validity and reliability of the *Uniform Crime Report* are jeopardized by numerous shortcomings in the FBI's record-keeping system. Nevertheless, without the UCR data it would be more difficult for researchers to conduct rigorous hypothesis-testing research about the prevalence of criminal behavior. In fact, users of the running record are often faced with the choice between using data that they know are flawed in some way and leaving a hypothesis untested because of the absence of a superior data source. Each researcher must ultimately decide whether the flaws in the written record are tolerable or not, since the running record is often a valuable source of information about political phenomena that are impossible to observe in any other way.

Content Analysis

Sometimes researchers extract excerpts, quotations, or examples from the written record to support an observation or relationship. Those who rely on the episodic record, such as Charles Beard and James David Barber, often use the written record in this way. At other times researchers use numerical measures calculated by record keepers and presented in the written record without altering these measures appreciably. Users of the *Uniform Crime Reports,* for example, often simply use the crime rates reported there as their independent and dependent variables, as do users of the Federal Election Commission's campaign spending reports. With both of these written records, very little conversion is done by the researcher.

Yet researchers may wish to extract numerical measures from an extensive written record that exists in nonnumerical form. For example, a researcher might want to study the news coverage of a presidential campaign to measure how favorable the tone of the coverage was for different candidates. This might require reducing hundreds of newspaper articles and news programs to a handful of numerical measures of the tone of news stories.

To derive numerical measures from a nonnumerical written record, researchers use a technique called *content analysis.* This procedure enables us to "take a verbal, nonquantitative document and transform it into quantitative data." A researcher "first constructs a set of mutually exclusive and exhaustive categories that can be used to analyze documents, and then records the frequency with which each of these categories is observed in the documents studied." [32] This is exactly what Segal and Cover had to do with a number of newspaper editorials in order to produce a quantitative measure of the political ideologies of Supreme Court justices. [33]

Content Analysis Procedures

The first step in content analysis is deciding what *sample of materials* to include in the analysis. If a researcher is interested in the political values of candidates for public office, a sample of political party platforms and campaign speeches might be suitable. If the level of sexism in a society is of interest, then a sample of television entertainment programs and films might be drawn. Or if a researcher is interested in what liberals are thinking about, liberal opinion magazines might be sampled. Actually, two tasks are involved at this stage: selecting materials germane to the researcher's subject (in other words, choosing the appropriate *sampling frame*) and sampling the actual material to be analyzed from that sampling frame. Once the appropriate sampling frame has been selected, then any of the possible types of samples described in Chapter 7—random, systematic, stratified, cluster, and nonprobability— could be used.

The second task in any content analysis is to *define the categories* of content that are going to be measured. A study of the prevalence of crime in the news, for example, might measure the amount of news content that either deals with crime or does not. Content that deals with crime might be further subdivided into the kinds of crime covered. A study of news coverage of a presidential campaign might measure whether news content concerning a particular presidential candidate is favorable, neutral, or unfavorable. Or a study might measure the personality traits of various prime-time television characters—such as strength, warmth, integrity, humility, and wisdom—and the sex, age, race, and occupation of those characters. This process is in many respects the most important part of any content analysis because the researcher must measure the content in such a way that it relates to the research topic, and he or she must define this content so that the measures of it are both valid and reliable.

The third task is to choose the *recording unit.* For example, from a given document, news source, or other material, the researcher may want to code (1) each word, (2) each theme, (3) each character or actor, (4) each sentence, (5) each paragraph, or (6) each item in its entirety. To measure concern with crime in the daily newspaper, the recording unit might be the article. To measure the favorableness of news coverage of presidential campaigns in news weeklies, the recording unit might be the paragraph. And to measure the amount of attention focused on different governmental institutions on television network news, the recording unit might be the story.

In choosing the recording unit, the researcher usually considers the ease of identifying the unit (words, sentences, and paragraphs are easier to identify than stories and themes) and the correspondence between the unit and the content categories (stories may be more appropriate than words in determining whether crime is a topic of concern, while individual words or sentences rather than larger units may be more appropriate for measuring the traits of political candidates). Generally, if the recording unit is too small, each case will be unlikely to possess any of the content categories. Furthermore, small recording units may obscure the context in which a particular content appears. For example, counting the number of mentions of "Dan Quayle" would lump together "Dan Quayle continues to be haunted by questions about his military service" with "Dan Quayle addressed another wildly enthusiastic rally today." On the other hand, if the recording unit is too large, it will be difficult to measure the single category of a content variable that it possesses (in other words, the case will possess multiple values of a given content variable). The selection of the appropriate recording unit is often a matter of trial and error, adjustment, and compromise in the pursuit of measures that capture the content of the material being coded.

Finally, a researcher has to devise a *system of enumeration* for the content being coded. The presence or absence of a given content category can be measured or the "frequency with which the category appears," or the "amount of space allotted to the category," or the "strength of intensity with which the category is represented." [34] For example, suppose we were coding the presence of Hispanics in televised entertainment programming, with the *program* as the recording unit. For each program we could count (1) whether there was at least one Hispanic present, (2) how many Hispanics there were, (3) how much time Hispanics were on the screen, and (4) how favorable or how important the portrayal of Hispanics was for the overall story.

The validity of a content analysis can usually be enhanced with a precise explanation of the procedures followed and content categories used. Usually the best way to demonstrate the reliability of content analysis measures is to show *intercoder reliability.* Intercoder reliability simply means that two or more analysts, using the same procedures and definitions, agree on the content categories applied to the material analyzed. The more the agreement, the stronger the researcher's confidence can be that the meaning of the content is not heavily dependent on the particular person doing the analysis. If different coders disagree frequently, then the content categories have not been defined with enough clarity and precision.

The following example of a content analysis may be helpful. Suppose you were interested in studying 1988 presidential campaign coverage by *Time* and *Newsweek* (the sampling frame). You could decide to analyze every article about the campaign from September 1 to election day, taking the article as the recording unit. The content categories could be (1) the subject of the article (that is, the "who"); (2) the topic of the article (that is, the "what"); and (3) the tone of the article (was it unfavorable or favorable?). To encode the content you could devise a coding sheet like the one presented in Table 9-2. It shows the content variables, the categories for each variable, the recording unit, and the system of enumeration. This is the type of sheet that would be used to quantify the data.

Table 9-2 Coding Sheet for Hypothetical Content Analysis of
Presidential Campaign Coverage

Magazine   1. *Time*_____   2. *Newsweek*_____
*Date*_____
Page no. _____
*No. of paragraphs*_____
*No. of paragraphs devoted
   to each candidate:*   1. Dukakis _____   3. Bush _____

                               2. Bentsen _____   4. Quayle _____

*Primary focus
   of article:*
                  1. Candidate prospects _____   3. Policy issues _____

                  2. Campaign events _____   4. Personalities _____
*Overall tone
   of article:*
              For Bush/Quayle: Negative 1 2 3 4 5 6 7 Positive
              For Dukakis/Bentsen: Negative 1 2 3 4 5 6 7 Positive

---

Although political scientists have used content analysis sparingly, it is a useful technique in some areas of inquiry. We will conclude this section with an example of a content analysis performed by two political scientists.

News Coverage of Presidential Campaigns

A frequent subject of content analysis is press coverage of election campaigns. Given the importance of how candidates are presented and how the electoral process is treated in the news, political scientists have been interested for some time in accurately and systematically describing and explaining campaign news coverage. Most of these studies have investigated whether candidates receive favorable or unfavorable coverage, whether news coverage relays useful information to the American electorate, whether the press accurately presents the complex and lengthy presidential nomination process, and whether journalists are, in general, objective, accurate, fair, and informative.

One good example of a content analysis of this type is a study of presidential campaign coverage in 1980 by Michael J. Robinson and Margaret A. Sheehan.[35] We will discuss the procedures they followed and some of the strengths and weaknesses of their analysis.

At the beginning Robinson and Sheehan had to select the news coverage to be included in their study. Given the overwhelming amount of print and broadcast coverage that a presidential election campaign stimulates, there was no way that they could carefully analyze it all. In

1980 there were more than 1,000 daily newspapers and 6,000 broadcast stations in the United States. Consequently, they had to select, or sample, a portion of the news coverage to analyze. Six different decisions were involved in choosing the sample.

First, the researchers decided what type of medium to analyze. Primarily because of their estimates of the audience reached by different media, they chose national network television and newspaper wire service copy. In the process, they decided not to select several regional daily newspapers and the news weeklies, as had been done in a study of the 1976 campaign, and not to draw a representative sample of daily newspapers, as had been done in a study of the 1974 congressional elections.[36]

Second, because Robinson and Sheehan's resources were limited, they had to decide which of the media outlets to select. In other words, which television network and which wire service would be chosen? Based again on audience size, as well as professional prestige, they selected CBS and the Associated Press (AP). But AP refused to cooperate—an example of one of those disturbing yet all too frequent developments that cause the best laid research plans to go awry. Consequently, the researchers switched reluctantly to United Press International (UPI), even though it had far fewer clients and generally placed fewer stories in daily newspapers. CBS and UPI, then, became their case studies for 1980.

What products of these two media outlets should be included in the study? This was the third decision facing Robinson and Sheehan. CBS produces several versions of the nightly news, as well as morning news shows, midday news shows, news interviews, and news specials. And UPI offers several news services, among them an "A" wire, which is the national wire; a city wire; and a radio wire. The "A" wire itself has two versions: the night cycle, which runs from noon to midnight, and the day cycle, which runs from midnight to noon. The researchers decided to use the day "A" wire, for reasons of scope of coverage as well as accessibility, and the CBS nightly news (the 7 p.m. Eastern Time edition), primarily for financial reasons and convenience.

Fourth, they had to decide which of the material from these news shows and wire copy to include. They decided to include only campaign or campaign-related stories. Thus they used any story that "mentioned the presidential campaign, no matter how tangentially; mentioned any presidential candidate in his campaign role; mentioned any presidential candidate or his immediate family in a noncampaign, official role (almost always a story about the president); or discussed to a substantial degree any campaign lower than the presidential level."[37] Just over 5,500 stories on UPI and CBS—22 percent of UPI and CBS total news coverage—met these selection criteria.

Fifth, Robinson and Sheehan had to decide what time period to include in their study. Although a presidential campaign has a fairly clear ending point, election day, the beginning date of the campaign is uncertain. The researchers decided to include weekday coverage throughout 1980 (that is, from January 1 to December 31). They give no justification for excluding the weekend news.

Finally, Robinson and Sheehan made an important decision to exclude some of the content of both CBS's and UPI's news coverage. They decided not to include any photographs, film, videotape, or live pictures and to rely exclusively on verbal (CBS) or written (UPI) expression. They defended this decision on the grounds that it is more difficult to interpret the meaning of visuals and that the visual message usually supports the verbal message. Moreover, they thought that comparing the visual component of CBS with that of UPI would be difficult.

Having selected the news content to be analyzed, Robinson and Sheehan then decided on the unit of analysis to use when coding news content. Generally, they analyzed the *story,* although at times they analyzed the content sentence by sentence and word by word. Most content analyses of this type have also used the story as the unit of analysis, but it is unfortunate that Robinson and Sheehan did not explain this choice in any detail or discuss how difficult it was to tell where one story ended and another began.

Having selected the news content to be used in the measurement of campaign news coverage, Robinson and Sheehan then had to decide the content categories to be encoded and the definitions of the values for these content categories. They coded some twenty-five different aspects of each 1980 campaign story. Some of these were straightforward, such as the story's date, length, and reporter. Other categories, which pertained · to the central subject matter of the study, were not as readily defined or measured.

The researchers were primarily concerned with five characteristics: Were CBS and UPI (1) objective, (2) equitable in providing access, (3) fair, (4) serious, and (5) comprehensive? Consequently, they needed to decide how to measure each of these attributes of news coverage.

Robinson and Sheehan measured the objectivity of the press's coverage in four ways: by the number of explicit and unsupported conclusions drawn by journalists about the personal qualities of the candidates; by the number of times the journalists expressed personal opinions concerning the issues of the campaign; by counting the number of sentences that were either descriptive, analytical, or judgmental; and by counting the number of verbs used by journalists that were either descriptive, analytical, or insinuative. Clearly, each of these content categories involved judgments by the researchers concerning what constituted an explicit and unsupported conclusion, what constituted a personal opinion, and what constituted a descriptive versus an analytical sentence. The researchers provide examples of different types of coded content, and they also give some brief definitions of what each of the categories meant to them: for example, *descriptive sentences* "present the who, what, where, when of the day's news, without any meaningful qualification or elaboration," *analytical sentences* "tell us *why* something occurs or predicts as to whether it might," and *judgmental sentences* "tell us how something ought to be or ought not to be." [38]

To determine whether the press granted appropriate access to each of the presidential candidates, Robinson and Sheehan measured how much coverage (in terms of seconds for CBS and column inches for UPI) each of the candidates received. They do not say whether this coding procedure presented any difficulties, although they do evaluate whether the amount of access granted each candidate was justified.

Determining whether press coverage was fair was much more difficult than measuring access since an evaluation of fairness requires that the tone of campaign coverage be measured. Establishing tone in a reliable and valid way is not easy. Robinson and Sheehan define tone and fairness in these terms:

> Tone pertains not simply to the explicit message offered by the journalist but the implicit message as well. Tone involves the overall (and admittedly subjective) assessment we made about each story: whether the story was, for the major candidates, "good press," "bad press," or something in between. "Fairness," as we define it, involves the sum total of a candidate's press tone; how far from neutrality the candidate's press score lies. [39]

They evaluated content in terms of whether it represented good press (a story that had three times as much positive information as negative information about a candidate) or bad press (a story that had three times as much negative as positive information). But they never discuss how they determined what constituted positive and negative information. Furthermore, in their effort to restrict their analysis to the behavior of journalists, Robinson and Sheehan excluded information about political events (such as the failure of the Iranian hostage rescue mission), polls, comments made by partisans, remarks of "criminals and anti-Americans" (such as Fidel Castro and the Ayatollah Khomeini), and statements made by the candidates themselves.[40] In short, their measurement of fairness depended upon the wisdom of a number of decisions regarding the encoding of campaign stories. Some of these decisions are questionable, such as using an arbitrary 3-to-1 ratio to determine good press/bad press and excluding political events, polls, and the words of the candidates themselves from the analysis.

The seriousness of press coverage was measured by coding each story and, at times, each sentence, according to whether it represented policy issues, candidate issues, "horse-race coverage," or something else. *Policy issues* were ones that "involve major questions as to how the government should (or should not) proceed in some area of social life," *candidate issues* "concern the personal behavior of the candidate during the course of his or her campaign," and *horse-race coverage* focuses on "any consideration as to winning or losing." Because of difficulty in encoding entire stories into only one of these categories, the researchers shifted to the more exacting sentence-by-sentence analysis. Some sentences did not fit into one and only one of these categories, but "the majority of sentences were fairly easy to classify as one form of news or another." [41] The seriousness of UPI and CBS campaign coverage in 1980 was then measured by comparing their amount of policy issue coverage with the policy issue coverage in other media in previous presidential election years.

Finally, to evaluate how comprehensive press coverage was in 1980, Robinson and Sheehan coded campaign stories in terms of the level of office covered: presidential, vice-presidential, senatorial, congressional, and gubernatorial. More than 90 percent of both CBS and UPI campaign coverage was of the presidential and vice-presidential races.[42]

Over the Wire and on TV represents one of the most thorough content analyses ever performed by political scientists. Certainly, in terms of the time period covered and the sheer quantity of material analyzed, it is an ambitious study. The value of the study is weakened, however, by the inadequate explanation of the content analysis procedures. The definitions of the categories used are brief and the illustrative material sketchy. Furthermore, Robinson and Sheehan dispense with the issue of measurement quality in only one paragraph, where they report that intercoder reliability figures among four members of the coding team averaged about 95 percent agreement.[43] However, they fail to report any details about how this reliability was measured or about the agreement scores for different content categories. Despite these shortcomings, this study exemplifies how content analysis can reveal useful information about a significant political phenomenon. It also illustrates how practical limitations—such as AP's refusal to participate, as well as financial constraints—all too often limit what researchers can actually accomplish.

Advantages and Disadvantages of the Written Record

Using documents and records, or what we have called the *written record,* has several advantages for researchers. First, it allows us *access* to subjects that may be difficult or impossible to research through direct, personal contact, because they pertain either to the past or to phenomena that are geographically distant. For example, the record keeping of the Puritans in the Massachusetts Bay Colony during the seventeenth century allowed Erikson to study their approach to crime control, and late eighteenth-century records permitted Beard to advance and test a novel interpretation of the framing of the U.S. Constitution. Neither of these studies would have been possible had there been no records available from these periods.

A second advantage of data gleaned from archival sources is that the raw data are usually *nonreactive*. In other words, those writing and preserving the records are often unaware of any future research goal or hypothesis or, for that matter, that the fruits of their labors will be used for research purposes at all. The record keepers of the Massachusetts Bay Colony were surely unaware that their records would ever be used to study how a society defines and reacts to deviant behavior. Similarly, state loan officers during the late 1700s had no idea that two hundred years later a historian would use their records to discover why some people were in favor of revising the Articles of Confederation. This nonreactivity has the virtue of encouraging more accurate and less self-serving measures of political phenomena.

Record keeping is not always completely nonreactive, however. Record keepers are less likely to create and preserve records that are embarrassing to them, their friends, or their bosses; that reveal illegal or immoral actions; or that disclose stupidity, greed, or other demeaning attributes. Richard Nixon, for example, undoubtedly wishes that he had destroyed the infamous Watergate tapes that revealed the extent of his administration's knowledge of the 1972 break-in at Democratic National Committee headquarters. Today many record-keeping agencies employ paper shredders to ensure that a portion of the written record does *not* endure. Researchers must be aware of the possibility that the written record has been selectively preserved to serve the record keepers' own interests. As noted earlier, police may underreport crimes because they know that the crime statistics they report to the FBI will be used to rate the relative safety of their cities.

A third advantage of using the written record is that sometimes the record has existed long enough to permit analyses of political phenomena *over time*. The before-and-after research designs discussed in Chapter 5 may then be used. For example, suppose you are interested in the impact of the 55-mile-per-hour speed limit (gradually adopted by the states) on the rate of traffic accidents. Assuming that the written record contains data on the incidence of traffic accidents over time in each state, you could compare the accident rate before and after the introduction of a 55 mph limit in those states that lowered their speed limit. These changes in the accident rate could then be compared with the changes occurring in states in which no change in the speed limit took place. The rate changes could then be "corrected" for other factors that might affect the rate of traffic accidents. (We will discuss how this is done in Chapter 13.) In this way an *interrupted time series research design* could be used, a research design that has some important advantages over cross-sectional designs. Because of the importance of time, and of changes in phenomena over time, for the acquisition of causal knowledge, a data source that supports longitudinal analyses is a valuable one. The written record more readily permits longitudinal analyses than either interview data or direct observation generally do.

A fourth advantage to researchers of using the written record is that it often enables us to *increase sample size* above what would be possible through either interviews or direct observation. For example, it would be terribly expensive and time consuming to observe the level of spending by all candidates for the House of Representatives in any given year. Interviewing candidates would require either a lot of travel, long-distance phone calls, or the design of a mail questionnaire to secure the necessary information. Direct observation would require gaining access to many campaigns. How much easier and less expensive to contact the Federal Election Commission in Washington, D.C., and request the printout of campaign spending for all House candidates! Without this written record, resources might permit only the inclusion of a handful of campaigns in a study; with the written record, all 435 campaigns can easily be included.

This raises the fifth main advantage of using the written record: *cost*. Since the cost of creating, organizing, and preserving the written record is borne by the record keepers, researchers are able to conduct research projects on a much smaller budget than would be the case if they had to bear the cost themselves. In fact, one of the major beneficiaries of the record-keeping activities of the federal government and of news organizations is the research community.[44] It would cost a prohibitive amount for a researcher to measure the amount of crime in all cities larger than 25,000 or to collect the voting returns in all 435 congressional districts. Both pieces of information are available at little or no cost, however, because of the record-keeping activities of the FBI and the Elections Research Center, respectively.

Similarly, using the written record often saves a researcher considerable *time*. It is usually much quicker to consult printed government documents, reference materials, computerized data, and research institute reports than it is to accumulate data ourselves. The written record is a veritable treasure for researchers. Collecting data in this manner, however, is not without some disadvantages.

One problem mentioned earlier is *selective survival*. For a variety of reasons, record keepers may not preserve all pertinent materials but rather selectively save those that are the least embarrassing, controversial, or problematic. It would be surprising, for example, if political candidates, campaign consultants, and public officials saved correspondence and memoranda that cast disfavor on themselves. Obviously, whenever a person is selectively preserving portions of the written record, the accuracy of what remains is suspect. This is less of a problem the less the connection between the record keeper's self-interest and the subject being examined by the researcher.

A second, related disadvantage of the written record is its *incompleteness,* for reasons other than the selectivity of the record keeper. There are large gaps in many archives due to fires, losses of other types, personnel shortages that hinder record-keeping activities, and the failure of the record maker or record keeper to regard a record as worthy of preservation. We all throw out personal records every day; political entities do the same. It is very difficult to know what kinds of records should be preserved, and it is often impossible for record keepers to bear the costs of maintaining and storing voluminous amounts of material.

Another reason why records may be incomplete is simply because no person or organization has assumed the responsibility for collecting or preserving them. For example, before 1930 national crime statistics were not collected by the FBI, and before the creation of the Federal Election Commission in 1971 records on campaign expenditures by candidates for the U.S. Congress were spotty and inaccurate.

A third disadvantage of the written record is that its content may be *biased.* Not only may the record be incomplete or selectively preserved, but it also may be inaccurate or falsified, either inadvertently or on purpose. For example, memoranda or copies of letters that were never sent may be filed, events may be conveniently forgotten or misrepresented, the authorship of documents may be disguised, and the dates of written records may be altered; furthermore, the content of governmental reports may tell more about political interests than empirical facts. For example, Soviet and Eastern European governments have apparently been releasing exaggerated reports of their economic performance for many years; scholars (and investigators) attempting to reconstruct the actions in the Watergate episode have been hampered by alterations of the record by those worried about the legality of their role in it. Often historical interpretations rest upon who said or did what, and when. To the extent that falsifications of the written record lead to erroneous conclusions, the problem of record-keeping accuracy can bias the results of a research project. The main safeguard against bias is the one used by responsible journalists: confirming important pieces of information through several dissimilar sources.

A fourth disadvantage is that some written records are *unavailable* to researchers. Documents may be classified by the federal government; they may be sealed (that is, not made public) until a legal action has ceased or the political actors involved have passed away; or they may be stored in such a way that they are difficult to use. Other written records—such as the memoranda of multinational corporations, campaign consultants, and Supreme Court justices—are seldom made public because there is no legal obligation to do so and the authors benefit from keeping them private.

Finally, the written record may *lack a standard format* because it is kept by different people. For example, the Chicago budget office may have different budget categories for public expenditures than the San Francisco budget office does. Or the Chicago budget office may have had different budget categories before 1960 than it had after 1960. Or the French may include different items in their published military defense expenditures than the Chileans do. Consequently, a researcher often must expend considerable effort to ensure that the formats in which records are kept by different record-keeping entities can be made comparable.

Despite these limitations, political scientists have generally found that the advantages of using the written record outweigh the disadvantages. The written record often supplements the data we collect through interviews and direct observation, and in many cases it is the only source of data on historical and cross-cultural political phenomena.

Conclusion

The written record includes personal records, archival collections, organizational statistics, and the products of the news media. Researchers interested in historical research, or in a particular event or time in the life of a polity, generally use the episodic record. Gaining access to the appropriate material is often the most resource-consuming aspect of this method of data collection, and the hypothesis testing that results is usually more qualitative and less rigorous (some would say more flexible) than with the running record.

The running record of organizations has become a rich source of political data as a result of the record-keeping activities of governments at all levels and of interest groups and research institutes concerned with public affairs. The running record is generally more quantitative than the episodic record and may be used to conduct longitudinal research. Measurements using the running record can often be obtained inexpensively, although the researcher frequently relinquishes considerable control over the data collection enterprise in exchange for this economy.

One of the ways in which a voluminous, nonnumerical written record may be turned into numerical measures and then used to test hypotheses is through a procedure called content analysis. Content analysis is most frequently used by political scientists interested in studying media content, but it has been used to advantage in studies of political speeches, statutes, and judicial decisions.

Through the written record researchers may observe political phenomena that are geographically, physically, and temporally distant from them. Without such records, our ability to record and measure historical phenomena, cross-cultural phenomena, and political behavior that does not occur in public would be seriously hampered.

Notes

1. Frank Way and Barbara J. Burt, "Religious Marginality and the Free Exercise Clause," *American Political Science Review* 77 (September 1983): 652-665; Samuel C. Patterson and Gregory A. Caldeira, "Getting Out the Vote: Participation in Gubernatorial Elections," *American Political Science Review* 77 (September 1983): 675-689; William Zimmerman and Glenn Palmer, "Words and Deeds in Soviet Foreign Policy: The Case of Soviet Military Expenditures," *American Political Science Review* 77 (June 1983): 358-367; and Alan P. L. Liu, "The Politics of Corruption in the People's Republic of China," *American Political Science Review* 77 (September 1983): 602-623.
2. Gary C. Jacobson, *Money in Congressional Elections* (New Haven, Conn.: Yale University Press, 1980); Jeffrey A. Segal and Albert D. Cover, "Ideological Values and the Votes of U.S. Supreme Court Justices," *American Political Science Review* 83 (June 1989): 557-565; and Manus I. Midlarsky, "Rulers and the Ruled: Patterned Inequality and the Onset of Mass Political Violence," *American Political Science Review* 82 (June 1988): 491-509.
3. Charles Beard reports that he was able to use some records in the U.S. Treasury Department in Washington "only after a vacuum cleaner had been brought in to excavate the ruins." See Beard, *An Economic Interpretation of the Constitution of the United States* (London: MacMillan, 1913), 22.
4. Sandra Van Burkleo, "My Own 'Desperate Deeds and Desperate Motives': How the Project Evolved," in W. Phillips Shively, ed., *The Research Process in Political Science.* Copyright © 1984, 214-218. Reprinted with permission of the publisher, F. E. Peacock Publishers, Inc., Itasca, Ill.
5. Kai T. Erikson, *The Wayward Puritans* (New York: Wiley, 1966).
6. The records of the governor were edited by Nathaniel B. Shurtleff and printed by order of the Massachusetts legislature in 1853-1854; the records of the courts were edited by George Francis Dow and published by the Essex Institute in Salem, Massachusetts.
7. Erikson, *The Wayward Puritans,* 209-210.
8. Beard, *An Economic Interpretation.*
9. Ibid., 324. Beard's interpretation has been challenged by several historians. Among his critics are Robert E. Brown, *Charles Beard and the Constitution* (Princeton, N.J.: Princeton University Press, 1956); Forrest McDonald, *We the People: The Economic Origins of the Constitution* (Chicago: University of Chicago Press, 1958); and Gordon Wood, *The Creation of the American Republic* (New York: W. W. Norton, 1972). Although Beard's interpretation continues to be controversial, the authors of one mainstream political science textbook have concluded that "although historical evidence does not fully support Beard's conclusions, most historians acknowledge that economic

interests were very much at issue in the framing and ratification of the Constitution" (Lewis Lipsitz and David M. Speak, *American Democracy,* 2d ed. [New York: St. Martin's, 1989], 76).

10. James David Barber, *The Presidential Character,* 3d ed. (Englewood Cliffs, N.J.: Prentice-Hall, 1985), 4, 5.

11. Ibid., 1st ed. (1972), ix.

12. A critique of Barber's analysis may be found in Garry Wills, *The Kennedy Imprisonment* (Boston: Little, Brown, 1982).

13. Andrew Hacker, *U/S: A Statistical Portrait* (New York: Viking, 1983).

14. Jacobson, *Money in Congressional Elections.*

15. George F. Bishop, Robert G. Meadow, and Marilyn Jackson-Beeck, eds., *The Presidential Debates* (New York: Praeger, 1980); Sidney Kraus, ed., *The Great Debates* (Gloucester, Mass.: Peter Smith, 1978); *Congressional Quarterly Weekly Report,* September 27, 1980, 2863-2869; *Congressional Quarterly Almanac,* 1980, 127B-137B; and *Congressional Quarterly Almanac,* 1984, 107B-127B.

16. Segal and Cover, "Ideological Values."

17. Midlarsky, "Rulers and the Ruled." The data on land ownership in Latin America were taken from James W. Wilkie and Adam Perkal, eds. *Statistical Abstract of Latin America,* vol. 24 (for 1985) (Los Angeles: University of California, 1986); the data on deaths due to political violence are in Charles L. Taylor and David A. Jodice, *World Handbook of Political and Social Indicators,* vols. 1 and 2 (New Haven: Yale University Press, 1983).

18. See C. Wright Mills, *The Power Elite* (New York: Oxford University Press, 1956); G. William Domhoff, *Who Rules America?* (Englewood Cliffs, N.J.: Prentice-Hall, 1967); and Andrew Hacker, "The Elected and the Anointed: Two American Elites," *American Political Science Review* 55 (September 1961): 539-549.

19. Marvin E. Wolfgang, "Uniform Crime Reports: A Critical Appraisal," *University of Pennsylvania Law Review* 111 (April 1963): 717-718.

20. Ibid; Sophia M. Robison, "A Critical View of the Uniform Crime Reports," *Michigan Law Review* 64 (April 1966); Marvin E. Wolfgang, "Urban Crime," in James Q. Wilson, ed., *The Metropolitan Enigma* (Garden City, N.Y.: Doubleday, 1970), 280; and U.S. President's Commission on Law Enforcement and Administration of Justice, *The Challenge of Crime in a Free Society* (New York: Dutton, 1968), 97.

21. Peter P. Lejins, "Uniform Crime Reports," *Michigan Law Review* 64 (April 1966): 1018.

22. Wolfgang, "Uniform Crime Reports," 715; Wolfgang, "Urban Crime," 280-281; President's Commission, *The Challenge,* 107-112; and Robison, "A Critical View," 1033-1037.

23. Wolfgang, "Uniform Crime Reports," 709-710.

24. Lejins, "Uniform Crime Reports," 1019-1020.

25. Wolfgang, "Uniform Crime Reports," 714, 716; and Robison, "A Critical View," 1040-1041.

26. Robison, "A Critical View," 1042.

27. Wolfgang, "Urban Crime," 279.

28. Wolfgang, "Uniform Crime Reports," 710.

29. Ibid., 721-724; and Wolfgang, "Urban Crime," 281.

30. Wolfgang, "Uniform Crime Reports," 709-710.

31. Ibid., 719-720; and Robison, "A Critical View," 1043-1045.

32. Kenneth D. Bailey, *Methods of Social Research,* 2d ed. (New York: Free

Press, 1982), 312-313.

33. Segal and Cover, "Ideological Values."
34. Bailey, *Methods of Social Research,* 319.
35. Michael J. Robinson and Margaret A. Sheehan, *Over the Wire and on TV* (New York: Russell Sage, 1983). On their survey decisions, discussed in the following paragraphs, see 17-27.
36. On the 1976 campaign, see Thomas Patterson, *The Mass Media Election: How Americans Choose Their President* (New York: Praeger, 1980). On the 1974 congressional elections, see Arthur Miller, Edie Goldenberg, and Lutz Erbring, "Type-Set Politics: Impact of Newspapers on Public Confidence," *American Political Science Review* 73 (March 1979): 67-84.
37. Robinson and Sheehan, *Over the Wire,* 20.
38. Ibid., 49-50.
39. Ibid., 92.
40. Ibid., 94-95.
41. Ibid., 144, 145, 155.
42. Ibid., 173.
43. Ibid., 22.
44. The proposed national budget for fiscal 1986 included the following amounts (in millions of dollars) for the major data collection agencies of the national government: Bureau of the Census, $88.0 (53 percent increase over 1981); National Center for Health Statistics, $48.0 (37 percent increase over 1981); Bureau of Justice Statistics, $16.7 (14 percent increase over 1981); Bureau of Labor Statistics, $148.3 (44 percent increase over 1981); and National Archives and Records Administration, $99.4 (17 percent increase over 1981). Consortium of Social Science Associations, *Washington Update,* vol. 2, no. 3, February 15, 1985.

Terms Introduced

Content analysis. A procedure by which verbal, nonquantitative records are transformed into quantitative data.
Episodic record. The portion of the written record that is not part of a regular, ongoing record-keeping enterprise.
Running record. The portion of the written record that is enduring and covers an extensive period of time.
Written record. Documents, reports, statistics, manuscripts, and other written, oral, or visual materials available and useful for empirical research.

Exercises

1. Find a recent volume of *The Statistical Abstract of the United States* and glance through its contents. Devise a testable hypothesis that could be evaluated with data contained therein.

2. Suppose the United Nations asked each member nation to supply data about its rates of illiteracy, infant mortality, and malnutrition. What problems would

there be with using such records as the basis for a measure of health in different nations?

3. Read Appendix D of Raymond E. Wolfinger and Steven J. Rosenstone's *Who Votes?* (New Haven, Conn.: Yale University Press, 1980). What difficulties did Wolfinger and Rosenstone encounter in using the written record to devise measures of election laws in each of the states? Do you think that their measures are both reliable and valid? Explain your answer.

4. In Jeffrey A. Segal and Albert D. Cover, "Ideological Values and the Votes of U.S. Supreme Court Justices," *American Political Science Review* 83 (June 1989): 557-565, the researchers rely on content analysis of newspaper editorials to measure the ideology of Supreme Court justices. How did the researchers decide which newspapers to use? What were the content categories they developed? What level of measurement resulted? How did they assess the reliability of their content analysis measures? What documents have been used by other researchers to measure the political attitudes of justices?

Suggested Readings

Hacker, Andrew, ed. *U/S: A Statistical Portrait of the American People*. New York: Viking, 1983.

Kalvelage, Carl, and Morley Segal. *Research Guide in Political Science*. 2d ed. Glenview, Ill.: Scott, Foresman, 1976.

Van Burkleo, Sandra. "My Own 'Desperate Deeds and Desperate Motives': How the Project Evolved." In *The Research Process in Political Science*, edited by W. Phillips Shively. Itasca, Ill.: F. E. Peacock, 1984.

Webb, Eugene J., et al. *Nonreactive Measures in the Social Sciences*. 2d ed. Boston: Houghton Mifflin, 1981.

CHAPTER 10

Observation

In the preceding two chapters we have discussed the two sources of data used most frequently by political scientists: interviews or questionnaires and the written record. In this chapter we consider a third method of collecting data about political phenomena: observation. Although observation is more generally a research tool of anthropologists, psychologists, and sociologists, political scientists have used it to good advantage as well. For example, observation has been used by political scientists to study political campaigning, community politics, leadership and executive decision making, program implementation, judicial proceedings, the U.S. Congress, and state legislatures. In fact, any student who has had an internship, kept a daily log or diary, or written a paper based on his or her experiences has used this method of data collection.

Every day we "collect data" using observational techniques. We observe some attribute or characteristic of people and infer some behavioral trait from that observation. For example, we watch the car in front of us sway between the traffic lanes and conclude that the driver has been drinking; we observe the dress, physical features, and facial expressions of a student in one of our classes and decide that the person is someone we would like to meet; or we decide not to try to sell encyclopedias at a house that is dilapidated and surrounded by junk. The observational techniques used by political scientists are really only extensions of this method of data collection. They resemble everyday observations, but are usually more self-conscious and systematic.

Observations may be classified in at least four different ways: *direct* or *indirect, participant* or *nonparticipant, overt* or *covert,* and *structured* or *unstructured.* The most basic distinction is whether an observation is direct—the actual behavior, verbal or nonverbal, is observed firsthand—or indirect—the results or physical traces of behavior are observed.[1] For example, an indirect method of observing college students' favorite studying spots in classrooms and office buildings would be to arrive on campus early in the morning before the custodial staff and measure the amount of food wrappers, soda cans, and other debris at various locations. A direct method of observing the same thing would be to go around the buildings and notice where students are.

In participant observation, the investigator is a regular participant in the activities or group being observed. For example, someone who studies political campaigns by becoming actively involved in them is a participant observer. A nonparticipant observer does not participate in group activities or become a member of the group or community. For example, an investigator studying children at play might sit quietly in the background and make no attempt to become a part of the play activity.

A third way to characterize observation is by noting whether it is overt or covert. In overt observation, those being observed are aware of the investigator's presence and intentions. In covert observation, the investigator's presence is hidden or undisclosed and his or her intentions are disguised. For example, two social scientists studying student conversations once hid under beds in students' rooms.[2] Covert observation may be the only way to observe some phenomena, but as you might imagine, the method often raises important ethical questions.

In structured observation, the investigator looks for and systematically records the incidence of specific behaviors. In unstructured observation, all behavior is considered relevant, at least at first, and recorded. Only later, upon reflection, will the investigator distinguish between important and trivial behavior.

In this chapter we shall discuss observation as a method of data collection and some of the ethical issues associated with it. As we will see, observation, like other research methods, has both advantages and disadvantages.

Direct Observation

The vast majority of observation studies conducted by political scientists have been the result of direct observation, either in a laboratory or in a natural setting.

Laboratory Settings

Observation in a laboratory setting gives a researcher the advantage of control over the environment of the observed. Thus the researcher may be able to employ more rigorous experimental designs than are possible in a natural, uncontrolled setting. Also observation may be easier and more convenient to record and preserve since one-way windows, video-tape machines, and other observational aids are more readily available in a laboratory.

A disadvantage of laboratory observation is that subjects usually know they are being observed and therefore may alter their behavior, raising questions about the validity of the data collected. The use of aids that allow the observer to be physically removed from the setting and laboratories that are designed to be as inviting and as natural as possible may lead subjects to behave more naturally and less self-consciously. In some cases, researchers have deceived subjects about the true purpose of the observation so that they will behave more naturally. This, of course, may be viewed as unethical.

A good example of an attempt to create a natural-looking laboratory setting may be found in Stanley Milgram and R. Lance Shotland's book *Television and Antisocial Behavior*.[3] These researchers were interested in the impact of television programming on adult behavior, specifically in the ability of television drama to stimulate antisocial acts such as theft. They devised four versions of a program called "Medical Center," each with a different plot, and showed the versions in a theater to four different audiences. Some of the versions showed a character stealing money, and the versions differed in whether the person was punished for his theft or not. The participants in the study were then asked to go to a particular office at a particular time to pick up a free transistor radio, their payment for participating in the research study. When they arrived in the office (the laboratory), they encountered a sign that said the radios were all gone. The researchers were then interested in how people would react and specifically in whether they would imitate any of the behaviors in the versions of "Medical Center" that they had seen (such as the theft of money from see-through plastic collection dishes). Their behavior was observed covertly via a one-way mirror. Once the subjects left the office, they were directed to another location where they were, in fact, given the promised radio.

Laboratory observation may be structured or unstructured. Only specific behaviors may be of interest and recorded, or all behavior may be recorded because it is considered potentially relevant. Recording aids in laboratory settings are helpful in this regard.

Researchers interested in child development often use laboratory observation to study parent-child interaction and other aspects of child behavior. The standard procedure in studies of the impact of violent movies or television programs on children is to divide the children into two groups, expose each group to a different type of video presentation, and then observe the play of the two separated groups, looking for instances of aggressive, violent, or antisocial behavior.[4]

Laboratory observation also has frequently been used to study group dynamics and the development of and response to power and authority. In Milgram's well-known study of obedience to authority, individuals were enlisted to help in an experiment. The purpose of the experiment, they were told, was to test the learning response of the subjects. The task of the individuals was to administer electric shocks to the subjects as instructed by the researcher. Actually the researcher's helpers were the real subjects and, unknown to the helpers, the electric shocks were fake. Many of the helpers complied with the researcher's requests to administer electric shocks despite the screams of the subjects: to have done otherwise, they thought, would have ruined the experiment. The real purpose of the study was to test obedience to authority even if it meant inflicting harm on others.[5] As you might imagine, this study has raised numerous ethical concerns, which we will discuss later in this chapter.

Field Studies

Political scientists have used direct observation as a data collection technique in natural settings or *field studies* more than in the laboratory. The advantage of observing people in a natural setting rather than in the artificiality of a laboratory setting is that people can generally be expected to behave as they would ordinarily. Furthermore, field studies permit the investigator to observe people for longer periods of time than would be possible in a laboratory. In fact, one of the striking features of field studies is the considerable amount of time an investigator may spend in the field. It is not uncommon for investigators to live in the community they are observing for a year or more. William F. Whyte's fascinating study of life in an Italian slum, *Street Corner Society,* was based on three years of observation (1937-1940), and Marc Ross's study of political participation in Nairobi, Kenya, took more than a year of field observation.[6] To study the behavior of U.S. representatives in their districts, Richard Fenno traveled intermittently for almost 7 years, making 36 separate visits and spending 110 working days in 18 congressional districts.[7]

Sometimes researchers have no choice but to observe political phenomena as they occur in their natural setting. Written records of events may not exist, or the records may not cover the behavior of interest to the researcher. Relying on personal accounts of participants may be unsatisfactory because of participants' distorted views of events, incomplete memories, or failure to observe what is of interest to the researcher.

Like laboratory observation, observation in field studies may be structured or unstructured. Hugh Lytton conducted a structured field study to compare parent-child interaction in families with twins and families with a single child. His assistants in this study learned an elaborate system of codes for various kinds of behaviors (for example, Code F57C3: Father romps with child, but in a gentle manner).[8] The codes were then quietly dictated into a tape machine. Another tape recorder taped the verbal interaction of family members. Dictation instead of note taking allowed the observers to see more, while the taped interaction provided a check on coded observation. Observer reliability was promoted through extensive training and by the use of a second observer on occasion. The two-tape-recorder method proved to be less intrusive than a videotape camera, which the observers discovered could not easily be kept focused on all relevant subjects anyway.

Lytton felt it was important to observe in the home since a laboratory setting would have reduced the validity of the observations. Data validity was further protected by conducting several lengthy observation sessions; it was felt that the families would be unlikely to maintain a front for the entire time period.

The term *field study* usually refers to open-ended and wide-ranging rather than structured observation in a natural setting. The studies by Whyte and Fenno were of this nature. Open-ended, flexible observation is appropriate if the research purpose of the field study is one of description and exploration. For example, Fenno's research purpose was to study "representatives' perceptions of their constituencies while they are actually in their constituencies...."[9] As Fenno explains, his visits with representatives in their districts

> were totally open-ended and exploratory. I tried to observe and inquire into anything and everything these members did. I worried about whatever they worried about. Rather than assume that I already knew what was interesting, I remained prepared to find interesting questions emerging in the course of the experience. The same with data. The research method was largely one of soaking and poking or just hanging around.[10]

In these kinds of field studies, researchers do not start out with particular hypotheses that they want to test. They often do not know enough about what they plan to observe to establish lists and specific categories of behaviors to look for and record systematically. The purpose of the research is to discover what these might be.

Some political scientists have used observation as a preliminary research method.[11] For example, James Robinson's work in Congress provided firsthand information for his studies of the House Rules Committee and of the role of Congress in foreign policy making.[12] Ralph Huitt's service on Lyndon B. Johnson's Senate majority leader staff gave Huitt inside access to information for his study of Democratic party leadership in the Senate.[13] And David Minar served as a school board member and used his experience to develop questionnaires in his comparative study of several school districts in the Chicago area.[14]

Most field studies involve participant observation. An investigator cannot, like a fly on the wall, observe a group of people for long periods of time. Usually he or she must assume a role or identity within the group that is being studied and participate in the activities of the group.

Acceptance by the group is necessary if the investigator is going to benefit from the naturalness of the research setting. An investigator who remains a stranger or complete outsider is unlikely to be privy to natural behavior, particularly behavior that is sensitive and could cause embarrassment or other harm if revealed to an outsider. If the observer can gain the trust of the observed, greater opportunities for observation arise. As noted earlier, many political scientists who have studied Congress have worked as staff members on committees and in congressional offices.

Field work using participant observation is also commonly referred to as *ethnography.* Cultural anthropologists and sociologists frequently use this method. Some well-known examples in addition to Whyte's study are Margaret Mead's *Coming of Age in Samoa,* Elliot Liebow's *Tally's Corner,* Herbert Gans's *The Levittowners,* and Arthur J. Vidich and Joseph Bensman's *Small Town in Mass Society.*[15]

Investigators using participant observation often depend on members of the group they are observing to serve as *informants,* persons who are willing to be interviewed about the activities and behavior of themselves and of the group to which they belong. An informant also helps the researcher interpret behavior. A close relationship between the researcher and informant may help the researcher gain access to other group members, not only because an informant may familiarize the researcher with community members and norms, but also because the informant, through close association with the researcher, will be able to pass on information about the researcher to the community.[16] Some participant observation studies will have one key informant; others will have several. For example, Whyte relied on the leader of a street corner gang whom he called "Doc" as his key informant, while Fenno's eighteen representatives all could be considered informants.

Although a valuable asset to researchers, informants may present problems. A researcher should not rely too much on one or a few informants since they may give a biased view of a community. And if the informant is associated with one faction in a multifaction community or is a marginal member of the community (and thus more willing to associate with the researcher), the researcher's affiliation with the informant may inhibit rather than enhance access to the community.[17]

Participant observers may be covert or overt about their activities. In covert observation, the participant investigator does not reveal his or her research purpose on the assumption that the presence of a researcher would not be accepted or that it would alter the behavior of the observed. In overt observation, members of the group are aware that they are being studied and are informed of the general purpose of the study. The line between covert and overt observation is not entirely clear, however. Those being observed may be told only in a general way the purpose of the research—not because the investigator wishes to deceive the group, but due to the open-ended nature of the research. In fact, the investigator may not decide on the actual direction of the research until much later. As Fenno puts it, "Only after prolonged, unstructured soaking is the problem formulated. Indeed, the reformulation of a problem or a question may be the end product of the research."[18] In other cases a researcher will be deliberately vague about the intended direction of the study for fear of rejection.

Some social scientists oppose covert observation as unethical.[19] The pursuit of knowledge does not justify deceit, they claim, even though researchers might not gain entry to a group or be able to observe natural, unaffected behavior if their research purposes were revealed. Subjects of the research may be harmed if they reveal damaging information about themselves—information they would have concealed if they had been aware that they were being studied. A second argument against covert participant observation is that subsequent revelation of deceit will lead to a backlash against social research and limit opportunities for other researchers.

Finally, a third argument against covert observation is that it is an unreliable and unsound research method. Deceit may alter the nature of the interaction between observed and observer. For example, covert participant observation of a flying saucer cult whose members predicted the end of the world probably damaged the validity of the data collected. In the study the researchers posed as cult members and believers. Since the cult was small in size, deceit very likely altered the behavior of the cult by reinforcing the beliefs of cult members. With enhanced expectations, harm to cult members was also increased when the prophesied end did not materialize. Thus ethical issues were raised as well.[20]

Participant observation offers the advantages of a natural setting, the opportunity to observe people for lengthy periods of time so that interaction and changes in behavior may be studied, and a degree of accuracy impossible with recall data such as that obtained in surveys. However, there are some noteworthy limitations to the method as well.

The main problem with direct, participant observation as a method of empirical research for political scientists is that many significant instances of political behavior are not accessible for observation. The privacy of the voter in the voting booth is legally protected, U.S. Supreme Court conferences are not open to anyone but the justices themselves, political consultants and bureaucrats do not usually wish to have political scientists privy to their discussions and decisions, and most White House conversations and deliberations are carefully guarded. Occasionally physical traces of these private behaviors become public—such as the Watergate tapes of Richard Nixon's conversations with his aides—and disclosures about some aspects of government decision making, such as congressional committee hearings and Supreme Court oral arguments; but typically access is the major barrier to directly observing consequential political behavior.

Another disadvantage of participant observation is lack of control over the environment. A researcher may be unable to isolate individual factors and observe their effect on behavior. Efforts to manipulate interactions among informants or subjects may be awkward and conflict with the expectations of subjects that the participant observer should remain a passive member of the social group. For example, to gain favor with a key member of a street gang, Whyte took the side of the member in a gang discussion. This antagonized the other side, and his plan backfired. Perceiving that Whyte was on his side, the member decided that he need not make an effort to establish closer relations with him. Thus Whyte failed to achieve his aim of greater rapport with this gang member.

Participant observation is also limited by the small number of cases that are usually involved. For example, Fenno observed only eighteen members or would-be members of Congress—too few for any sort of statistical analysis. He chose "analytical depth" over "analytical range"; in-depth observation of eighteen cases was the limit that Fenno thought he could manage intellectually, professionally, financially, and physically.[21] Whyte observed one street-corner gang in-depth, although he did observe others less closely. Because of the small numbers of cases, the representativeness of the results of participant observation has been questioned.

Unstructured participant observation also has been criticized as invalid and biased. A researcher may selectively perceive behaviors, noting some, ignoring others. The interpretation of behaviors may reflect the personality and culture of the observer rather than the meaning attributed to them by the observed themselves. Moreover, the presence of the observer may alter the behavior of the observed no matter how skillfully the observer attempts to become accepted as a nonthreatening part of the community.

Field workers attempt to minimize these possible threats to data validity by immersing themselves in the culture they are observing and by taking copious notes on everything going on around them no matter how seemingly trivial. Events without apparent meaning at the time of observation may become important and revealing upon later reflection. Of course, copious note taking leads to what is known as a *high dross rate:* much of what is recorded is not relevant to the research problem or question as it is finally formulated. It may be painful for the investigator to discard so much of the material that was carefully recorded, but this is a standard practice with this method.

Another way to attain more valid data is to allow the observed to read and comment on what the investigator has written and point out events and behavior that may have been misinterpreted. This check on observations may be of limited or no value if the observed cannot read or if the written material is aimed at persons well versed in the researcher's discipline and therefore is over the observed's head.

Researchers' observations may be compromised, however, if the researchers begin to overidentify with their subjects or informants. "Going native," as this phenomenon is known, may lead them to paint a more complimentary picture of the observed than is warranted. Researchers combat this problem by returning to their own culture to analyze their data and by asking colleagues or others to comment on their findings.

By now you should have some understanding of various types of field studies and their advantages and disadvantages. We now will focus on four common aspects of all fieldwork experiences: gaining access, learning the ropes, maintaining relations, and leaving the field.[22] This section should be especially helpful to novice researchers and to students doing observational studies as part of an internship.

How to Conduct Fieldwork

If you have served as an intern for a government agency, a private organization, or an elected representative, you may recall your initial uneasiness as you learned your way around and became acquainted with your co-workers. If you were supposed to write a report based on your internship experiences, you may have felt additional pressure to understand what was going on and to be accepted. Those you were observing as part of your internship may have attempted to influence information you obtained, the content of your report, or the audience to whom it would be given. Perhaps this description of the rigors of fieldwork rings true with your own experience in the field:

> Fieldwork must certainly rank with the more disagreeable activities that humanity has fashioned for itself. It is usually inconvenient, to say the least, sometimes physically uncomfortable, frequently embarrassing and, to a degree, always tense. Sociologists and anthropologists, among others in the social sciences, have voluntarily immersed themselves for the sake of research in situations all but a tiny minority of humanity goes to great lengths to avoid....
>
> For most researchers the day-to-day demands of fieldwork are regularly fraught with feelings of uncertainty and anxiety. The

process of becoming immersed over an extended period of time in a way of life that is often both novel and strange exposes the researcher to situations and experiences that are usually accompanied by an intense concern with whether the research is conducted and managed properly.[23]

As this quote indicates, doing fieldwork can be a physically and mentally demanding task. The first challenge usually involves *gaining access* to those you wish to study. There is no single way of gaining entry; access depends on the characteristics of the fieldworker and of his or her subjects. Usually a fieldworker must receive permission to observe activities or assume a role within the group that allows the opportunity for observation. Fenno used the direct approach of writing letters to members of Congress. In the letter he described his research topic in general terms, gave personal references, and requested permission to accompany the representative on district visits. After he had conducted several district visits, his letters included references to representatives whom he had already accompanied.[24]

But such a direct approach will not always work. Those you wish to study may not comprehend or sympathize with your research needs, or they may suspect you as an outsider (even Fenno experienced these problems). Here access may be facilitated by a member of the subject group who acts as a reference or initial go-between. Whyte gained access to the street-corner gang by talking to social workers in the local settlement house. One of the social workers introduced him to Doc, who became his key informant and entrée into the community. Doc also provided tips on appropriate behavior for Whyte. Commenting on his success, Whyte explains, "At the time I found it hard to believe that I could move in as easily as Doc had said with his sponsorship. But that indeed was the way it turned out." [25]

Whyte's previous efforts at gaining entry had not been successful. In one attempt he followed a Harvard colleague's suggestion that access could be obtained by picking up a young woman at a local bar.

There I encountered a situation for which my adviser had not prepared me. There were women present all right, but none of them was alone. Some were there in couples, and there were two or three pairs of women together. I pondered this situation briefly. I had little confidence in my skill at picking up one female, and it seemed inadvisable to tackle two at the same time. Still, I was determined not to admit defeat without a struggle. I looked around me again and now noticed a threesome: one man and two women. It occurred to me that here was a maldistribution of females which I might be able to rectify. I approached the group and opened with something like this: "Pardon me. Would you mind if I joined you?" There was a moment of silence while the man stared at me. He then offered to throw me downstairs. I assured him that this would not be necessary and demonstrated as much by walking right out of there without any assistance.[26]

In other cases a researcher may assume a role within a community before making the research role known (if ever). For example, Laud Humphreys studied homosexual behavior in public restrooms by assuming the role of a "lookout" (someone who watches for the approach of police, youths, or others who may harass homosexuals). David Karp hung around Times Square to study behavior in public places. And William Chambliss claimed to be a truck driver and frequented an amusement parlor in Seattle's skid-row area to begin his study of crime in that city.[27]

Gaining entry is only the first step in achieving access. In *learning the ropes,* a researcher must learn appropriate behavior and gain acceptance from those being studied. Rapport must be established between the observer and the observed. Without a mutual feeling of trust and understanding, a researcher may move into a community and not be threatened or asked to leave, yet be unable to carry out his or her research. For example, Myron and Penina Glazer moved to Chile to study the professional and political attitudes of Chilean university students, but they found that students were extremely suspicious of North Americans and were reluctant to agree to be interviewed.[28] Fenno found that he had to establish rapport with representatives' gatekeepers (wives, friends, district staff) as well as with the representatives. Acceptance was facilitated by his active participation in district activities, such as telephone polling and handing out campaign material, and his willingness to be patient and not compete with gatekeepers for access to a member of Congress.

Gaining acceptance may require changes in a researcher's behavior and attitudes. For example, in her study of army life, Arlene K. Daniels found that she had to conform with military officers' ideas of appropriate female behavior and change her critical attitude toward career officers before she could conduct her research.[29] It is not always necessary for the researcher to behave exactly as the researched, however. The researcher may be accepted without assuming the language and behavior of those being studied. Whatever the circumstances and conditions of the fieldwork, this is a stressful stage for the researcher since the success of the research effort hinges on the ability to establish rapport.

Maintaining relations is the process of building upon the rapport the researcher has established with the observed. A researcher must take care not to speak or act in a way that will damage this rapport. If confidentiality has been promised to informants, the researcher must be careful not to reveal knowledge to other members of the informants' group that will violate that confidence.

Appropriate behavior for the researcher may change as the informants' views of the researcher evolve. In their study of the Unification Church and the anticult organization called the National Ad Hoc Committee Engaged in Freeing Minds, David Bromley and Anson Shupe found that rapport diminished as they became more knowledgeable about the organizations. Both groups "developed a sense of uneasiness that we had seen so much and yet remained unconvinced, and the failure to embrace their respective points of view tended to threaten their faiths (and our positions, dependent as they were on our informants' cooperation and good will) in the self-evident rightness of their causes." [30]

Another problem in maintaining relations may stem from achieving too much rapport. In his study of members of Congress, Fenno preferred to create and maintain business friendships rather than personal friendships with his informants. In one case where Fenno was treated as a personal friend, he found that he could not ask probing questions important for his research. The representative was in a close reelection contest and would have considered such behavior by a personal friend unacceptable and callous. [31]

In some situations a researcher has to choose between engaging in unacceptable or illegal behavior and losing rapport. For example, Harold Pepinsky chose not to expose a policeman who to save face used a trumped-up charge against a youth. Pepinsky didn't disclose the crime because he wanted to maintain relations with the police on whom he depended for his dissertation research. [32] Whyte became so involved in one election in Cornerville that he cast four votes for his candidate and came close to being arrested. [33]

In *leaving the field* a researcher may confront a new set of problems. [34] Some researchers report that it is difficult to adjust, that they miss their research settings. [35] In overt participation observation, terminating relationships and coping with personal obligations that may have developed during a study may be difficult. A researcher may feel he or she is abandoning the observed. Yet usually the observed understand that the researcher has come into a setting to study it, not to stay. Some investigators continue friendships with informants and find that they enjoy these friendships more after completion of their research since they are freed from the role of observer. [36]

Of course, those who are covertly observed do not have expectations concerning the researcher's activities and departure. The researcher may find natural reasons for leaving the field and choose not to continue contact for fear of revealing his or her true identity. Leaving the field in covert observation may be problematic if the researcher is not in control of his or her departure. A researcher's cover role may be terminated before the completion of the research. If the cover role is terminated by the group being observed, gaining reentry may be extremely difficult.

A major problem associated with leaving the field is the writing and publication of the research findings. Researchers must confront the possibility that their observations will offend the observed. Care must be exercised to honor promises of anonymity and confidentiality given to informants. If the research report takes a long time to complete and informants have been promised a copy, the researcher may avoid contact with the informants until the report is in hand, further exacerbating the awkwardness of leaving the field.

One professor who observed the filming of a series of political commercials encountered great hostility upon the publication of his report.[37] This professor was asked by a friend and former student to go to the Southwest and help him film a series of commercials for a congressional candidate, a series the former student was hoping would further his own career as a film maker. Based on his participant observation, the professor wrote a report, published in an academic journal, that criticized the whole filming enterprise and elicited a highly negative reaction from his former student. It is most unlikely that the professor will ever be invited, by his former student at least, to observe the same type of activity again.

All researchers engaged in observational studies face some problems in gaining entry, learning the ropes, maintaining rapport, and leaving the field. But these problems must be weathered if the full advantages of gaining knowledge and understanding through participant observation are to be realized.

Another demanding yet essential part of a field study is *taking field notes*. Note taking can be divided into three types: mental notes, jotted notes, and field notes. *Mental note taking* involves orienting one's consciousness to the task of remembering things one has observed, such as "who and how many were there, the physical character of the place, who said what to whom, who moved about in what way, and a general characterization of an order of events."[38] Since mental notes may fade rapidly, researchers use *jotted notes* to preserve them. Jotted notes consist of short phrases and key words that will activate a researcher's memory later when the full field notes are written down.

Since note taking may disrupt observation, researchers often use restrooms, cars, and other private settings to make jotted notes. Note taking may be especially awkward while gaining rapport. Once rapport has been achieved field researchers may be able to jot down field notes or to use a recording device during observation. Field researchers may arrange interviews with informants to probe for desired information. For example, after Chambliss had spent a considerable amount of time in the bar and in the entertainment district in Seattle, he revealed his true identity and purpose to a bar manager and arranged interviews with a number of individuals engaged in criminal activity. Chambliss recorded these interviews and later revealed them to his informants, giving them the choice to keep the tapes. Only one informant, who had revealed a murder, refused to allow Chambliss to keep the recorded conversation.[39]

Taped interviews do not constitute full *field notes,* which should include a running description of conversations and events. John Lofland advises that researchers should be factual and concrete, avoid making inferences, and employ participants' descriptive and interpretative terms. Full field notes should include material previously forgotten and subsequently recalled. Lofland suggests that researchers distinguish between verbal material that is exact recall, paraphrased or close recall, and reasonable recall.[40]

Field notes should also include a researcher's analytic ideas and inferences, personal impressions and feelings, and notes for further information.[41] Because events and emotional states in a researcher's life may affect observation, they should be recorded. Notes for further information provide guidance for future observation, either to fill in gaps in observations, call attention to things that may happen, or test out emerging analytic themes.

Full field notes should be legible and should be reviewed periodically, since the passage of time may present past observations in a new light to the researcher or reveal a pattern worthy of attention in a series of disjointed events. Creating and reviewing field notes is an important part of the observational method. Consequently, a fieldworker should expect to spend as much time on field notes as is spent observing in the field.

Indirect Observation

Indirect observation, the observation of physical traces of behavior, is essentially detective work.[42] Based on physical traces, inferences about people and their behavior can be drawn. An unobtrusive research method, indirect observation is nonreactive: subjects do not change their behavior because they do not know they are being studied. Among indirect observation methods, Webb et al. distinguish between *erosion measures,* created by selective wear on some material, and *accretion measures,* created by the deposition and accumulation of materials.

Erosion Measures

An example of an erosion measure is the selective wearing of floor tiles in a museum.[43] Tiles around popular exhibits will tend to be more worn than those around less popular exhibits. Similarly, the rate at which carpeting and stairs are worn will indicate relative use. We know of at least one university where campus planners observed paths worn in grassy areas and then rerouted paved walkways to correspond to the most heavily trafficked routes. Other examples of natural erosion measures include wear on library books, wear and tear on selected articles within volumes, depletion of items in stores, and wear on upholstery.

In some cases the researcher may intervene in an erosion measure without impairing its nonreactivity. This may be done to reduce the problem of materials that erode too slowly to be measured in the desired time frame or to make sure that the materials are equivalent before the wearing activity occurs. For example, in a study measuring the activity level of children by how quickly their shoes wear out, children could be given identical shoes.[44]

Accretion Measures

Archeologists and geologists commonly use accretion measures in their research by measuring, mapping, and analyzing accretion of materials. Other professions find them useful as well. Webb et al. report a study in which mechanics in an automotive service department recorded radio dial settings to estimate radio station popularity.[45] This information was then used to select radio stations to carry the dealer's advertising. Popularity of television programs could be measured by drops in water levels during commercials since for very popular shows viewers tend to use the toilets only during commercials. Similarly, declines in telephone usage could indicate television program popularity. The presence of fingerprints and nose prints on glass display cases may indicate interest as well as reveal information about the size and age of those attracted to the display. The effectiveness of various antilitter policies and conservation programs could also be measured using physical trace evidence, and the amount and content of graffiti may represent an interesting measurement of the beliefs, attitudes, and mood of a population.

One of the best known examples of the use of accretion measures is W. L. Rathje's ongoing study of people's garbage.[46] He has been studying people's behavior from what they discard in their trash cans. One project involved investigating whether poor people waste more food than those better off: they do not.

Indirect observation typically raises fewer ethical issues than direct observation since the measures of individual behavior are taken after the individuals have left the scene, thus assuring anonymity in most cases. But Rathje's studies of garbage raised ethical concerns because some discarded items (such as letters and bills) identified the source of the garbage. Although the court ruled in Rathje's favor by declaring that when people discard their garbage, they have no further legal interest in it, one might consider sorting through one's garbage an invasion of privacy. In a study in which data on households were collected, consent forms were obtained, codes were used to link household information to garbage data, and then the codes were destroyed. Rathje's assistants in another garbage study were instructed not to examine closely any material.

It is also possible that garbage may contain evidence of criminal wrongdoing. Twice during Rathje's research, body parts were discovered, although not in the actual bags collected as part of the study. Rathje has taken the position that evidence of victimless crimes should be ignored; evidence of serious crimes should be reported. Of course, the publicity surrounding Rathje's garbage study may deter disposal of such evidence. This raises the problem of reactivity: to what extent might people change their garbage-disposing habits if they know there is a small chance that what they throw away will be examined?

This example also illustrates the possibility that indirect observation of physical traces of behavior may border on direct observation of subjects if the observation of physical traces quickly follows their creation. In some situations, extra measures may have to be taken to preserve the anonymity of subjects.

Another good example of the use of accretion measures is Kurt and Gladys Lang's study of the MacArthur Day parade in Chicago in 1951.[47] Gen. Douglas MacArthur and President Harry S. Truman were locked in an important political struggle at the time, and the Langs wanted to find out how much interest there was in the parade. They used data on mass-transit passenger fares, hotel reservations, retail store and street vendor sales, parking lot usage, and the volume of tickertape on the streets to measure the size of the crowd attracted by MacArthur's appearance.

Validity Problems with Indirect Observation

Although physical-trace measures generally are not as subject to reactivity as are participant observation and survey research, threats to the validity of these measures do exist. Also, erosion and accretion measures may be biased. For example, certain traces are more likely to survive because the materials are more durable. Thus physical traces may provide a selective, rather than complete, picture of the past. Differential wear patterns may be due not to variation in use but to differences in material. Researchers studying garbage must be careful not to infer that garbage reflects all that is used or consumed. Someone who owns a garbage disposal, for example, will generally discard less garbage than someone who doesn't.

Researchers should exercise caution in linking changes in physical traces to particular causes. Other factors may account for variation in the measures. Webb et al. suggest that several physical-trace measures be used simultaneously or that alternative data collection methods be used to supplement physical-trace measures.[48] For example, physical-trace measures of use of recreational facilities, such as which trash cans in a park fill up the fastest, could be supplemented with questionnaires to park visitors on facility usage.

Caution should also be used in making inferences about the behavior that caused the physical traces. For example, wear around a particular museum exhibit could be indicative either of the number of people viewing the exhibit or of the amount of time people spent near the exhibit shuffling their feet. Direct observation could determine the answer; but in cases where the physical-trace measures occurred in the past, this solution is not possible.

Examples of the use of indirect observation in political science research are not numerous. Nevertheless, this method has been used profitably, and you may be able to think of cases where it would be appropriate, such as in a study of the number of campaign posters put up in communities, how long they remained posted, and how long before they were defaced. A comparative measure of the number of visitors and office activity of elected representatives might be obtained by noting carpet wear in office entryways. This would not be as precise as counting visitors, but it would avoid posting observers or questioning office staff.

Indirect observation, when used ingeniously, can be a low-cost research method free from many of the ethical issues that surround direct observation. Let us now turn to a consideration of some of these ethical issues that develop in the course of fieldwork and in simple, nonexperimental laboratory observations.

Ethical Issues in Observation

Ethical dilemmas arise primarily when there is a potential for harm to the observed. They also may arise if researchers observe behavior or conditions that they feel they should report but in doing so would jeopardize their research. For example, what if a researcher during the course of observation views a crime? Should it be reported, or is the researcher obligated not to report it if he or she has requested and received permission to observe activities that are not normally accessible to an outsider? Or, for example, what if researchers observe deplorable living conditions or severe political repression? Should they abandon their research to devote their efforts to the improvement of the conditions? Or is it acceptable to continue the research by rationalizing that it will ultimately benefit the observed? [49]

The potential for serious harm to subjects in most observational studies is quite low. Observation generally does not entail investigation of highly sensitive, personal, or illegal behavior because people are reluctant to be observed in those circumstances. In addition, fieldwork and simple laboratory observation do not involve experimental manipulations of subjects and exposure to risky experimental treatments. Nonetheless, harm or risks to the observed may result. They include (1) negative repercussions from associating with the researcher due to the researcher's sponsors, nationality, or outsider status; (2) invasion of privacy; (3) stress during the research interaction; and (4) disclosure of behavior or information to the researcher resulting in harm to the observed during or after the study. Each of these possibilities will be considered in turn.

In some fieldwork situations, contact with outsiders may be viewed as undesirable behavior by an informant's peers. Cooperation with a researcher may violate community norms. For example, a researcher who studies a group known to shun contact with outsiders exposes informants to the risk that they will be censured by their group.

Social scientists from the United States have encountered difficulty in conducting research in countries with hostile relations with the United States.[50] Informants and researchers may be accused of being spies, and informants may be exposed to harm for appearing to sympathize with "the enemy." Harm may result even if hostile relations develop after the research has been conducted. Military, CIA, or other government sponsorship of research may particularly endanger the observed.

A second source of harm to the observed results from the invasion of privacy that observation may entail. Even though a researcher may have permission to observe, the role of observer may not always be remembered by the observed. In fact, as a researcher gains rapport, there is a greater chance that informants may reveal to the researcher as a friend something that could prove to be damaging. A researcher does not always warn, "Remember, you're being observed!" Furthermore, if a researcher is being treated as a friend, such a warning may damage rapport. Researchers must consider how they will use the information gathered from subjects. They must judge whether use in a publication will constitute a betrayal of confidence.[51]

Some harm to informants may occur if a researcher encourages them to talk about topics that cause them anxiety or embarrassment. Although informants can exercise control over what they say, they may reveal something in the flow of a conversation that they later regret.[52]

In some situations, informants may welcome the opportunity to talk to a sympathetic listener even if the subject is a painful one. For example, in her study of American widows, Helena Lopata found that widows were not reluctant to discuss widowhood. Protective relatives and friends, however, tried to keep Lopata from interviewing some widows because they feared the subject would upset them.[53]

The potential for harm to those being observed is the greatest in covert observation studies, which, by definition, involve an invasion of privacy. Mary Henle and Marian B. Hubble's eavesdropping in dormitory rooms mentioned at the beginning of the chapter is clearly an unacceptable invasion of privacy, but is eavesdropping and observation in public places unethical? Consider the ethics of Humphreys's study of homosexual encounters in park restrooms.[54] Humphreys disguised himself and assumed the role of a lookout. Then, with the cooperation of authorities who were not aware of the nature of his research, Humphreys traced automobile license plate numbers to identify and locate participants. Was this a legitimate use of this information? A year later Humphreys had a number of these men included in a community health study so he could interview them without their ever being aware of his knowledge of their homosexual activities.

Humphreys's study has been criticized for the risk of discovery he created for these homosexuals. Public or family discovery of their homosexual encounters could have resulted in serious harm to these men. Luckily, Humphreys exercised a great deal of caution and was never required by law enforcement officials to disclose his subjects' identities, but the risk was real.[55] Humphreys conducted his research out of sympathy for homosexuals, and he presented a sympathetic portrait of these men as posing no threat to others. Yet would they have agreed to take the personal risk of participation in the study in return for the possibility that they would be better understood and persecuted less? Even if Humphreys had acted as a lookout and not followed through on his observations, was this unjustifiable snooping? Some critics think so.[56] Finally, should Humphreys be criticized for not reporting observed illegal behavior to the authorities?

In Milgram's violence/obedience experiment, subjects were deceived about the purpose of their participation. The harm to the subjects stemmed from their awareness that they had been obedient to an authority even to the extent of "harming" another person. Milgram has contended that his subjects were not harmed. When interviewed after the experiment, his subjects claimed they were happy to have participated. Milgram's experiment also might be condoned by some on the grounds that knowledge about obedience to authority is socially beneficial. Others, however, conclude that balancing harms against benefits is off target; his subjects were wronged, they contend, by being exposed "to unwanted and unasked-for self-knowledge," whether or not they were harmed. This position is similar to the one that arises when an informant reveals embarrassing information or experiences psychological stress during or after a conversation with an investigator. Questions that are potentially embarrassing or stressful are potentially harmful. Even if no harm is felt and no deceit is involved, do researchers have the right to expose subjects to the possibility of harm?[57]

Much of the harm to subjects in fieldwork occurs as a result of publication. They may be upset at the way they are portrayed, subjected to unwanted publicity, or depicted in a way that embarrasses the larger group to which they belong. Moreover, disclosures about individuals or groups may be used by others in an exploitative manner.[58] Carelessness in publication may result in the violation of promises of confidentiality and anonymity. And value-laden terminology may offend those being described.[59]

Although subjects may be upset at discovering how they are perceived by others, published research has helped individuals see and change their objectionable qualities.[60] For example, Whyte depicted one Cornerville individual as self-centered, ambitious, and insensitive to others. While this portrayal hurt the feelings of the person who recognized himself, he accepted Whyte's description and appeared to alter his behavior in response.[61]

Carole Johnson has prepared the following guidelines for the "ethical proofreading" of manuscripts prior to publication. To diminish the potential for harm to the observed, researchers should keep in mind these nine points:

1) Assume that both the identities of the location studied and the identities of individuals will be discovered. What would the consequences of this discovery be to the community? To the individuals? What would the consequences be both within the community and outside the community? Do you believe that the importance of what you have revealed in your publication is great enough to warrant these consequences? Could you, yourself, live with these consequences should they occur?

2) Look at the words used in your manuscript. Are they judgmental or descriptive? How accurate are the descriptions of the phenomena observed? A judgment, for example, would be to say that a community is backward. A description might be to say that 10% of the adult population can neither read nor write. The latter is preferable both scientifically and ethically....

3) Where appropriate in describing private or unflattering characteristics, consider generalizing first and then giving specifics.... This tends to make research participants feel less singled out. It also adds to the educational value of the writing.

4) Published data may affect the community studied and similar communities in a general way even though the identities of the community and individuals may remain unknown. In the case of West's book on Plainville, for example, people were described as backward. Some people were said to live like animals. Some men were said to be as dirty as animals. West also related that many people from Plainville left the community to seek employment in the cities. What if such descriptive information about rural communities affected individuals' opportunities for employment due to the creation of negative stereotypes about people from rural areas? Therefore, ask yourself how your information might be used in a positive way? In a negative way? And again ask if the revelations are worth the possible consequences.

5) Will your research site be usable again or have you destroyed this site for other researchers? Have you destroyed other similar sites? Is such destruction worth the information obtained and disseminated?

6) What was your perspective toward subjects? What were your biases? How did your perspective and biases, both positive and negative, affect the way you viewed your subjects and wrote about them?...

7) In what ways can research participants be educated about the role of fieldworkers and the nature of objective reporting of fieldwork? It may be advisable to caution your subjects at various stages of the research that it is not easy to read about oneself as one is described by another.

8) When conducting research within a larger project, know the expectations of other project members concerning what each member will be permitted to publish both in the short and long run, i.e., are there any limitations? If not, what limits ought ethically to be imposed? Who will have the final say about publication? Who will own the data? Who will have access to the data and on what terms? What will happen to the data after publication? Most important, see that agreements are set forth in writing in a legally enforceable contract.

9) Have several people do "ethical proofreading" of your manuscript. One or two of those people might be your subjects. They should read it for accuracy and should provide any general feedback they are inclined to offer. One or two of your colleagues should also read the manuscript. Preferably those colleagues should not be ones who are particularly supportive or sympathetic to your research but colleagues who can be constructively critical.[62]

Ethical proofreading of manuscripts will protect informants from some of the worst examples of researcher carelessness or insensitivity, but it does not protect the observed from the harm that might arise during observation. Protecting the observed against harm and assessing the potential for harm to the observed prior to starting observation may be difficult. The risk to subjects posed by observation cannot be precisely estimated, nor may concrete measures to avoid all harm be easily specified and enforced. It is up to the researcher to behave ethically. An appropriate ethical framework for judging fieldwork should be "constructed on respect for the autonomy of individuals and groups based on the fundamental principle that persons always be treated as ends in themselves, never merely as means" to a researcher's own personal or professional goals.[63]

Conclusion

Observation is an important research method for political scientists. Observational studies may be direct or indirect. Indirect observation is less common but has the advantage of being a nonreactive research method. Direct observation of people by social scientists has produced numerous studies that have enhanced knowledge and understanding of human beings and their behavior. Fieldwork—direct observation by a participant observer in a natural setting—is the best known variety of direct observation, although direct observation may take place in a laboratory setting. Observation tends to produce data that are qualitative rather than quantitative. Because the researcher is the measuring device, this method is subject to particular questions about researcher bias and data validity. Since there is an evolving relationship between the observer and the observed, participant observation is a demanding and often unpredictable research endeavor. Part of the demanding nature of fieldwork stems from the difficult ethical dilemmas it raises.

As a student you may find yourself in the position of an observer, but it is more likely that you will be a consumer and evaluator of observational research. In this position you should base your evaluation on a number of considerations: Does it appear that the researcher influenced the behavior of the observed or was biased in his or her observation? How many informants were used? A few or only one? Does it appear likely that the observed could have withheld significant behavior of interest to the researcher? Are generalizations from the study limited because observation was made in a laboratory setting or because of the small number of cases observed? And were any ethical issues raised by the research? Could they have been avoided, and what would you have done in a similar situation? These questions should help you evaluate the validity and ethics of observational research.

Notes

1. Eugene J. Webb et al., *Nonreactive Measures in the Social Sciences,* 2d ed. (Boston: Houghton Mifflin, 1981).
2. Mary Henle and Marian B. Hubble, "Egocentricity in Adult Conversation," *Journal of Social Psychology* 9 (May 1938): 227-234.
3. Stanley Milgram and R. Lance Shotland, *Television and Antisocial Behavior: Field Experiments* (New York: Academic, 1973).
4. H. J. Eysenck and D. K. B. Nias, *Sex, Violence and the Media* (London: Temple Smith, 1978).
5. Stanley Milgram, "Behavioral Study of Obedience," *Journal of Abnormal and Social Psychology* 67 (October 1963): 371-378.
6. William F. Whyte, *Street Corner Society: The Social Structure of an Italian Slum,* 3d ed. (Chicago: University of Chicago Press, 1981); and Marc H. Ross, *Grass Roots in an African City: Political Behavior in Nairobi* (Cambridge, Mass.: MIT Press, 1975).
7. Richard F. Fenno, Jr., *Home Style: House Members in Their Districts*

(Boston: Little, Brown, 1978).

8. Hugh Lytton, *Parent-Child Interaction: The Socialization Process Observed in Twin and Singleton Families* (New York: Plenum, 1980), 295.

9. Fenno, *Home Style*, xiii.

10. Ibid., xiv.

11. Jennie-Keith Ross and Marc Howard Ross, "Participant Observation in Political Research," *Political Methodology* 1 (Winter 1974): 65-66.

12. James A. Robinson, *The House Rules Committee* (Indianapolis: Bobbs-Merrill, 1963); and James A. Robinson, *Congress and Foreign Policy-making* (Homewood, Ill.: Dorsey, 1962). Also extensive firsthand observations of Congress are reported in many of the articles in Raymond E. Wolfinger, ed., *Readings on Congress* (Englewood Cliffs, N.J.: Prentice-Hall, 1971).

13. Ralph K. Huitt, "Democratic Party Leadership in the Senate," *American Political Science Review* 55 (June 1961): 333-344.

14. David W. Minar, "The Community Basis of Conflict in School System Politics," in Scott Greer et al., eds., *The New Urbanization* (New York: St. Martin's, 1968), 246-263.

15. Margaret Mead, "Coming of Age in Samoa," in *From the South Seas* (New York: Morrow, 1939); Elliot Liebow, *Tally's Corner* (Boston: Little, Brown, 1967); Herbert Gans, *The Levittowners: Ways of Life and Politics in a New Suburban Community* (New York: Pantheon, 1967); and Arthur J. Vidich and Joseph Bensman, *Small Town in Mass Society: Class, Power and Religion in a Rural Community* (Princeton, N.J.: Princeton University Press, 1958).

16. Ross and Ross, "Participant Observation," 70.

17. Ibid.

18. Fenno, *Home Style*, 250.

19. Joan Cassell, "Harms, Benefits, Wrongs and Rights in Fieldwork," in J. E. Sieber, ed., *The Ethics of Social Research: Fieldwork, Regulation and Publication* (New York: Springer-Verlag, 1982), 18, 19.

20. Leon Festinger, Henry Riecken, and Stanley Schacter, *When Prophecy Fails* (Minneapolis: University of Minnesota Press, 1956).

21. Fenno, *Home Style*, 255.

22. These categories are the same as those used by William B. Shaffir, Robert A. Stebbins, and Allan Turowitz, eds., *Fieldwork Experience: Qualitative Approaches to Social Research* (New York: St. Martin's, 1980). For a discussion of fieldwork experiences, see also Myron Glazer, *The Research Adventure: Promise and Problems of Field Work* (New York: Random House, 1972).

23. Shaffir, Stebbins, and Turowitz, *Fieldwork Experience*, 3.

24. Fenno, *Home Style*, 257-258.

25. Whyte, *Street Corner Society*, 293.

26. Ibid., 289.

27. Laud Humphreys, *Tearoom Trade: Impersonal Sex in Public Places* (Chicago: Aldine, 1970); David A. Karp, "Observing Behavior in Public Places," in *Fieldwork Experience*, 82-97; and William J. Chambliss, *On the Take: From Petty Crooks to Presidents* (Bloomington: Indiana University Press, 1978).

28. Glazer, *The Research Adventure*, 21.

29. Ibid., 32-36.

30. David G. Bromley and Anson D. Shupe, Jr., "Evolving Foci in Participant Observation: Research as an Emergent Process," in *Fieldwork Experience*, 201.

31. Fenno, *Home Style*, 272-273.
32. The youth pleaded guilty in exchange for a small fine. Harold E. Pepinsky, "A Sociologist on Police Patrol," in *Fieldwork Experience*, 201.
33. See account in Whyte, *Street Corner Society*, 313-317.
34. In general, see Shaffir, Stebbins, and Turowitz, *Fieldwork Experience*, 257-310.
35. Alan Roadburg, "Breaking Relationships with Research Subjects: Some Problems and Suggestions," in *Fieldwork Experience*, 257-310.
36. Peter Letkemann, "Crime as Work: Learning the Field," in *Fieldwork Experience*, 281-290.
37. Thomas W. Benson, "Another Shooting in Cowtown," *Quarterly Journal of Speech* 67 (November 1981): 347-406.
38. John Lofland, *Analyzing Social Settings: A Guide to Qualitative Observation and Analysis* (Belmont, Calif.: Wadsworth, 1971), 102-103.
39. Chambliss, *On the Take*, 49.
40. Lofland, *Analyzing Social Settings*, 105.
41. Ibid., 106-107.
42. Webb et al., *Nonreactive Measures*, 4.
43. Ibid., 7.
44. Ibid., 24.
45. Ibid., 10-11.
46. See discussion of Rathje's work in ibid., 15-17.
47. Kurt Lang and Gladys Engel Lang, *Politics and Television* (Chicago: Quadrangle, 1968).
48. See Webb et al., *Nonreactive Measures*, 27-32.
49. See Glazer, *The Research Adventure*, 59-72.
50. Ibid., 25-48, 97-124.
51. See Fenno, *Home Style*, 272.
52. Myron Glazer, "The Threat of the Stranger: Vulnerability, Reciprocity, and Fieldwork," in *The Ethics of Social Research*, 50-53.
53. Helena Znaniecki Lopata, "Interviewing American Widows," in *Fieldwork Experience*, 68-81.
54. Humphreys, *Tearoom Trade*.
55. See Glazer's account in *The Research Adventure*, 107-116.
56. Cassell, "Harms, Benefits," 18.
57. Ibid., 21.
58. Carole Gaar Johnson, "Risks in the Publication of Fieldwork," in *The Ethics of Social Research*.
59. For a discussion and examples of value-laden terminology in published reports of participant observers, see ibid.
60. See Brian Miller and Laud Humphreys, "Keeping in Touch: Maintaining Contact with Stigmatized Subjects," in *Fieldwork Experience*, 212-222.
61. Whyte, *Street Corner Society*, 350-354.
62. Carole Garr Johnson, "Risks in the Publication of Fieldwork," in J. E. Sieber, ed., *The Ethics of Social Research: Fieldwork, Regulation and Publication* (New York: Springer-Verlag, 1982), 87-88. This passage is reprinted with permission from the publisher.
63. Cassell, "Harms, Benefits," 14.

Terms Introduced

Accretion measures. Measures of phenomena through/indirect observation of the accumulation of materials.
Covert observation. Observation in which the observer's presence or purpose is kept secret from those being observed.
Direct observation. Actual observation of behavior.
Erosion measures. Measures of phenomena through indirect observation of selective wear of some material.
Ethnography. Participant observation in a natural setting.
Field study. Observation in a natural setting.
Indirect observation. Observation of physical traces of behavior.
Overt observation. Observation in which those being observed are informed of the observer's presence and purpose.
Participant observation. Observation in which the observer becomes a regular participant in the activities of those being observed.
Structured observation. Systematic observation and recording of the incidence of specific behaviors.
Unstructured observation. Observation in which all behavior and activities are recorded.

Suggested Readings

Fenno, Richard F., Jr. *Home Style: House Members in Their Districts.* Boston: Little, Brown, 1978. See the Introduction and Appendix "Notes on Method: Participant Observation."
Glazer, Myron. *The Research Adventure: Promise and Problems of Field Work.* New York: Random House, 1972.
Ross, Jennie-Keith, and Marc Howard Ross. "Participant Observation in Political Research." *Political Methodology* 1 (Winter 1974): 63-88.
Shaffir, William B., Robert A. Stebbins, and Allan Turowitz, eds. *Fieldwork Experience: Qualitative Approaches to Social Research.* New York: St. Martin's, 1980.
Sieber, J. E., ed. *The Ethics of Social Research: Fieldwork, Regulation, and Publication.* New York: Springer-Verlag, 1982.
Whyte, William F. *Street Corner Society: The Social Structure of an Italian Slum.* 3d ed. Chicago: University of Chicago Press, 1981. See Appendix A, "On the Evolution of *Street Corner Society.*"

CHAPTER 11

Univariate Data Analysis and Descriptive Statistics

In the preceding chapters we have discussed the initial stages of a social science research project. We have examined the nature of scientific knowledge, the formulation of testable hypotheses, the development of a suitable research design, the process of measuring variables, and the many ways in which empirical observations may be made and data collected. The remainder of this book will cover the final steps of a research project: analyzing the data that have been collected and putting together a research report.

The major purpose of making empirical observations is to test hypotheses about political phenomena and behavior. This requires the analysis of observations on two or more variables. In addition to performing this sort of analysis, however, researchers often investigate the distribution of observed values for a single variable, then summarize or describe those values. This activity is called *univariate data analysis,* and the measurements used to summarize the observed values of one variable are called *descriptive statistics.*

You are undoubtedly already familiar with quite a few instances of univariate data analysis and descriptive statistics. For example, if you make a list of all of the grades you have received in the college courses you have taken and then group all the identical grades together (for example, 2 A's, 4 A−'s, 7 B's, 3 C+'s, 1 D), you are conducting a univariate data analysis of the observed values of your grades. If you then use the numerical value of each grade (for example, A = 4.0, A− = 3.7, B = 3.0, C+ = 2.3, D = 1.0) to calculate your cumulative grade-point average, you have calculated a descriptive statistic that

Table 11-1 Distributions of Political Ideology and of Civil Liberties Votes among Supreme Court Justices

Justice	Values[a]	Votes[b]
Warren	.50	78.1
Harlan	.75	41.9
Brennan	1.00	77.9
Whittaker	.00	43.4
Stewart	.50	51.5
White	.00	43.4
Goldberg	.50	89.6
Fortas	1.00	80.4
Marshall	1.00	79.7
Burger	−.77	29.7
Blackmun	−.77	42.9
Powell	−.67	37.9
Rehnquist[c]	−.91	19.5
Stevens	−.50	56.3
O'Connor	−.17	30.9
Rehnquist[d]	−.91	23.0
Scalia	−1.00	34.7
Kennedy	−.27	40.0

Source: Jeffrey A. Segal and Albert D. Cover, "Ideological Values and the Votes of U.S. Supreme Court Justices," *American Political Science Review* 83 (June 1989): 560.

[a] Derived by Segal and Cover. The range is −1.00 (extremely conservative) to 1.00 (extremely liberal).

[b] Percentage liberal in civil liberties cases, 1953-1988.

[c] Values and votes as Nixon appointee.

[d] Values and votes as Reagan appointee.

summarizes your academic performance.

Univariate data analyses and descriptive statistics are often encountered in the daily news. Charting the unemployment rate over time to see if it is rising or falling is a case of univariate data analysis where the unemployment rate is a descriptive statistic.

Recall the four research examples introduced in Chapter 1 and referred to throughout this book. In several of those cases, the researchers present information on the distribution of the observed values on a single variable before testing the hypothesized relationship between two or more variables. In Segal and Cover's article about the political ideology and decision making of selected Supreme Court justices, the first table (Table 11-1) shows the observed values for each justice on the authors' political ideology measure (remember that this measure was derived from their content analysis of newspaper editorials) and on their measure of support for civil liberties as reflected in the justices' case opinions.[1] This type of data presentation is called an *enumerative table*

Table 11-2   Number of Deaths from Political Violence and the Presence of Patterned Land Inequality in Latin America

Mean Death Rate from Political Violence, 1948-1977	Patterned Inequality	
	Absent	Present
225.0		Bolivia
210.8	Dominican Republic	
116.5		Colombia
100.9	Cuba	
89.6	Argentina	
54.5	Nicaragua	
38.1	Venezuela	
21.4	Guatemala	
20.0	Paraguay	
17.2	Panama	
16.8	Honduras	Peru
15.3	Haiti	
12.8	Costa Rica	
12.6		Chile
6.7	Ecuador	
6.4		El Salvador
3.4	Uruguay	
3.2	Mexico	
.5	Brazil	

Source: Edward N. Muller, Mitchell A. Seligson, and Hung-der Fu, "Land Inequality and Political Violence," *American Political Science Review* 83 (June 1989): 585.

since it basically lists the values of a variable for all of the cases. It does not represent a test of a hypothesis.

A similar data display may be found in one of the recent articles concerning the relationship between land inequality and political violence. Muller, Seligson, and Hung-der Fu, in their critique of Midlarsky's analysis of the effects of land inequality, present the data shown in Table 11-2.[2] These data simply show the number of deaths due to political violence and the presence or absence of land inequality (called "patterned" inequality) for the Latin American countries included in their analysis. This display does not indicate whether there is a relationship between the two variables, but it does familiarize the reader with the distribution of values on each variable.

The two data displays just discussed include a relatively small number of cases and observed values. Sometimes, however, the number of cases and observed values of a variable is far too large to be presented listwise in an enumerative table. Consequently, researchers often present

Table 11-3   Frequency Distributions: Two Examples

Categories (Values)	Frequency (Number of Observations)
A. Variable: gender	
Male	117
Female	124
Total	241
B. Variable: color perceived as most restful	
Blue	55
Red	17
Green	72
Yellow	60
Total	204

Source: Hypothetical data.

frequency distributions of their variables and use a variety of graphic devices to depict the contents of a frequency distribution. We also often use *descriptive statistics*—which are ways of mathematically summarizing numerous observed values in a clear and meaningful fashion—to represent a distribution of observed values on a variable.

Frequency Distributions

The beginning point of any univariate data analysis is the frequency distribution of the observed values on a variable. A frequency distribution is nothing more than a table that shows the number of observations for each of the values of a variable. The number of observations is also called the frequency, which is often represented by the small letter *f*.

Table 11-3 shows two hypothetical frequency distributions. The first is a variable (gender) with only two values (called a *dichotomous variable*). The second is a variable with four values. In both cases the frequency distribution shows the number of cases (observations) that had each value on the variable being measured.

Usually a frequency distribution is accompanied by a column of numbers that transforms the frequencies into proportions or percentages of the total number of observations. Proportions are calculated by dividing the number of observations in each category by the total number of observations. Percentages are calculated by multiplying proportions by 100. Proportions and percentages communicate information that is often more meaningful and easier to remember than a raw frequency distribu-

Table 11-4 Frequency Distribution, Proportion, and Percentage of Delegate Votes, 1984 Democratic National Convention

Categories (Values)	Frequency	Proportion	Percentage
Variable: Roll call vote for 1984 Democratic presidential nomination			
Mondale	2,191.0	.568	56.8
Hart	1,200.5	.311	31.1
Jackson	465.5	.121	12.1
Total	3,857.0	1.000	100.0

Source: New York Times, July 20, 1984, A12.

Note: Abstentions, absences, and votes for others are not included. Fractions are rounded off to tenths of a delegate.

tion. Table 11-4 presents the frequency distribution, proportion, and percentage of delegate votes at the 1984 Democratic National Convention for the three major presidential candidates: Walter Mondale, Gary Hart, and Jesse Jackson.

Proportions and percentages are often preferred to simple frequency distributions because they make it easier to compare two populations of different size. For example, Table 11-5 shows two hypothetical student populations of different size, but with the same proportions of selected majors. It would be difficult to discern this fact from the frequency distributions alone. The percentages reveal this information immediately. In many tables, only percentages are shown for each category. Frequency distributions are omitted, but the total number of observations is given, making it possible to calculate a frequency distribution.

For example, recall the researchers in Chapter 1 who were inter-

Table 11-5 Frequency Distribution and Percentage for Student Populations

Categories (Values)	College A		College B	
	f	%	f	%
Variable: Student majors				
Political science	35	25.9	105	25.9
Biology	30	22.2	90	22.2
English	45	33.3	135	33.3
Math	25	18.5	75	18.5
Total	135	99.9	405	99.9

Source: Hypothetical data.

Note: Percentages do not add to 100 due to rounding.

ested in the relationship between changes in public opinion and changes in public policy decisions.[3] They were especially interested in whether changes in policy were in the same direction as significant changes in public opinion. The first step in the presentation of their data was to display the frequency distribution of the number of cases of opinion-policy change in the same direction, opinion-policy change in opposite direction, no policy change, and policy change that was impossible to categorize. These results are shown in Table 11-6. There we can see that of the 357 cases the authors had to analyze, in 153 or 43 percent of the cases policy and opinion changed in the same direction. In 78 or 22 percent of the cases opinion and policy changed in opposite directions, and in 120 or 33 percent of the cases there was no discernible policy change. If one concentrates only on the cases in which there was policy change (the right-hand side of the table) we can see that policy was about twice as likely to change in the direction of opinion change as it was to change in the opposite direction (66 percent versus 34 percent).

Usually, researchers use computer software programs to retrieve information on the observed values of a variable and to display the contents in a frequency distribution. Table 11-7 shows a frequency distribution that was produced by one such software program, called *SPSS*.[4] There we can see the distribution of responses to a question asked in a 1984 national survey of Americans about whether they thought their lives were exciting or dull. This format shows the meaning of each value (value label), the number assigned to each value (value), the number of observations in each category (frequency), the percentage of the total number of observations in each category (percent) and the percentage of observations in each category after excluding meaningless observations (valid percent). The final column shows the percentage of observations included in the values that have been displayed thus far in the frequency table (cum percent, which stands for *cumulative percentage*). Such software programs allow researchers to produce frequency distributions quickly and accurately.

Bar charts and *pie diagrams* are other ways of presenting the information in a frequency distribution. A bar chart is a series of bars where each bar represents the number or percentage of observations that are in a category. Figure 11-1 is a bar chart of student majors in college A from Table 11-5. A pie diagram is a circular representation of a set of observed values where the entire circle (or pie) stands for all of the observed values and where each portion of the circle (or pie slice) represents the proportion of the observed values in each category. Figure 11-2 is a pie diagram of the roll call vote for the 1984 Democratic presidential nomination shown in Table 11-4. Both a bar chart and a pie

Table 11-6 Congruence between Changes in Public Opinion and Changes in Public Policy, 1935-1979

	Total Cases		Cases with Policy Change	
	%	f	%	f
Congruent change in opinion and policy	43	(153)	66	(153)
Noncongruent change in policy	22	(78)	34	(78)
No change in policy	33	(120)		
Uncertain	2	(6)		
	100	(357)	100	(231)

Source: Benjamin I. Page and Robert Y. Shapiro, "Effects of Public Opinion on Policy," *American Political Science Review* 77 (March 1983): 178.

Note: Each case is an instance in which public policy preferences changed significantly according to repeated administration of identical survey items.

diagram are most useful when the number of values for a variable is small.

An interesting example of data presented in the form of a bar chart may be found in a recent article investigating regime (actually, ruler) stability in African countries.[5] Two researchers were interested in understanding the length of time that African rulers remained in power. Figure 11-3 shows how a bar chart can efficiently present the frequency distribution of African rulers' years in office. In this case, the use of the hatching technique (which creates a *segmented* bar chart) allows the simultaneous presentation of two frequency distributions: one covering all 165 cases and one representing the subset of 63 cases in which a ruler died in office of natural causes or was still in office when the analysis was

Table 11-7 Frequency Distribution Produced by the SPSS Software Program

Value Label	Value	Frequency	Percent	Valid Percent	Cum Percent
Exciting	1	684	46.4	46.8	46.8
Pretty routine	2	704	47.8	48.2	95.0
Dull	3	73	5.0	5.0	100.0
Missing data	9	12	.8	Missing	
Total		1,473	100.0	100.0	

Valid Cases: 1,461
Missing Cases: 12

Source: Marija J. Norusis, *SPSS/PC + Studentware* (Chicago: SPSS, Inc., 1988), 82.
Note: Question asked was: Is life exciting or dull?

Figure 11-1 Bar Chart of Frequencies of Student Majors at College A

Source: Hypothetical data from Table 11-5.

Figure 11-2 Pie Diagram of Roll Call Vote on 1984 Democratic Presidential Nomination

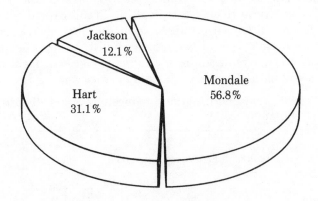

Source: *New York Times,* July 20, 1984, A-12.
Note: N = 3,857.

conducted (termed censored cases by the authors).

Visual displays such as these can help a reader understand or visualize the distribution of values on a variable. Care must be taken, however, to ensure that they are honest representations that clarify rather than distort

Figure 11-3   Distributions of African Leaders' Years in Power

All   Censored

Totals = 165 (63)

Source: Henry Bienen and Nicolas van de Walle, "Time and Power in Africa," *American Political Science Review* 83 (March 1989): 25.

Note: Censored observations include leaders who died of natural causes while in office.

the meaning of the data. An excellent discussion of the use of graphic displays to present and summarize quantitative data may be found in Edward Tufte's *The Visual Display of Quantitative Information.*[6]

The frequency distributions and graphic displays considered so far have contained relatively few values for each of the variables presented (for example, there are three categories of votes for the 1984 Democratic nomination in Table 11-4 and Figure 11-2, four categories of opinion-policy change in Table 11-6, and twelve categories of African leaders' duration in power in Figure 11-3). Some variables, however, are measured in such a way that the number of values is far too large to be presented in a bar chart, in a pie diagram, or even in a frequency distribution. Most such variables are interval or ratio level measures. If we prepared a frequency distribution of the ages of the respondents in a typical survey of eligible voters in the United States, for example, there might be as many as seventy age categories (Table 11-8). This is far too many to present either in a frequency distribution or in one of the graphic displays considered thus far. In such a case a *line diagram* or *frequency curve* is

Table 11-8 Frequency Distribution of the Ages of a National Sample of Americans

Value	Frequency	Percent	Cum Percent
18	2	0	0
19	20	1	1
20	23	2	3
21	37	3	6
22	29	2	8
23	50	3	11
24	47	3	14
25	39	3	17
26	32	2	19
27	44	3	22
28	37	3	25
29	33	2	27
30	28	2	29
31	28	2	31
32	37	3	33
33	39	3	36
34	31	2	38
35	37	3	40
36	41	3	43
37	38	3	46
38	31	2	48
39	24	2	50
40	28	2	51
41	25	2	53
42	21	1	55
43	25	2	56
44	23	2	58
45	20	1	59
46	18	1	60
47	19	1	62
48	22	1	63
49	21	1	65
50	8	1	65
51	16	1	66
52	21	1	68
53	14	1	69
54	17	1	70
55	19	1	71
56	19	1	72

(continued)

Table 11-8 *(Continued)*

Value	Frequency	Percent	Cum Percent
57	19	1	74
58	24	2	75
59	16	1	76
60	27	2	78
61	20	1	80
62	20	1	81
63	15	1	82
64	13	1	83
65	18	1	84
66	14	1	85
67	25	2	87
68	24	2	88
69	9	1	89
70	18	1	90
71	12	1	91
72	14	1	92
73	6	0	93
74	15	1	94
75	9	1	94
76	14	1	95
77	13	1	96
78	6	0	96
79	4	0	97
80	6	0	97
81	12	1	98
82	8	1	98
83	5	0	99
84	4	0	99
85	2	0	99
86	2	0	99
87	1	0	99
88	2	0	100
89	7	0	100

Missing Data

Value	Frequency
99	6

Valid Cases: 1,467   Missing Cases: 6

Source: Marija J. Norusis, *SPSS/PC + Studentware* (Chicago: SPSS, Inc., 1988), 97.

often used.

A frequency curve is simply a graph of a frequency distribution in which the values of the variable are arrayed along the X-axis and the number of observations is depicted along the Y-axis. Each data point represents the number of observations for each value, and the data points are then joined together to form a line diagram or frequency curve. This can be done for interval or ratio level measures because of the mathematical properties of the values at this level of measurement.

Figure 11-4 is a line diagram of the age distribution from Table 11-8. Clearly, this way of presenting the distribution of observed values is more informative than the frequency distribution itself.

Line diagrams are often used to present the values of a variable that has been measured many different times. In Figure 11-5, for example, the responses to the Gallup poll question regarding citizen approval of presidential job performance are shown for dozens of measurements taken between January 1981 and January 1986. Each data point represents the frequency distribution for one measurement (with values of approve, disapprove, or other responses) and the data points have been connected in order to show the trend in Ronald Reagan's approval ratings.

Figure 11-6 is a line diagram that shows the distribution of observed values on *three* variables on the same graph. Each variable is a measurement of the amount of political information possessed by the American electorate, as measured in three different years. This type of graphic permits the comparison of the distribution of observed values across variables.

Frequency curves and line diagrams come in an unlimited number of shapes. As Figure 11-7 shows, they may be symmetrical (a, b, f) or asymmetrical (c, d, e). A symmetrical distribution is the same shape on either side of the midpoint in the range of observed values. Asymmetrical distributions may be positively skewed (also called "skewed to the right") (c) or negatively skewed (also called "skewed to the left") (d). In a positively skewed distribution, there are fewer observations to the right of the midpoint, but those observations are farther from the midpoint. In a negatively skewed distribution, there are fewer observations on the left part of the curve.

Descriptive Statistics

As we have seen, there are a number of ways in which the information contained in a frequency distribution can be displayed and presented. Sometimes, however, the information in a frequency distribution is too extensive for us to expect anyone to appreciate, or we may

Figure 11-4 The Frequency Distribution of Age in a U.S. Adult Sample

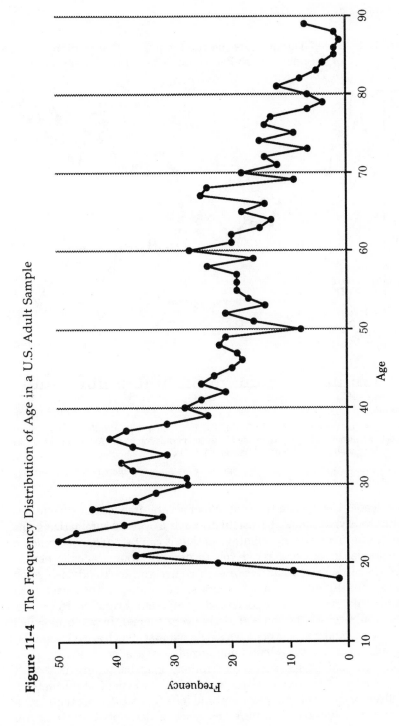

Source: Data are from Table 11-8.

Figure 11-5   Line Diagram Showing the Frequency Distribution
of Presidential Job Performance Measure at Many Points
in Time

Source: Jerry L. Yeric and John R. Todd, *Public Opinion: The Visible Politics*, 2d. ed.
(Itasca, Ill.: Peacock, 1989), 97. Reprinted with the permission of the American Enterprise
Institute for Public Policy Research, Washington, D.C.

Note: The question asked was: Do you approve or disapprove of the way Ronald Reagan is
handling his job as president?

want a reader to compare the contents of several frequency distributions
simultaneously. It would be useful to have a way of summarizing the
contents of a frequency distribution so that it can be understood readily.
For example, if someone asked you to describe your academic performance in college, you could recite each course you took and each grade
you received. But after about ten courses, the listener might have a hard
time formulating a clear understanding of your overall performance
(unless you received the same grade in every course). It would be much
easier if you could give the person a single number—such as your cumulative grade-point average—that summarized your academic performance.

The content of frequency descriptions may be summarized with
descriptive statistics. Descriptive statistics are mathematical calculations
that attempt to capture, precisely and efficiently, the contents of a
frequency distribution. Two different types of descriptive statistics are

Figure 11-6 Frequency Curves of Citizen Information Levels, 1952, 1976, 1984

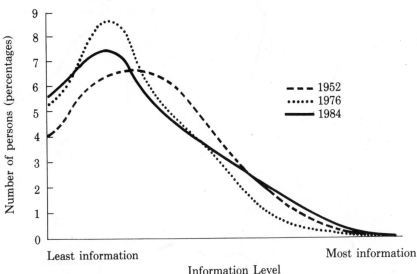

Source: John H. Kessel, *Presidential Campaign Politics*, 3d edition. Copyright © John H. Kessel, 1980, 1984, and 1988. Reprinted by permission of Brooks/Cole Publishing Company.

commonly used to summarize a collection of measurements: one measures *central tendency* (that is, what value is most frequent, middle, or central in the distribution of data values); the other measures *dispersion* (that is, how closely or remotely data values are distributed around the most frequent, middle, or central value).

Summarizing data with descriptive statistics has a disadvantage, however: information about single measurements is inevitably lost. For example, if you say you have a grade-point average of 3.0 (in a 4.0 grade scale), it is impossible to learn from that single descriptive statistic whether you have excelled in some courses and struggled in others or whether you have been a consistent student receiving all B's. To minimize the loss of information, researchers often use several descriptive statistics together to summarize different aspects of their data. When used together these descriptive statistics yield a clearer picture of the individual measurements than could be obtained from a single statistic.

Different descriptive statistics are appropriate for different levels of measurement. Therefore, we will discuss in turn those that are appropriate for nominal, ordinal, and interval or ratio level measures.

Figure 11-7 Six Examples of Frequency Curves

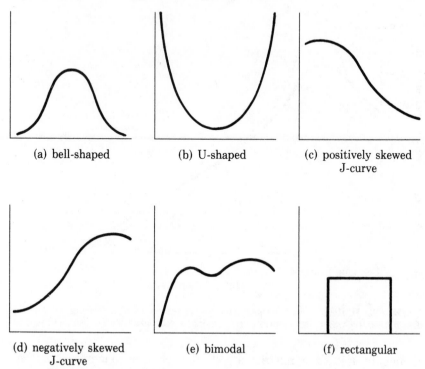

(a) bell-shaped (b) U-shaped (c) positively skewed
J-curve

(d) negatively skewed (e) bimodal (f) rectangular
J-curve

Descriptive Statistics for Nominal Level Measures

A nominal level measure is one that divides observations into arbitrarily ordered categories. Summarizing nominal level data is quite straightforward. The measure of central tendency is called the *mode* or *modal category* and it is simply the category with the greatest frequency of observations. In section *a* of Table 11-3, female is the modal category; in section *b*, it is the color green.

For nominal level data, the greatest dispersion occurs when the observations are distributed equally among the categories. In section *a* of Table 11-3, the data are markedly dispersed since there is an almost equal number of males and females. The dispersion in section *b* of Table 11-3 is not as high as it could be since there are relatively few observations in the red category. A total lack of dispersion is indicated if all the observations fall into one category. A measure of dispersion for nominal level measures is the proportion of the observed values that are in the modal category. The smaller the number of observations in the modal category, the greater the dispersion.

Descriptive Statistics for Ordinal Level Measures

The same descriptive statistics used to summarize nominal level data may also be used to summarize ordinal level data. Ordinal level data involve categories of observations that are ordered, however (from more of some attribute to less of some attribute). Thus, there are some additional descriptive statistics that summarize information about the ordering of measurements.

The *median* as well as the *mode* is used to indicate the central tendency of an ordinal measure. The median is the category or value in a distribution of values above and below which one-half of the frequencies fall. Put in another way, it is the category to which the middle observation belongs.[7] For example, the age of respondents may be measured ordinally by grouping ages as shown in Table 11-9. With 729 respondents, the middle observation is 364.5. Respondents 364 and 365 fall into the "35-44" category, so this is the median age group.

Dispersion for ordinal measures may be indicated by the *range*, the distance between the highest and lowest observations or the range of categories into which observations fall. The range of ages in Table 11-9 is "18-24" to "60 and over." One extreme observation may cause the range to be quite large even when most of the observations are included in only a small range of categories. For this reason, the *interquartile range*, which is not as sensitive to a few observations at the extreme ends of a distribution, is the preferred measure of dispersion. The interquartile range reflects the middle 50 percent of the observations: 25 percent are above, 25 percent are below. To calculate the interquartile range, remove the bottom quarter and the top quarter of the observations. For example, one-quarter of 729 is 182.25; removing 182.25 respondents from the low end of the age scale puts one end of the interquartile range in the "25-34" age group. Removing the same number from the high end puts the other end of the interquartile range in the "45-59" age group. Thus the interquartile range is "25-34" to "45-59."

Notice that the statistics for ordinal level measures are more informative than those for nominal level measures. For ordinal level measures, the central tendency of a frequency distribution may be judged with both the mode and the median; for nominal level measures, only the mode is appropriate. For ordinal level measures, the dispersion of a frequency distribution may be indicated with the range and the interquartile range; for nominal level measures, dispersion can be judged only by the percentage of cases within the modal category.

Table 11-9 Ordinal Grouping of Age of Respondents

Ages	18-24	25-34	35-44	45-59	60 and over	Total
Number	91	196	128	154	160	729

Source: Hypothetical data.

Descriptive Statistics for Interval and Ratio Level Measures

Interval and ratio level measures can be summarized in ways that take advantage of the mathematical properties of the observed values.

Measures of central tendency for interval and ratio level measures are the mode, the median, and the *arithmetic mean*. The arithmetic mean or average is the sum of the values of a variable divided by the number of values. This is represented algebraically as follows:

$$\bar{X} = \frac{X_1 + X_2 + \ldots + X_N}{N} = \frac{\Sigma X}{N} = \frac{\text{sum of scores}}{\text{number of scores}} \quad (11.1)$$

Where

$\bar{X}$ = the mean and is referred to as X bar
X = a raw score in a set of scores
N = the number of scores, and
Σ = sigma and directs us to sum the score[8]

Although the mean is a commonly used statistic, it can be a misleading indicator of central tendency if there is a handful of extreme observed values in a frequency distribution. For example, the incomes in two hypothetical communities shown in Table 11-10 are identical except for the income of one person. The mean income of Community A is $37,500, of Community B, $20,500. Knowing just the mean income of the communities would give you the erroneous impression that people in Community A are much better off than people in Community B, when in reality there is only one person in A who is much better off than anyone in B. In this case the median is a better indicator of central tendency than the mean. The median income in both communities is the same: $21,000. If the mean and the median are not close in value, one or a few extreme values are affecting the value of the mean.

Indicators of dispersion for interval and ratio level data include the *mean deviation, variance,* and *standard deviation* as well as the range and interquartile range discussed earlier. For interval and ratio level data these indicators are represented by a single number (rather than a range

Table 11-10 Incomes for Two Communities

Case Number	Community A	Community B
1	$ 10,000	$10,000
2	10,000	10,000
3	12,000	12,000
4	18,000	18,000
5	20,000	20,000
6	22,000	22,000
7	25,000	25,000
8	28,000	28,000
9	30,000	30,000
10	200,000	30,000
	$\overline{X} = 37,500$	$\overline{X} = 20,500$

Source: Hypothetical data.

of values as with ordinal data) because of the mathematical properties of the level of measurement. For example, if the highest score on a test was 100 and the lowest was 25, the range of test scores would be 100 − 25 or 75. If 25 percent of the test scores were above 80, and 25 percent were below 60, then the interquartile range would be 80 − 60 or 20. If the range of scores on another test was 90, and the interquartile range was 40, this would indicate a greater dispersion of scores on the second test. The range and interquartile range are less useful indicators of variability in scores than the mean deviation, variance, and standard deviation, however, and consequently they are used less often as indicators of dispersion with interval and ratio level measures.

The mean deviation (MD) is a measure of dispersion that is based on the deviation of each score from the mean. Its calculation is shown in Table 11-11. If we take each score and subtract it from the mean, we calculate the amount each score deviates from the mean (column 2). The sum of these deviations is always zero—an important mathematical property of the mean. (Check this by adding the numbers in column 2 for yourself.) Because we are interested only in the amount of deviation and not the direction or sign of the deviation, we can add up the *absolute values* of the deviations (column 3). Then we take this sum and divide by the number of scores to find the mean deviation of scores from the mean. The larger the mean deviation, the greater the dispersion of scores around the mean.

The equation for the mean deviation is:

$$MD = \frac{\Sigma \mid X - \overline{X} \mid}{N}$$

Table 11-11   Distribution, Deviation, and Mean Deviation of
Incomes in Community B

	X	X − X̄	|X − X̄|
1.	$10,000	−10,500	10,500
2.	10,000	−10,500	10,500
3.	12,000	−8,500	8,500
4.	18,000	−2,500	2,500
5.	20,000	−500	500
6.	22,000	1,500	1,500
7.	25,000	4,500	4,500
8.	28,000	7,500	7,500
9.	30,000	9,500	9,500
10.	30,000	9,500	9,500

X̄ = 20,500
Σ(X − X̄) = 0
Σ\|X − X̄\| = 65,000
MD = $\dfrac{65,000}{10}$ = 6,500

Source: Hypothetical data from Table 11-10.

Where

   \| \| = the symbol for an absolute value

Even though the mean deviation indicates dispersion, the standard deviation and the variance are used more often than the mean deviation. One reason for this is that the standard deviation and variance are used in advanced statistics, which we discuss later in this chapter and in Chapters 12 and 13.[9]

The *variance* (s^2) is the sum of the squared deviations from the mean divided by the number of scores:

$$s^2 = \frac{\Sigma(X - X)^2}{N}$$

The standard deviation (s) is the square root of the variance:

$$s = \sqrt{\frac{\Sigma(X - X)^2}{N}}$$

The greater the dispersion of data points about the mean, the higher the value of s^2 and s. If all the data points are the same, s^2 and s will be equal to zero.

To calculate the variance and standard deviation, follow these seven steps:

1. Calculate the mean.

2. Calculate the distance between the mean and each value.

3. Square the distances calculated in step 2.

4. Multiply the squared distances by the frequency of observations for each value.

5. Sum the squared distances calculated in step 4.

6. Divide the sum of squares from step 5 by N. This equals the variance.

7. Take the square root of the number calculated in step 6. This equals the standard deviation.

A sample calculation of the variance and standard deviation is presented in Table 11-12.[10]

The standard deviation is an important statistic, especially in conjunction with the normal or bell-shaped distribution, which we will discuss in the next section.

The Normal Distribution

The normal distribution is a special symmetrical, bell-shaped frequency curve with two interesting properties. First, the mean, the mode, and the median all coincide at the peak of the curve. Second, a fixed proportion of observations or cases lies between the mean and any distance from the mean measured in terms of the standard deviation. This is shown in Figure 11-8. Thus 34.13 percent of the cases in any normal distribution lie between the mean and one standard deviation to the right of the mean. Since the normal curve is symmetrical, we know that 68.26 percent of the cases lie between the mean and plus or minus one standard deviation from the mean. Also 95.44 percent of the cases lie between the mean and plus or minus two standard deviations. It is not necessary to use only even multiples of the standard deviation. For example, exactly 95 percent of the cases lie between the mean and 1.96 standard deviations on either side of the mean. Ninety-nine percent lie within plus or minus 2.58 standard deviations of the mean.

The Normal Distribution and Probability Sampling

The normal distribution and its properties are important to probability sampling. If we take a large number of random samples and calculate the mean of each sample, the distribution of these sample

Table 11-12 Sample Calculation of Variance and Standard Deviation

f	X	f(X)	$X - \bar{X}$	$(X - \bar{X})^2$	$f(X - \bar{X})^2$
2	1	2	-2	4	8
1	2	2	-1	1	1
4	3	12	0	0	0
1	4	4	1	1	1
2	5	10	2	4	8

$\Sigma X = 30$
$\bar{X} = 30/10 = 3$
$f(X - \bar{X})^2 = 18$
$s^2 = 18/10 = 1.8$
$s = \sqrt{1.8} = 1.34$

Source: Hypothetical data.

means (the *sampling distribution*) will resemble a normal curve. In other words, most of the sample means will cluster around the mean of all the sample means. Furthermore, according to the *Central Limit Theorem*, the mean of all the sample means will be equal to the mean of the population (designated by the Greek letter mu or μ).[11]

Most of the sample mean values will cluster around the true population mean, although the mean of some samples may differ substantially from the true population mean. Thus, we can use the information that we get from one sample to estimate the mean of the population. (For a discussion of confidence levels and margins of error, see Chapter 7.)

In order to estimate the mean of the population from sample information, we need to calculate the standard deviation of the distribution of the sample means around the population mean. This is called the standard deviation of the mean or *standard error* (S.E. or σ) and is equal to $\sigma/\sqrt{N}$ where σ is the standard deviation of the population and N is the size of each of the samples.

In probability sampling, a proportion of the population is selected at random and then a population parameter is estimated. For example, we can estimate the mean amount of financial aid received by students at a large university by taking a sample of those students. In a sample survey of 100 college students, let's say the mean amount of financial aid ($\bar{X}$) is $750 and the standard deviation (s) is 50. What does this tell us about the mean amount of financial aid received by all students in the college? How certain are we that our sample estimate of the mean is accurate? Luckily mathematics tells us that where our sample size is large, we may substitute s (the sample standard deviation) for σ in the formula for standard error. Therefore the standard error is

$$\text{S.E.} = s/\sqrt{N} \text{ or } 50/\sqrt{100} \text{ or } \$5 \tag{11.5}$$

Figure 11-8 Normal Distribution and Percent of Cases between
Selected Points under the Curve

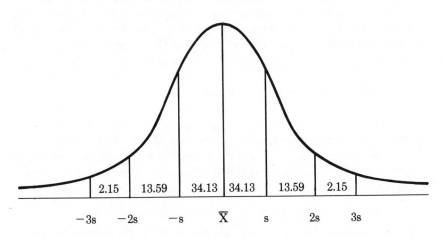

	2.15	13.59	34.13	34.13	13.59	2.15	

| $-3s$ | $-2s$ | $-s$ | $\overline{X}$ | s | $2s$ | $3s$ |

Because the sample distribution is a normal curve, roughly 68 percent of the sample estimates will lie between the mean and plus or minus one standard error. (Remember that the standard error is a standard deviation, which is why we can substitute standard error for standard deviation in this discussion of the normal distribution.) Therefore, we can say that we are 68 percent confident that the true population mean, or average financial aid award, is $750 ± $5, or between $745 and $755. We are about 95 percent certain that the true average financial aid award is between $740 and $760 (750 ± 2 S.E.).

To emphasize this important aspect of probability sampling, we will explain the process slightly differently. Three different distributions are involved: the distribution of a characteristic in a population, the distribution of the same characteristic in a single sample taken from the population, and the sampling distribution, that is, the distribution of sample means if we take many samples and calculate a mean for each sample.

For each distribution a standard deviation can be calculated. For the population, it is called σ, and normally its numerical value is unknown. For the sample it is s, and it can be calculated. For the sampling distribution we can calculate the standard deviation of the sample means around the mean of all the sample means. This is called the standard error.

Since the sampling distribution is normally distributed, we can calculate the probability of obtaining a single sample mean that lies between the mean of all sample means and any number of standard errors from it. The formula for the standard error is $\sigma\sqrt{N}$. We know the value of N (the size of the sample), but we do not know σ (the standard deviation of the population), nor do we know the mean of all sample means. But we may substitute the mean of the sample, $\bar{X}$, for the mean of all sample means (which equals the mean of the population), and the standard deviation of the sample, s, for the standard deviation of the population, σ. Because a probability sample can be linked to the normal distribution in this way, the characteristics of the normal distribution can be used to estimate the accuracy of a probability sample.

The Standard Normal Distribution

Standard normal distributions are normal distributions with a mean of zero and a standard deviation and variance of one. We can convert any normal distribution into a standard normal distribution by converting scores into *z scores*. A z score is the number of standard deviations that a score varies from the mean. The calculation for a z score is represented by

$$Z = \frac{X - \bar{X}}{s}$$

(11.6)

Where
X = a single score
$\bar{X}$ = mean of all scores
s = standard deviation of scores

For example, in Table 11-12, where $\bar{X} = 3$ and s = 1.34, the z score for X = 5 would be $(5 - 3)/1.34 = 2/1.34 = 1.49$. Thus the observation X = 5 is 1.49 standard deviations from the mean.

All z scores have some of the properties of a standard normal distribution; that is, the mean of the z scores is zero, and the standard deviation and variance of z scores are equal to one. Z scores will also be normally distributed if the original scores are normally distributed. Converting raw data scores to z scores will not normalize a nonnormal distribution, however.[12]

Z scores make it easier to compare groups of scores or variables. For example, suppose some people were given three tests, and the scores for each test were normally distributed. A person who received scores of 80, 85, and 87 is interested in comparing his performance on each test to the performance of the others.

For each test, a mean grade and standard deviation are calculated. For the first test, $\bar{X} = 80$, s = 3. For the second test, $\bar{X} = 75$, s = 5. For the third test, $\bar{X} = 80$, s = 3.5. The individual's scores can be converted to z scores of 0, 2, and 2. Thus the individual is zero standard deviations from the mean score on the first test, two on the second, and two on the third. This means that although the individual's score on the third test was closer to the mean than his score on the second (7 points versus 10 points), his relative performance compared with the rest of the group was the same. The individual outperformed 97.72 percent of the group in both the second and the third tests. The normal distribution tells us that 97.72 percent of all test scores fall below (or to the left of) two standard deviations above the mean (50 + 34.13 + 13.59 = 97.72). Z scores also have an important role in more advanced statistical analysis of data.

Conclusion

In this chapter we have discussed the presentation and analysis of the observed values of a single variable. A frequency distribution presents the number of observations on each value of a variable, and a variety of techniques—such as bar charts, pie diagrams, and frequency curves—are used to graphically display this information. Such graphic displays should be designed carefully to ensure that they clearly and accurately summarize the data in a frequency distribution.

Descriptive statistics are also used to summarize the observed values of a variable. Univariate descriptive statistics indicate the central tendency and the dispersion of data values for a single variable. A single number or a few numbers communicate these important characteristics and thus make the task of describing large amounts of data more manageable. Different univariate statistics are appropriate for use with nominal, ordinal, and interval or ratio level data.

Of the statistics that were discussed, the mean and the standard deviation are among the most important because they provide a foundation for more complex statistical analyses and for exploring relationships between variables. In Chapters 12 and 13, we will discuss statistical analyses that allow researchers to test for relationships between two or more variables.

Notes

1. Jeffrey A. Segal and Albert D. Cover, "Ideological Values and the Votes of U.S. Supreme Court Justices," *American Political Science Review* 83 (June 1989): 557-565.
2. Edward N. Muller, Mitchell A. Seligson, and Hung-der Fu, "Land Inequality and Political Violence," *American Political Science Review* 83 (June 1989): 577-586.
3. Benjamin I. Page and Robert Y. Shapiro, "Effects of Public Opinion on Policy," *American Political Science Review* 77 (March 1983): 175-190.
4. *SPSS,* which stands for *Statistical Package for the Social Sciences,* is the trademark of a company that has developed computer software to perform data analysis. It is one of several software packages used by social scientists.
5. Henry Bienen and Nicolas van de Walle, "Time and Power in Africa," *American Political Science Review* 83 (March 1989): 19-34.
6. Edward R. Tufte, *The Visual Display of Quantitative Information* (Cheshire, Conn.: Graphics, 1983).
7. Kirk W. Elifson, Richard P. Runyon, and Audrey Haber, *Fundamentals of Social Statistics* (Reading, Mass.: Addison-Wesley, 1982), 100.
8. Ibid., 95.
9. Ibid., 118.
10. For formulas for the standard deviation that involve fewer rounding errors, see Hubert M. Blalock, Jr., *Social Statistics,* 2d ed. (New York: McGraw-Hill, 1972), 82-83.
11. Ibid., 181.
12. Elifson, Runyon, and Haber, *Fundamentals,* 133.

Terms Introduced

Bar chart. A graphic display of the data in a frequency or percentage distribution.
Central tendency. The most frequent, middle, or central value in a frequency distribution.
Descriptive statistic. The mathematical summary of measurements for one variable.
Dichotomous variable. A variable with only two categories of values.
Dispersion. The distribution of data values around the most frequent, middle, or central value.
Enumerative table. A table listing the observed values of a variable.
Frequency curve. A line graph summarizing a frequency distribution.
Frequency distribution (f). The number of observations per value or category of a variable.
Interquartile range. The middle 50 percent of observations.
Line diagram. Another name for a frequency curve.
Mean. The sum of the values of a variable divided by the number of values.
Mean deviation. A measure of dispersion of data points for interval and ratio level data.
Median. The category or value above and below which one-half of observations lie.

Mode. The category with the greatest frequency of observations.

Negatively skewed. A distribution of values in which fewer observations lie to the left of the middle value and those observations are fairly distant from the mean.

Normal distribution. A frequency curve showing a symmetrical, bell-shaped distribution in which the mean, mode, and median coincide and in which a fixed proportion of observations lies between the mean and any distance from the mean measured in terms of the standard deviation.

Percentage distribution. The percent of observations in all categories of a variable.

Pie diagram. A circular graphic display of frequency distribution.

Positively skewed. A distribution of values in which fewer observations lie to the right of the middle value and those observations are fairly distant from the mean.

Range. The distance between the highest and lowest values or the range of categories into which observations fall.

Standard deviation(s). A measure of dispersion of data points about the mean for interval and ratio level data.

Standard error. The standard deviation of sample means about the mean of sample means.

Standard normal distribution. Normal distribution with a mean of zero and a standard deviation and variance of one.

Univariate data analysis. The analysis of a single variable.

Variance (s^2). The measure of dispersion of data points about the mean for interval and ratio level data.

Z score. The number of standard deviations by which a score deviates from the mean score.

Exercises

1. Suppose you have surveyed 1,000 people about their attitudes toward Eastern Europe. Three hundred people think that the United States should offer unilateral economic aid to the countries of Eastern Europe, 250 people think any increased aid should be part of an international aid package overseen by the United Nations, 400 people think that the United States should not offer any aid until it is certain that democratic governments have been established in Eastern Europe, and 50 people are not sure what the United States should do. Design a table showing the frequency distribution and percentage distribution of these responses. Then recalculate the percentage distribution of the responses excluding those who said *don't know* and add that information to the table. What level of measurement does this table represent?

2. Draw a line diagram and describe the shape of the curve for the following data points: 1, 1, 2, 5, 1, 1, 6, 1, 2, 3, 1, 0, 1, 0, 1, 4, 1, 6, 1.

3. Find the mean, mode, median, range, and interquartile range for the data points in Exercise 2. Locate these on the line diagram. Is the mean to the left or the right of the mode?

4. What is the mean percentage of liberal votes cast by the Supreme Court

justices as shown in Table 11-1? What is the median? What does the comparison between the two numbers indicate?

5. What measures of central tendency and dispersion would be appropriate for the data shown in Table 11-8? What is the mode?

6. Calculate the mean and standard deviation for the following scores: 0, 1, 1, 2, 2, 2, 3, 3, 3, 3, 4, 4, 4, 5, 5, 6. Calculate the z score for the score of 4. What does this tell you about the score of 4 with respect to the mean?

7. In a normally distributed population of scores with a mean of 50 and standard deviation of 5, what percentage of the scores are between 45 and 55? If a score is 1.2 standard deviations above the mean, what is this score?

8. Calculate the percentages for the following frequency distribution of partisan affiliation. Calculate the appropriate measures of central tendency and dispersion.

Strong Democrat	Moderate Democrat	Weak Democrat	Weak Republican	Moderate Republican	Strong Republican
123	156	64	80	125	60

9. A researcher gathered data on the number of school strikes fifty cities had experienced in the last five years. The frequency distribution that resulted is shown below. Calculate the mode, median, mean, and standard deviation for the frequency distribution. (You may express the standard deviation in terms of a fraction and/or square root sign if necessary.) What does the comparison of the median and mean tell you? Is this a normal distribution?

Number of School Strikes	Number of Observations
0	8
1	18
2	5
3	2
4	1
5	2
6	3
7	4
8	7

Suggested Readings

Blalock, Hubert M., Jr. *Social Statistics.* Rev. 2d ed. New York: McGraw-Hill, 1979.

Elifson, Kirk W., Richard P. Runyon, and Audrey Haber. *Fundamentals of Social Statistics.* Reading, Mass.: Addison-Wesley, 1982.

Tufte, Edward R. *The Visual Display of Quantitative Information.* Cheshire, Conn.: Graphics, 1983.

CHAPTER 12

Measuring Relationships and Testing Hypotheses: Bivariate Data Analysis

In this chapter and the next we will discuss how to test the hypotheses that we have developed and refined. In testing hypotheses five general questions must be addressed: Is there a *relationship* between the independent and dependent variables in the hypothesis? What is the direction or shape of the relationship? How strong is the relationship? Is the relationship statistically significant? Is the relationship a causal one? Each of these questions will be considered in turn.

A relationship exists if the values that observations take on for the independent variable are associated with the values that they take on for the dependent variable. For example, if as people get older they vote more frequently, then the cases (people) take on a value for the dependent variable (voting or not voting) that is associated with a value for the independent variable (age). Therefore, the values for the two variables are related.

Once it is established that there is some pattern in the observed values for the independent and dependent variables, the nature of that pattern becomes important. The direction or shape of a relationship tells the researcher which values of the independent variable are associated with which values of the dependent variable, rather than simply whether the two are connected. For example, if the chances of people voting change as their ages change, there is a relationship between age and turnout. However, the direction of the relationship tells us which values of the independent variable (age) are associated with which values of the dependent variable (turnout). The shape of the relationship when graphed tells us whether the relationship is linear, exponential, logarithmic, or something else. To conclude that "the younger you are, the more likely you are to vote" is quite different from concluding that "the older you are, the more likely you are to vote." In both cases there is a relationship between the two variables, but the nature of the relationship is different.

A relationship is strong if most of the observed values for the independent variable are connected with values for the dependent variable. If only a few of the observed values show this association, then we refer to the relationship as a weak one. The notion of strength, therefore, depends upon how many of the observed values of the dependent variable may be understood, accounted for, or explained with values of the independent variable.

There is always a possibility that a relationship observed in a researcher's data is due only to chance. A sample from some target population may be an inaccurate indication of what we would have observed in the entire population. We test the possibility that an observed relationship is the result of chance rather than systematic factors by measuring the relationship's *statistical significance*. This measurement tells us the probability that we could have observed the results we did even if there were no real relationship between the two variables. When working with sample data, we calculate the probability that no relationship exists in the target population given the observed relationship in our sample. If the relationship observed in the sample is too weak for us to be confident that there is a relationship in the population, then we discount the importance of our sample results. When working with nonsample data, we must also generally be concerned with the statistical significance of our results since observed results may also be the product of random chance alone.

That a relationship exists between independent and dependent variables does not necessarily mean that the independent variable is a cause of the dependent variable. There are a number of other possible reasons for the existence of such a relationship. For example, there is a relationship between the league of the baseball team that wins the World Series in presidential election years and the political party that wins the U.S. presidency: when National League teams win, a Democratic presidential candidate tends to win. No one seriously thinks that one causes the other, however. The observation of a relationship, then, is really only the beginning of the search for causal knowledge, a search that is generally long and difficult.

In this chapter we will show you how to answer the first four questions. Observing the existence, direction, strength, and statistical significance of a relationship is a fairly objective process in which there are well-established analytical techniques and sensible conventions for evaluating evidence. Reaching conclusions about causal relationships, however, is more subjective and problematic and will be discussed in Chapter 13.

The procedure for measuring relationships and testing hypotheses depends upon the level of measurement of the independent and dependent variables. When the independent and dependent variables are both nominal or ordinal level measures, *contingency table analysis* (also called *crosstabulation*) is generally used. When one of the variables is nominal or ordinal and the other is interval or ratio, the *difference of means test* or *analysis of variance* is the preferred technique. And when both variables are interval or ratio level measures, *regression* or *correlation analysis* is often used.[1]

Crosstabulation

A crosstabulation or "crosstab" takes each case in a set of observations and displays the value of that case for both variables in a table. This is done by putting the values for one of the variables along one side of the table and the values for the other variable along the other side of the table. Each case is then placed in the cell in the table that corresponds to the case's values for both variables.

Suppose, for example, a researcher is interested in testing the hypothesis that blondes are more likely than brunettes to vote Republican. Data are collected that measure the hair color and vote choice of a sample of voters. The first ten cases in this sample look like this:

Case Number	Hair Color	Vote
1	Blonde	Republican
2	Blonde	Democrat
3	Blonde	Republican
4	Brunette	Democrat
5	Brunette	Republican
6	Blonde	Republican
7	Brunette	Democrat
8	Brunette	Democrat
9	Brunette	Democrat
10	?	Republican

We can construct a table showing each case's value for both variables by putting the independent variable across the top and the dependent variable down the side. (This is the conventional format, but the independent variable could instead be located down the side.) In section *a* of Table 12-1, the cases have been placed in the appropriate box or cell in the crosstab.

Now, what is important in testing the hypothesis is not which cases have particular values for the independent and dependent variables, but how many cases have each combination of values. The number of observations in each cell is shown in section *b* of Table 12-1.

Table 12-1 Relationship between Hair Color and Vote: A Simple Crosstabulation

Dependent Variable: Vote	Independent Variable: Hair Color		
	Blonde	Brunette	Total
a.			
Republican	1, 3, 6	5	
Democrat	2	4, 7, 8, 9	
b.			
Republican	3	1	4
Democrat	1	4	5
Total	4	5	9

Source: Hypothetical data.

Note: Case number 10 is not included because hair color is unknown.

How does section *b* of Table 12-1 help us measure a relationship and test the hypothesis? The hypothesis with which we began was that blondes vote differently from brunettes. We have separated the blondes from the brunettes so that we can compare their voting behavior. Our expectation is that blondes will be more likely to vote Republican than brunettes are. Of the four blondes in the table, three or 75 percent voted Republican. Of the five brunettes in the table, one or 20 percent voted Republican. Therefore, a greater proportion of blondes voted Republican (75 percent) than did brunettes (20 percent), indicating that blondes and brunettes did vote differently. Therefore, the value of the independent variable matters (whether blonde or brunette) and knowing a person's hair color would help us account for that person's presidential vote.

Crosstabs almost always contain many more than nine cases and often contain more than four cells. No matter what the number of cases and categories, however, the procedure remains the same: (1) separate the cases into groups based on their values for the independent variable, (2) compare the values of the dependent variable for those groups, and (3) decide whether the values for the dependent variable are different for the different groups of cases.

Now let us take a slightly more complicated crosstab and see how we would use it to assess the existence, direction, and strength of the relationship between hair color and party voting. Consider Table 12-2.

The first question we need to answer is whether a relationship between hair color and presidential vote does, in fact, exist. In other words, do the votes of blondes differ from the votes of brunettes? To answer that question, we need to calculate the percentage of people in each column who voted a particular way because each column contains people with the same hair color. Of the 500 blondes, 300 or 60 percent

Table 12-2 Relationship between Hair Color and Vote: A More Complex Crosstabulation

Dependent Variable: Vote	Independent Variable: Hair Color		
	Blonde	Brunette	Total
a.			
Republican	300	400	700
Democrat	200	600	800
Total	500	1,000	1,500
b.			
Republican	60%	40%	47%
Democrat	40	60	53
Total	100	100	100

Source: Hypothetical data.

voted Republican; 200 or 40 percent voted Democratic. Of the 1,000 brunettes, 400 or 40 percent voted Republican; 600 or 60 percent voted Democratic. Table 12-2 with the column percentages in section *b* shows at a glance that blondes do vote Republican more often than brunettes do. Not all blondes vote Republican and not all brunettes vote Democratic, but the two groups defined by their values on the independent variable do differ. Consequently, we can conclude that there is a relationship—in this sample—between hair color and party vote.

Table 12-3 is a crosstab that shows no relationship between the independent and dependent variables. The cases in all the categories of the independent variable behaved the same on the dependent variable. And the percentage of cases with a particular value of the dependent variable is the same for every category of the independent variable: an equal proportion of blondes and brunettes voted Republican. Conse-

Table 12-3 A Crosstabulation Showing No Relationship between Hair Color and Vote: Column Percentages

Dependent Variable: Vote	Independent Variable: Hair Color			
	Blonde	Brunette	Total	(n)
Republican	47%	47%	47%	(700)
Democrat	53	53	53	(800)
Total	100	100	100	
(n)	(500)	(1,000)		(1,500)

Source: Hypothetical data.

Table 12-4   A Crosstabulation Showing No Relationship between Hair
Color and Vote: Row Percentages

Independent Variable: Hair Color	Dependent Variable: Vote			
	Republican	Democrat	Total	(n)
Blonde	47%	53%	100%	(500)
Brunette	47%	53%	100%	(1,000)
Total	47%	53%	100%	
(n)	(700)	(800)		(1,500)

Source: Hypothetical data.

quently, the hypothesis that hair color affects voting behavior would not
be confirmed by this evidence.

As we mentioned earlier, the categories of the independent variable
may be either the rows or columns in a crosstab. The convention is to
place the independent variable across the top of a crosstab, thereby
creating the categories of the independent variable in the columns of the
table. However, to fit a crosstab on one page, it sometimes will be
constructed so that the variable with the most categories runs down the
side of the table. It really does not matter whether a crosstab is
constructed with the independent variable across the top or down the
side. Either way, the percentages in the table must be calculated for the
values of the independent variable in order to test the existence of a
relationship.

Table 12-4, for example, presents exactly the same information as
Table 12-3, except that the independent variable is down the side of the
table rather than across the top. Therefore, the row rather than the
column percentages indicate the lack of a relationship between hair color
and vote.

After determining whether a relationship exists between the independent and dependent variables, a researcher should investigate its
direction. The direction of a relationship shows which values of the
independent variable are associated with which values of the dependent
variable. The direction of the relationship presented in Tables 12-1 and
12-2 is that blondes, not brunettes, are more likely to vote Republican.
Had we gotten different results, the direction of the relationship between
hair color and party vote might have been different, with brunettes being
more likely to vote Republican.

Table 12-5 displays hypothetical relationships between party identification and attitudes toward military spending. In section *a* of Table 12-
5, the Republicans are more likely to favor increased military spending; in
section *b* of Table 12-5, the Democrats are more likely to favor increased

Table 12-5 Negative and Positive Relationships between Party
Identification and Attitude toward Military Spending

Dependent Variable: Attitude toward Military Spending	Independent Variable: Party Identification				
	Democrats	Independents	Republicans	Total	(n)
a.					
Increase	20%	40%	60%	40%	(240)
Remain same	50	40	30	40	(240)
Decrease	30	20	10	20	(120)
Total	100	100	100	100	
(n)	(200)	(200)	(200)		(600)
b.					
Increase	60%	40%	20%	40%	(240)
Remain same	30	40	50	40	(240)
Decrease	10	20	30	20	(120)
Total	100	100	100	100	
(n)	(200)	(200)	(200)		(600)

Source: Hypothetical data.

military spending. In both cases there is a relationship between the two
variables, but the direction of the relationship differs. Since the direction
of the relationship yields important information for understanding the
association between the two variables, its assessment is often a crucial
part of testing a hypothesis.

When low values of one variable are associated with low values of
another, a *positive relationship* exists between the variables; for example,
"the more education one has, the higher one's political interest is." When
low values of one variable are associated with high values of another, a
negative relationship exists between the two variables; for example, "the
higher one's income is, the less liberal one is." Of course, this type of
statement is possible only when the variables are measured at the ordinal
level or higher. Since the values of nominal level measures do not
represent more or less of anything, we cannot talk about positive or
negative relationships involving nominal level measures.

Most computer programs print crosstabs with low values to the left
and top of the table and high values to the right and bottom. Therefore, if
the top left and bottom right corners are filled with more observations a
positive relationship is indicated (as was the case in section *b* of Table 12-
5, since 60 percent and 30 percent are higher than 20 percent and 10
percent). But if the top right and lower left corners of a table are filled
with more observations, a negative relationship is generally indicated, as
was the case in section *a* of Table 12-5. The direction of the relationship

Table 12-6 Relationship between Party Identification and Attitude
toward Military Spending: Different Table Construction

Dependent Variable: Attitude toward Military Spending	Independent Variable: Party Identification				
	Republicans	Independents	Democrats	Total	(n)
a.					
Increase	20%	40%	60%	40%	(240)
Remain same	50	40	30	40	(240)
Decrease	30	20	10	20	(120)
Total	100	100	100	100	
(n)	(200)	(200)	(200)		(600)

Source: Hypothetical data.

does not tell us how significant or important the relationship is, but it
does tell us the nature of the relationship and it helps us test a hypothesis
in which the direction has been proposed.

The *meaning* of a positive or negative relationship, however, cannot
be determined without referring to how a crosstab is constructed. The
meaning of the relationship in Table 12-6 is identical to the meaning of
the relationship in section *b* of Table 12-5. The only difference is in how
the values of the independent variable are displayed. Therefore, a
crosstab must be inspected before the meaning of the direction of the
relationship can be interpreted.

The *strength* of a relationship refers to how different the observed
values of the dependent variable are in the categories of the independent
variable. If blondes are voting much differently from brunettes, then we
can say that there is a strong relationship between the two variables. If
they are voting only a little bit differently, a weak relationship exists.

The strongest relationship possible between two variables is one in
which the value of the dependent variable for every case in one category
of the independent variable differs from that of every case in another
category of the independent variable. We call such a relationship a
perfect relationship because the dependent variable is perfectly associated with the independent variable; that is, there are no exceptions to the
pattern. A perfect relationship between the independent and dependent
variables enables a researcher to predict accurately a case's value on the
dependent variable if the value on the independent variable is known. A
perfect relationship for the hair color-vote example is illustrated in Table
12-7. Either a perfect positive or a perfect negative relationship between
variables may exist since the direction and the strength of a relationship
are two different properties.

A weak relationship would be one in which the differences in the
observed values of the dependent variable for different categories of the

Table 12-7 Perfect Relationship between Hair Color and Vote

Dependent Variable: Vote	Independent Variable: Hair Color			
	Blonde	Brunette	Total	(n)
Republican	100%	0%	33%	(500)
Democrat	0	100	67	(1,000)
Total	100	100	100	
(n)	(500)	(1,000)		(1,500)

Source: Hypothetical data.

independent variable are slight. In fact, the weakest relationship is one in which the distribution is identical for all categories of the independent variable—in other words, one in which a relationship does not exist. Table 12-3 is an example.

In reality, the strength of most relationships falls somewhere in between perfect and nonexistent relationships. How strong a relationship is may be judged from how much the column percentages in a crosstab differ as one looks across the rows (when the independent variable has been placed across the top of the table and column percentages have been calculated). In section *b* of Table 12-2, for example, there is a 20 percent difference in the column percentages across the rows. In Table 12-8, however, there is a 70 percent difference in the column percentages. The relationship in Table 12-8, then, is much stronger than the one in section *b* of Table 12-2 since the difference more closely approximates the 100 percent difference in the perfect relationship shown in Table 12-7. Essentially, the larger the differences across the rows, the stronger the relationship.

The statistical significance of a relationship indicates whether the observed relationship could have occurred by chance alone. The determination of statistical significance requires the calculation of a statistic

Table 12-8 A Strong but Imperfect Relationship between Hair Color and Vote

Dependent Variable: Vote	Independent Variable: Hair Color			
	Blonde	Brunette	Total	(n)
Republican	80%	10%	33%	(500)
Democrat	20	90	67	(1,000)
Total	100	100	100	
(n)	(500)	(1,000)		(1,500)

Source: Hypothetical data.

Table 12-9 Relationship between Education and Voter Turnout
(in percent)

Independent Variable: Education	Dependent Variable: Turnout			
	Voted	Did Not Vote	Total	Percent of Total
0-4 years	38	62	100	4
5-7 years	49	51	100	6
8 years	59	41	100	10
9-11 years	55	45	100	16
12 years	69	31	100	38
1-3 years college	79	21	100	14
4 years college	86	14	100	7
5+ years college	91	9	100	4

Source: Raymond E. Wolfinger and Steven J. Rosenstone, *Who Votes?* (New Haven, Conn.: Yale University Press, 1980), 17. Reprinted with permission.

called *chi-square,* which will be discussed later in this chapter. The stronger a relationship is, the more likely it is to be statistically significant. Hence, a strong relationship is especially desirable. Moreover, the larger the number of cases in a crosstab, the more likely an observed relationship is to be statistically significant. Consequently, large samples are more likely to yield statistically significant results than are small samples.

Example of a Crosstab Analysis

So far we have illustrated crosstabulation exclusively with hypothetical data. Let us take a look now at an example of an actual observed relationship between a nominal and an ordinal level measure.

Raymond Wolfinger and Steven Rosenstone, in their analysis of why people vote, use crosstab analysis to test their hypothesis that the more education one has, the more likely one is to vote.[2] Table 12-9 shows that only 38 percent of those with 0-4 years of formal education voted while more than 86 percent of those who completed four years of college voted, and that generally the higher a group's years of formal education, the larger the percentage of that group voting. Therefore, the relationship between education and voter turnout exists, the direction is *as hypothesized,* and the strength of the relationship is fairly strong. (This is a good example of a crosstab that has the independent variable down the side because of its many categories. In this case, then, the table is percentaged across the rows, and comparisons are made down the columns.)

Researchers often use readily available computer software packages to produce the crosstabulations that will indicate relationships between nominal and ordinal level measures. Table 12-10, for example, shows a

Table 12-10   Sample Crosstabulation Produced by SPSS Software
Program: The Relationship between Gender and Attitudes
toward Life

Count/ Column Percent		Gender		Row Total
		Male	Female	
		1	2	
Exciting	1	300	384	684
		50.3	44.4	46.8
Pretty routine	2	267	437	704
		44.8	50.5	48.2
Dull	3	29	44	73
		4.9	5.1	5.0
Column total		596	865	1,461
		40.8	59.2	100.0

Number of missing observations = 12

Source: Marija J. Norusis, *SPSS/PC + Studentware* (Chicago: SPSS, Inc., 1988), 127.
Note: Question asked was: Is life exciting or dull?

crosstab table produced by the *SPSS* program. There we can see that the
crosstab displays the relationship between gender (the independent
variable—displayed across the top of the table) and attitudes toward how
exciting life is (the dependent variable—displayed down the side of the
table). Of the 865 women in the sample 44 percent think life is exciting
and 56 percent think life is pretty routine or dull. Of the 596 men in the
sample, 50 percent think life is exciting and 49 percent think life is pretty
routine or dull. There is a weak relationship, then, between these two
variables; men are slightly more likely to think life is exciting than
women are. At this point, however, we do not know whether this
relationship is statistically significant.

Measures of Association

So far we have measured the relationship between two variables by
inspecting a crosstabulation percentaged on the categories of the independent variable. However, if a researcher's analysis involves many
crosstabs or crosstabs that are so large that a way of summarizing the
information is needed, *measures of association* may be used. These
measures summarize efficiently the existence, direction, strength, and
statistical significance of the relationship between two variables in a
crosstab.

Measures of association take the number of observations in each of
the cells and combine them arithmetically to produce a summary

Table 12-11   Relationship between Education and Political Interest: Concordant, Discordant, and Tied Pairs

Dependent Variable: Political Interest	Independent Variable: Education		
	Low	Medium	High
Low	1		4
Medium		2	
High	5	3	6

	Type		
	Concordant	Discordant	Tied
	1, 2	3, 4	1, 5
	1, 6	2, 4	1, 4
	1, 3	2, 5	2, 3
	2, 6	4, 5	3, 5
			3, 6
			4, 6
			5, 6

Source: Hypothetical data.

measure of the distribution of cases. Some of these measures indicate the direction and strength of a relationship and can vary from −1 to +1. The closer the value is to 0, the weaker the relationship; the closer the value is to ±1 the stronger the relationship. The direction of the relationship is indicated by the sign + or − that precedes the statistic.

The particular measure of association that is used to summarize a crosstab depends on the level of measurement of the variables and the intent of the researcher. When both variables in a crosstab are ordinal level measures, the most frequently used measures of association are *Kendall's tau, Somer's d,* and *Goodman and Kruskal's gamma*—named after the people who developed them. Most computer programs will calculate at least these statistics for any crosstab and print the value out for the researcher's use. Tau, d, and gamma are similar, but not identical, in how they summarize the contents of a crosstab. Each of them uses pairs of cases in the crosstab and measures whether those pairs are concordant, discordant, or tied.

Let us take the relationship between education and political interest. In Table 12-11 we have placed six cases in a crosstab so that we can illustrate the identification of concordant, discordant, and tied pairs. A *concordant pair* is a pair of cases in which one case is higher on both variables than the other case. The pair of observation 1 and observation 2 is concordant because 2 is higher on both education and interest than 1 is. A *discordant pair* is one in which one case is lower on one of the variables but higher on the other variable. The pair of observation 3 and observation 4 is discordant because 4 is higher on education than 3 but lower than 3 on political interest. Therefore, this pair violates the expectation that as education increases, so does political interest. A *tied pair* is a pair in which both observations are tied on at least one of the variables. The pair consisting of observations 1 and 5 is tied because both observations have the same value on education.

Tau, d, and gamma all use this evaluation of pairs to summarize the relationship in the crosstab. The basic comparison made is between the number of concordant and discordant pairs. If both types of pairs are equally numerous, the statistic will be 0, indicating no relationship. If concordant pairs are more numerous, there will be a positive statistic; if discordant pairs are more numerous, there will be a negative statistic. The degree to which one type of pair is more frequent than the other will result in the size of the statistic, which is indicative of the strength of the relationship. Hence if only the main diagonal were filled with observations, all of the pairs would be concordant, and the statistic would be +1—a perfect, positive relationship. If only the minor diagonal were filled with observations, all of the pairs would be discordant, and the statistic would be −1—a perfect, negative relationship.

The formulas for tau, d, and gamma are as follows:

$$\text{tau b} = \frac{P - Q}{\sqrt{(P + Q + T_2)(P + Q + T_1)}}$$

$$\text{tau c} = \frac{P - Q}{1/2(n)^2\,[(m - 1)/m]}$$

$$\text{Asymmetric d} = \frac{P - Q}{P + Q + T_1} \quad \text{(row variable is dependent)}$$

$$= \frac{P - Q}{P + Q + T_2} \quad \text{(column variable is dependent)}$$

$$\text{Symmetric d} = \frac{P - Q}{P + Q + (T_1 + T_2)/2}$$

$$\text{Gamma} = \frac{P - Q}{P + Q} \tag{12.1}$$

Where

P = number of concordant pairs
Q = number of discordant pairs
T_1 = number of ties on row variables
T_2 = number of ties on column variables
m = the smaller of the number of rows and columns
n = number of cases

For all of these measures, the numerator in the equation is simply the comparison of the number of concordant and discordant pairs $(P - Q)$. The denominators differ, however, with the equation for gamma ignoring ties altogether and the equations for the others taking ties into consideration in many different ways. Tau b is suitable for square tables (that is, tables with the same number of rows and columns); tau c is suitable for nonsquare tables; and Somer's d has both a symmetric and an asymmetric version, depending on which variable in the crosstab is dependent.[3]

We can illustrate the calculation of these statistics by using the data in Table 12-12. The number of concordant pairs may be found by multiplying the number of cases in each cell by the number in each cell below and to the right, and summing the result:

$$60(100 + 80 + 50 + 100) + 30(50 + 100)$$
$$+ 50(80 + 100) + 100(100) = 43,300$$

The number of discordant pairs may be calculated by multiplying the number of cases in each cell by the number in each cell above and to the right and summing the result:

$$30(50 + 20) + 10(50 + 20 + 100 + 80)$$
$$+ 100(20) + 50(20 + 80) = 11,600$$

The number of ties for the row variable may be found by multiplying the number of cases in each cell by the number of cases in the remaining cells

Table 12-12 Relationship between Education and Political Interest: Calculating Measures of Association

Dependent Variable: Political Interest	Independent Variable: Education			
	Low	Medium	High	Total
Low	60	50	20	130
Medium	30	100	80	210
High	10	50	100	160
	100	200	200	500

Source: Hypothetical data.

in that row, and summing the result:

$$60(50 + 20) + 50(20) + 30(100 + 80)$$
$$+ 100(80) + 10(50 + 100) + 50(100) = 25,100$$

The number of ties for the column variable is the number of cases in each cell multiplied by the number of cases in the remaining cells in that column, added together:

$$60(30 + 10) + 30(10) + 50(100 + 50)$$
$$+ 100(50) + 20(80 + 100) + 80(100) = 26,800$$

Once these calculations are completed, each of the measures of association can be calculated as follows:

$$\text{tau b} = \frac{43,300 - 11,600}{\sqrt{(43,300 + 11,600 + 26,800)(43,300 + 11,600 + 25,100)}}$$

$$= \frac{31,700}{80,846} = +.39$$

$$\text{tau c} = \frac{43,300 - 11,600}{1/2\ (500)^2\ [(3 - 1)/3]} = \frac{31,700}{83,333} = +.38$$

$$\text{Asymmetric d} = \frac{43,300 - 11,600}{43,300 + 11,600 + 25,100}$$

$$= \frac{31,700}{80,000} = +.40 \tag{12.2}$$

$$\text{Symmetric d} = \frac{43,300 - 11,600}{43,300 + 11,600 + (25,100 + 26,800)/2}$$

$$= \frac{31,700}{80,850} = +.40$$

$$\text{gamma} = \frac{43,300 - 11,600}{43,300 + 11,600} = \frac{31,700}{54,900} = +.58$$

Tau, d, and gamma will generally take on similar but not identical values for any given crosstab. They will all have a value of zero when there is no relationship between the two variables, and they will all have the same sign for a given relationship. Values of gamma, however, are generally higher than the other statistics and may yield a misleading overestimation of the strength of a relationship. When a researcher is uncertain about the properties of the three measures of association, tau is probably the safest measure to use.

When one or both of the variables in a crosstab is a nominal level measure, tau, d, and gamma may not be used because the identification of concordant and discordant pairs requires that the variables possess an ordering of values (one value higher than another). Hence a different measure of association, called *Goodman and Kruskal's lambda*, is generally used.

Lambda is designed to indicate whether the values of one variable tend to cluster with certain values of the other variable so that knowing a case's value for the independent variable would help one predict that case's value for the dependent variable.

The formula for lambda is

$$\text{Lambda} = \frac{L - M}{L} \tag{12.3}$$

where L is the number of mistakes one would make in predicting the values of the dependent variable without taking the independent variable into consideration, and M is the number of mistakes one would make in predicting values of the dependent variable when the independent variable is taken into consideration. The best prediction for values of the dependent variable without knowing the value of the independent variable is the modal value for the dependent variable. The best prediction for values of the dependent variable when taking the independent variable into consideration is the modal value for each category of the independent variable. Let us consider an example of how these calculations are performed.

Suppose we are interested in the relationship between race and primary votes for the 1984 Democratic presidential candidates. Table 12-13 shows a hypothetical crosstabulation of this relationship without any cases inside the cells. Our best prediction of how particular people voted, based only on the information in Table 12-13, would be that the cases in every category of race voted for Mondale since that is the most numerous (or modal) value on the dependent variable. Such a prediction would yield 410 correct predictions and 590 errors, not a very impressive performance.

Now suppose we know something about the relationship between race and 1984 primary votes as shown in section *a* of Table 12-14. The primary votes of the voters in each category of race can be predicted based on how the observations are distributed or clustered within the table. We would predict that each racial group voted for the modal value in that racial category: all white voters would vote for Mondale, all black

Table 12-13   Relationship between Race and 1984 Democratic Primary
Votes: Predicting without the Help of an Independent
Variable

Dependent Variable: 1984 Democratic Primary Vote	Independent Variable: Race				
	White	Black	Hispanic	Oriental	Total
Mondale					410
Hart					295
Jackson					295
Total	600	300	50	50	1,000

Source: Hypothetical data.

voters for Jackson, all Hispanic voters for Jackson, and all Oriental voters
for Mondale. This prediction would be correct in 551 of the cases (300 +
201 + 25 + 25) and incorrect in 449 of the cases. We have improved our
prediction from 590 incorrect predictions to 449. Consequently, lambda
would be

$$\Lambda = \frac{590 - 449}{590} = \frac{141}{590} = .24$$

The extent of this improvement in prediction is dependent upon the
extent to which the cases in each category of the independent variable
cluster within particular categories of the dependent variable. It is this
improvement on the original prediction that lambda is designed to
measure. If all of the cases clustered within only one category of the
dependent variable for each category of the independent variable, as in
section *b* of Table 12-14, our prediction would be perfect and lambda
would be 1. Since nominal measures do not have an ordering, we cannot
speak of positive or negative relationships, and lambda therefore has no
sign. The direction of the relationship in this case is simply which
category of the dependent variable goes with which category of the
independent variable.

The extent of this improvement Although lambda is the generally preferred measure of association
for relationships involving nominal level measures, it yields a misleading
result in two situations. First, if the best prediction (mode) for each
category of the independent variable is the same as the overall mode of
the dependent variable, lambda will always be 0, even if the column
percentages for the categories differ markedly across the rows, as in
section *c* of Table 12-14. In that case inspection of the column percentages would seem to indicate a relationship between the two variables even
though the calculation of lambda indicates no relationship. Second,
whenever there are more categories for the dependent variable than there
are for the independent variable, lambda cannot take on a value of 1.0,

Table 12-14 1984 Democratic Primary Votes: Predicting with the Help of an Independent Variable

Dependent Variable: 1984 Democratic Primary Vote	*Independent Variable: Race*					
	White	Black	Hispanic	Oriental	Total	(n)
a.						
Mondale	50%	23%	30%	50%	41.0%	(410)
Hart	40	10	20	30	29.5	(295)
Jackson	10	67	50	20	29.5	(295)
Total	100	100	100	100	100.0	
(n)	(600)	(300)	(50)	(50)		(1,000)
b.						
Mondale	100%	0%	0%	0%	60.0%	(600)
Hart	0	0	100	100	100.0	(100)
Jackson	0	100	0	0	30.0	(300)
Total	100	100	100	100	100.0	
(n)	(600)	(300)	(50)	(50)		(1,000)
c.						
Mondale	90%	80%	70%	60%	84.5%	(845)
Hart	5	0	10	40	5.5	(55)
Jackson	5	20	20	0	10.0	(100)
Total	100	100	100	100	100.0	
(n)	(600)	(300)	(50)	(50)		(1,000)

Source: Hypothetical data.

even if the cases are clustered as much as the marginals permit. As both cases show, the result of any measure of association should not be taken at face value without inspecting the distribution of the observed values upon which that measure is based.

Statistical Significance

Whether a relationship is statistically significant—that is, whether it is the result of systematic factors rather than just chance—usually cannot be determined by inspecting a crosstab; instead, a statistic called chi-square (χ^2) must be calculated. Chi-square measures whether the observed relationship in the crosstab differs significantly from the relationship we might have observed by chance alone between the two variables. Chi-square is usually used to indicate the probability that a relationship observed among data drawn from a sample would also be observed among the target population.

Table 12-15 presents a crosstab exhibiting the observed relationship between gender and attitudes toward nuclear power plants among a

Table 12-15 Relationship between Gender and Attitudes toward Nuclear Power Plants: Observed Table, Observations

Dependent Variable: Attitudes toward Nuclear Power Plants	*Independent Variable: Gender*			
	Male	Female	Total	(n)
Open more plants	Cell a: 200	Cell d: 100	30%	(300)
Retain status quo	Cell b: 100	Cell e: 200	30%	(300)
Close plants	Cell c: 100	Cell f: 300	40%	(400)
Total	40%	60%	100%	
(n)	(400)	(600)		(1,000)

Source: Hypothetical data.

sample of 1,000 people. *Among that sample* it appears that there is a relationship between gender and attitudes toward nuclear power plants, with women being more opposed to the plant. Table 12-16, an *expected values table,* will include the number of cases that we would expect in each cell if there were no relationship between the two variables. This table has the same marginals as Table 12-15, but the cell entries will probably be different. The expected values in each cell are calculated from the marginals in Table 12-15.

Recall that no relationship is present in a crosstab when the column percentages are identical across the rows and when the column percentages are identical to the marginal percentages at the far right-hand side of the table. If there were no relationship in Table 12-16, 30 percent of both males and females would be in favor of opening more plants, 30 percent of both males and females would be in favor of retaining the status quo, and 40

Table 12-16 Relationship between Gender and Attitudes toward Nuclear Power Plants: Expected Values Table, Marginals Only

Dependent Variable: Attitudes toward Nuclear Power Plants	*Independent Variable: Gender*			
	Male	Female	Total	(n)
Open more plants			30%	(300)
Retain status quo			30%	(300)
Close plants			40%	(400)
Total	40%	60%	100%	
(n)	(400)	(600)		(1,000)

Source: Hypothetical data.

Table 12-17   Relationship between Gender and Attitudes toward
Nuclear Power Plants: Expected Values Table, Cell
Frequencies

Dependent Variable: *Attitudes toward* *Nuclear Power Plants*	*Independent Variable: Gender*			
	Male	Female	Total	(n)
Open more plants	Cell a: 120	Cell d: 180	30%	(300)
Retain status quo	Cell b: 120	Cell e: 180	30%	(300)
Close plants	Cell c: 160	Cell f: 240	40%	(400)
Total	40%	60%	100%	
(n)	(400)	(600)		(1,000)

Source: Hypothetical data.

percent of both males and females would be in favor of closing plants.
The distribution of cases in the crosstab, then, would look like Table 12-17.

In general, the expected number of cases in each cell may be calculated by multiplying the marginals for each cell together and dividing by the total sample size. Hence the expected values in Table 12-17 would be:

$$\text{Cell a: } (300)(400)/1000 = 120$$

$$\text{Cell b: } (300)(400)/1000 = 120$$

$$\text{Cell c: } (400)(400)/1000 = 160$$

$$\text{Cell d: } (300)(600)/1000 = 180$$

$$\text{Cell e: } (300)(600)/1000 = 180$$

$$\text{Cell f: } (400)(600)/1000 = 240$$

The next step is to calculate how much difference there is between the observed table (Table 12-15) and the expected values table with cell frequencies (Table 12-17). This will tell us how far the observed relationship is from the expected distribution if there were no relationship between the two variables. To do this, we subtract the number of cases in each cell of Table 12-17 from the number of cases in the corresponding cell of Table 12-15, square the difference, and then divide the difference by the number of cases in that cell in Table 12-17. These calculations should be done separately for each cell in the two tables and then summed across all the cells to yield the chi-square value. The formula for chi-square, then, is

$$\chi^2 = \frac{(O - E)^2}{E} \tag{12.4}$$

For Table 12-15 and Table 12-17, the calculations would look like this:

Cell	Observed Value	Expected Value	Difference	(Difference)²	$\dfrac{(Difference)^2}{Expected\ Value}$
a	200	120	80	6400	53.33
b	100	120	−20	400	3.33
c	100	160	−60	3600	22.50
d	100	180	−80	6400	35.56
e	200	180	20	400	2.22
f	300	240	60	3600	15.00
				Sum	131.94

The value of chi-square in this example is 131.94. To determine whether the relationship is statistically significant, we must calculate a number called the *degrees of freedom,* which is the number of columns in a table minus one $(C - 1)$ times the number of rows in a table minus one $(R - 1)$ or in this case $(2 - 1)$ $(3 - 1)$ or 2. Then we must look up the value of our chi-square on a chi-square table to determine whether it is high enough to indicate a statistically significant relationship. (See the Appendix for a chi-square table.) For a given value of chi-square and degrees of freedom, the chi-square table will indicate the probability that a χ^2 value of at least that magnitude would have been observed if there were no relationship between the two variables (or, in other words, if the *null hypothesis* were true). The lower this probability, the better; to reject the null hypothesis the probability that the null hypothesis is true generally must be less than .01. The value of chi-square in our example, 131.94, is well above the criterion value, 9.21, and therefore the relationship is statistically significant at the .01 level.

Researchers generally want their chi-square value to be large so that they can reject the null hypothesis. Large values of chi-square result when the observed and expected tables are quite different and when the sample size upon which the tables are based is large. A weak relationship among a large sample may attain statistical significance while a strong relationship within a small sample may not. In other words, statistical significance is not the same as strength or substantive significance, and chi-square values should not be used as a measure of substantive importance. Rather, chi-square values tell us the probability that an observed relationship could have occurred by chance or would not have been observed in the target population.

Difference of Means Test and Analysis of Variance

Crosstabulation is the appropriate analysis technique when both variables are nominal or ordinal level measures. When the independent variable is nominal or ordinal and the dependent variable is interval or ratio, however, a crosstab would have far too many columns or rows to permit a straightforward and meaningful analysis. Therefore, two similar analysis techniques—the *difference of means test* and *analysis of variance*—are used.

Both of these techniques help test the researcher's hypothesis that the dependent variable, which is measured at the interval or ratio level, is related to the independent variable. First the cases are divided into categories based on the values of the independent variable. Then, if the values of the dependent variable are (1) less varied within each category of the independent variable than they were before *and* (2) quite different in general for different values of the independent variable, a relationship exists.

A simple example will illustrate this point. Suppose we have hypothesized that there is a relationship between gender and the amount of money contributed to political campaigns. And suppose that we measure these two variables for a sample of ten people and receive the following results:

Gender	Money Contributed (in thousands of dollars)	Gender	Money Contributed (in thousands of dollars)
Male	10	Male	15
Female	8	Male	20
Female	5	Female	2
Male	10	Female	5
Female	10	Male	15

Now if we ignore the independent variable, we can see that the mean amount of money for all ten observations is 10 (thousand dollars) and that the variation around that mean looks like this:

It is this variation (the actual variance is 26.8) that we are trying to explain.

Now let us consider whether the independent variable helps us account for this variation. The independent variable is clearly a nominal level measure. If we divide the cases into two groups based on this measure, we find that the original variation is distributed across the two groups in the following way:

Males	Females
10	2
10	5
15	5
15	8
20	10

Total	= 70	Total	=	30
$\overline{X}$	= 14	$\overline{X}$	=	6
s^2	= 14	s^2	=	7.6

The average amount of money contributed by the two groups is quite different, and the variation in the amount contributed is much smaller within both groups than it was originally. In other words, the independent variable has been helpful in grouping the observations into categories that are different from each other on the dependent variable and that contain observations that are similar to each other. The analysis has revealed a pattern in the data and has reduced the amount of unexplained variation.

This is the basic logic of both analysis techniques. We begin with a certain amount of unexplained variance in the dependent variable. We use the measurement of the independent variable to divide the cases into analysis groups and then determine if the groups created are dissimilar from each other and more homogeneous than the original data were. The difference of means test involves comparing the means of the groups created with the independent variable to see if the difference is statistically significant. The analysis of variance involves comparing the variance in each of the analysis groups with the total variance in the dependent variable to see how much variance has been explained by the independent variable.

Edward Tufte's study of the relationship between automobile inspection policy and traffic fatality rates contains a good example of a hypothesis involving a nominal and a ratio level measure.[4] Tufte was interested in whether states with mandatory auto inspections experienced lower auto fatality rates than states without mandatory inspections. His initial test of this hypothesis was to measure the relationship between auto inspection policy (a nominal level independent variable with only two categories) and auto fatality rates (a ratio level dependent variable).

Tufte began with a distribution of fifty observed values (one for each state) on the dependent variable, motor vehicle deaths per 100,000 people. These observed values had a mean value of 29.8 deaths per 100,000 and a variance of 60.55. He then divided the cases (states) into two categories: states with and states without mandatory automobile inspections. This resulted in mean death rates of 26.1 for the eighteen

Figure 12-1 Using the Difference of Means Test: Average Death Rates in Inspected versus Uninspected States

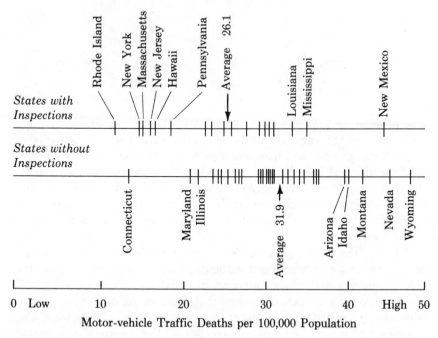

Source: Edward R. Tufte, *Data Analysis for Politics and Policy* © 1974, 13. Adapted by permission of Prentice-Hall, Inc., Englewood Cliffs, New Jersey.

states with inspections (with a variance of 66.07) and 31.9 for the thirty-two states without inspections (with a variance of 45.56). Therefore, the two analysis groups defined by the values of the independent variable differed somewhat. Furthermore, visual inspection of the distributions within the two categories suggested that the variation within each group was smaller than it was for the whole set of observations (see Figure 12-1). Initially, then, it appears that dividing the cases into the two analysis groups is worthwhile and that there is a relationship between the two variables.

Since the number of cases analyzed is generally larger than Tufte's fifty, visual inspection of the distribution of cases in the analysis groups is not usually adequate. Furthermore, more precise measures of the direction, strength, and statistical significance of the relationships are desirable. Both the difference of means test and the analysis of variance have been developed to provide a more precise measure of relationships between variables of this type.

The initial step in both the difference of means test and the analysis of variance is to calculate the mean and variance for the cases on the dependent variable. This variance is called the *total variance*. The cases are then divided into two or more groups based on the independent variable and the mean and variance for each group are calculated. If the means of the groups are quite different, and the possibility that the difference in the means has occurred because of chance can be eliminated, then a relationship between the two variables is indicated by the difference of means test.

One can get an idea of the direction and strength of the relationship revealed by these procedures by noting which group (or groups) has the higher mean and by comparing the variances of the analysis groups with the total variance for all the observations. In Tufte's case, the direction of the relationship is that those states with mandatory auto inspections have fewer traffic fatalities, and the strength of the relationship is indicated by the variation left in the categories of the independent variable. However, a more precise measure of the relationship is given by an analysis of variance and a correlation called *eta-squared*.

Eta-squared is similar to lambda for a crosstabulation. It represents the amount of reduction that has occurred in the total variance as a result of dividing the cases into groups based on the independent variable. To calculate eta-squared, take the total variance, subtract from it a weighted sum of the variances left in the analysis groups (the *unexplained variance*), and divide this difference by the total variance. The numerator of this ratio is the *explained variance*, and the higher this number, the stronger the relationship:

$$E^2 = \frac{\text{total SS} - \text{unexplained SS}}{\text{total SS}} = \frac{\text{explained SS}}{\text{total SS}} \qquad (12.5)$$

Where SS = sum of squares.

In the gender-money contributed example, the total variance was 26.8. The unexplained variance left after the cases were divided into males and females was an average of the two variances left (14 and 7.60 weighted by the number of cases in each group):

$$(5(14) + 5(7.6))/10 = (70 + 38)/10 = 108/10 = 10.8$$

The unexplained variance is then subtracted from the total variance to get the explained variance, and the result is divided by the total variance:

$$\frac{26.8 - 10.8}{26.8} = \frac{16.0}{26.8} = .60$$

This value of eta-squared means that 60 percent of the variance in the dependent variable has been explained by the independent variable, indicating a fairly strong relationship.

In Tufte's analysis of auto inspection policy the total variance with which he began was 60.55. The unexplained variance left after the states were divided into categories was

$$\frac{(45.56)(32) + (66.07)(18)}{50} = 52.94$$

The explained variance, as a proportion of the total variance, was

$$\frac{60.55 - 52.94}{60.55} = .13$$

Eta-squared was .13, indicating a weak relationship, with 13 percent of the variance in the dependent variable explained by the independent variable. Remember that the closer eta-squared is to 0 the weaker the relationship, and the closer it is to 1 the stronger the relationship.

Both a difference of means test and an analysis of variance allow us to assess the direction and strength of a relationship between a nominal or ordinal level independent variable and an interval or ratio level dependent variable. The relative means for the analysis groups tell us the direction of the relationship, while the eta-squared, derived from the comparison of the explained and unexplained variance, tells us the strength of the relationship. In an analysis of variance, the strength of the relationship is indicated by the amount of variance left in the dependent variable when the cases are divided into groups based on the independent variable.

The statistical significance of a relationship also may be determined with a difference of means test and an analysis of variance. The test involves determining when the difference in the means on the dependent variable for the analysis groups could have occurred by chance. The larger the difference in means relative to the variances involved and the larger the sample size, the greater the chance that a given difference will be statistically significant.

Statistical significance may be calculated with a statistic called the *F ratio*. Like chi-square for a crosstab, the F ratio indicates the probability that the null hypothesis is true. The F ratio must be greater than a particular criterion level to show a statistically significant relationship between the independent and dependent variables. The criterion level depends upon the degrees of freedom (calculated from the sample size and the number of analysis groups) and the probability of rejecting the null hypothesis. Once the F ratio is calculated, then the result may be compared with an F-ratio table to decide whether to accept or reject the null hypothesis in the population.[5]

Table 12-18 Relationship between Income and Contacts with Public
Officials: A Regression Analysis

Case	Independent Variable: Income	Dependent Variable: Number of Contacts
a	$ 3,000	0
b	15,000	3
c	42,000	3
d	22,000	2
e	10,000	1
f	85,000	7
g	30,000	4
h	70,000	6
i	100,000	4
j	55,000	6

Source: Hypothetical data.

Regression and Correlation Analysis

When both the independent and the dependent variables are interval or ratio level measures, regression and correlation analysis are the standard techniques for measuring relationships and testing hypotheses. Both procedures are similar to crosstabulation, the difference of means test, and analysis of variance; although the terms regression and correlation may seem imposing, the analyses are really quite easy to understand.

Regression Analysis

To illustrate the technique of regression analysis, we will test the hypothesis that there is a positive relationship between people's income and the number of times they personally contact public officials. We will consider just the first 10 cases in a sample of 500 people. The values on the independent and dependent variables for these 10 cases are presented in Table 12-18.

The first step is to display all of the cases in the sample so that we can see each case's values on both the independent and the dependent variables. In crosstabulation, this is done by putting each case into its proper category or cell in a table. In regression analysis, a graph called a *scattergram* is drawn and each case is placed at the point that corresponds to the value of the independent and dependent variables for that case.

Figure 12-2 Scattergram of Relationship between Income and Political
Contacts: Ten Cases Only

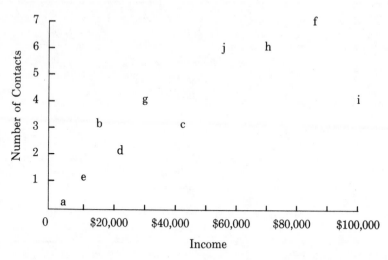

Source: Hypothetical data.

The first ten cases in our example are presented in Figure 12-2. The
values of the independent variable are placed along the bottom of the
graph on the *X-axis,* and the values of the dependent variable are placed
along the side of the graph on the *Y-axis.* Each case is then placed at the
point that corresponds to the intersection of that case's values on the
independent (X-axis) and dependent (Y-axis) variables and a line is
drawn through the points to show the overall pattern of the data. This
regression line is usually calculated for you by a computer program in a
way that *minimizes* the vertical distances between the data points and
the line drawn. This line will be the best *linear* representation of the
relationship between the two variables.

Any straight line may be represented by the *regression equation*

$$Y = bX + a \qquad (12.6)$$

Where

    Y = any case's value on the dependent variable
    X = any case's value on the independent variable
    a = the *Y-intercept* or the place at which the line crosses the Y-axis
    b = the *slope* of the line across the graph

As the regression equation indicates, there are two unknowns, a and
b. From the observed values, b may be calculated directly:

$$b = \frac{N\Sigma XY - (\Sigma X)(\Sigma Y)}{N\Sigma X^2 - (\Sigma X)^2} \qquad (12.7)$$

Figure 12-3 Regression Line for Relationship between Income and
Political Contacts: All 500 Cases

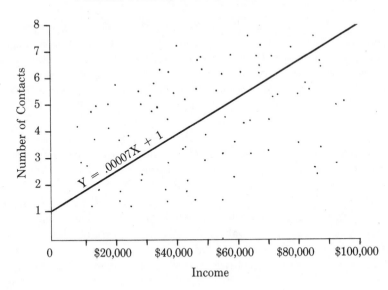

Where
  X = the observed values of the independent variable
  Y = the observed values of the dependent variable
  Σ = summation
  N = the number of observed values

Once b has been calculated, then it is a relatively simple step to calculate
a, since

$$a = \overline{Y} - b\overline{X}$$

After b and a have both been determined, the regression line that
minimizes the squared distances between observed and predicted values
of Y may be drawn. Computer programs designed to perform regression
analysis accomplish these calculations quickly and accurately.

Let us suppose that after we have graphed all 500 data points testing
the relationship between income and contacts with public officials, we
end up with the *regression line* shown in Figure 12-3 and a regression
equation of Y = .00007X + 1. What does this tell us about the relationship between the two variables and the hypothesis linking the two?

The slope of the line (also called the *regression coefficient*) and the
Y-intercept tell us the nature of the relationship between the two
variables. The Y-intercept tells us what the value of the dependent
variable should be when the value of the independent variable is 0. In this
case, a Y-intercept of 1 tells us that when a person's income (the
independent variable) is 0, that person is likely to have contacted a public

official one time (that is, the dependent variable at that point on the graph is 1). This is the place at which the regression line crosses the Y-axis.

The slope of the line tells us how much the dependent variable changes when the independent variable changes or how much change will take place in values of Y for every change in X of 1 unit. In this case, the slope of .00007 tells us that for every change in X of $1, there is a change in Y of .00007. Or if we compare two people—one with $15,000 more income than the other—the expected value of Y will be different by (.00007 x 15,000) or 1.05. Therefore, we expect a difference of $15,000 in income to be associated with a difference of about one personal contact with a public official. The slope shows how responsive, in a mathematical sense, the dependent variable is to changes in the independent variable.

Finally, the sign of the slope tells us the direction of the relationship. A *positive sign* indicates a positive relationship: as the values of one of the variables increase, the values of the other variable increase. A *negative sign* indicates a negative relationship: as the values of one of the variables increase, the values of the other variable decrease. Because most graphs are drawn with the lowest values for both variables at the bottom and left-hand side, a positive relationship is usually represented by a line that rises from lower left to upper right, and a negative relationship is represented by a line that falls from upper left to lower right.

The regression equation contains a lot of useful information. It gives the expected value of the dependent variable for any value of the independent variable and the general relationship between the two variables. In this case we could substitute any value of X (income) into the equation and calculate the expected value of Y (number of personal contacts with public officials). For example, someone who made $40,000 would have contacted a public official 3.8 times—(.00007 x 40,000) + 1.

The regression coefficient is not a good measure of the strength of the relationship between interval level measures because it is dependent upon the units in which the variables are measured. The regression coefficient in the income-political contacts example looks very small: .00007. But it is a small number because the independent variable is measured in terms of dollars, and most of the observed values of income were in the thousands of dollars range. If we measured income in thousands of dollars instead of dollars, the regression equation would change to $Y = .07X + 1$. This change in the regression coefficient does not mean that the relationship is any stronger; it means only that the units of measurement have changed. Although the regression coefficient indicates how much change in the dependent variable is generally associated with change in the independent variable, it does not indicate how strong that association is. *Correlation analysis,* discussed in the next section, measures the strength of the relationships between the independent and dependent variables.

A good example of the use of regression analysis may be found in a recent investigation of the performance of the fifteen regional governments in Italy.[6] The researchers were interested in explaining why some of the Italian governments performed their governmental duties better than others did. First they devised a measure of institutional performance (the dependent variable) for each of the fifteen governments based on eight indicators of legislative activity, bureaucratic efficiency, programmatic innovation, and governmental stability. Then they measured the relationships between this measure and a number of possible explanations for governmental performance. One of the researchers' hypotheses was that performance would depend on socioeconomic development. Using per capita income, literacy, nonagricultural employment, and television and automobile ownership as measures of socioeconomic development, they graphed the relationship between development and performance, shown in Figure 12-4.

Clearly, a positive relationship exists between socioeconomic development and institutional performance. Although there are a few cases distant from the regression line, the best approximation of the data appears to be a straight line.

Since the researchers provide neither the regression equation that corresponds to the regression line nor the units of the measures along the axes, it is impossible to tell what the exact mathematical relationship is between the measures of socioeconomic development and institutional performance. Because the measures are indices consisting of many different individual attributes, they lack a straightforward, intuitive meaning. Although the researchers have uncovered a fairly strong, positive relationship between development and performance, we cannot conclude that one is the cause of the other. Much more analysis would be necessary to establish a causal relationship.

Another good example of the use of regression analysis is Ted Robert Gurr's research concerning why some nations exhibit more domestic violence and turmoil than others do.[7] He hypothesized that there is a relationship between the size of a country's internal security force and the amount of civil strife. Figure 12-5 indicates that a relationship exists (the data approximate a straight line), that the relationship is positive (as the size of the coercive forces increases, so does the magnitude of civil strife), and that the relationship is fairly strong (most of the data points are fairly close to the regression line).

Again remember that the discovery of a positive relationship between the size of coercive forces and the magnitude of civil strife does not necessarily mean that one is causing the other. As Gurr himself concludes:

Figure 12-4 Regression Line for Relationship between Socioeconomic
Development and Institutional Performance of Italian
Regional Governments

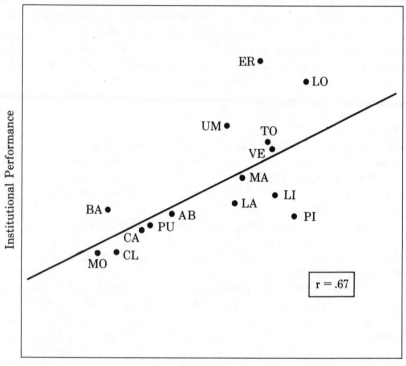

Socioeconomic Development

Source: Robert D. Putnam et al., "Explaining Institutional Success: The Case of Italian Regional Government," *American Political Science Review* 77 (March 1983): 64. Reprinted with permission.

Note: AB = Abruzzo, BA = Basilicata, CA = Campania, CL = Calabria, ER = Emilia-Romagna, LA = Lazio, LI = Liguria, LO = Lombardia, MA = Marche, MO = Molise, PI = Piemonte, PU = Puglia, TO = Toscana, UM = Umbria, VE = Veneto.

The correspondence of force size and levels of strife does not necessarily imply a simple causal connection between the two. The military establishment is relatively large in most Western countries because of cold-war tension, not because of the threat of internal disorder. Nonetheless, the investment of large portions of national budgets in armaments; military conscription policies; and involvement in foreign conflict have directly generated widespread popular opposition in the United States and France in the past decade, and may have provided a similar though less dramatic impetus to public protest in other Western nations.[8]

Figure 12-5   Regression Line for Relationship between Coercive Force
Size and Magnitude of Civil Strife in Twenty-one Western
Communities

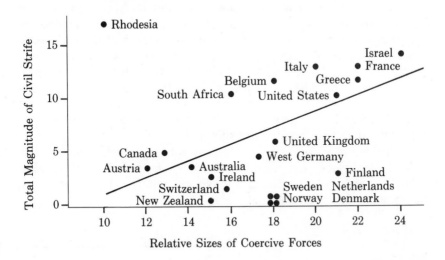

Source: Ted Robert Gurr, "A Comparative Study of Civil Strife," in Hugh Davis Graham
and Ted Robert Gurr, eds., *Violence in America: Historical and Comparative Perspectives,
A Report to the National Commission on the Causes and Prevention of Violence* (Washington, D.C.: U.S. Government Printing Office, 1969), 477.

Correlation Analysis

A straight line can be drawn through any set of data points, and as long
as the slope of the line drawn is not 0, we can say that there is a
relationship between the independent and dependent variables. However,
that does not necessarily mean that the line is a close approximation of
the data points or that the relationship is a statistically significant one. It
may be that the line drawn is the best one possible, but that the data
points are so scattered that no line would come close to very many of
them. The test of the strength of a relationship is how close the data
points are to the regression line that is drawn. The further away from the
line the data points are, the weaker the relationship is. The closer to the
line the data points are, the stronger the relationship is. If all of the data
points are right on the regression line, then there is a perfect linear
relationship between the two variables.

  With hundreds of data points it is often difficult to tell visually
exactly how close the regression line is to the points and how strong the
relationship is between the variables. Consequently, there is a statistic,
called the *Pearson product-moment correlation* (r), that may be calculated for any regression line. It tells you at a glance how good the fit is

between the data points and the line. This correlation varies from 0 for no relationship to ±1 for a perfect relationship. It is calculated from the vertical distances between each of the data points and the regression line.

The product-moment correlation is very similar to eta-squared. It is based on the variance in the dependent variable (*total variance*) that we are trying to explain. We attempt to explain as much of the variance as possible by drawing a regression line through the points and approximating the values of the dependent variable from the values of the independent variable. The squared vertical distances from the data points to this line represent the variance in the dependent variable that is not accounted for by the regression line. The sum of these squared distances for all the data points is the *unexplained variance*.

The *square* of the product-moment correlation (r^2) shows exactly how much variance has been explained by the independent variable. Therefore, r^2 is exactly analogous to eta-squared; the closer it is to $+1$, the stronger the relationship is.

$$r = \sqrt{\frac{1 - \text{unexplained variance}}{\text{total variance}}} \quad \text{or} \quad \sqrt{\frac{1 - \sum_{i=1}^{N} (Y_i - Y_p)^2}{\sum_{i=1}^{N} (Y_i - \bar{Y})^2}} \tag{12.14}$$

$$r^2 = \frac{1 - \text{unexplained variance}}{\text{total variance}} \quad \text{or} \quad \frac{1 - \sum_{i=1}^{N} (Y_i - Y_p)^2}{\sum_{i=1}^{N} (Y_i - \bar{Y})^2}$$

Where
Y_i = actual observations
Y_p = predicted observations

It is also possible to calculate r directly from the observed data:

$$r = \frac{N\Sigma XY - (\Sigma X)(\Sigma Y)}{[N\Sigma X^2 - (\Sigma X)^2][N\Sigma Y^2 - (\Sigma Y)^2]} \tag{12.8}$$

As we mentioned earlier, the slope of a regression line and the correlation coefficient for a regression line indicate two quite different things. The slope shows how much change in the dependent variable is associated with change in the independent variable; the correlation coefficient shows how much variance in the dependent variable is explained with the independent variable. It is quite possible to have a steep slope but a low correlation, indicating that the dependent variable changes a lot for every unit change in the independent variable but that the regression line does not approximate the data very well. It is also possible to have a very small slope but a very high correlation, indicating that the dependent variable does not change very much for every unit change in the independent variable but that the regression line is a good representation of the data.

The magnitude of the slope is heavily dependent upon the variables involved and the units of measurement being used; almost always, however, researchers hope that the correlation is high, that is, that the regression line shows a close fit with the data points.

Figure 12-6 illustrates six different types of analytical results using regression and correlation analysis: a weak and positive relationship with a small slope (a), a weak and positive relationship with a large slope (b), a weak and negative relationship with a large slope (c), a strong and positive relationship with a small slope (d), a strong and negative relationship with a large slope (e), and no relationship between the independent and dependent variables (f). In this last example, the predicted value of the dependent variable is the same no matter what the value of the independent variable is.

A good example of the use of correlation analysis may be found in Segal and Cover's study of Supreme Court justices' votes on civil liberties cases. Recall that they were interested in the relationship between the justices' ideology, as inferred from newspaper editorials about them, and their decisions once they reached the bench. Since both variables were conceived as ratio level measures, it was possible for Segal and Cover to calculate a regression equation relating the two variables and the product-moment correlation representing the strength of the relationship. Their result was a correlation of .80 between ideological values and votes, indicating a strong relationship between the two. Figure 12-7 displays this relationship on a scattergram. Those justices positioned *above* the regression line had cast more liberal votes than expected on civil liberties cases; those justices positioned *below* the line had been less liberal than expected.

The correlation coefficient also may be used to indicate the statistical significance of the observed relationship. Once the coefficient has been calculated, it can be checked against the appropriate table to determine if it is above or below the criterion level of statistical

Figure 12-6 Six Different Types of Regression and Correlation Results

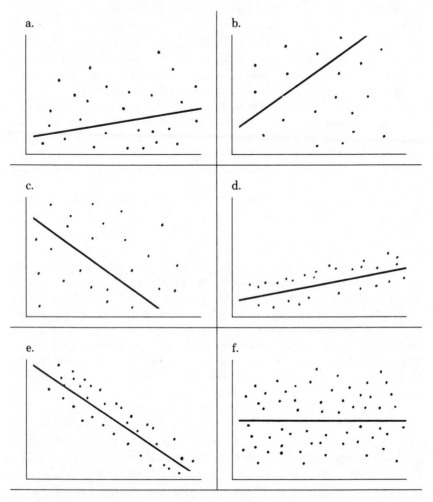

Source: Hypothetical data.

significance. This criterion level is dependent upon the size of the sample from which the data are drawn, and it indicates the probability that the null hypothesis is true. Again remember that statistical significance is not the same as substantive importance; very weak relationships observed in very large samples readily attain statistical significance.

Researchers often use correlation analysis to determine the strength of the relationships among many different variables. In this case they are less concerned with the mathematical function associating independent and dependent variables than with how much variance in a dependent variable is explained by a number of independent variables. The results

Figure 12-7 Example of Correlation Analysis: The Relationship between Justices' Ideology and Decisions on Civil Liberties Cases

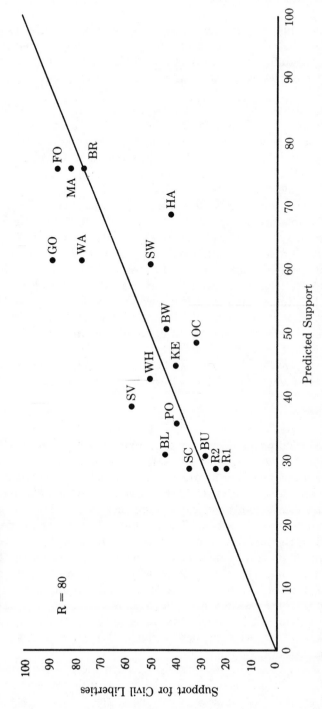

Source: Jeffrey A. Segal and Albert D. Cover, "Ideological Values and the Votes of U.S. Supreme Court Justices," *American Political Science Review* 83 (June 1989).

Key: WA = Warren, HA = Harlan, BR = Brennan, WH = Whittaker, SW = Stewart, BW = White, GO = Goldberg, FO = Fortas, MA = Marshall, BU = Burger, BL = Blackmun, PO = Powell, R1 = Rehnquist (1971), SV = Stevens, OC = O'Connor, R2 = Rehnquist (1986), SC = Scalia, KE = Kennedy.

of a correlation analysis are often used to eliminate some variables from an analysis so that those most useful in accounting for the dependent variable can be studied more easily. A *correlation matrix* shows relationships *among* variables, whereas a scattergram shows only each individual relationship.

Gurr constructed a correlation matrix to test the relationship between a number of variables—such as economic deprivation, coercive force size, past strife levels, and system legitimacy—and civil strife. The matrix, presented in Table 12-19, shows the strength of the relationships among the independent variables, among the different measures of the dependent variable, and between the independent and dependent variables. Gurr then used this initial test of his hypothesis to guide him in the search for a more efficient explanatory model of civil strife by eliminating from further analysis those variables weakly related to civil strife.

Another example of correlational analysis may be found in John McConahay's analysis of attitudes toward busing.[9] McConahay was interested in the relationships between a person's personal involvement in busing, racial attitudes, and attitudes toward busing. His initial analysis of these relationships involved calculating the product-moment correlation between a number of independent variables and the dependent variable (attitudes toward busing). The correlations, reported in Table 12-20, led McConahay to an initial conclusion that racial attitudes rather than personal involvement is associated with attitudes toward busing.

Other Issues

Before concluding our discussion of correlation and regression analysis, we will address two remaining issues. First, the information contained in a regression analysis may help a researcher analyze variation in the dependent variable. Recall that the regression equation indicates the expected value of the dependent variable for each case, given that case's value on the independent variable. The difference between this expected value and the actual observed value is called the *residual* (the variation left over), and it measures how well the regression line fits the data points. Residuals also may be used to explain why the cases did not take on the value for the dependent variable that was predicted from the regression line. The researcher might be able to identify a second independent variable that could account for a portion of the unexplained variance left by the first independent variable. (We examine this procedure in more detail in Chapter 13.)

In our example of the relationship between income and personal contacts with public officials, consider the case of a person who earned $80,000 and made three contacts. According to the regression equation describing the relationship between income and personal contacts, we

Table 12-19 Correlation Matrix Showing the Correlates of Civil Strife [a]

Variable[b]	1	2	3	4	5	6	7	8	9	10	11	12	13	14
1 Economic deprivation (+)		48	83	-02	-17	-16	-36	-09	26	32	34	31	25	44
2 Political deprivation (+)			88	08	-18	03	-37	-20	33	27	44	18	30	38
3 Short-term deprivation (+)				04	-20	-07	-42	-17	34	34	46	28	32	48
4 Persisting deprivation (+)					-04	-21	-14	-37	-04	17	29	26	27	36
5 Legitimacy (−)						25	48	02	-05	-15	-29	-23	-29	-37
6 Coercive force size (±)							53	27	31	04	-23	-11	-01	-14
7 Coercive potential (−)								41	-14	-37	-44	-39	-35	-51
8 Institutionalization (−)									-19	-40	-35	-23	-26	-33
9 Past strife levels (+)										41	24	16	30	30
10 Facilitation (+)											42	57	30	67
11 Magnitude of conspiracy												30	32	59
12 Magnitude of internal war													17	79
13 Magnitude of turmoil														61
14 Total magnitude of strife														

Source: Ted Gurr, "A Causal Model of Civil Strife: A Comparative Analysis Using New Indices," *American Political Science Review* 2 (December 1968): 1117. Reprinted with permission.

[a] Product moment correlation coefficients, multiplied by 100. Underlined r's are significant, for n = 114, at the .01 level. Correlations between 18 and 23, inclusive, are significant at the .05 level.

[b] The proposed relationships between the independent variables, nos. 1 to 10, and the strife measures are shown in parentheses, the +/- for coercive force size signifying a proposed curvilinear relationship. Examination of the r's between the independent and dependent variables, in the box, shows that all are in the predicted direction with the anticipated exception of coercive force size, and that all but one are significant at the .05 level.

Table 12-20   Relationship between Self-Interest Measures, Racial
                  Attitudes, and Attitudes toward Busing: Product-
                  Moment Correlations

Independent Variable	Correlation
Parents of school-age children	.12[a]
Parents of public-school children	.10[b]
Parents of bused children	.03
Homeowner	.09[b]
Relatives in area	.04
Lived in area long time	.09[b]
Happy with neighborhood	−.06[c]
Intent to stay in area	−.01
Self interest index	.11[a]
Modern racism	.51[a]
Old-fashioned racism	.36[a]
Affect for blacks	−.15[a]

Source: John B. McConahay, "Self-Interest versus Racial Attitudes as Correlates of Anti-Busing Attitudes in Louisville: Is It the Buses or the Blacks?" *Journal of Politics* 44 (August 1982): 711. Reprinted with permission.

[a] $p \leq .001$. This correlation indicates that parents of school-age children are slightly more likely to oppose busing than are parents without school-age children.
[b] $p \leq .01$
[c] $p \leq .05$

would expect such a person to have made 6.6 contacts. Consequently, this person made 3.6 fewer contacts than expected; -3.6 is the residual of this case. This residual might stimulate our curiosity. Why did this particular person contact public officials so many fewer times than his income alone would have predicted? This question might lead us to analyze all of those who contacted public officials fewer times than expected and to develop a hypothesis that would explain this discrepancy. In this way residuals may be used to extend a researcher's analysis and provide a more complete understanding of the phenomenon under investigation. Residual scores may themselves become dependent variables in hypotheses designed to explain the amount of discrepancy between the expected and observed values for some dependent variable.

The second issue we need to address is the deceptive simplicity of linear regression. A computer can draw a straight line through any set of data points, yielding a regression equation purporting to capture the relationship between two variables. However, some data points may be better described by a parabola, sine curve, U-curve, or J-curve than by a straight line. If a researcher fails to consider these other possibilities without first inspecting the graph of the data points and has a computer calculate only the best-fitting straight line, a more representative characterization of the relationship may never be discovered.

An actual example of a curvilinear relationship may be found in

Figure 12-8 A Curvilinear Relationship between Age and Vote Turnout in 1972

Age	% Who Voted
18-24	53
25-31	62
32-36	67
37-69	74
70-78	68
79+	52

Source: Raymond E. Wolfinger and Steven J. Rosenstone, *Who Votes?* (New Haven, Conn.: Yale University Press, 1980), 38. Copyright © 1980. Reprinted with permission.

Wolfinger and Rosenstone's study of voter turnout. They hypothesized a relationship between age and voter turnout.[10] A scattergram of this relationship indicated that there was, indeed, a relationship, but that it was a curvilinear rather than a linear one, as Figure 12-8 shows. It is the middle-aged who vote most frequently, and the young and old alike who vote least frequently. Therefore, a straight line would not have been the best approximation of the relationship between age and turnout.

Like regression analysis, correlational analysis can disguise strong, nonlinear relationships. All the correlation coefficient indicates is the fit between the data points and the best-fitting straight line. Drawing a straight line through a set of data points better represented with a curve will often result in a very low product-moment correlation, perhaps leading the researcher to ignore a nonlinear relationship. Had the researcher checked the scattergram upon which the correlation coefficient was calculated, it would have become evident that a curvilinear relationship was a better representation of the data points. Researchers are well advised, therefore, to inspect the scattergrams corresponding to every regression equation and product-moment correlation that they calculate.

Conclusion

In this chapter we have shown how to measure the existence,

direction, strength, and statistical significance of relationships between two variables. The particular techniques used—crosstabulation, difference of means test, analysis of variance, regression analysis, and correlation analysis—depend, in part, on the levels of measurement—nominal, ordinal, interval, or ratio—of the independent and dependent variables. Just because a relationship is present, however, does not mean that a cause of the dependent variable has been discovered. We will explain this in more detail in Chapter 13.

Notes

1. In reality there are many techniques for analyzing relationships at a given level of measurement. The ones presented in this chapter are the most common, and least complicated, ones.
2. Raymond E. Wolfinger and Steven J. Rosenstone, *Who Votes?* (New Haven, Conn.: Yale University Press, 1980).
3. For further information about the calculation of each of these statistics, see Hubert M. Blalock, Jr., *Social Statistics*, rev. 2d ed. (New York: McGraw-Hill, 1979).
4. Edward R. Tufte, *Data Analysis for Politics and Policy* (Englewood Cliffs, N.J.: Prentice-Hall, 1974).
5. A more complete discussion of the calculation of the F ratio may be found in Blalock, *Social Statistics*, chap. 16.
6. Robert D. Putnam et al., "Explaining Institutional Success: The Case of Italian Regional Government," *American Political Science Review* 77 (March 1983): 55-74.
7. Ted Robert Gurr, "A Comparative Study of Civil Strife," in Hugh Davis Graham and Ted Robert Gurr, eds., *Violence in America: Historical and Comparative Perspectives* (New York: New American Library, 1969). See also Ted Gurr, "A Causal Model of Civil Strife: A Comparative Analysis Using New Indices," *American Political Science Review* 2 (December 1968): 1104-1124.
8. Gurr, "A Comparative Study," 580-581.
9. John B. McConahay, "Self-Interest versus Racial Attitudes as Correlates of 'Anti-Busing' Attitudes in Louisville: Is It the Buses or the Blacks?" *Journal of Politics* 44 (August 1982): 692-720.
10. Wolfinger and Rosenstone, *Who Votes?*

Terms Introduced

Analysis of variance. A technique for measuring the relationship between one nominal or ordinal level variable and one interval or ratio level variable.

Chi-square. A measure used with crosstabulation to determine if a relationship is statistically significant.

Correlation matrix. A table showing the correlations (usually Pearson product-moment correlations) among a number of variables.

Crosstabulation. A technique for measuring the relationship between nominal and ordinal level measures.

Degrees of freedom. A measure used in conjunction with chi-square and other measures to determine if a relationship is statistically significant.

Difference of means test. A technique for measuring the relationship between one nominal or ordinal level variable and one interval or ratio level variable.

Direction of a relationship. An indication of which values of the dependent variable are associated with which values of the independent variable.

Eta-squared. A measure of association used with the analysis of variance that indicates the proportion of the variance in the dependent variable explained by the variance in the independent variable.

Explained variance. That portion of the variation in a dependent variable that is accounted for by the variation in the independent variable(s).

F ratio. A measure used with the analysis of variance to determine if a relationship is statistically significant.

Goodman and Kruskal's gamma. A measure of association between ordinal level variables.

Goodman and Kruskal's lambda. A measure of association between one nominal or ordinal level variable and one nominal level variable.

Kendall's tau. A measure of association between ordinal level variables.

Measures of association. Statistics that summarize the relationship between two variables.

Negative relationship. A relationship in which high values of one variable are associated with low values of another variable.

Pearson product-moment correlation. The statistic computed from a regression analysis that indicates the strength of the relationship between two interval or ratio level variables.

Positive relationship. A relationship in which high values of one variable are associated with high values of another variable.

Regression. A technique for measuring the relationship between two interval or ratio level variables.

Regression coefficient. Another name for the slope of a regression equation.

Regression equation. The mathematical formula describing the relationship between two interval or ratio level variables.

Relationship. A relationship is established when the values of one variable covary with or are dependent upon the values of another variable.

Residual. The difference between the observed and predicted values of Y (the dependent variable) in a regression analysis.

Scattergram. A technique for displaying graphically the relationship between two interval or ratio level variables.

Slope. The part of a regression equation that shows how much change in the value of Y (the dependent variable) corresponds to a one-unit change in the value of X (the independent variable).

Somer's d. A measure of association between ordinal level variables.

Statistical significance. An indication of whether an observed relationship could have occurred by chance.

Strength of a relationship. An indication of how consistently the values of a dependent variable are associated with the values of an independent variable.

Total variance. The variation in a dependent variable that a researcher is attempting to account for.

Unexplained variance. That portion of the variation in a dependent variable that is not accounted for by the variation in the independent variable(s).

Y-intercept. The value of Y (the dependent variable) in a regression equation when the value of X (the independent variable) is 0.

Exercises

1. A researcher interested in the relationship between city size and mass transit systems takes a random sample of 100 cities of varying sizes and finds that 20 of the small cities have transit systems and 30 do not; 12 of the mid-size cities have transit systems and 18 do not; and 8 of the large cities have transit systems and 12 do not.

Construct a crosstabulation showing the relationship between the independent and dependent variables. Place the independent variable across the top of the table and calculate the percentages in the correct way. What do the table percentages indicate about the relationship between city size and the existence of a mass transit system?

2. Senator Blowchill, Democrat from Massachusetts, has charged that the Bush administration is directing more federal funds to the Sunbelt states than to those in the Frostbelt. Senator Dryheat, Republican from Arizona, disagrees and challenges Senator Blowchill to prove his claim. So Senator Blowchill tells his research assistant to select randomly ten states and analyze the relationship between the region and amount of federal funds spent. The research assistant produces the following crosstabulation and then hands it to you, a summer intern, for your interpretation. What would you say about the relationship in the table? Be sure to discuss the statistical significance, direction, and strength of the observed relationship.

	Sunbelt States	Frostbelt States
State has received an above average amount of federal funds	3	2
State has received a below average amount of federal funds	1	4

3. Suppose that you conducted a sample survey of 100 respondents and produced the following crosstabulation showing the relationship between religion and attitudes toward abortion. With 95 percent certainty, is there a relationship between the two variables? Is the relationship weak, moderate, or strong? What is

the direction of the relationship? Which of the following correlation coefficients is correct for this crosstabulation: $+.8$, $-.2$, $+.2$, $-.6$? How would you express verbally the results of this crosstabulation?

	Catholic	Protestant
Oppose right to have an abortion	36	44
Favor right to have an abortion	4	16

4. What does the following crosstabulation of the relationship between education and ideology tell you about the strength, direction, and statistical significance of the relationship?

EDUCATION

	Low	*Medium*	*High*	
Liberal	20	50	80	150
Moderate	40	80	80	200
Conservative	40	70	40	150
	100	200	200	500

Which of the following correlation coefficients is the most likely: $+.20$, $-.70$, $+.10$, $-.25$? How would you express verbally the meaning of this relationship?

5. In Benjamin I. Page and Robert Y. Shapiro, "Effects of Public Opinion on Policy," *American Political Science Review* 77 (March 1983): 175-190, the authors test the relationship between the size of changes in public opinion and the congruence of opinion/policy change (Table 3). What does this crosstabulation indicate about this relationship? What measure of association is used?

6. The relationship between inequality in land ownership and political violence is tested in Manus I. Midlarsky, "Rulers and the Ruled: Patterned Inequality and the Onset of Mass Political Violence," *American Political Science Review* 82 (June 1988): 491-509. In Table 3 the relationship is displayed for twenty Latin American countries in a modified crosstabulation. What do the crosstab and the measures of association indicate about the relationship?

7. Suppose you want to know if there is a relationship between the unemployment rate in cities and the number of robberies that occur within the city limits. You take a random sample of cities and plot the unemployment rates and number of robberies as shown in Figure 12-9 on page 338. Answer the following questions about the graph and the regression line drawn to best approximate the data.

   a. What is the strength and direction of the relationship between the two variables? How do you know this? What does it mean?

   b. If the unemployment rate in a given city increases by 1 percent, about how many additional robberies will occur?

   c. If there were no unemployment in a city, how many robberies would you expect to occur?

   d. What other factors might make a city experience more robberies or fewer robberies than you would expect based on the unemployment rate alone?

Figure 12-9 Regression Line for the Relationship between
Unemployment and Robberies

Source: Hypothetical data.

8. You observe that there is a statistically significant relationship between the amount of television Americans watch and the number of violent crimes Americans commit. Therefore, you conclude that watching television causes Americans to commit violent crimes. What is wrong with your conclusion?

Suggested Readings

Blalock, Hubert M. *Social Statistics*. 2d ed. New York: McGraw-Hill, 1972.

Elifson, Kirk W., Richard P. Runyon, and Audrey Haber. *Fundamentals of Social Statistics*. Reading, Mass.: Addison-Wesley, 1982.

Healey, Joseph F. *Statistics: A Tool for Social Research*. Belmont, Calif.: Wadsworth, 1984.

Mueller, John, Karl Schuessler, and Herbert Costner. *Statistical Reasoning in Sociology*. 2d ed. Boston: Houghton Mifflin, 1970.

Nie, Norman H., et al. *SPSS*. 2d ed. New York: McGraw-Hill, 1975.

Phillips, John L. *Statistical Thinking*. San Francisco: W. H. Freeman, 1973.

Watson, George, and Dickinson McGraw. *Statistical Inquiry*. New York: Wiley, 1980.

CHAPTER 13

Searching for Complete Explanations and Causal Knowledge: Multivariate Data Analysis

Introduction

Chapter 12 discussed how to measure the existence, strength, direction, and statistical significance of a relationship between one independent variable and a dependent variable using various data analysis techniques. Measuring a single relationship between two variables is a fairly straightforward procedure. Most political science research, however, involves the measurement of many variables and the testing of several hypotheses involving more than two variables. As a result, *multivariate data analysis* techniques are required.

Most of the political scientists whose research we have discussed in previous chapters used multivariate data analysis to investigate the relationships between a number of independent variables and the dependent variable of interest. Gary Jacobson, for example, found that the variation in votes received by candidates for the U.S. Congress could be explained in a number of ways. Although he was most interested in the impact of candidate spending on electoral outcomes, he also considered the relationships between the distribution of the vote and the challenger's party, the challenger's prior political experience, the number of years the incumbent had held office, the challenger's district party strength, and whether the candidates had run in a primary election. Only by considering the relations among these variables could Jacobson reach some firm conclusions about campaign spending and its effect on the vote for congressional candidates.[1]

Ted Gurr also used a number of independent variables to explain the dependent variable of interest to him: cross-national variation in civil strife. Although his major independent variable was relative deprivation, he also tested the relationships between civil strife and legitimacy (the amount of popular support for and acceptance of the decisions made by the regime); coercive potential (the ability of the regime to punish those participating in civil strife); institutionalization ("the extent to which societal structures beyond the primary level are broad in scope, command substantial resources and/or personnel, and are stable and persisting"); and facilitation (the existence of social and environmental conditions that would encourage or enhance civil strife).[2] Gurr used all of these independent variables to account for levels of civil strife because he believed that each one would have some impact on the dependent variable. He measured the individual relationships between each of the independent variables and civil strife, and he also measured the relationships between all of the independent variables combined and civil strife. He concluded that persistent deprivation did have an impact on the magnitude of civil strife, even when other possible explanations were taken into account.

Multivariate analysis techniques were also used by McConahay in his attempt to explain attitudes toward compulsory school busing (refer back to Table 12-20 on page 332). McConahay used eight measures of the respondent's "self-interest" regarding busing (such as whether the respondent had children, had children attending public schools, had children who were being bused, owned his or her own home, or planned to move out of the neighborhood soon); three measures of each respondent's racial attitudes (what the author called modern racial attitudes, old-fashioned racial attitudes, and feelings for blacks); and a host of other variables thought to be related to attitudes toward busing (such as measures of a respondent's education, income, sex, and union membership).[3] The relationship between *each* independent variable and attitudes toward busing was measured, and the relationships between *all* of the independent variables simultaneously and busing attitudes were observed. McConahay concluded that racial attitudes had a much greater impact on attitudes toward busing than did indicators of "self-interest."

Page and Shapiro's article on the relationship between public opinion change and public policy change also concludes with a multivariate analysis designed to explain why there is more congruence between opinion and policy in some cases than in others.[4] The authors used a variety of independent variables measuring aspects of the opinion change, the type of policy, and the political context in which the policy response occurred in an attempt to explain the variation in opinion-policy congruence.

There are essentially two reasons for measuring relationships involving more than two variables: to provide more complete explanations for political phenomena and to gain *causal knowledge*. For most political phenomena more than one independent variable is needed to explain the variation in the observed values of the dependent variable or to predict accurately particular observed values of the dependent variable. Interesting political behavior is usually so complex that researchers need to rely on a number of concepts to explain it adequately.

Moreover, if a researcher is interested in acquiring *causal knowledge,* a number of possible explanations for the phenomenon of interest must be tested. Simply because an independent variable exhibits a strong relationship with a dependent variable does not mean that the former caused the latter. Both the independent and dependent variables might be caused by a third variable, which could create the appearance of a relationship between the first two and lead to an erroneous conclusion about the effect of the independent variable on the dependent variable. The possibility that a third variable is the real cause of both the independent and dependent variables must be considered before one makes causal claims. Only by eliminating this possibility can a researcher achieve some confidence that a relationship between an independent and dependent variable is a causal one.

In Tufte's study of automobile fatalities, for example, a relationship between the existence of mandatory automobile inspections and a lower auto fatality rate was observed (refer back to Figure 12-1 on page 316).[5] This does not necessarily mean, however, that inspections cause a decline in auto fatality rates. There may be another phenomenon related to inspections and auto deaths that is causing the relationship between the two. Tufte discovered a strong, inverse relationship between population density and auto fatality rates, and he also discovered that those states with mandatory inspections tend to be more densely populated. Therefore, until population density was eliminated as a possible cause of the relationship between inspections and auto fatalities, he could not make a causal claim about the observed bivariate relationship.

Similarly, Jacobson could not conclude that campaign spending caused an increase in the votes received by congressional candidates until he had evaluated other possibilities. For example, partisan strength in a district might influence both campaign spending and the vote distribution and therefore be the real cause of the relationship between spending and votes received. Although disconfirming this possibility still did not permit Jacobson to conclude with certainty that challenger spending increases votes, it did allow him to be somewhat more confident that the relationship is a causal one.

In this chapter we will explain how political scientists use multivariate data analysis techniques to *control for* the effects of a third variable. This means that the impact of other variables is removed or taken into account when researchers observe the relationship between an independent and dependent variable. Generally, the impact of a third variable may be controlled either experimentally or statistically. Experimental

Table 13-1 Relationship between Attitudes toward Government
Spending and Presidential Vote

	Independent Variable: Attitudes toward Government Spending		
Dependent Variable: Presidential Vote	Decrease Spending	Keep Spending the Same or Increase It	(n)
Republican	64%	46%	(555)
Democratic	36	54	(445)
Total	100	100	
(n)	(550)	(450)	(1,000)

Source: Hypothetical data.

control is introduced by assigning the participants in an experiment to
different groups and controlling each group's exposure to the experimental stimulus. Statistical control, the procedure used more frequently by
political scientists, involves measuring each observation's values on the
control variables and using these measures to make comparisons between
observations.

Multivariate Crosstabulation

How to display and measure the relationship between two nominal
or ordinal level variables was explained in Chapter 12. The joint
distribution of observations on the two variables is displayed in a crosstab
table, and the researcher looks for different values of the dependent
variable across the different categories of the independent variable. The
extent to which the cases in the different categories of the independent
variable exhibit different values on the dependent variable indicates the
strength and direction of the relationship.

Suppose, for example, that we have hypothesized a relationship
between attitudes toward government spending and presidential voting.
Our hypothesis is that "the more in favor of decreasing government
spending a person is, the more likely she is to vote Republican." Table 13-
1 seems to confirm the hypothesis, since 64 percent of those who favor
decreased spending voted Republican while only 46 percent of those who
favored keeping spending the same or increasing it voted Republican.
This difference of 18 percentage points among a sample of 1,000 suggests
that there is a weak relationship between attitudes toward government
spending and presidential voting behavior.

At this point, a researcher might ask, "Can I improve upon my
explanation of presidential voting by including another independent
variable?" Thirty-six percent of those who favored decreased spending

voted contrary to the hypothesis, as did 46 percent of those in favor of maintaining or increasing spending levels. Perhaps it would be possible to provide an explanation for those voters' behavior and hence improve the understanding of presidential voting behavior.

A second question a researcher might ask is, "Does this analysis mean that attitudes toward government spending *caused* people to vote Republican?" Or, put another way, "Would people still have voted Republican if they had had different attitudes toward government spending?" These two questions acknowledge the possibility that the observed relationship may not be a causal one, and they imply that an additional explanation of presidential voting should be considered.

A second independent variable that might affect presidential voting is income. People with higher incomes might favor decreased government spending because they feel they gain little from most government programs. Those with higher incomes might also be more likely to vote Republican because they perceive the GOP to be the party that favors government policies that benefit the affluent. Therefore, income might influence both attitudes toward government spending *and* presidential voting and thus could create the appearance of a relationship between the two.

To consider the impact of income we need to control for it and then observe the resulting relationship between government spending attitudes and presidential voting. In crosstab analysis we control for a third variable by holding it constant; that is, by grouping the observations into categories of the third variable and then observing the original relationship within each of these categories. This has the effect of removing the impact of the variation in the third variable since we observe the original relationship within each group of identical or similar observations on the third variable. In this case we can observe the relationship between government spending attitudes and presidential vote separately among those with low, medium, and high incomes.

Table 13-2 shows what might happen were we to control for income. Within each of the categories of income there is now no relationship between government spending attitudes and presidential voting. Regardless of their attitudes on spending, 80 percent of respondents with high incomes voted Republican, 60 percent with medium incomes voted Republican, and 30 percent with low incomes voted Republican. Once the variation in income was removed by grouping those with similar incomes together, the relationship between government spending attitudes and presidential voting disappeared.

What does this reveal about the original relationship between government spending attitudes and presidential voting? First, there is clearly a relationship between income and attitudes toward spending. Eighty-three percent of those with high incomes favored cutting spending

Table 13-2 Relationship between Attitudes toward Government
Spending and Presidential Vote: Controlling for Income

Dependent Variable: Presidential Vote	*Independent Variable: Attitudes toward Government Spending*		
	Decrease Spending	Keep Spending the Same or Increase It	(n)
High income			
Republican	80%	80%	(240)
Democratic	20	20	(60)
Total	100	100	
(n)	(250)	(50)	(300)
Medium income			
Republican	60%	60%	(210)
Democratic	40	40	(140)
Total	100	100	
(n)	(200)	(150)	(350)
Low income			
Republican	30%	30%	(105)
Democratic	70	70	(245)
Total	100	100	
(n)	(100)	(250)	(350)

Source: Hypothetical data.

while only 57 percent of those with medium incomes and 29 percent of those with low incomes did. Therefore, those who favored reducing spending were also more likely to be wealthy; they differed from those opposed to spending cuts not only on their attitudes toward spending but also on their incomes. In other words, the two groups with different spending attitudes differ in other ways.

Second, it is also clear that income is related to presidential voting. Eighty percent of the wealthy voted Republican, while only 60 percent of middle-income respondents and 30 percent of low-income respondents did. Consequently, income is a possible alternative explanation for the variation in presidential voting.

Third, when we control for income by grouping those with similar incomes together and observing the relationship between spending attitudes and presidential voting within each group, the original relationship disappears. This indicates that the only reason for the original relationship was the variation in income. The original relationship was spurious, that is, it was due entirely to a third variable. Therefore, government spending attitudes cannot be a cause of presidential voting because

Table 13-3   Relationship Between Income and Presidential Vote:
Controlling for Government Spending Attitudes

Dependent Variable: *Presidential Vote*	*Independent Variable: Income*			
	High	Medium	Low	(n)
Decrease spending				
Republican	80%	60%	30%	350
Democratic	20	40	70	200
Total	100	100	100	
(n)	(250)	(200)	(100)	(550)
Keep spending same or increase it				
Republican	80%	60%	30%	205
Democratic	20	40	70	245
Total	100	100	100	
(n)	(50)	(150)	(250)	(450)

Source: Hypothetical data.

spending attitudes had no effect on voting above and beyond the effect of income. Respondents did not vote the way they did because of their different attitudes toward government spending.

This does not mean that there is no relationship between spending attitudes and presidential voting; we observed such a relationship in Table 13-1. It does, mean, however, that the original relationship occurred because of the variables' relationships with a third variable, income. It also means that the original relationship was not a causal one; spending attitudes cannot possibly be a cause of presidential voting because within income groups they make no difference whatever. The only reason for the relationship between spending attitudes and presidential voting is the effect of income differences.

Given the relationships between each pair of variables in this model, how do we know whether it is spending attitudes or income that has a larger impact on presidential voting and has causal priority? We have already seen that the relationship between spending attitudes and presidential voting disappears when we control for income. Now what happens if we observe the relationship between income and presidential voting while controlling for spending attitudes? Table 13-3 contains the answer.

The relationship between income and presidential voting persists after controlling for spending attitudes. In fact, the relationship is identical in both control groups to the original, "uncontrolled" relationship; controlling for spending attitudes does not alter the relationship. This suggests that, *of the two independent variables,* income is by far the more important in accounting for variations in the presidential vote.

Figure 13-1 Impact of Income on the Relationship between
Government Spending Attitudes and Presidential Voting

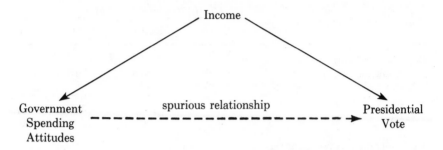

Income

Government
Spending
Attitudes

spurious relationship

Presidential
Vote

Income is also more likely than attitudes toward government spending to
have causal priority since a person's attitudes toward government spending are more likely to be caused by his or her income than vice versa.
Since it is difficult to imagine that a person's income could be altered by
attitudes of this type, it is more plausible that spending attitudes are
dependent upon income, as Figure 13-1 illustrates.

A good example of an actual multivariate crosstabulation analysis
may be found in Raymond Wolfinger and Steven Rosenstone's study of
voter turnout.[6] They observed a positive relationship between education and turnout (the higher the education, the higher the turnout) and
a curvilinear relationship between age and turnout (the older a person,
up to an age of about seventy, the higher the turnout; after seventy, turnout declined). However, since there is also a relationship between age and education (older people tend to have fewer years of formal education since they grew up at a time when high school and college
educations were rarer), the researchers wondered whether it was age,
or education, or both, that affected turnout most. In other words,
they were interested in testing the three-variable model presented in
Figure 13-2.

Figure 13-2 Impact of Age on the Relationship between Education and
Voter Turnout

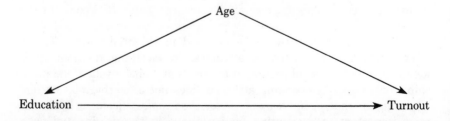

Age

Education

Turnout

Table 13-4 Relationship between Age, Education, and Turnout, 1972

	Age						
Education	18-24	25-31	32-36	37-69	70-78	78+	Total
0-8 (grammar school)	14	26	36	56	58	44	52
9-12 (high school)	44	55	63	75	76	63	65
1-3 college	72	76	79	87	85	72	79
4 college	76	84	89	90	85	75	86
5+ college	85	86	91	93	94	80	91
Total	53	62	67	74	68	52	67

Source: Raymond E. Wolfinger and Steven J. Rosenstone, *Who Votes?* (New Haven, Conn.: Yale University Press, 1980), 47. Reprinted with permission.

Note: The entry in each cell is the percentage of people voting with the given combination of age and education. For example, 36 percent of people aged 32 to 36 who had not attended high school voted.

The last column on the right-hand side of Table 13-4 shows the bivariate relationship between education and turnout; the bottom row shows the bivariate relationship between age and turnout. The relationship between education and turnout, controlling for age, may be observed by looking *down* each column of the table. Since each column contains observations grouped by age, age is being *held constant* (or nearly so). Turnout levels generally increase as one looks down each column. Thus the relationship with education persists after controlling for age. The relationship between age and turnout, controlling for education, may be observed by looking *across* each row. Since each row contains observations grouped by education, education is being *held constant* (or nearly so). Turnout levels increase, up to age seventy, and then decrease in each row. Thus the relationship with age persists after controlling for education.

In this case, then, the relationship between education and turnout is not spurious. Both independent variables exhibit relationships with turnout independent of the other. Therefore, education and age together account for more of the variation in turnout than does either variable alone.

When a researcher controls for a third variable, five general situations can arise. First, the original relationship may disappear entirely, indicating that it was spurious. This was the case with the government spending attitudes and presidential voting example. Second, the original relationship may decline somewhat but not completely disappear, indicating that it was partly spurious. That is, some but not all of the original relationship may be accounted for with the control variable. Third, the original relationship may remain *unchanged*, indicating that the third variable was not responsible for the original relationship. This suggests that the relationship between the independent and dependent variables may be causal, as in Wolfinger and Rosenstone's analysis of education, age, and voter turnout. Fourth, the original relationship may increase, indicating that the control variable was disguising or deflating the true relationship between the independent and dependent variables. Fifth, the controlled relationship may be different for different categories of the control variable. This is called a *specified relationship*. It indicates that the relationship between two variables is dependent upon the values of a third variable. For example, the relationship between residential mobility and turnout may be strong only when education is low. People with high education may vote no matter how geographically mobile they are, while for people of low education, mobility may interfere with voting. If the relationship between two variables differs significantly for different categories of a third, then we say that the third variable has specified the relationship.

Table 13-5 presents a summary of the possible results when a third variable is held constant. It displays the appropriate measures of association and statistical significance for the original, uncontrolled relationship between two variables. The same information for each category of the control variable is shown. Comparing the uncontrolled results with the controlled results indicates whether the relationship is spurious (a), partially spurious (b), unchanged (c), has increased (d), or has been specified (e).

Multivariate crosstabulation analysis, then, may be used to assess the impact of one or more control variables when those variables are measured at the nominal or ordinal level. Although this is a relatively straightforward and frequently used procedure, it has several disadvantages.

First, it is difficult to interpret the numerous crosstabs required when a researcher wishes to control for a large number of variables at once and the control variables have a large number of categories. Suppose, for example, that you wanted to observe the relationship between television news exposure and political knowledge while controlling for education (five categories), newspaper exposure (four categories), and political interest (three categories). You would need to construct sixty different crosstabs to accomplish this very reasonable analytical objective!

Second, controlling by grouping similar cases together can rapidly deplete the sample size for each of the control situations, producing less accurate and statistically insignificant estimates of the relationships. Suppose that we had started out with a standard sample size of 1,500 respondents in our example of the relationship between television news exposure and political knowledge. By the time we had divided the sample into the sixty discrete control groups, each crosstab measuring the

Table 13-5   Five Results When Controlling for a Third Variable

Uncontrolled Relationship	Measure of Association	Significance Level
a.	+.35	.001
Category 1	+.05	.07
Category 2	−.03	.14
Category 3	+.01	.10
b.	+.42	.001
Category 1	+.20	.01
Category 2	+.17	.05
Category 3	+.26	.001
c.	−.28	.01
Category 1	−.30	.05
Category 2	−.35	.01
Category 3	−.27	.05
d.	−.12	.08
Category 1	−.42	.001
Category 2	−.30	.01
Category 3	−.35	.001
e.	+.31	.001
Category 1	+.55	.001
Category 2	+.37	.01
Category 3	+.16	.05

Source: Hypothetical data.

relationship between news exposure and political knowledge would have, on average, only 25 people in it. This would make it virtually impossible to observe a statistically significant relationship between news exposure and political knowledge.

Third, control groups in multivariate crosstabulation analysis often disregard some of the variation in one or more of the variables. For example, to control for income in our government spending attitude/ presidential voting example, we put all those with low incomes into one group. This grouping ignored what might be important variations in actual income levels. Similarly, when Wolfinger and Rosenstone measured the combined effect of age and education on turnout, they combined people of different ages and educations into their control categories. This is often done because of the first two problems mentioned earlier—number of tables and sample size—but it has the unfortunate consequence of eliminating what might be consequential variations in the control variables.

Despite these three limitations, multivariate crosstabulation is used whenever the variables are measured at the nominal or ordinal level. It usually yields more insight into a researcher's hypothesis than would a simple bivariate crosstabulation alone. Multivariate crosstabulation helps explain the dependent variable and addresses the question whether an observed relationship is a causal one.

Two-Way Analysis of Variance

Two-way analysis of variance may be used to assess the extent to which two or more independent variables measured at the nominal or ordinal level can explain the variance in a dependent variable measured at the interval or ratio level. The logic of this procedure is very similar to the one-way analysis of variance described in Chapter 12. Recall that in the one-way analysis of variance, we began with a certain amount of observed variance in the dependent variable. This variance may be calculated from the mean for this variable since it is measured at the interval or ratio level. Then we divided the observations into categories based on the measurement of the independent variable and measured the mean and variance within each of these categories. If the means for the categories were quite different and the variance within the categories was much less than the variance in the "ungrouped" dependent variable, then the categorization was judged successful in accounting for the dependent variable. The more different the means across categories and the smaller the variances within categories of the independent variable, the stronger the relationship between independent and dependent variables.

A two-way analysis of variance proceeds in a similar fashion. Again we begin with a certain amount of variance in the dependent variable. In this case, however, we have more than one independent variable with which to explain that variation. Consequently, the first step in measuring the impact of a control variable is to divide the observations into categories based on the values of the cases on each of the independent variables. The mean and variance on the dependent variable is then calculated for the cases in each of these categories.

For example, recall that Tufte hypothesized that those states with mandatory automobile inspections would have fewer auto fatalities than those without them. A one-way analysis of variance showed that there was a weak relationship between the two variables. To provide a more complete explanation of auto fatalities and to confirm his suspicion that inspection policy was an important cause of variations in auto fatalities, Tufte then considered the effect of another independent variable—population density—on auto fatalities (see Figure 13-3).

Tufte argued that the population density of a state has numerous effects on behavior related to auto fatalities—such as the speed at which cars are driven, the distances they are driven, and the proximity of

Figure 13-3 Impact of State Population Density on the Relationship between State Inspection Policy and State Auto Fatality Rate

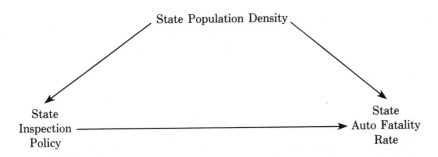

medical services to crash victims. When he calculated the state-level relationship between population density and auto fatality rates, he discovered a fairly strong, negative relationship; that is, as the density of a state increases, the auto fatality rate decreases. Furthermore, he found that there is a relationship between population density and the existence of auto inspection policies; eight of the nine most densely populated states had mandatory inspections. Therefore, the relationship between auto inspections and auto fatality rates may be spurious. Population density may be a much more important explanation for auto deaths than the lack of inspection policies.

We can measure the impact of both population density and auto inspection policy on auto fatality rates by dividing the fifty observations (states) into categories based on their population density and on their inspection policies. If we then calculate the mean auto fatality rate and the variance around that rate for each of the categories, we can assess the impact of the independent variables, both individually and in combination.

Table 13-6 shows the mean and variance for each of the six categories of states created by the two independent variables. An inspection of the means for those categories shows that auto fatality rates for categories of states of differing population density are still quite different even after one has controlled for inspection policies (this can be seen by looking across the rows). In addition, the fatality rates for states with auto inspections continue to be lower than those for states without inspections, even controlling for population density. The states without inspections have higher mean fatality rates by 2.5, 3.2, and 5.3 in each of the density categories, while the "uncontrolled" difference was 5.8. Therefore, although there has been some reduction in the relationship with auto inspections, the relationship has not disappeared entirely.

Table 13-6 Relationship between State Auto Inspection Policy and State Auto Fatality Rates: Controlling for Population Density

Auto Inspection Policy	Density			
	Thin (<25 people/ square mile)	Medium (25-125 people/ square mile)	Thick (>125 people/ square mile)	Total
States without inspections	37.4	31.6	23.6	31.9
(n)	(10)	(16)	(6)	(32)
(s^2)	(47.0)	(11.5)	(29.5)	(31.9)
States with inspections	34.9	28.4	18.3	26.1
(n)	(3)	(9)	(6)	(18)
(s^2)	(77.6)	(33.6)	(23.1)	(26.1)
Total	36.8	30.5	21.0	29.8
(n)	(13)	(25)	(12)	(50)
(s^2)	(49.4)	(20.8)	(31.8)	(61.8)

Source: Edward R. Tufte, *Data Analysis for Politics and Policy,* copyright 1974, 23. Adapted by permission of Prentice-Hall, Inc., Englewood Cliffs, New Jersey.

Note: Entries are mean auto fatality rates for each group of states in each cell. Tufte eliminates Alaska in his analysis, but it is included here in the "thin, without inspections" cell.

With the information in Table 13-6, a precise estimate of the impact of each independent variable on auto fatality rates can be calculated. A measure of the extent to which the two variables together account for the variation in auto fatality rates can also be calculated. In this case the relationship between population density and auto fatalities remains strong even when inspection policies are controlled for, and the relationship between inspection policies and auto fatality rates is diminished and becomes modest when population density is controlled for. The two variables combined account for a substantial portion (57 percent) of the variance in auto fatality rates across the fifty states.

Like multiple crosstabulation, two-way analysis of variance measures the relationship between one independent variable and a dependent variable while controlling for one or more other independent variables. Also like crosstabulation, it controls for a third variable by grouping together cases identical or similar on the control variable. The only major difference is that the dependent variable is measured at the interval or ratio level. Consequently, the variance is a mathematical one rather than one involving the distribution of cases across categories. For the specific mathematical calculations involved in the two-way analysis of variance, consult the readings at the end of this chapter.

Figure 13-4 Impact of Age on Relationship between Education and Liberalism

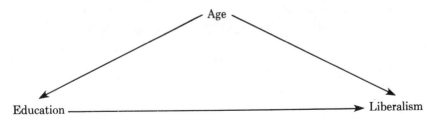

Multiple Regression and Partial Correlation

So far we have described how to control for a third variable by grouping cases together that have identical or similar values on the control variable. Although this is an adequate procedure when the values of the control variable are discrete and homogeneous and is the only appropriate procedure when variables are measured at the nominal or ordinal level, control by grouping does cause two major problems: the proliferation of control groups in a complex multivariate model and the reduction in the sample size within each control group.

Suppose, for example, that we are interested in the relationship between education and liberalism, controlling for age, where each of the variables is measured at the interval or ratio level (see Figure 13-4). Fortunately, there is an alternative. When variables are measured at the interval or ratio level (and even sometimes when they are not), controlling may be done by *adjustment*. This is accomplished using the techniques of *multiple regression* and *partial correlation*. A partial correlation is a measure of the relationship between two variables after the effect of a third variable on both has been removed.

First, we would measure the relationship between age (the independent variable) and education (the dependent variable) using the regression equation described in Chapter 12. We could then calculate the residual value for each case on education. This would be the variance in education unexplained by age. Then, with a second regression equation, we could measure the relationship between age and the second dependent variable, liberalism, and calculate the residuals for this equation for each case. This is the variance in liberalism unexplained by age. Finally, we could use a third regression equation to calculate the relationship between the residuals from the first equation and the residuals from the second equation. This third equation would indicate the relationship between education and liberalism once the effects of age have been removed. The correlation associated with this final regression equation between the two sets of residuals is called a *partial correlation,* and it indicates the variance in the dependent variable explained by the independent variable once the effects of the control variable have been removed. The partial correlation must be squared to equal the actual "percent of variance explained."

Actually, there is a much simpler way to calculate the partial correlation coefficient:

$$r_{ij,k} = \frac{r_{ij} - (r_{ik})(r_{jk})}{\sqrt{1 - r^2_{ik}}\,\sqrt{1 - r^2_{jk}}}$$

Where

    k = the control variable
    i and j = the independent and dependent variables
    and the correlation coefficients on the right-hand side of the equation are calculated from the bivariate analysis involving i and j

Thus, if the correlation between age and education was +.38, the correlation between age and liberalism was +.20, and the correlation between education and liberalism was +.50, then the partial correlation coefficient between education and liberalism, while controlling for age, would be

$$r = \frac{+.50 - (+.38)(+.20)}{\sqrt{1 - .38^2}\,\sqrt{1 - .20^2}}$$

$$= \frac{+.50 - .076}{\sqrt{.8556}\,\sqrt{.96}}$$

$$= +.47$$

Partial correlations may be calculated for any number of control variables, as long as the sample sizes and variances permit. They are useful indicators of whether a relationship has persisted after controlling for one or more control variables. However, the partial correlation does not reveal very much about the mathematical relationship between an independent and a dependent variable, after controlling for a control variable. For example, Jacobson did not want to know only how strong a relationship existed between campaign spending and votes received (after controlling for the partisan strength of a district); he also wanted to know how much money would have to be spent to receive a winning percentage of the vote.

A second multivariate data analysis technique, *multiple regression,* provides this type of information. Recall that regression analysis involves the display of data points in a two-dimensional space and the calculation of the line that best approximates the data points (a regression line). The algebraic equation corresponding to this best-fitting line describes the nature of the relationship between the independent and dependent variables, and the product-moment correlation coefficient indicates the strength and statistical significance of that relationship. This regression equation may be used to calculate the predicted value on Y (the dependent variable) for any value of X (the independent variable), and the residual or distance between the predicted and observed value of Y can be calculated for each observation.

Multiple regression does exactly the same thing, only the regression equation contains more than one variable, and the regression coefficient expresses the relationship between one independent variable and the dependent variable while controlling for all other variables in the equation. But control is done by adjusting the values of each case to take into account the effect of all the other variables rather than by grouping similar cases together.

The general form of a *linear multiple regression equation* is

$$Y = b_1X_1 + b_2X_2 + b_NX_N + a \tag{13.3}$$

Here a indicates the Y-intercept or the value of Y when the values of all of the other variables are zero, and the b's indicate how much Y changes for a unit change in each of the independent variables, when the other variables are being held constant. Hence each b indicates the relationship between X and Y while controlling for all of the other independent variables simultaneously, and the expected value of Y may be calculated by substituting any values of the various independent variables into the equation.

The solution to the linear multiple regression equation is the mathematical relationship between the independent variables and the dependent variable. Usually by a computer, a and b are calculated to minimize the squared distances between each data point and its predicted Y-value. As a result, the multiple regression equation contains the same wealth of information as a bivariate regression equation does.

Remember, however, that it is difficult to judge the relative importance of the independent variables based on the multiple regression equation alone. The b's are calculated in tandem with the units of measurement for each of the independent variables and are therefore sensitive to how those variables are measured. One b may be much larger than another b, not because the independent variable is more strongly related to the dependent variable but because the independent variable is measured in much smaller units.

To assess the relative importance of a series of independent variables, the b's from a regression equation may be *standardized* to reflect the mean and variance of each of the independent variables. When this is done, the b's are converted into *standardized regression coefficients*— also called *beta weights*—that indicate the relative importance of each independent variable in explaining the variation in the dependent variable, when controlling for all of the other variables in the equation.

Table 13-7 Multivariate Explanation of Vote for Congressional Challengers: Multiple Regression Analysis, 1972-1978

	Regression Coefficient	t Ratio[a]	Standardized Regression Coefficient (Beta)	
1972				
CV^b = a	20.7			
b_1 Challenger's expenditures	.112	9.42	.51	
b_2 Incumbent's expenditures	−.002	−.14	−.01	R^2 = .49
b_3 Challenger's party	−.47	−.61	−.03	
b_4 Challenger's district party strength	.299	6.94	.33	
1974[c]				
CV = a	15.6			
b_1 Challenger's expenditures	.121	10.45	.48	
b_2 Incumbent's expenditures	−.028	−2.34	−.11	R^2 = .65
b_3 Challenger's party	9.78	11.19	.42	
b_4 Challenger's district party strength	.351	7.75	.28	

(continued)

Betas may vary from −1 to +1 so they indicate not only the direction of the controlled relationship with an independent variable but also the amount of variance in the dependent variable accounted for by each of the independent variables.

The statistical significance of a controlled relationship with an independent variable may also be derived from a multiple regression equation. The computer program that calculates a regression equation will print out the standard error of the regression coefficients. The usual test for a statement with 95 percent certainty is that the regression coefficient be at least twice its standard error. If the test is met, then the relationship is statistically significant. If it is not met, then the null hypothesis involving that relationship (controlling for the other independent variables in the equation) must be accepted.

The overall success of a multiple regression equation in accounting for the variation in the dependent variable is indicated with the multiple correlation coefficient (R) and its square (R^2). R^2 is the ratio of the explained variance in the dependent variable to the total variance in the

Table 13-7   *(continued)*

	Regression Coefficient	t Ratio[a]	Standardized Regression Coefficient (Beta)	
1976				
CV[b] = a	14.8			
b₁ Challenger's expenditures	.074	9.57	.45	
b₂ Incumbent's expenditures	−.003	−.27	−.01	R² = .60
b₃ Challenger's party	.26	.32	.01	
b₄ Challenger's district party strength	.441	10.84	.48	
1978				
CV[b] = a	14.8			
b₁ Challenger's expenditures	.063	11.10	.51	
b₂ Incumbent's expenditures	−.002	−.35	−.02	R² = .61
b₃ Challenger's party	−1.76	−2.15	−.08	
b₄ Challenger's district party strength	.454	9.70	.42	

Source: Gary C. Jacobson, *Money in Congressional Elections* (New Haven, Conn.: Yale University Press, 1980), 42, 235. Copyright © 1980. Reprinted with permission.

[a] A t ratio of at least 1.98 is necessary for a .05 level of significance, 2.58 for .01, and 3.35 for .001.

[b] CV is challenger's share of the vote.

[c] Variables are the same as those in the 1972 analysis.

dependent variable; hence it equals the proportion of the variance in the dependent variable that may be explained by the independent variables acting together in the multiple regression equation:

$$R^2 = \frac{\text{Sum of squares for Y} - \text{Sum of squares for residuals}}{\text{Sum of squares for Y}} = \frac{\text{Sum of squares for regression}}{\text{Sum of squares for Y}} = \frac{\text{Explained variance in Y}}{\text{Total variance in Y}} \quad (13.4)$$

R^2 itself can vary from 0 to 1.0, and it also has a corresponding significance test that indicates whether the entire regression equation permits a statistically significant explanation of the dependent variable.

Multiple regression is currently the preferred technique in political science for observing multivariate relationships. In fact, most of the

Table 13-8   Multivariate Explanation of Civil Strife: Multiple
Regression Analysis

	Regression Coefficient	Standardized Regression Coefficient (Beta)
Total magnitude of strife = a	−3.110	
b_1 Economic deprivation, short-term	1.770	.24
b_2 Political deprivation, short-term	.660	.09[a]
b_3 Persisting deprivation	.271	.39
b_4 Coercive forces loyalty	.140	−.17
b_5 Institutionalization	.056	.07[a]
b_6 Past civil strife	.024	.04[a]
b_7 Facilitation	.481	.55
b_8 Legitimacy	−.184	−.26
R^2 = .650		

Source: Ted Gurr, "A Causal Model of Civil Strife: A Comparative Analysis Using New Indices," *American Political Science Review* 2 (December 1968): 1119. Reprinted with permission.
[a] Not significant at the .05 level.

political science researchers whose work we have been discussing used multiple regression. Gary Jacobson, for example, used this analytical tool to determine the relationships between campaign spending, partisan strength, political party, and the vote for congressional candidates, shown in Table 13-7. He discovered that the strongest relationships are generally between challengers' expenditures and the vote, and between the challengers' district party strength and the vote, when controllin: for the other variables. Incumbent spending and the challengers' party exhibit much weaker relationships with the distribution of the vote. Table 13-7 also shows that Jacobson's four-variable model generally explains over half of the variation in votes cast for challengers and that challengers have gained about 1 percent of the vote for every $5,000 to $10,000 spent (depending on the year).

Gurr used multiple regression to assess the impact of relative deprivation and other factors on cross-national measures of civil strife. The result of one of Gurr's multiple regression analyses intended to explain the variation in civil strife is shown in Table 13-8. Gurr's eight-variable equation explains 65 percent of the variation in strife, with persisting deprivation, short-term economic deprivation, social and political facilitation, and legitimacy contributing the most to the explanation. Because of the way the independent variables are measured in this case—with multimeasure scales and indices—the regression coefficients do not have a straightforward interpretation.

Table 13-9 Multivariate Explanation of Congruence of Public Opinion with Public Policy: Multiple Regression Analysis

Variables	Bivariate Correlation[a]	Regression Standardized Beta
Size of opinion change (%)	.23	.06
No fluctuation [b]	.19	.11
How long change took (months)	.18	.01
Low salience (% DKs)	−.10	−.09
Social issues	.14	.00
Economy	.01	.03
Defense	−.09	−.03
World War II	.13	.15
Other foreign policy	−.14	−.11
Liberal opinion change	.28	.25
States' policy	.11	−.05
1969-1979 period	.14	.06
Multiple R		.40
R²		.16

Source: Benjamin I. Page and Robert Y. Shapiro, "Effects of Public Opinion on Policy," *American Political Science Review* 77 (March 1983): 184.

Note: The dependent variable is direction of policy change from T1 to one year after T2, scored 0 (noncongruent) or 1 (congruent). Some independent variables with insignificant bivariate correlations are omitted. The excluded category of issue types consists of remaining domestic policies.

[a] Correlations with magnitudes of .11 or better are significant at the .05 level; those .07 or greater, at the .1 level.

[b] Three categories; cases with insufficient time points to detect fluctuation were coded in a middle category.

Page and Shapiro also employ multiple regression analysis to understand better the relationship between public opinion change and public policy change. In their analysis the presence or absence of opinion-policy congruence is the dependent variable and various measures of the opinion change, policy type, and political context of the policy response are used as independent variables. Their analysis reviewed statistically significant relationships between policy congruence and several measures of the size of opinion change, the type of issue under consideration, and the ideological direction of the opinion/policy change (Table 13-9). Fully explaining policy congruence is not an easy task, however. Page and Shapiro's multiple regression equation, employing all of the relevant independent variables, explains only 16 percent of the variation in policy congruence.

A final example of multiple regression analysis is McConahay's study of attitudes toward busing, shown in Table 13-10. The variable with the strongest relationship to busing attitudes is modern racial attitudes,

Table 13-10 Multivariate Explanation of Attitudes toward Busing: Multiple Regression Analysis

Predictors of Busing Attitudes	Standardized Regression Coefficient (Beta)
Self-Interest	
Parents	.11
Children in public school	−.06
Children being bused	.03
Homeowner	.07
Relatives in neighborhood	.00
Time lived in neighborhood	.02
Happy with neighborhood	−.02
Planning to stay in neighborhood	.01
Racial Attitudes	
Modern	.40[a]
Old-fashioned	.10[c]
Feelings for blacks	.07
Demographics and Other Attitudes	
Education	−.08
Family job status	−.11[b]
Union membership	.02
1975 income	−.01
Southern socialization	.08[c]
Sex	−.05
Political efficacy	.05
Authoritarianism	−.02
Life-style conservatism	−.01
$R^2 = .32$	

Source: John B. McConahay, "Self-Interest versus Racial Attitudes as Correlates of Anti-Busing Attitudes in Louisville: Is It the Buses or the Blacks?" *Journal of Politics* 44 (August 1982): 713. Reprinted with permission.

[a] Significant at .001 level.

[b] Significant at .01 level.

[c] Significant at .05 level.

followed at a considerable distance by family job status, parental status, and old-fashioned racial attitudes. In addition, this regression analysis is not especially successful since it explains only 32 percent of the variation in attitudes toward busing.

Conclusion

As we have seen, multivariate data analysis helps researchers provide more complete explanations of political phenomena and produce causal knowledge. Observing the relationship between an independent and a dependent variable while controlling for one or more control variables allows researchers to assess more precisely the effect attributable to each independent variable and to accumulate evidence in support of a causal claim. Being able to observe simultaneously the relationship between a number of independent variables and a dependent variable also helps researchers construct more parsimonious and complete explanations for political phenomena.

Multivariate data analysis techniques vary in how they control for the control variable. Multivariate crosstabulation and two-way analysis of variance control by grouping similar observations; partial correlation and multiple regression control by adjustment. Both types of procedures have their advantages and limitations. Control by grouping can result in the proliferation of analysis tables, the reduction of the number of cases within categories to a hazardous level, and the elimination of some of the variance in the control variables. Control by adjustment, on the other hand, can disguise important specified relationships; that is, relationships that are not identical across the range of values observed in the control variables.

Notes

1. Gary C. Jacobson, *Money in Congressional Elections* (New Haven, Conn.: Yale University Press, 1980).
2. Ted Gurr, "A Causal Model of Civil Strife: A Comparative Analysis Using New Indices," *American Political Science Review* 2 (December 1968): 1104-1124. The quote is on 1105.
3. John B. McConahay, "Self-Interest versus Racial Attitudes as Correlates of Anti-Busing Attitudes in Louisville: Is It the Buses or the Blacks?" *Journal of Politics* 44 (August 1982): 692-720.
4. Benjamin I. Page and Robert Y. Shapiro, "Effects of Public Opinion on Policy," *American Political Science Review* 77 (March 1983): 175-190.
5. Edward R. Tufte, *Data Analysis for Politics and Policy* (Englewood Cliffs, N.J.: Prentice-Hall, 1974).
6. Raymond E. Wolfinger and Steven J. Rosenstone, *Who Votes?* (New Haven, Conn.: Yale University Press, 1980).

Terms Introduced

Analysis of variance. A technique for measuring the relationship between one nominal or ordinal level variable and one interval or ratio level variable.

Control by adjustment. A form of statistical control in which a mathematical adjustment is made to assess the impact of a third variable.

Control by grouping. A form of statistical control in which observations identical or similar for the control variable are grouped together.

Experimental control. Manipulation of the exposure of experimental groups to experimental stimuli in order to assess the impact of a third variable.

Multiple regression. A technique for measuring the mathematical relationships between more than one independent variable and a dependent variable, while controlling for all other independent variables in the equation.

Multivariate crosstabulation. A procedure by which crosstabulation is used to control for a third variable.

Multivariate data analysis. Data analysis techniques designed to test hypotheses involving more than two variables.

Partial correlation. A mathematical adjustment in the relationship between two variables, designed to control for the effect of a third.

Partly spurious relationship. A relationship between two variables caused partially by the impact of a third.

Specified relationship. A relationship between two variables that varies with the values of a third.

Spurious relationship. A relationship between two variables caused entirely by the impact of a third.

Statistical control. Assessing the impact of a third variable by comparing observations across the values of a control variable.

Two-way analysis of variance. An extension of the analysis of variance procedure to allow controlling for a third variable.

Exercises

1. Refer to Table 13-9. What are the independent variables with which the authors are trying to explain opinion/policy congruence? What do the numbers in the column labeled *Bivariate Correlation* mean? Which variables are the most successful in explaining the variation in opinion/policy congruence? How much of the total variation in opinion/policy congruence is accounted for by the independent variables included in this analysis?

2. Read pages 185-189 in Benjamin I. Page and Robert Y. Shapiro, "Effects of Public Opinion on Policy," *American Political Science Review* 77 (March 1983). What do the authors say about their evidence that changes in public opinion *cause* changes in public policy?

3. In Alan I. Abramowitz, "Explaining Senate Election Outcomes," *American Political Science Review* 82 (June 1988): 385-403, an attempt is made to provide a multivariate explanation for the percentage of the major party vote received by candidates for the U.S. Senate. What variables are used in this explanation? What analysis technique is used to investigate the hypothesized relationships? How successful is this explanation for votes for the U.S. Senate?

4. In Douglas A. Hibbs, Jr., and Christopher Dennis, "Income Distribution in the United States," *American Political Science Review* 82 (June 1988): 467-490, the authors present an explanation for the difference in the amount of income earned by the richest 20 percent of American families and the poorest 40 percent of American families. What factors do the authors believe affect this income inequality? What hypotheses do they advance? What do their results show?

Suggested Readings

Anderson, T. W. *Introduction to Multivariate Statistical Analysis.* New York: Wiley, 1958.

Blalock, Hubert M. *Causal Inference in Non-Experimental Research.* Chapel Hill: University of North Carolina Press, 1964.

———. *Social Statistics,* 2d ed. New York: McGraw-Hill, 1972.

Draper, N. R., and H. Smith. *Applied Regression Analysis.* New York: Wiley, 1966.

Kendall, M. G., and A. Stuart. *The Advanced Theory of Statistics,* vol 2. Griffin: London, 1961, chap. 27.

Kerlinger, F. N., and E. Pedhazer. *Multiple Regression in Behavioral Research.* New York: Holt, Rinehart & Winston, 1973.

Overall, J. E., and C. Klett. *Applied Multivariate Analysis.* New York: McGraw-Hill, 1973.

Scheffe, Henry A. *The Analysis of Variance.* New York: Wiley, 1959.

CHAPTER 14

The Research Report:
An Annotated Example

In the preceding chapters we have described important stages in the process of conducting a scientific investigation of political phenomena. In this chapter we will discuss the culmination of a research project: writing a research report. A complete and well-written research report that covers each component of the research process will contribute to the researcher's goal of creating transmissible, scientific knowledge.

This chapter examines how one researcher conducted and reported his research activities. We will evaluate how well he performed each component of the research process and how adequately he described and explained the choices he made during the investigation. To help you evaluate the report, the major components of the research process and some of the criteria by which they should be analyzed are presented here as a series of numbered questions. Refer to these questions while you read the article and jot the number of the question in the margin next to the section of the article in which the question is addressed. For easier reference, the sections of the article have been assigned letters and numbers.

1. Does the researcher clearly specify the main research question or problem? What is the "why" question?
2. Has the researcher demonstrated the value and significance of his research question and indicated how his research findings will contribute to scientific knowledge about his topic?
3. Has the researcher proposed clear explanations for the political phenomena that interest him? What types of relationships are hypothesized? Does he discuss any alternative explanations?

4. Are the independent and dependent variables identified? If so, what are they? Has the author considered any alternative or control variable? If so, please identify them. Can you think of any that the researcher did not mention?
5. Are the hypotheses empirical, general, and plausible?
6. Are the concepts in the hypotheses clearly defined? Are the operational definitions given the variables valid and reasonable?
7. What method of data collection is used to make the necessary observations? Are the observations valid and reliable measurements?
8. Has the researcher made empirical observations about the units of analysis specified in the hypotheses?
9. If a sample is used, what type of sample is it? Does the type of sample seriously affect the conclusions that can be drawn from the research? Does the researcher discuss this?
10. What type of research design is used? Does the research design adequately test the hypothesized relationships? For example, if the researcher hypothesizes a causal relationship, does the research design permit the researcher to show a causal relationship?
11. Are the statistics that are used appropriate for the level of measurement of the variables?
12. Are the research findings presented and discussed clearly? Is the basis for deciding whether a hypothesis is supported or refuted clearly specified?

GLOBAL NEWS FLOWS
Dependency and Neoimperialism
A

1 During the past decade, the political context for communication in the Third World has been set by nonaligned diplomats who advocate creation of a New World Information Order (NWIO), and by structural theorists of communication such as Johan Galtung and Herbert Schiller.[1] The research presented here is designed to assess the validity of certain descriptive statements and causal arguments that have been advanced in the midst of these policy debates and theoretical discourses. The first set of claims, those of a descriptive nature, holds that Third World media have come to replicate the "news values" of the Western media. Evidence of this media homogenization is said to be found in the dependency of Third World nations on Western media products, and in the way that nonaligned media follow the West's lead in the focus of their media coverage (Masmoudi, 1981). Those claims of a more causal nature posit media dependency

William H. Meyer, "Global News Flows: Dependency and Neoimperialism," *Comparative Political Studies* (October 1989): 243-264. Reprinted with permission.

as a further source of cultural imperialism (Galtung, 1979, 1980) and as a tool for creating regional spheres of informational hegemony (Becker et al., 1986; Schiller, 1976). Cultural imperialism is said to be evident in the tendency of the mass media to cover events of interest to a westernized audience (e.g., violence) while largely excluding issues of utmost concern to a non-Western public (e.g., development). Finally, media dependency is said to follow the geographic patterns of older forms of imperialism, dividing the world's communication traffic according to the hegemonic domains of the Americans, the British, and the French (i.e., controllers of the four largest transnational news agencies, or TNNAs).

2 This study addresses three research questions. 1. Are the nonaligned media dependent on the West for international news, and does the nonaligned press follow Western media in its patterns of news coverage? 2. Do Western and westernized media display traits of cultural imperialism in their selection of topics, while non-Western topics must come from alternative sources? 3. Is the global traffic in international communication divided into neocolonial spheres of influence?

Media Dependency and
B   Patterns of News Coverage

1 The data used in this study have been taken from three English-language African dailies: the *Daily Nation* (Nairobi, Kenya), the Zimbabwe *Herald*, and the *Times of Zambia;* and from three Latin American dailies: *Excelsior* (Mexico City), *La Nacion*, and *La Prensa* (both from Buenos Aires). These dailies have the largest circulations or have been ranked as the "most influential" journals in their respective nations (Kurian, 1982: 89, 630). Each also ranks among the largest, in terms of circulation, in its respective region. All six papers cater primarily to local urban elites, with little or no rural circulation (Kurian, 1982). According to Kurian, these papers serve a local audience, not foreigners. Therefore, they are more comparable to the prestige press of the West than to global media such as the *International Herald Tribune*.[2]

2 Sub-Saharan Africa is one region neglected in most prior news flow studies (Harris, 1981; Harris et al., 1982; IPI, 1953; Rogers and Schement, 1984; Schramm and Atwood, 1981; Stevenson and Cole, 1980; Stevenson and Shaw, 1984). Furthermore, news flows in this part of Africa represent the best-case test[3] of the structuralist's charge that international communications are neocolonial (Galtung, 1979; McPhail, 1987; Schiller, 1976). Nations in this area are the countries that as a group, have received their independence most recently. If the patterns of communication that were established during the age of imperialism (see Meyer, 1988a: chapter two) persist to this day, then evidence of that fact is most likely to remain in sub-Saharan Africa. If imperial powers still control information flows in and out of their former colonies (as specified by structural theory), evidence of such a trend is most likely to show up in news reports from Africa and in news reported within Africa.

3 The African papers, published in a European language, served the residents of European extraction in the days before independence (Kurian, 1982).

Hence, if any local newspapers are linked to the existing world information order in a neoimperial manner, it should be these. Evidence of the sorts of things that structuralists look for (e.g., Galtung's alleged link between the news interests of Center and Periphery elites) should be most readily apparent in these particular publications.[4]

4 On the other hand, Latin American states have enjoyed their independence from colonialism longer than any other region of the Third World. This is another geographic area that is underrepresented in prior news flow studies. Therefore, a focus on these two regions not only fills in some of the gaps in the prior literature, it also gives us samples that reflect the diversity of the Third World's colonial experience.

C The Samples

1 The data presented are taken from: five issues of each African paper for 1984; five issues of each African paper for 1985; and four issues of each Latin American publication for 1985 (for a total of forty-two issues altogether). The basic unit of analysis is the international news story. A total of 1596 reports regarding international affairs, roughly half from each region, were coded from stratified samples.

2 The population this research seeks to describe is that of international news stories as carried in the African and Latin American prestige presses. The samples are stratified in two senses. First news items were stratified by issue, rather than randomly selecting news stories individually, regardless of which issue they appeared in. Second, the issues themselves were stratified in the sense that no two issues were taken from the same week. While the news story is our basic indicator of news as carried in the Third World (i.e., the unit of analysis), the units that were sampled were the daily issues. This is similar to the methodology used by Harris, Schramm, and others. Once an issue had been randomly selected for inclusion in the sample, all news items regarding international events in that issue were coded.[5]

3 Prior news flow studies encountered difficulties because their samples were often skewed toward coverage of one or two major events (see, for example, Schramm, 1980: 613). Because studies by Harris, the International Press Institute, Schramm, and others took their samples from only one week (or at most one month) of the year, the distribution of news items was commonly dominated by one or two recurring stories. This fact casts doubts upon the validity of generalizing from such samples. Schramm's influential study of Asian media employs a sample that is admitted to be unique in some respects, in that coverage of a certain airline disaster dominated much of the international news. Therefore, that sample is less representative of average news coverage than might be desired.

4 The samples used here avoid such problems by drawing on a more representative distribution of the Third World press. In order to do this, papers were sampled from a six-month time period.[6] By using a random sample from all available issues for a larger time-frame, a more balanced and accurate portrayal of the nonaligned press is possible.[7] It is more representative because it is not skewed by one or two major events. It is, therefore, closer to the norm for all reporting.

Table 1 Reports with Western Newswires Identified as Sources

	Africa		Latin America	Asia
Wire Service	(1984) %	(1985) %	(1985) %	(1981) %
AFP	23%	13%	11%	
AP	14%	19%	19%	
Reuters	36%	29%	4%	
UPI	3%	1%	22%	
Totals	76%	62%	56%	76%
	(N = 230)	(N = 184)	(N = 296)	

Note: The Asian figure, included for ease of comparison, is taken from Schramm, 1981.

5 Each story in the sample was coded for the paper and date of publication, the wire service carrying the story,[8] the nation and region covered in the story, the theme, the total column-inches and lines for the story, the column-inches/lines devoted to spot news, and the column-inches/lines for developmental news. Spot news is generally regarded as raw facts about diplomacy, wars, crime, unrest, and disasters. Developmental news is not just news about modernization or other forms of development. The style known as developmental journalism attempts to imbue all news stories with the links between a raw data-event and projects of economic or political modernization. Developmental journalism also addresses the historical background and long-range implications of an isolated event (Aggarwala, 1979; see also the discussion of news as a social good in Meyer, 1988a: chapter two).[9]

6 The data analysis presented here has been organized according to the three research questions at hand: media dependency and patterns of news coverage; differences in news reporting between the Western TNNAs (i.e., AFP, AP, Reuters, UPI) and the local or regional, nonaligned agencies; and the structure of international news flows. Let us address the nature of media dependency and patterns of coverage first.

D Media Dependency

1 Evidence of media dependency could presumably take many forms. Prior study by this researcher has shown that LDCs are not generally dependent on electronic media from the West (Meyer, 1988a). The developing nations of the Third World do import roughly two-thirds of their television broadcasting. However, in radio broadcasting, that area generally accepted to be of greatest importance for development (Schramm, 1964), LDCs are, on average, almost self-sufficient.[10] To assess the state of dependency in the area of the print media, one would do well to start with the sources of international reports that appear in the Third World dailies (see Table 1).

2 Table 1 shows the distribution of all news stories that cited TNNAs as their source. Percentages signify that portion of the total number of international

news reports with identified sources that were provided by each service. News items without a wire service byline, and news from non-TNNA sources (24-44% of total news), were excluded from Table 1. Special attention should be given to the row containing totals: 56-76% of all international news items that identified their sources in these six dailies came from the four Western international agencies combined.[11] We now know that this is a pattern repeated in other areas of the Third World, as these results are very close to Schramm's findings of 76% for Asian dailies. Schramm's figure is included in Table 1 simply for ease of comparison.[12] From my samples we can also see that the African press tends to be more reliant on the Big Four (AFP, AP, Reuters, UPI) than is Latin America. The latter takes more news off the regional wire services, especially from EFE, the Spanish service and from IPS, a specialist in developmental news.

3 Special note should also be taken of the totals in Table 1 for news supplied to Africa by Reuters, and for news to Latin America from AP and UPI. Twenty-nine to thirty-six percent, the largest single group, of all identified newswire stories on international relations as reported in the Kenyan, Zambian, and Zimbabwean press, came from the British newswire. Recall that each of these nations is also a former British colony. Similarly, 41% of all global news in the Latin American press came from the two U.S. TNNAs, AP and UPI, combined. Of course, Central and South America are often argued to be within the "imperial sphere" of the United States. These are key points that will be expanded upon below when considering whether global news flows follow neoimperial patterns.

4 While the evidence from Table 1 tends to support the descriptive claim that developing nations are heavily reliant upon Western newswires for international coverage, it is by no means conclusive. At best, this is only prima facie evidence that structuralists and NWIO advocates are correct. However, while frequencies alone are far from conclusive, they are helpful in taking a first cut at the data used here. Presentation of frequency distributions is also essential in order to provide comparability between the data from Africa and Latin America, and the prior literature on news flows provided by Schramm and others, a body of literature in which frequencies are a preferred methodology. Therefore, while tests of significance and measures of association will be required when evaluating the causal arguments of structuralists and NWIO advocates, we must restrict ourselves to frequency distributions for a short while longer in order to describe the overall distribution of topics covered in the international press.

E Patterns of News Coverage

1 Another descriptive claim often advanced by critics of the West and by advocates of a new international order in communication is that the global print media is becoming homogenized in its coverage of world events (MacBride Commission, 1981a). Newspapers from different regions of the Third World are said to resemble each other (Schramm, 1980: 583), and Third World papers are said to be close to Western prestige dailies (Stevenson, 1981) in terms of the topics selected for coverage. If this were indeed the case, then one should be able to point to certain similarities between the African and Latino media in this study

Table 2   Percentage of All News Devoted to International Reporting

	Africa			Latin America		
D. Nation 1984/85	Herald 1984/85	Times 1984/85	Excelsior 1985	La Nacion 1985	La Prensa 1985
Issue						
1. 15% 33%	11% 21%	21% 37%	32%	31%	39%
2. 23% 24%	36% 27%	31% 45%	38%	35%	35%
3. 24% 23%	18% 34%	39% 52%	32%	22%	22%
4. 31% 28%	26% 39%	26% 31%	32%	27%	16%
5. 22% 43%	23% 33%	31% 31%			
Averages						
23% 30%	24% 31%	30% 39%	33%	29%	28%

and these other papers. Once again, the search begins with a look at the surface appearance (frequencies) of these dailies.

2 The first question one might pose is whether international news is treated any differently, in terms of its relative importance, by the Third World press than it is in the West. Table 2 shows that these dailies devoted between 11% and 52% of all news to reports on international affairs, with average coverage ranging from 23% to 39%. Figures for average coverage of interstate news are close to those of Schramm's 1980 study in Asia (18% to 28%) and Pinch's 1978 study of the *New York Times, Washington Post,* and *Los Angeles Times* (20% to 30%). Note that the averages for Africa increase from 1984 to 1985, indicating a rising interest in international affairs over that period. Average international coverage in the 1985 Latin American press is greater than that of Africa for 1984, but roughly equivalent to African dailies for 1985.

3 When looking at the regions covered in the Southern presses (see Table 3 for Third World versus non-Third World coverage), one finds, again, results similar to Schramm's (1981: 205) for the Asian press. The presses in Africa and Latin America devote 41-47% of all international news to the local region; and both of these regions, along with the Asian press, devote roughly one-half to two-thirds of international coverage (i.e., 48-68%) to news involving at least one Third World nation. As Schramm (1981: 209) points out, these results also correlate strongly with coverage by the Big Four (see also Weaver and Wilhoit, 1984: 159). Therefore, Third World dailies in Africa, Asia, and Latin America all show evidence of following the lead of Western papers and Western wire services in focusing on certain regions and countries.

4 Turning now to the subjects covered, Table 4 shows the distribution of news items according to topics. Once again the African and Latin American presses exhibit striking similarities to the Asian and U.S. presses. Thirteen to eighteen percent of all stories focused on economics and development in the African/Latin American samples, compared to 19% for Asian dailies, and 14% to 25% for U.S. dailies (Pinch, 1978). In another area of similarity, 9-18% of the

Table 3 Regions Covered in the Third World Press

	Africa		Latin America	Asia
Region	(1984) %	(1985) %	(1985) %	(1981) %
Africa	47%	41%	1%	
Asia	8%	13%	6%	
Latin Am.	3%	4%	42%	
Middle East	8%	7%	3%	
U.S.	9%	7%	20%	
USSR/E. Europe	2%	4%	6%	
W. Europe	21%	21%	22%	
Other	2%	3%	1%	
Totals	100%	100%	100%	
	(N = 420)	(N = 470)	(N = 706)	
Third World	39%	39%	34%	24%
T.W. + Other	29%	26%	32%	24%
Non-Third W.	32%	35%	34%	51%
Totals	100%	100%	100%	100%
	(N = 420)	(N = 470)	(N = 706)	(N = 920)

Note: The Asian figure is taken from Schramm, 1981.

Table 4 International News Items According to Topics

	Africa		Latin America	Asia
Topic	(1984) %	(1985) %	(1985) %	(1981) %
Development/Economics	16%	13%	18%	19%
Diplomatic Relations	20%	15%	14%	29%
Disasters	4%	6%	2%	7%
Politics/Government	9%	9%	9%	12%
Science and Culture	7%	12%	15%	9%
Sports	17%	23%	23%	12%
Unrest and Crime	18%	15%	9%	7%
War/Military Affairs	9%	6%	10%	5%
Totals	100%	100%	100%	100%
	(N = 420)	(N = 470)	(N = 706)	(N = 920)

Note: The Asian figure is taken from Schramm, 1981.

stories in my samples were about crimes and unrest (a paradigm of spot reporting), almost identical in range to the results of Schramm (7% in Asia) and Pinch (17% in the U.S.).

5 On the basis of results such as these, Schramm and Pinch have argued that there is no significant difference between Western papers and Third World dailies when it comes to coverage of developmental news versus coverage of other news. Results from this study, combined with those of the earlier news flow studies, suggest that Asian, African, Latin American, and Western dailies also approximate one another in percentages of news devoted to interstate reporting, and in regions covered. These conclusions are shared by many who see little difference between Western and Third World newspapers in general (Stevenson and Cole, 1980; Stevenson, 1981). My findings support the claim that Third World *dailies* treat developmental news much like Western papers do but, as we shall see, Third World and Western *newswires* differ significantly in their treatment of reports.

F   Media Dependency and Cultural Imperialism

1 Evidence from Third World regions around the globe points to a heavy reliance by LDCs on the West for international news. If the samples discussed above are accurate indicators, one might be led to the conclusion that Western news values have come to dominate media in the South. According to Stevenson and Cole (1980: 13), "Western agencies ... set the agenda for [Third World] media at the level of influencing what topics get covered." Western TNNAs invariably focus on crises, armed conflict, and crime when reporting from either developed or developing nations (Weaver and Wilhoit, 1984: 185). Tables 2−4 indicate that dailies in Africa and Latin America may indeed reflect this Western mass media mentality. A reliance on the West for news becomes a form of cultural imperialism if and when it reaches that point at which media producers and consumers in the South begin to think like their counterparts in the West.

2 If media dependency leads to cultural imperialism, and if the effect of Western media items flooding into the South has been to impose foreign news values upon those peoples, then media producers in the South do not just cover topics similar to those in the Western press. They also come to think about world events through the same perceptual paradigms. They come to see the world "through Western eyes." If this is the case, then one would expect to find that Third World news agencies approach their work with the same priorities as do the TNNAs.

3 In other words, the similarities in news coverage among the many regions of the world outlined above could be due to random variation. Furthermore, similarities between presses in the North and the South could be due to the finite number of stories to cover. On the other hand, if communication imperialism leads directly to cultural imperialism, as Galtung argues (1979: 166), then similarities from North to South must be more than just random or skin-deep. If media dependency has a necessary causal impact on cultural imperialism, then Third World news agencies, as well as newspapers, would tend to follow the West's lead.

Table 5   Topics According to Source

Sample =	Diplomatic Relations A84/A85	Crime & Unrest A84/A85	Wars & Military A84/A85	Disaster A84/A85	Development A84/A85
AFP	16/11%	35/21%	13/18%	4/ 5%	6/ 0%
AP	19/14%	17/28%	17/ 2%	10/ 9%	2/ 5%
Reuters	27/20%	19/15%	14/ 9%	4/ 6%	6/ 2%
UPI	22/ 0%	22/50%	11/ 0%	0/ 0%	0/ 0%
Local/ Regional	20/24%	16/ 6%	12/ 3%	8/21%	20/15%
Paper's Reporter	29/17%	4/ 3%	2/ 3%	0/ 3%	27/23%
Sample =	LA85	LA85	LA85	LA85	LA85
AFP	11%	21%	0%	4%	0%
AP	12%	14%	7%	5%	1%
Reuters	21%	10%	21%	5%	5%
UPI	13%	14%	14%	1%	1%
Local/ Regional	15%	3%	7%	0%	8%
Paper's Reporter	18%	5%	13%	0%	5%

A84 = Africa, 1984
A85 = Africa, 1985
LA84 = Latin America, 1985

4 To what extent do reports drawn from the nonaligned newswires reflect the news values of the Western TNNAs? Table 5 presents data for each of the international newswires, as well as national and regional (nonaligned) wire services, and coverage supplied by the papers' correspondents and stringers. The coverage taken from each source is broken down according to subject matter. As one can see, the categories of Diplomatic Relations, War, and Crime and Unrest (spot news categories) rank at the top for reports drawn from each of the TNNAs. Conversely, development news ranks significantly higher for both national/regional newswires and local coverage.

5 Table 6 presents a slightly more sophisticated treatment of the same question. Here the columns are divided into TNNA news sources and non-TNNA sources. The row of Spot News contains all stories coded originally as diplomacy, crime and unrest, domestic politics (from other nations), wars, or disasters. Developmental Reports are those in which either the subject was one of national modernization, or more than half the item was devoted to the developmental journalistic style. The category of Other contains mostly social, cultural, or scientific news, and a few human interest stories. Sports news was not counted for the purposes of this table because it does not fall neatly into either the category of spot news or that of developmental news.

6 Cross-tabular analysis of TNNA versus non-TNNA news sources shows

Table 6 Spot News Versus Developmental Reporting

	TNNAs	Local-Regional	
Spot News	85%	57%	
Developmental Reports	5%	24%	Africa (1984)
Other	10%	19%	
Totals	100% (N = 229)	100% (N = 72)	

Chi-square = 29.72; significant at less than .001 level
Cramer's V = .22

Spot News	73%	55%	
Dev. News	3%	20%	Africa (1985)
Other	24%	25%	
Totals	100% (N = 184)	100% (N = 99)	

Chi-square = 25.53; significant at less than .001
Cramer's V = .21

Spot News	59%	55%	
Dev. News	1%	5%	Latin America (1984)
Other	40%	40%	
Totals	100% (N = 295)	100% (N = 290)	

Chi-square = 7.57; significant at .02
Cramer's V = .08

Note: D.F. = 2.

that there is a statistically significant difference between reports taken from these two sources. The chi-square tests show that the probability of there being no relationship between news source and subject matter is less than .05 for all three samples. Values for Cramer's V show that the strength of association between wire service and type of report is constant across time in Africa, but weaker in the case of Latin America.[13]

7 The clear trend is for stories with a TNNA byline to center on spot news, while those with a nonaligned news service byline display a greater interest in

Table 7 Mean Values for Length of Developmental Reports—Analysis of Variance

Africa (1984)

	MEANS				ANOVA	
	TNNA	Non-TNNA		D.F.	F-Ratio	Significance
Total Lines	3.38	25.39	Between Within	1 300	31.41	.000*
Total Inches	.43	4.65	Between Within	1 300	27.28	.000*

Africa (1985)

	MEANS				ANOVA	
	TNNA	Non-TNNA		D.F.	F-Ratio	Significance
Total Lines	2.70	11.20	Between Within	1 323	13.10	.000*
Total Inches	.53	1.80	Between Within	1 323	8.46	.003

Latin America (1985)

	MEANS				ANOVA	
	TNNA	Non-TNNA		D.F.	F-Ratio	Significance
Total Lines	2.80	16.60	Between Within	1 619	13.37	.000*
Total Inches	.41	2.30	Between Within	1 619	13.65	.000*

Note: * = significant at less than the .001 level.

developmental news. But what of those few developmental reports that are taken off the TNNA newswires? Table 7 compares the mean values for length of developmental reports taken from TNNAs with those from a non-TNNA news service.

8 Reports taken from nonaligned news services are more likely to cover developmental news (see Table 6), and will also go into much greater detail in their developmental reports (see Table 7). F-ratios for the ANOVA (analysis of variance) tests, comparing the mean values for developmental reports acquired from the two types of news sources, show that there is a statistically significant difference in both total column-inches and total lines at less than the .01 level for all three samples. Not only do the articles that cite the nonaligned agencies as sources focus more on developmental news than those citing TNNAs, but these reports also go into the subject of development at much greater length and in

more detail.

9 It would seem that media dependency has not produced cultural imperialism in the form of nonaligned newswires fully adopting the news values of Western wire services. In fact, many Third World editors have gone to great lengths to produce for themselves the developmental journalism that they see lacking in the Western services (Roser and Brown, 1986). One could view this trend as a journalistic backlash against Western news values.

G   Neoimperialism in Global News Flows

1 The last question to be addressed by this news flow study is the one that is most central to the view of structural communications theory. Media dependency allegedly takes the form of a neoimperial structure for news flows. The Big Four control the bulk of international news. This may allow the Americans, the British, and the French to carve out their own individual hegemonic spheres of informational influence. Furthermore, the claim is repeatedly made that international communications are a prime—even paradigmatic—example of the overall neocolonial structure of world affairs. If one were to find clear evidence of structural imperialism in the area of communication, this fact would tend to support the claim of Galtung and others that a feudal structure characterizes North-South relations in general. On the other hand, if the structural view of communication were found to be inaccurate, then structural theory in general would be seriously undermined.

2 The testing of structural theories of international relations has itself become a controversial issue. Theorists of dependency and structuralism have claimed that the validation of their work can only be found in its relative ability to promote new forms of political action (Galtung, 1980: chapter 9) and socioeconomic organization (Cardoso and Faletto, 1979: xiv). Cardoso and Faletto (1979: xii) decry past attempts at empirical testing as being efforts to quantify what may be inherently unquantifiable. Furthermore, the neocolonial interaction structure of information flows is something that has already been "amply demonstrated" in Galtung's view (1980: 129), although he cites no empirical studies to support this point.

3 Adequate quantitative studies of international communication flows have tended to be few and far between (for recent efforts see Cioffi-Revilla et al., 1987; Stevenson and Shaw, 1984). Mass communication researchers who purport to have tested structural theory have been particularly unsophisticated in their analyses, with a clear tendency to oversimplify structural claims before proceeding to "refute" them (Haynes, 1984; Link, 1984). Haynes believes that he can demonstrate the invalidity of structural thought by calling our attention to the fact that the Latin American press carries news about other Third World regions (i.e., interactions exist between the Peripheral states). Any Periphery-to-Periphery (horizontal) linkages of this sort, according to Haynes, refute Galtung's claim that neocolonial information flows always follow a Center-to-Periphery (vertical) structure. However, one cannot hope to counter structural claims with evidence as meager as this.

4 What Galtung is trying to show us is that flows from one region of the

Periphery to another must normally be channeled through the Center, which acts as the intermediary for all economic sectors of the Periphery (and profits nicely in the bargain). If news from former British colonies comes to Africa and South America through Reuters (the British service), and events from former French colonies are reported primarily by AFP (the French agency), while news from within the U.S. sphere of influence comes mainly via AP or UPI, one would find strong evidence to support the notion of feudal, Periphery-to-Center-to-Periphery (vertical) interaction patterns. Such structures would be consistent with Haynes' findings, yet they would also stand as confirmation of Galtung's thought.

5 On the other hand, there is no reason one should be expected to accept structural theses as true, a priori, as NWIO advocates tend to do; and structural theory deserves no special dispensation from the scientific tasks of empirical validation and critical evaluation. Therefore, while it may be the case that structuralism has been unjustly slighted and inadequately comprehended by the mainstream of international relations literature, nevertheless, new steps toward empirically testing this school of thought, remain necessary.

6 To state the structural thesis in its broadest form, the claim is that British multinational corporations (MNCs) are still dominant in the political economies of former British colonies, French MNCs hold a similar position in former French colonies, and U.S. MNCs hold dominance in areas historically under U.S. hegemony. The multinationals of the news industry, the TNNAs, are cited as clear examples of this trend. Tables 8 and 9 present data from the news flow study relevant to these claims.

7 Simple extensions of the prior data (see Table 8) show that, when looking at regions covered in international reports carried in the major dailies of three former British colonies (Kenya, Zambia, Zimbabwe), one-half to three-fourths (i.e., 56-76%) of the news covers other nations or regions that were also formerly under British imperial control. In Latin America, an area widely accepted to be part of the U.S. sphere of influence, a full 85% of all international news concerns this and other regions under American hegemony.[14] However, these facts do not necessarily indicate neocolonial spheres of "informational influence." It could be that commonalities of interest and common problems make these states more attentive to one another (not to mention the fact that most of their immediate neighbors have had similar colonial histories).

8 Table 9 presents information that more directly addresses this question. Each news item was coded for the former colonial ruler of the nation or region that was the subject of the report. Each story was also coded for the nationality of the TNNA if any, carrying the report. The association of former imperial power in the area to nationality of TNNA reporting from the area was then evaluated.

9 It is true that Latin America and Africa carry a great deal of news about LDCs beyond their own region (as Haynes has shown). However, from Table 9 we see that these flows clearly follow a vertical structure. Seventy-one percent of all news about areas formerly or currently under U.S. hegemony comes to the South via AP and UPI. This pattern is also repeated in regions historically dominated by England or France. Almost half (48%) of the stories about areas that have been part of the vast British empire have been channeled to the six papers in this study by Reuters. A comparable figure also holds for the French imperial domain (44%). Therefore, when we look beneath the surface appearances of the Third

Table 8 Regions Covered According to their Colonial History

	Africa				Latin America	
	1984		1985		1985	
Imperial Power	N	%	N	%	N	%
France	48	12%	24	8%	14	4%
United Kingdom	236	56%	227	76%	28	8%
United States	50	12%	19	6%	301	85%
More Than One	33	8%	10	3%	6	2%
West European (Not UK or France)	30	7%	10	3%	4	1%
Other or None	23	5%	9	3%	2	.5%

World press, when we look beyond the mere fact of which regions are covered and compare the sources of international news to the geopolitics of colonialism, we find that a vertical flow does characterize news inputs into the media of the developing world.

H   Conclusions

1 Fifty-six to seventy-six percent of the international news reports carrying a byline in the Latin American and African presses came from a TNNA, indicating a continued reliance on the Western newswires. Furthermore, Third World dailies generally show close similarities to one another and to U.S. "prestige" dailies in regard to the geographic areas and topics covered. These findings are consistent with prior news flow studies, and point to media dependency as well as Western news values being replicated by the major dailies in the South.

2 Through a comparative analysis of Western and nonaligned newswires,

Table 9 News Flows Compared to Imperial Hegemony

	Imperial Power for Nation/Region in Report			
Wire Service	United States	United Kingdom	France	Other
U.S.	71%	29%	25%	26%
British	12%	48%	31%	35%
French	17%	23%	44%	39%
Totals	100% (N = 134)	100% (N = 205)	100% (N = 54)	100% (N = 31)

Chi-square = 84.96; significant at less than the .001 level
Cramer's V = .32

Note: D.F. = 6.

stories taken from TNNAs were shown to focus on spot reports of diplomacy, unrest, crime, and disasters. Local and regional, nonaligned services seem to be more concerned with developmental news. When one looks at developmental reports in particular, the finding is that articles from the nonaligned agencies display more in-depth reporting than do those taken from the TNNAs. Therefore, local and regional services provide usable information to Third World editors which is different from that of the Big Four in this important respect. If editors want in-depth developmental coverage, they will find that it is not generally available from the TNNAs and they must seek it elsewhere, either from national or regional services or from their own reporters. To assume that "one Third World country is not interested in development news of another Third World country" (Merrill, 1981: 156) would be a mistake.

3 On the other hand, this study confirms a point advanced by Stevenson (1981: 5): Third World dailies do not lack informational alternatives to the TNNAs. Western news agencies do not have anything like a stranglehold on the news supplied to Southern papers (as some of the more extreme structuralists would seem to imply). There does appear to be, however, a clear "shortage of coverages or [different] kind[s] of coverage," as found by Schramm (1981: 214). That is to say, nonaligned nations do have available to their news media a number of alternatives to TNNA newswires. Unfortunately, it seems that Third World papers remain in a position of heavy reliance upon the TNNAs for timely, up-to-the-minute coverage of most of the globe. Editors of these dailies are in the unenviable position of relying on TNNA coverage, even though this research shows that reports taken from the Big Four are inadequate from the standpoint of both journalists and political leaders of developing nations (see Roser and Brown, 1986 for an overview of editorial opinion in the South on these matters).

4 Looking at the final question, the data clearly show that a vertical flow does characterize the structure of international communication. International news flows are neocolonial in at least two respects. First, three former British colonies get their largest percentage of international news (roughly one-third) from the British wire service. Similarly, four out of every ten foreign reports in the Latin American press are carried by the two American agencies combined. Therefore, information coming into these Third World nations follows a moderately neocolonial pattern. Second, in regard to information flowing out of LDCs, the evidence indicates interactions of an even more pronounced neoimperial nature. A strong relationship exists between a Third World nation's former colonial power and the Western wire service that gathers information within that LDC. Roughly 70% of the news from the U.S. sphere of influence, 50% of the news from the British domain, and 45% of news from areas formerly under French suzerainty has been directed to the developing presses studied here by the TNNAs of each respective power (see Figure 1 on page 381).

5 Figure 1 presents a picture of the neocolonial structure of news flows. One can clearly see that the *framework* is essentially the same as the "feudal interaction patterns" described by Galtung and others. Periphery-to-Center and Center-to-Periphery vertical flows are evident within each imperial sphere. On the other hand, related studies have found that the *effects* that structuralists have said must follow from this framework of domination do not hold. The neocolonial structure has been said to destroy indigenous cultures and promote

Figure 1 Neoimperialism in Global News Flows

Source: William H. Meyer, *Comparative Political Studies* 22, no. 3 (October 1989): 243-264. Copyright © 1989 by Sage Publications, Inc. Reprinted by permission of Sage Publications, Inc.

domestic instability in LDCs. Prior research has shown Western media to be unrelated to cultural hegemony in the Third World (Meyer, 1987). Furthermore, a free flow of media into and within the developing countries is associated with political stability there, not with increasing domestic unrest (Meyer, 1988b).

I   **Notes**

1. The platform for the NWIO was worked out at a series of meetings held between 1977 and 1980 by the International Commission for the Study of Communication Problems (or the MacBride Commission) which was created by UNESCO (see MacBride Commission, 1981b; Meyer, 1988a: chapter one; UNESCO, 1980).

2. These particular dailies are among the few papers from the nonaligned world that consistently identify the sources of their news stories in the byline (an important consideration for reasons that will soon become apparent). They also represent both government-owned and independent presses. The *Herald* and *Times* are in the former category, the *Daily Nation* and the Latin American dailies are in the latter.

3. A best-case test is one that would most fairly and clearly evaluate the validity of a given claim (on the basis of its own arguments). Tests described here provide results directly relevant to the claims made within UNESCO in favor of the NWIO.

4. There are certain obvious constraints placed upon the generalizability of findings from this study, given the fact that no papers from francophone Africa are included. The conditions of print media in those nations are not addressed directly, but results from this study will have direct implications regarding post-colonial communication in LDCs of all regions. See the section below on tests of the claim that interstate communications are neocolonial in structure.

5. For those wishing to know more about the actual dates for the samples, the exact topics or stories covered, and intercoder verification (sampling error), complete data are available from the author upon request.

6. Each paper was sampled from all available issues for the periods of December, 1983 to May, 1984; or from December, 1984 to May, 1985. Problems with access to African dailies during 1984 created a situation under which issues were available for the *Daily Nation* only for the months of December (1983), January, February, March, and May. For the Zimbabwe *Herald,* issues were available for January through May. The *Times of Zambia* was available only for the months of April and May. No such problems existed for the samples drawn during 1985 from all issues published by the African and Latin American papers within that time-frame.

7. The random sample was generated by numbering all issues in succession and then relying on a random numbers table to select the particular issues to be included.

8. This task was complicated somewhat by the fact that both the *Herald* and

the *Times* report all of their stories by including their respective national news agencies in every byline. For the purposes of coding, it was assumed that the majority of that portion of the report coming from overseas was carried via the TNNAs.

9. For a particularly instructive example of developmental journalism, see Meyer, 1988a: chapter three.

10. For a fuller discussion of broadcasting in the Third World, and for a comparison of the print data discussed here to both television and radio imported into LDCs (e.g., imbalances in media flows), see "Flows of News and Broadcasting to the Third World" in Meyer, 1988a.

11. Cf. Note 8.

12. The Asian figure represents that percentage of all news stories with identifiable sources that were taken off the Western newswires.

13. Cramer's V is a measure of the strength of association that controls for both sample size and number of categories in an R x C table. While there is no intuitive meaning for a Cramer's V value, as that value approaches 1.00 the strength of association is greater. Cramer's V is particularly useful, therefore, when comparing strength of association across more than one R x C table.

14. In those areas where colonial powers did not have formal colonies, but in which one imperial nation historically held sway in matters of military hegemony or international communication (e.g., the United Kingdom in Egypt), stories were coded according to the Western power that was dominant in the area.

J   References

AGGARWALA, N. (1979) "What is development news?" J. of Communication 29 (2): 115-126.

BECKER, J., G. HEDEBRO, and L. PALDIAN [eds.] (1986) Communication and Domination: Essays to Honor Herbert I. Schiller. Norwood, NJ: Ablex-Norwood.

CARDOSO, F. H. and E. FALETTO (1979) Dependency and Development in Latin America. Berkeley: Univ. of California Press.

CIOFFI-REVILLA, C., R. MERRITT, and D. A. ZINNES [eds.] (1987) Communication and Interaction in Global Politics. Beverly Hills, CA: Sage.

GALTUNG, J. (1979) "A structural theory of imperialism," in G. Modelski (ed.) Transnational Corporations and World Order. San Francisco: W. H. Freeman.

GALTUNG, J. (1980) The True Worlds. New York: Free Press.

HARRIS, P. (1981) Reporting Southern Africa. Paris: UNESCO.

HARRIS, P., H. MALCZEK, and E. OZKOK (1982) Flow of News in the Gulf. Documents on the New Communication Order #3. New York: Unipub.

HAYNES, R. D., Jr. (1984) "Test of Galtung's theory of structural imperialism," pp. 200-216 in R. L. Stevenson and D. L. Shaw (eds.) Foreign News and the New World Information Order. Ames: Iowa State Univ. Press.

International Press Institute (1953) The Flow of News. Zurich: Author.

KURIAN, G. T. (1982) World Press Encyclopedia. New York: Facts on File.

LINK, J. H. (1984) "Test of the cultural dependency hypothesis," pp. 186-199 in R. L. Stevenson and D. L. Shaw (eds.) Foreign News and the New World Information Order. Ames: Iowa State Univ. Press.

MacBride Commission (1981a) "Communication problems today," pp. 35-55 in J. Richstad and M. A. Anderson (eds.) Crisis in International News: Policies and Prospects. New York: Columbia Univ. Press.

MacBride Commission (1981b) "Communication tomorrow," pp. 380-401 in J. Richstad and M. A. Anderson (eds.) Crisis in International News: Policies and Prospects. New York: Columbia Univ. Press.

MASMOUDI, M. (1981) "The new world information order," pp. 77-98 in J. Richstad and M. A. Anderson (eds.) Crisis in International News: Policies and Prospects. New York: Columbia Univ. Press.

McPHAIL, T. (1987) Electronic Colonialism: The Future of International Broadcasting and Communication (2nd rev. ed.). Beverly Hills, CA: Sage.

MERRILL, J. C. (1981) "A growing controversy: the 'free flow' of news among nations," pp. 151-161 in J. Richstad and M. A. Anderson (eds.) Crisis in International News: Policies and Prospects. New York: Columbia Univ. Press.

MEYER, W. H. (1987) "Testing theories of cultural imperialism." International Interactions 13 (4): 353-374.

MEYER, W. H. (1988a) Transnational Media and Third World Development: The Structure and Impact of Imperialism. Westport, CT: Greenwood.

MEYER, W. H. (1988b) "International information flows as a determinant of political violence in third world nations: fact or fiction?" Social Sci. Q. 69 (1): 24-39.

PINCH, E. T.(1978) A Brief Study of News Patterns in Sixteen Third World Countries. Occasional Papers. Medford, MA: Tufts University, Edward R. Murrow Center of Public Diplomacy.

ROGERS, E. M. and J. R. SCHEMENT [eds.] (1984) Media Flows in Latin America. Beverly Hills, CA: Sage.

ROSER, C. and L. BROWN (1986) "African newspaper editors and the new world information order." Journalism Q. 63(1): 114-121.

SCHILLER, H. I. (1976) Communication and Cultural Domination. White Plains, NY: M. E. Sharpe.

SCHRAMM, W. L. (1964) Mass Media and National Development. Stanford, CA: Stanford Univ. Press.

SCHRAMM, W. L. (1980) "Circulation of news in the third world: a study of Asia," pp. 589-619 in G. C. Wilhoit and H. de Bock (eds.) Mass Communication Review Yearbook. Beverly Hills, CA: Sage.

SCHRAMM, W. L. (1981) "International news wires and third world news in Asia," pp. 197-218 in J. Richstad and M. A. Anderson (eds.) Crisis in International News: Policies and Prospects. New York: Columbia Univ. Press.

SCHRAMM, W. L. and E. ATWOOD (1981) Circulation of News in the Third World: A Study of Asia. Hong Kong: Chinese Univ. Press.

STEVENSON, R. L. (1981) "Beyond Belgrade: prospects for a balanced flow of information." Presented to the International Studies Association, Philadelphia.

STEVENSON, R. L. and R. R. COLE (1980) "Patterns of world coverage by the major western agencies." Presented to the Inter-Cultural Communication Division, International Communication Association, Acapulco.

STEVENSON, R. L. and D. L. SHAW [eds.] (1984) Foreign News and the New World Information Order. Ames: Iowa State Univ. Press.

UNESCO (1980) Many Voices, One World. New York: Unipub.

WEAVER, D. H. and G. C. WILHOIT (1984) "Foreign news and the western agencies," pp. 153-185 in R. L. Stevenson and D. L. Shaw (eds.) Foreign News and the New World Information Order. Ames: Iowa State Univ. Press.

Now that you have read this example of a research report and noted whether and where the author has addressed each of the twelve research questions, compare your findings with ours. The letters and numbers after each question refer to where in the article the question under discussion is addressed.

1. *Does the researcher clearly specify the main research question or problem?* (A-2, A-4) *What is the "why" question?* (F-6, F-8, G-8)

Three research questions are clearly specified. They are not presented as "why" questions, however. As an investigation of claims about the domination of Third World news by Western media, much of Meyer's research is descriptive and is intended to test the claims with appropriate empirical data. Some of Meyer's research can be phrased in terms of "why" questions. For example: Why does the content of news stories vary (being either spot news or developmental news)? Why are some developmental news stories longer than others? Why do the wire services vary with respect to the national or regional focus of their news stories?

2. *Has the researcher demonstrated the value and significance of his research question* (A-1, H-5) *and indicated how his research findings will contribute to scientific knowledge about his topic?* (B-2, B-4, G)

Yes, Meyer's discussion presents three general reasons why his research is significant. First, it addresses concern about Western media dominance over Third World media. This concern has led nonaligned diplomats to call for changes in international news reporting and for the creation of a New World Information Order. There is concern about the impact of Western-style news and Western media values on developing nations.

Second, the research will provide a basis for testing structural communications theory. Meyer argues that his research provides a "best-test" case of the charge by structuralists that international communications follow patterns established in imperial or colonial days. Meyer notes that prior quantitative studies of international communications flows have been inadequate and that NWIO advocates have not supported their positions with scientific information. A third contribution is that Meyer's research presents data from geographic areas underrepresented in prior news flow studies.

The person unfamiliar with structural theories of international relations will find it difficult to judge the theoretical significance of Meyer's research. The article is directed at a specialized audience that is likely to be familiar with structural theory and the NWIO debate.

3. *Has the researcher proposed clear explanations for the political phenomena that interest him? (F-3) What types of relationships are hypothesized? (D, E, F, G) Does he discuss any alternative explanations? (G-7)*

The author is interested in comparing news coverage in different regions of the world. The explanation presented by Meyer for similarities in news coverage is that Western news media are dominant. He does present alternative explanations for his observations. He notes that similarities in news coverage among the many regions of the world could be due to random variation or to the finite number of stories available. Commonalities of interest and problems as well as proximity are given as alternative explanations for news flow patterns.

Although he does not specifically present his research as hypothesis testing, much of the research can be phrased using null hypotheses:

1. No matter what the daily newspaper's region of the world, most international news stories come from a Western newswire.

2. There is no difference among newspapers in the relative importance of international news.

3. There is no difference among newspapers in their focus on regions and countries.

4. There is no difference among newspapers from different regions of the world with regard to the subjects covered in international news reports.

5. There is no difference in terms of topic or length between reports drawn from nonaligned newswires and those drawn from TNNA sources.

Meyer's next to last hypothesis is correlative:

6. The geographic focus of international reports in Third World dailies is related to the territorial sphere of influence of the former colonial power or imperial nation.

The last hypothesis is causal:

7. The choice of newswire source for stories about a nation or region is caused by that nation's or region's colonial history.

4. *Are the independent and dependent variables identified? If so,*

what are they? Has the author considered any alternative or control variable? If so, please identify them. Can you think of any that the researcher did not mention? (D-2, E-2, E-3, E-4, F-4, F-5, F-7, G-7, G-8)

The independent and dependent variables are identified. They are listed below by hypothesis number along with the level of measurement for each variable.

	Dependent variable	*Independent variable*
1	Newswire or source of news story (nominal)	Region of published newspaper carrying story (nominal)
2	Percentage of news devoted to international news (ratio)	Name of newspaper (nominal)
3	Region covered in news story (nominal)	Region of newspaper (nominal)
4	News topic (nominal)	Region of newspaper (nominal)
5a	News story topic (nominal)	Type of newswire (nominal)
5b	Length of developmental news story (ratio)	Type of newswire (nominal)
6	Geographic focus of story (nominal)	Colonial power of newspaper's country (nominal)
7	Nationality of wire service carrying story (nominal)	Colonial power of nation mentioned in news story (nominal)

Meyer does not mention any alternative or control variables and none are obviously left out.

5. *Are the hypotheses empirical, general, and plausible?* (D, E, F, G)

The hypotheses are empirical. All hypotheses relate characteristics of the news stories, and each characteristic can be measured empirically. The hypotheses can be objectively evaluated based on the data. Reasons are given to support the plausibility of each hypothesis. As discussed above, the hypotheses embody claims made about the relationship between Western and Third World media. The hypotheses are general in that they apply to many Third World nations. Meyer does not discuss, however, whether there exist Third World nations for which these hypotheses would not apply. In his discussion of the New World Information Order debate, Meyer mentions "nonaligned" nations, but it is not clear how many of these there are.

6. *Are the concepts in the hypotheses clearly defined? Are the operational definitions given the variables valid and reasonable?* (C-5, F-4, F-5, G-7, G-8, G-9)

The most important definitional task faced by the author is to define domination of the Third World media by the Western media. The meaning of such domination is clarified as he develops specific expectations or hypotheses about the similarities of newspapers and the differences between TNNAs and non-TNNAs. These similarities or differences are operational definitions of domination. The concepts in the hypotheses need very little further definition. The meaning of concepts such as region or type of newswire is quite clear. The difference between spot news and developmental news is explained, but examples would have made the distinction clearer. Because the concepts are not complex, operationalization of the variables is not problematic.

7. *What method of data collection is used to make the necessary observations?* (C-5) *Are the observations valid and reliable measurements?* (C-5)

Content analysis of news stories is used to make most of the necessary measurements. Each story was coded for a number of variables. While measurement of some of the variables, such as wire service, does not require much judgment, measurement of other variables concerning the regional or substantive focus of stories is subject to validity and reliability problems. Meyer notes that he will supply complete information about his data upon request (I-5). Identification of previous colonial power or nation with imperial domain is not discussed in great detail. There probably is not much argument over nations with recent colonial histories, but for other nations there may be some questions.

The categories used by Meyer for the nominal level variables seem to be straightforward and reasonable.

8. *Has the researcher made empirical observations about the units of analysis specified in the hypotheses?* (C)

The unit of analysis in all but one of the hypotheses is the international news story. All measures were either specific attributes of the news story (such as wire service source of story, theme, length, and topic) or contextual attributes (such as region of newspaper, former colonial power of country of a newspaper). In the second hypothesis, the unit of analysis is the news story (all news stories, not just international news stories).

9. *If a sample is used, what type of sample is it?* (B, C) *Does the type of sample seriously affect the conclusions that can be drawn from the research? Does the researcher discuss this?*

Meyer uses a sample, but it is not a probability sample of all Third World newspapers. First, he selected six daily newspapers from two regions of the world: sub-Saharan Africa and Latin America. These daily newspapers were not drawn randomly from a sample of all daily newspapers in those regions, but rather were selected on the basis of circulation, prestige, or language. In the second step the author selected a six-month time period from which to sample newspapers. He does not explain how this particular six-month time period was selected. In the next step Meyer stratified the issues for each of the six dailies during this period by week and selected issues at random to avoid selecting any two issues from the same week. A total of five issues for each African paper for 1984, five issues of each African paper for 1985, and four issues of each Latin American paper for 1985 were selected. Once an issue was selected, all stories in that issue were coded. As a result, Meyer has a probability cluster sample of newspapers from six dailies from six-month periods in 1984 and 1985. Each week is a cluster of issues and each issue is a cluster of stories or units of analysis. All units were sampled within each issue selected.

Problems with the sampling process (missing issues during the six-month time period) are discussed in I-6. It is difficult to judge whether the missing issues seriously affected the study. It would be interesting to know why the issues were missing, but lack of a complete record is one of the problems of document analysis. Meyer points out that his sampling procedure improves upon those of prior news flow studies because he selected issues over a longer period of time. In addition his sample includes two regions of the world underrepresented in earlier news flow studies.

The author notes that generalization of some of his findings is limited because no French-language African newspapers are included. We do not know whether French language newspapers in former French colonies derive most of their international news from the French wire service. One may also question if his results in Africa can be generalized to African nations with other colonial histories (Dutch, Portuguese) because none are included in his sample.

10. *What type of research design is used? (C) Does the research design adequately test the hypothesized relationships? For example, if the researcher hypothesizes a causal relationship, does the research design permit the researcher to show a causal relationship?*
The research design is cross-sectional. All the variables are measured at roughly the same time. The main independent variable, the wire service source of a news story, is not manipulated by the investigator and is measured at the same time as the dependent variables.

The investigation of neoimperialism in global news flows also is based on cross-sectional research design. Meyer does not manipulate the independent variable (colonial power). However, differences in this variable already existed and occurred prior to the measurement of the dependent variable. This allows the author to advance a causal argument about patterns of news flows. Note that there is no "control" group—that is, there is no Third World nation without a colonial or imperial power included in the study, if such a place exists.

11. *Are the statistics that are used appropriate for the level of*

measurement of the variables? (Tables 1-9)

The statistics used by the author to analyze the data are appropriate for the levels of measurement for the variables. A criticism that could be made about the statistics in this research report concerns their interpretation.

Table 1 shows the percentage of international news stories that have various Western newswires identified as sources. These results are compared with another researcher's results for Asian dailies. Meyer concludes that the total percentages of reports coming from TNNAs for each of the regions are similar. We are left to conclude that the differences between the regions (56 percent versus 76 percent) are not significant, substantively or statistically.

In Table 2 the author compares the percentage of news reports devoted to international news among the dailies in his sample and in previously published reports for Asian and U.S. dailies. No statistical analysis of the differences in these percentages is conducted—probably because the differences are not very large and because the number of cases in each category of the independent variable is rather small. Simple percentages communicate the basic finding.

Table 3 examines the regions covered by international news stories. It indicates that Third World dailies devote most of their coverage to their own region, which is hardly surprising. Meyer concludes after collapsing regions covered into three categories (Third World, Third World, and other, non-Third World) that the dailies in Asia, Latin America, and Africa follow the lead of Western papers "in focusing on certain regions and countries." This conclusion is hardly supported by the data presented, since no other countries except the United States are identified. Furthermore, if Western presses devote at least half of their international coverage to Third World nations, what would a significant difference in level of coverage by Third World dailies look like? Meyer implies that a 20 percentage point difference (48 percent to 68 percent) is not a significant difference. (E-3) The standards by which the reader should judge differences in the percentage of stories devoted to different regions of the world are not at all clear.

This is less of a problem in Table 4, which shows the percentage of news stories devoted to different topics. The difference among Third World presses is generally less than 10 percentage points. Meyer compares his percentages for development/economics reports (13 percent to 18 percent) with those reported for U.S. dailies (14 percent to 24 percent) and concludes that there is no significant difference.

Table 5 compares the coverage of topics by nonaligned newswires to that of the TNNAS. Here we are told that development news ranks significantly higher for national/regional newswires and local coverage. This conclusion is more appropriate for the African newspapers than for the Latin American ones, but even here the difference in percentages is as low as 14 points (6 percent for AFP and Reuters versus 20 percent for Local/Regional).

Simple percentages give us a pretty clear picture in Table 8, which shows that news reports are generally about nations with histories of colonial or imperial influence similar to that of the newspaper's country.

We are given more help in interpreting differences in percentage distributions in Table 6, where Meyer compares the reporting of TNNAs with that of local-regional newswires in terms of spot news versus developmental reporting. For the African dailies in 1984, of the news drawn from TNNAs, 85 percent was spot news, while only 5 percent was developmental. Of the news drawn from local or regional sources, 57 percent was spot news and 24 percent was developmental. This is a 19 percentage point difference in developmental news reporting. For each of the crosstabulations in Table 6, additional statistics are calculated. The chi-square test of statistical significance is appropriate for use with nominal level data and tells us that the difference in the first crosstabulation is significant at less than the .001 level. Cramer's V is used appropriately to measure strength of association. Cramer's V is highest for Africa in 1984 (.22) and lowest for Latin America (.08). Thus while the association between newswire and type of report is statistically significant at fairly high levels, the strength of association is not very great. Crosstabulation along with the chi-square test and Cramer's V are used appropriately also in Table 9, where Meyer presents evidence of vertical news flows.

Because the dependent variables are ratio level measures and the independent variable is a nominal level measure, it is appropriate that mean values are calculated for the dependent variable and that F-ratios are used as the test of statistical significance in Table 7.

12. Are the research findings presented and discussed clearly? Is the basis for deciding whether a hypothesis is supported or refuted clearly specified? (E, F, G)

In general the research findings are presented and discussed very clearly. The basis for deciding whether a hypothesis is supported or refuted is not always clear, as discussed above. To be fair to Meyer, he did not set out to explain some of the research questions or relationships that we have phrased as null hypotheses. His purpose was to present descriptive data and see whether it conformed to expectations or assumptions about the dominance of Western media. He does not say why he does not calculate tests of statistical significance or measures of association for the relationships he evaluates in many of his tables, and the standards he uses in his interpretation of percentages are not always clear. A final criticism is that he does not explain where the percentages used in Figure 1 came from.

Conclusion

A research report rarely answers all the questions that can be raised about a topic. But a well-written report, because it carefully explains how the researcher conducted each stage in the research process, makes it easier for other researchers to evaluate the work. Other investigators may build upon it by varying the method of data collection, the operationalization of variables, or the research design.

The question of effects of Western media domination is a logical extension of Meyer's research presented here. Meyer discusses some prior research that shows predicted effects have not been borne out by the empirical evidence. Other lines of further research include investigating presses in more Third World nations, explaining why local-regional presses in Latin America did not differ from the TNNAs with respect to the number of developmental reports, and investigating whether there is any substantive difference among the TNNAs with regard to which former colonies they report more often on—their country's or another country's.

By now you should understand how scientific knowledge about politics is acquired. You should know how to formulate a testable hypothesis, choose valid and reliable measures for the concepts that you relate in a hypothesis, develop a research design, conduct a literature review, and make empirical observations. You should also be able to analyze data using appropriate univariate, bivariate, and multivariate statistics. Finally, you should be able to evaluate most research reports as well as write a research report yourself.

We encourage you to think up research questions of your own. Some of these may be feasible projects for a one- or two-semester course. You will learn much more about the research process by doing research than by just reading about it. We wish you success.

Exercises

1. Choose one of the following research articles, or one assigned to you by your instructor, and try to answer the series of questions on pages 365–366 on your own.

> Lawrence Bobo and Franklin D. Gilliam, Jr., "Race, Sociopolitical Participation, and Black Empowerment," *American Political Science Review* 84 (June 1990): 377-393.

Norman Frohlich and Joe A. Oppenheimer, "Choosing Justice in Experimental Democracies with Production," *American Political Science Review* 84 (June 1990): 461-477.

Jon A. Krosnick and Donald R. Kinder, "Altering the Foundations of Support for the President through Priming," *American Political Science Review* 84 (June 1990): 497-512.

William P. Browne, "The Aged Agenda in State Legislatures: A Comparative Perspective," *Policy Studies Journal* 17 (Spring 1989): 495-513.

Cathy Marie Johnson, "New Wine in New Bottles: The Case of the Consumer Product Safety Commission," *Public Administration Review* 50 (January/February 1990): 74-81.

2. Using the article assigned in Exercise 1, describe how you would build upon the research and mount a related investigation of your own.

Appendix   Table of Chi-square (X^2) Values

Degree of Freedom (df)	0.10	0.05	0.02	0.01
1	2.706	3.841	5.412	6.635
2	4.605	5.991	7.824	9.210
3	6.251	7.815	9.837	11.341
4	7.779	9.488	11.668	13.277
5	9.236	11.070	13.388	15.086
6	10.645	12.592	15.033	16.812
7	12.017	14.067	16.622	18.475
8	13.362	15.507	18.168	20.090
9	14.684	16.919	19.679	21.666
10	15.987	18.307	21.161	23.209
11	17.275	19.675	22.618	24.725
12	18.549	21.026	24.054	26.217
13	19.812	22.362	25.472	27.688
14	21.064	23.685	26.873	29.141
15	22.307	24.996	28.259	30.578
16	23.542	26.296	29.633	32.000
17	24.769	27.587	30.995	33.409
18	25.989	28.869	32.346	34.805
19	27.204	30.144	33.687	36.191
20	28.412	31.410	35.020	37.566
21	29.615	32.671	36.343	38.932
22	30.813	33.924	37.659	40.289
23	32.007	35.172	38.968	41.638
24	33.196	36.415	40.270	42.980
25	34.382	37.652	41.566	44.314
26	35.563	38.885	42.856	45.642
27	36.741	40.113	44.140	46.963
28	37.916	41.337	45.419	48.278
29	39.087	42.557	46.693	49.588
30	40.256	43.773	47.962	50.892

Source: Kirk W. Elison, Richard P. Runyon, and Audrey Haber, *Fundamentals of Social Statistics* (Reading, Mass.: Addison-Wesley, 1982), 476. Reprinted with permission of McGraw-Hill, Inc.